MASTERS PROGRAMME IN EDUCATION

RESEARCH METHODS IN EDUCATION

Collated from:

E824 Educational Research Methods, Study Guide *(authors: Martyn Hammersley, Roger Gomm and Peter Woods) and*

E621 Professional Development in Action, Methodology Handbook *(authors: Dorothy Faulkner, Joan Swann, Sally Baker, Margaret Bird and Joan Carty).*

Additional material provided by Neil Mercer, Michelle Perrott and Joan Swann

HANDBOOK

The Open University, Walton Hall, Milton Keynes MK7 6AA
First published 2001. Reprinted 2003

Edited, designed and typeset by The Open University.
Printed in the United Kingdom by The Alden Group, Oxford.
ISBN 0 7492 3638 8
1.2
23168B/E839maresearchhandbooki1.2

CONTENTS

INTRODUCTION

Welcome to the *Research Methods in Education Handbook* for The Open University Masters Programme in Education. This is supplied to all students on entry to the Programme. It is designed to assist you in your study at postgraduate level. All of the modules in the Masters Programme demand an ability to interpret and assess evidence, and often this evidence comes from research studies. In addition, some of the modules also require students to carry out small-scale investigations. Guidance is provided in the modules about both these types of activity. However, as a result of limitations on space and time, the modules are not able to supply an in-depth introduction to research methodology. This research methods handbook is designed to provide such an introduction, and thereby to supplement the materials in individual modules and to serve as an important resource in your work on the Masters Programme.

As with any resource, we expect you to use it flexibly and selectively. Much will depend on what knowledge you already have of educational research methods. If your background is strong in this area, then you will need to check the contents offered here and use the Handbook to update and extend your knowledge in those areas where this is necessary. If, on the other hand, you have little background knowledge of methodology, you may well want to work your way systematically through some parts of this material.

While we would recommend that, in using the Handbook, you do some work at the beginning of the year, ideally before the start of your course, you will also find it useful to consult the Handbook later, to address specific methodological issues as they arise. This may be especially important if you are required to do a research project as part of the course.

The *Research Methods in Education Handbook* falls into three parts. The first, entitled 'Principles and debates', is a general introduction to the nature of educational research and to the methodological issues surrounding it. It outlines the history of educational research, the division into quantitative and qualitative approaches, and the debates surrounding such key issues as objectivity and the relationship between research and educational policymaking or practice. In addition, it provides a detailed introduction to how to read and understand educational research studies. Many of the original activities have been retained to offer an opportunity to engage with the content. Finally, it outlines the basic principles of both qualitative and quantitative analysis.

The second part of the Handbook, entitled 'Practical guidelines for practitioner research', is much more directly concerned with doing the kind of small-scale project that you may be required to carry out as part of your module. It begins with an introduction to the notion of practitioner research. It then discusses what is involved in carrying out interviews and observations, as well as some of the practicalities of doing both qualitative and quantitative forms of analysis, of a relatively simple kind. It is primarily designed to assist teachers doing research in classrooms; but what it offers is actually of wider relevance.

The final part of the Handbook, 'Resources for the analysis of talk as data', is specifically concerned with the analysis of talk in educational settings. It begins with a section on the different approaches to talk as data that can be found in the field of educational research, outlining their strengths and weaknesses. The other section is concerned with the practical and theoretical aspects of recording and transcribing talk for analysis. This is an expansion of the section dealing with this topic in Part 2.

It is worth noting that, because these materials were originally written for various purposes by different authors, you will find the attitudes taken to key issues in the three parts differ somewhat. However, this reflects the heterogeneous nature of the field of educational research. There are many different kinds of work in this area, and conflicts in approach are not uncommon.

Needless to say, this Handbook will not deal with every issue or method that may be relevant for your module work. However, it covers a great deal of ground, and we hope that you will find it a useful resource.

PART 1 PRINCIPLES AND DEBATES

CONTENTS

1 INTRODUCTION

Part 1 of this Handbook is concerned with the goals of inquiry into educational issues, and with the techniques available for pursuing it. This is a large area and we cannot hope to do more than provide an introduction, giving an overall view and outlining directions in which more specialized topics can be pursued. The structure of the first part of the Handbook is relatively straightforward. Following this Introduction, we begin in Sections 2 and 3 by looking at the nature of educational research and at its relationship to practice. As will become clear, these are by no means uncontentious issues. We consider the history and current state of educational research, focusing on the influence of the methodology of the natural sciences and reactions against that influence. We look at quantitative educational research of various kinds and trace the more recent emergence of qualitative approaches. Then, in Section 3, we examine views about the nature and extent of the contribution made by research to educational practice and at attempts to increase or modify this contribution. We explore the debates surrounding this issue in some depth.

Section 4 examines the relationship between quantitative and qualitative approaches to educational research and looks at how to set about understanding and assessing such research. The distinction between quantitative and qualitative approaches is very widely employed in the literature and we use it ourselves to structure much of the discussion about research methods in the Handbook. It captures an important aspect of the diversity of educational research today. However, it is important to recognize its dangers. To think of educational research as if there were just two ways of doing it would be misleading. We examine some of the arguments surrounding this distinction between quantitative and qualitative approaches and the implications for how educational research should be assessed. We argue that the same standards should be applied to all research, and we explore and illustrate what is involved in applying them to particular studies.

Sections 5 and 6 look in detail at some of the techniques of research design, data collection and data analysis that are employed by educational researchers. Section 5 outlines the nature and variety of qualitative research in education. It discusses the particular strategies used by qualitative researchers, but, equally important, it is designed to give a sense of the spirit of this approach, emphasizing how individual researchers are themselves closely involved in the research process and its products. Section 6 is an introduction to some of the methods used in quantitative data analysis. The aim is to provide an elementary introduction to the basic principles of such analysis, covering some of the statistical techniques commonly used in educational research. This is done through close examination of examples and through worked activities.

Finally, Section 7 is concerned with the planning of educational research. We look briefly at various different aspects of the research process – formulating problems for investigation, selecting cases for study, producing the data, analysing it and writing research reports. In the course of this discussion we draw together many of the ideas introduced earlier in this Part of the Handbook.

2 WHAT IS EDUCATIONAL RESEARCH?

We must begin by recognizing that the term 'research' is not one that has a well-defined meaning shared by everyone. It is used to cover a wide range of activities that differ substantially in all sorts of ways; and there is considerable disagreement about what should and should not count as research. At one extreme, the term covers forms of educational inquiry designed to contribute to disciplinary knowledge in, for example, the psychology or sociology of education. Equally, though, educational research may be primarily intended to inform policy making or practice, or it may take the form of inquiries carried out *by* policy makers, school managers, or teachers, in order to further their own activities.

'Research' is a status-laden term, and including or not including something under this heading may have an effect on how people view it. This status-loading gives debates about research a political charge that we cannot neglect. Our aim in this section, though, will be not so much to decide definitively what does and does not count as educational research, as to sketch some of the criteria that are typically applied and the arguments for and against them. In doing so, we shall touch on most of the major controversies that surround educational research. For the purposes of this Handbook, then, we shall interpret 'research' in a rather broad sense, using it to refer to the selection and analysis of data with a view to the provision of valid and useful information.

We shall start from what has been the axis around which much methodological thinking about educational research has revolved: the methodological approach of the natural sciences. Our focus will be both on its influence and on the reactions against it.

2.1 EDUCATIONAL RESEARCH AS SCIENTIFIC

Much of the work of educational researchers, like that of social scientists generally, has been modelled on what were taken to be the methods of the natural sciences. In many ways this has been the most important influence of all shaping the ways in which educational researchers have thought about and carried out their research.

Activity 1

What characteristics do you associate with research in the natural sciences? Make a list of such features before you read on.

We shall probably not have succeeded in anticipating all of the features that you have thought of and we may have listed some that you overlooked, or that you do not associate with natural scientific methods, but here are some methodological features commonly identified with the natural sciences:

- The testing of claims against empirical evidence.
- The provision of an explicit account of the methods of testing, thereby providing the basis for replication.
- The quantitative measurement of phenomena.
- Experimental or statistical manipulation of variables to test causal hypotheses.
- A focus on facts rather than values.
- A concern to maintain objectivity, to avoid bias due to personal preferences.

These are the sorts of characteristics often associated with the natural sciences. We shall not consider here the question of the extent to which they constitute an accurate representation of either the ideas or the practices of natural scientists. What is more important for our purposes is that the conception of natural scientific method outlined above has guided and continues to guide the work of many educational researchers, although the features listed have been given varying emphases and been interpreted in different ways.

METHODOLOGICAL DEVELOPMENTS IN THE PSYCHOLOGY OF EDUCATION

We can illustrate the impact of what we have called the scientific model by looking briefly at the history of methodological ideas in educational research. To a large extent educational research as we know it today had its origins in the work of psychologists in the late nineteenth century, when psychology was itself only just emerging as an independent form of inquiry. During this period, the experimental method was widely regarded as the essence of a scientific approach to research. As a result, experimental psychology was seen by many as laying a theoretical basis for understanding the processes of learning, which would thereby revolutionize education by putting it on a scientific footing.

Another important aspect of the early history of educational research, again reflecting the influence of psychology, was the development of mental tests of various kinds: for example, of intelligence, personality, attitude, and academic achievement. Such tests were believed to be able to offer teachers, educational administrators and others valuable information of an objective kind about the characteristics of the pupils and students to be educated. It was believed that this information would enable both effective educational planning and the monitoring of educational processes to assess their success. The emergence of the testing movement led to a great deal of methodological work on the construction of tests, as well as to the development and use of novel sorts of statistical analysis.

Psychology, in a variety of forms, but all influenced in one way or another by the approach of the natural sciences, has continued to have a substantial influence on educational thinking up to the present day. A well-known example is the contribution to progressive ideas in primary education of the research of the Swiss psychologist Jean Piaget. He developed an influential account of child development, which portrayed the child as evolving through various stages, each stage providing for more complex capabilities. This encouraged forms of teaching attuned to individual differences in levels of development and to an emphasis on *facilitating* cognitive development rather than *transmitting* information or instilling skills.[1]

A contrasting example of the influence of psychology on educational thinking is the behaviour-modification movement. This drew on behaviourist psychology and was concerned with effective treatment of children's disorderly behaviour in school. It recommended highly structured ways of dealing with pupils, these being designed to reinforce conformity and to give no reward for deviance.[2] The existence of these strands of psychological research, which seem to carry very different implications for educational practice, suggests that the dream of the pioneers of educational research that science would provide a single determinate set of recommendations for the efficient pursuit of education has not come true. Whether this is something to be disappointed or relieved about we leave as an open question.

Psychology and the methodological ideas associated with it have thus had an enormous influence on educational inquiry and, in methodological terms, this has generally been in the direction of encouraging a 'scientific approach', broadly defined in terms of the list of characteristics we outlined earlier. However, the impact of at least some of the characteristics of that approach is also to be found more widely, notably in the sociology of education.

[1] For a critical analysis of Piaget's influence on education see Egan (1983).
[2] For analysis of the influence of behaviour modification see the discussions and references in Fink and Hyde (1985) and Seborg and Hosford (1985).

METHODOLOGICAL DEVELOPMENTS IN THE SOCIOLOGY OF EDUCATION

When the sociology of education came to be established in the UK in the 1950s, its primary concern was with measuring the inputs into and outputs from the educational system. In particular, researchers were interested in the extent to which children from different social classes enjoyed equality of opportunity within the educational system. A major interest among researchers in England and Wales was the impact of the 1944 Education Act. (Similar measures were introduced in Scotland in 1945 and Northern Ireland in 1947.) Previously, most pupils had received all their education in elementary schools, with only a minority receiving a secondary education, either funded by private means or through the award of scholarships. The 1944 Act replaced this structure with a tripartite system in which, at the age of eleven, children were allocated on the basis of an examination, a test and/or teachers' recommendation to grammar or secondary modern schools and a few to technical schools, although private schools continued to exist. Grammar and technical schools catered for those who passed this 'eleven-plus' test; secondary modern schools were for those who did not. The earlier system had clearly disadvantaged children from the working class and much sociological research of the 1950s was designed to discover how far the new system rectified this. For instance, there was investigation of the extent to which able working-class children gained access to grammar schools and thereby had a chance of pursuing middle-class careers.

Although this sociological research was not experimental in character, it employed similar measurement techniques (e.g. of pupils' ability and social class) to those used in psychological research. It also used statistical analysis designed to simulate the manipulation of variables involved in experimental research. Quantitative research relying on these techniques continues today, though now the focus is as likely to be on differences between girls and boys, or between pupils from different ethnic groups, or on the contribution that schools make to pupils' levels of achievement.

The last of these, measurement of 'school effects', is an area of research that has come to have great salience in recent years. One of the original stimuli for this was the report in the United States by Coleman (1966). This was based on a survey of a large sample of schools, documenting their material circumstances and the home backgrounds and levels of achievement of their pupils. Comparison was made mainly between schools that had predominantly white pupils and those with predominantly black pupils, reflecting concern about the fact that black people tended to be concentrated at the bottom of the occupational structure and suffered a disproportionate level of unemployment. Analysis of these data suggested that the differences between predominantly black and predominantly white schools were surprisingly small and that school characteristics seemed to have little effect on the levels of pupils' achievement. This led Coleman to the controversial conclusion that family background is much more important than school characteristics in explaining differences in pupils' achievements.

The limited contribution of schools to reducing inequality was also emphasized by some other research, such as that of Jencks *et al.* (1972); but later quantitative studies have questioned this conclusion. An early example in the UK was the work of Rutter *et al.* (1979), which claimed to discover significant 'school effects' arising from such factors as the extent to which schools laid down clear rules for pupils' behaviour and the degree to which such rules were enforced. Other studies, employing more refined statistical techniques than those available to Coleman and Jencks, have also claimed to discover significant differences among schools in their effects on pupils' achievements (e.g. Smith and Tomlinson, 1989).

Another area outside of psychology where quantitative research and the influence of 'the scientific approach' were very important was in the field of educational evaluation. In the UK in the 1960s many large-scale projects for curriculum development were sponsored by the Schools Council and by private funding agencies, such as the Nuffield Foundation. Very often these projects were subject to evaluation as part of the process of implementation. This usually took the form of a translation of the objectives of the project into quantitative terms and an investigation relying on quantitative measurement of pupils' achievements, attitudes, etc., to determine whether those objectives had been achieved. This quantitative approach to evaluation has continued to be influential, notably in government circles, even though, as we shall see, qualitative conceptions of evaluation also became prominent in later years.

2.2 REACTIONS AGAINST THE SCIENTIFIC APPROACH

Much educational research, on both sides of the Atlantic, has been quantitative in character. This has reflected in varying ways the influence of what we called the 'scientific method' or 'scientific approach'. There have, however, been strong reactions against such research. We can identify two broad sorts of criticism, one concerned with validity and the other with ethical and political issues. We shall look at each in turn.

VALIDITY CRITICISMS

The first area of criticism concerns the extent to which the results of 'scientific' educational research are valid. It has often been argued that, although the numerical evidence produced by such research has the appearance of being 'hard data' of the kind used in the natural sciences, there are, in fact, fundamental doubts about its validity; about whether it represents accurately what it claims to represent. We can get a sense of these criticisms by looking briefly at the work of Piaget, mentioned earlier. Interestingly, this was not strongly quantitative in character, and it has been criticized by some for being insufficiently rigorous from an experimental point of view; reflecting, at least in part, a difference between Piaget and commentators on his work about the requirements of scientific research. This highlights the point we made earlier: that although it is convenient to refer to the 'scientific method', there is, in fact, a variety of interpretations of what is involved in a scientific approach to research and of how it should be applied to the study of human beings and their behaviour.

Piaget carried out a number of experiments on the basis of which he developed the idea that children go through different stages of development, and that only when they have reached the necessary stage of development can they carry out the most advanced forms of cognitive operation. A famous experiment of his required children to compare the amount of liquid held by different shaped containers. The containers had the same capacity, and even when young children were shown that the same amount of liquid could be poured between the two containers, many claimed that one was larger than the other. Piaget's interpretation of this was that the children were *unable* to perform the logical task involved in recognizing that the two containers, while different in shape, were the same in capacity; this being because their cognitive development had not reached the necessary stage. Critics of his work have questioned this conclusion (see, for instance, Donaldson, 1978). They raise the possibility that the children were simply unwilling to play the experimenter's game, or that the children misunderstood what the experimenter was asking. These criticisms point to the fact, obvious enough, but important in its implications, that experiments are social situations in which interpersonal interactions take place. The implication is that Piaget's work and attempts to replicate it are not only measuring the children's capacities for logical thinking, but also the extent to which they have understood what was required, their willingness to comply with these requirements, the experimenters' success in communicating what was required, in motivating the children, etc.

Similar criticisms have been applied to psychological and educational tests. For example, Mehan points out how test questions may be interpreted in ways different from those intended by the researcher:

> [In a] language development test, children are presented with a picture of a medieval fortress – complete with moat, drawbridge, and parapets – and three initial consonants: D, C, and G. The child is supposed to circle the correct initial consonant. C for 'castle' is correct, but many children choose D. After the test, when I asked those children what the name of the building was, they responded 'Disneyland'. These children used the same line of reasoning intended by the tester, but they arrived at the wrong substantive answer. The score sheet showing a wrong answer does not document a child's lack of reasoning ability; it only documents that the child indicated an answer different from the one the tester expected.
>
> (Mehan, 1973, pp. 249–50)

Here we have questions being raised about the validity of the sort of measurements on which the findings of quantitative research are typically based. Some, including for example Donaldson, regard these as technical problems that can be overcome by more rigorous experimentation. Others, however, including Mehan, believe them to be not simply problems with particular experiments or tests, but serious threats to validity that potentially affect all research of this kind.

At the same time, questions have also been raised about the assumption built into the 'logic' of quantitative educational research that causes can be identified by physical and/or statistical manipulation of variables. Critics suggest that this fails to take account of the very nature of human social life, assuming it to consist of fixed, mechanical causal relationships, whereas in fact it involves complex processes of interpretation and negotiation that do not have determinate outcomes. From this point of view, it is not clear that we can understand why people do what they do in terms of the simple sorts of causal relationships on which quantitative research focuses. Social life, it is suggested, is much more contextually variable and complex.

Such criticisms of quantitative educational research have been the stimulus for an increasing number of educational researchers, over the past thirty or forty years, to adopt more qualitative approaches. These researchers have generally rejected attempts to measure and control variables experimentally or statistically. Qualitative research can take many forms, loosely indicated by such terms as 'ethnography', 'case study', 'participant observation', 'life history', 'unstructured interviewing', 'discourse analysis', etc. In general, though, it has the following characteristics:

- A strong emphasis on exploring the nature of particular educational phenomena, rather than setting out to test hypotheses about them.
- A tendency to work with 'unstructured data': that is, data that have not been coded at the point of collection in terms of a closed set of analytical categories. When engaging in observation, qualitative researchers therefore audio- or video-record what happens or write detailed open-ended field-notes, rather than coding behaviour in terms of a predefined set of categories, as would a quantitative researcher employing 'systematic observation'. Similarly, when interviewing, open-ended questions will be asked rather than questions requiring predefined answers of the kind typical, for example, of postal questionnaires. In fact, qualitative interviews are often designed to be close in character to casual conversations.
- Typically, a small number of cases will be investigated in detail, rather than any attempt being made to cover a large number, as would be the case in most quantitative research, such as systematic observational studies or social surveys.
- The analysis of the data involves explicit interpretations of the meanings and functions of human actions, and mainly takes the form of verbal descriptions and explanations. Quantification and statistical analysis play a subordinate role at most.

The two areas of educational research where criticism of quantitative research and the development of qualitative approaches initially emerged most strongly were the sociology of education and evaluation studies. The trend towards qualitative research in the sociology of education began in the UK in the 1960s with studies of a boys' grammar school, a boys' secondary modern school, and a girls' grammar school by Lacey (1966 and 1970), Hargreaves (1967), and Lambart (1976, 1982 and 1997). They employed an ethnographic or participant observation approach, though they also collected some quantitative data on, for example, friendship patterns among the pupils. These researchers observed lessons, interviewed teachers and pupils, and drew on school records. They studied the schools for relatively long periods, spending many months collecting data and tracing changes over time.

The studies by Hargreaves and Lacey became very well-known and widely influential.[3] Their research focus was the effects of streaming on pupils' motivation and achievements, which they claimed became polarized. They argued that streaming increased the motivation and achievements of pupils in the top stream and depressed those of pupils in the bottom stream. They also argued that a similar effect occurred within streams, with the differences in motivation and achievement between those ranked high or low by the teacher being amplified. Although the work of Hargreaves and Lacey contrasted with earlier research in the sociology of education, in being focused on intra-school processes and being largely qualitative in character, it shared the concern of previous researchers in this field with social-class inequalities. Both authors looked at the way in which differentiation and polarization processes within the schools largely reinforced social-class differences in pupils' achievements. This theme has been continued in more recent work by Ball (1981), Abraham (1989) and others.

In the late 1960s and early 1970s other qualitative researchers within sociology broke more sharply with the earlier tradition of quantitative sociological research on education. They argued that this research did not ask deep enough questions about the phenomena it investigated, that it took too much for granted. For instance, it simply assumed that the education that schools dispensed was of positive value. Rather than giving attention to the nature of school knowledge and pupils' learning, it concentrated exclusively on the distribution of educational opportunities. By contrast, these 'new sociologists of education' sought to place the question of who defines what constitutes education on the research agenda. They suggested that the nature of the teaching and learning processes in schools reflects the cultural and, ultimately, the political and economic dominance of some groups in society over others. This change in theoretical orientation in the sociology of education had methodological relevance: it was widely believed that only qualitative research could provide the necessary understanding of the cultural and political processes involved in schooling.[4] Both the example of Hargreaves and Lacey and the writings of the 'new sociologists' encouraged the growth of ethnographic and other forms of qualitative research in the 1970s and 1980s.

Similar developments also took place in curriculum evaluation. As we noted earlier, the original approach to evaluation was one in which the goals of an innovation were specified in terms of measurable features of the situation. Gains in knowledge and changes in attitude on the part of pupils were then assessed by comparing the results of tests before and after the innovation. This approach was criticized on a variety of grounds. The most fundamental criticism paralleled directly criticisms of quantitative research in the sociology of education: that such an approach made false assumptions about the nature of human beings and their social interaction and that, as a result, it could not capture the effects of innovations. There were other criticisms, too. For instance, it was argued that

[3] Lambart's work did not have the same impact at the time, though it anticipated later interest both in the effects of setting and in gender differences in school experience and achievement.
[4] For a more recent example of this argument in the field of research on the experience of ethnic-minority children in British schools see Troyna (1991). See also Hammersley (1992b).

being concerned solely with outcomes, this type of quantitative evaluation failed to document the processes that had led to those outcomes and, consequently, failed to understand *how* they had been produced (Hamilton *et al.*, 1977). It was also suggested that the narrow focus of quantitative research meant that unanticipated, but perhaps very significant, outcomes were unlikely to be discovered (Rist, 1984).

As a result of these trends, the amount of qualitative research in education grew considerably in the 1970s and 1980s, spreading beyond the areas of sociology and evaluation. It is worth emphasizing, though, that while they rejected exclusive reliance on quantitative techniques, most qualitative researchers at this time retained a commitment to at least some of the features of what we have referred to as 'the scientific approach'. For instance, there remained a general interest in the testing of empirical claims and a concern to maintain objectivity of analysis.

In recent years this has started to change; with a small, but increasing, number of qualitative researchers coming to question virtually all aspects of that approach. For example, it has been denied that educational research can rely on testing claims against evidence, on the grounds that no evidence can be independent of the presuppositions of the researcher. In part, this argument reflects changes in the philosophy of science in the past few decades, in particular discrediting of the idea that there is a body of data (e.g. direct observation of physical behaviour) whose validity is given to us independently of all theoretical presuppositions. The consensus among philosophers of science today is that all observational data rely on theoretical presuppositions. Not only may these presuppositions be wrong, but which ones are taken to be true varies across cultures and over historical periods. Thus, for example, work in the history of science has shown how, in the past, scientists have interpreted the same data very differently from modern scientists. Moreover, it is argued that this cannot be accounted for simply in terms of our better knowledge of the natural world today.[5]

Some have drawn the conclusion from these ideas that we must simply accept that there are different perspectives on the world, based on different presuppositions, and that a key assumption built into the scientific approach, that research can provide us with conclusive evidence to judge between competing accounts, is false. Thus, some educational researchers reject the whole idea that the goal of educational inquiry can be the production of accurate representations of educational phenomena. Instead, it is argued that the accounts produced by researchers are constructions that reflect their personal characteristics and socio-historical circumstances. It is sometimes inferred from this that these accounts should be judged by ethical, aesthetic, or political, not cognitive, criteria. Another important element of this trend has been to question the distinction between factual and fictional accounts, stressing the reliance of both on similar rhetorical forms and devices. Furthermore, it is suggested by some that the educational value of research reports often depends heavily on those rhetorical devices, and that fictional accounts may be able to fulfil much the same functions. Indeed, they may be more effective than research-based accounts – see, for example, Barone (1990).

One important area of debate concerns whether research and its findings can be objective, and what the term 'objective' means. We can explore this by looking at some of the work of two influential writers on educational research methodology: Elliott Eisner and Denis Phillips (see, for instance, Eisner, 1992, and Phillips, 1990). Eisner criticizes what he takes to be the traditional conception of objectivity underlying much educational research. This treats as the aim what he calls 'ontological objectivity': producing an account that captures the phenomena investigated as they truly are, independently of the researcher. And this is believed to be achievable by means of what he refers to as 'procedural objectivity': the following of a method that eliminates, or at least minimizes, the scope for personal judgement and therefore for subjective bias. Eisner criticizes

[5] For a now classic example of this work see Kuhn (1970).

both these aspects of objectivity. He argues that in order to show whether ontological validity has been achieved we need to have direct access to the area of reality being represented, so that we can compare representation with reality to check that they correspond. This is clearly impossible and, if it were possible, it would make research unnecessary. He adds other reasons in support of this argument: for example, that perception and understanding are always framework-dependent, so that the framework of presuppositions on which we rely allows us to perceive and understand some things, but not others. More than this, the framework plays a role in actually *constituting* what it is we see and understand. From this point of view, knowledge and experience are achievements, products of the transaction between our frameworks of understanding and features of a 'world-out-there' that we cannot know directly. Eisner claims that unwillingness to relinquish the notion of objectivity stems from the feeling that this would leave us without bearings in the world. He argues that this is not so, and that we can and must learn to live with this sort of relativism. He suggests that it does not prevent us using the concept of truth, so long as we understand that what we regard as true depends upon shared frameworks of perception and understanding. While we cannot have knowledge whose validity is certain, we can still judge whether beliefs are more or less sound. Furthermore, we must remember that the literal conception of truth as correspondence only applies to those forms of inquiry directed towards achieving literal truth and that these are not the only valuable ones. He is thinking here of artistic representation as an alternative model.

Phillips adopts what, on the face of it at least, is a contrary position. He explicitly criticizes Eisner, claiming that the relativism which the latter advocates leaves us in a position where we cannot make reasonable judgements between competing empirical claims. He sets out to demonstrate that relativism does not necessarily follow from the absence of some foundation of data whose validity is absolutely certain. He is at some pains to show that the concept of truth is legitimate and desirable, and that so too is the concept of objectivity.

To some extent, what we have here are two writers who, though they address the same issues, do not seem to join in argument; a fact that might be taken to support Eisner's claim that 'when people do not share frameworks, there is no common ground; they cannot understand each other' (1992, p. 14). We can get a sense of what is involved in the disagreement if we recognize that the two authors are criticizing opposite polar positions that each regards the other as exemplifying. To call the target of Eisner's critique 'objectivity' is potentially misleading because, as he points out, that term is used to cover a variety of considerations. We would do better to see him as criticizing what he refers to elsewhere in his 1992 article as 'naïve realism'. This is the idea that all knowledge, to be justifiably referred to as such, must constitute a full representation of the objects known and a representation whose validity is absolutely certain. Furthermore, this view seems to require that knowledge can only be gained by following a procedure that excludes subjective influences and thereby gives direct access to reality. However, it is important to emphasise that Phillips also rejects this position.

By contrast, Phillips takes as his target relativism; but this is not synonymous with the relativism that Eisner admits to; and, for this reason, we shall call it 'extreme relativism'. Extreme relativism is the view that all 'knowledge' is a construction based on a particular framework of presuppositions, that these presuppositions can never be fully assessed because all assessments themselves rely on presuppositions, and that all empirical claims must be treated as equally valid in their own terms. From this point of view, we cannot talk of validity as correspondence to a reality that stands outside of any framework of assumptions, nor of a procedure that provides access to any such reality.

We are not faced, then, with a conflict between two positions each represented by one of these authors, but rather with two authors attacking opposite polar positions that neither of them seems to occupy. Thus Eisner suggests that quantitative educational research is founded on naïve realism. Yet the philosophical ideas associated with quantitative research have been quite diverse and have included rejection of naïve realism in favour of approaches that seek to avoid all reference to any reality beyond our experience. Indeed, what Eisner refers to as procedural objectivity has been regarded by some quantitative researchers as the only form of objectivity there is, agreeing in this respect with him that this is 'all we can ever have' and that we must 'recognize it for what it is'.

Similarly, Phillips treats Eisner as effectively claiming that any view is as good as any other, that this is what the abandonment of objectivity implies. Yet Eisner clearly does not see his position in these terms. He quotes the philosopher of science Stephen Toulmin to the effect that even in the absence of knowledge that is certain we can still make reasonable assessments of competing claims (Eisner, 1992, p. 15). It must be said, though, that Eisner does not spell out how this is to be done and, in particular, how judgements of validity are to be justified; nor does he address the issue that Phillips raises about whether it is possible to offer rational justification for the selection of frameworks.[6]

This debate between two influential authors indicates the sort of philosophical issues that are at the heart of much discussion about validity among qualitative educational researchers today. Our analysis of them shows that the differences of view are often complex and subtle.

POLITICAL AND ETHICAL CRITICISMS

The debates about the nature of educational research and the scientific approach have not been concerned only with the *validity* of research findings, but also with political and ethical aspects of educational research. For example, in the 1970s and 1980s many educational researchers rejected earlier work in the psychology and sociology of education on the grounds that it had effectively served to preserve the political status quo, rather than challenging it. This was true, it was claimed, even of sociological work concerned with whether working-class children received equality of opportunity, since this research drew attention away from the fact that the educational system serves to reproduce an unequal society. In other words, the focus had been on the *distribution* of education rather than on the functions performed for capitalism by the educational system. The effect of this, it was suggested, was to reinforce the widespread belief in the political neutrality and value of the education offered in schools, when this should have been challenged.

These criticisms symbolized the emergence of a tradition of 'critical' educational research, on this and the other side of the Atlantic. Such research is concerned not just with exposing educational inequalities and the ways in which the educational system reinforces wider *social* inequalities, but also with questioning dominant views about the character and role of education in modern capitalist societies. While initially focused on the reproduction of the social-class structure, this perspective has come to be applied to aspects of inequality previously neglected, notably those produced by sexism and racism. One consequence of this has been an increased amount of research, largely qualitative in character, on women's and girls' experiences of the educational system – see, for example, Deem (1980), Stanworth (1981), Griffin (1985), Weiner (1985), Arnot and Weiner (1987), Weiner and Arnot (1987). Similarly, there has been a growing amount of research looking at the experience of ethnic-minority children in schools – see, for example, Eggleston *et al.* (1986), Mac an Ghaill (1988), Foster (1990) and Gillborn (1990).

At the same time, the feminist and anti-racist movements have also had an important effect on methodological thinking about educational research. Many feminists have argued for a distinctively feminist methodology, characterized for instance by a commitment to taking women's experience more seriously, to

[6] More extensive presentations of these arguments are to be found in Eisner (1991) and Phillips (1992).

practising 'non-hierarchical' forms of research, and to directing research towards the emancipation of women.[7] Similar developments have become evident in anti-racist research (Troyna and Carrington, 1989) and among advocates of critical ethnography.

A useful illustration is an article by Gitlin, Siegel and Boru (1989). This is located firmly within the 'critical' tradition of research on education. But the authors criticize previous work in that tradition for failing to give sufficient attention to methodology; and, in particular, for adopting ethnographic method without taking sufficient notice of methodological arguments among anthropologists concerning both the capacity of ethnography to produce objective accounts of the world, and the way in which all research methods involve political commitments. The first of these criticisms relates to an issue we discussed earlier in connection with the articles by Eisner and Phillips. The second concerns, more directly, the political and ethical aspects of research. What the authors challenge is the separation of what they call understanding and application; they challenge the idea that it is the researcher's task simply to understand events rather than also to participate in them in order to bring about 'emancipatory change'.

There seem to be three reasons for Gitlin *et al.*'s rejection of the distinction between understanding and application. One, hinted at rather than spelled out in any detail, is that being a spectator rather than a participant does not give access to knowledge or at least impairs such access. It must be remembered, however, that they reject the idea that knowledge consists of representations of events that are independent of the researcher, in favour of the view that 'the rightness of educative research is based on the *relation* between normative frameworks established by a dialogical community and the specific practices of the study' (1989, p. 207). This has the effect of collapsing the issue of cognitive validity into the political and ethical aspects of research. The second reason for their redefinition of the task of research is the claim that previous research, even that carried out from a committed leftist position, has not had an emancipatory effect. The final reason is that they believe the division of labour between researcher and researched in conventional qualitative (and other) research to be unethical, since it involves an unequal distribution of power.

On the basis of these arguments, the authors advocate what they call 'educative research', research that is not only committed to bringing about 'emancipation', conceived in terms of egalitarian and democratic forms of social organization, but which also seeks to implement those forms within the research process. In other words, they argue for a kind of research in which researcher and researched collaborate, to the point where the differences between them disappear.

There are a number of questions that might be raised about this argument. For one thing, these authors seem to adopt an even more extreme anti-realist position than Eisner, apparently denying the possibility of knowledge in any sense independent of ideas that prove successful in the political struggle. Symptomatic here is the statement that 'the question is not whether the data are biased; the question is whose interests are served by the bias' (p. 200). The authors also comment that 'clearly a consideration of ethnography's "objectivity" is an attempt to gain legitimacy in relation to the more positivist paradigm' (p. 192), as if this were obviously true and as though (even if it were true) it exhausted the interest we might have in objectivity. Phillips' arguments seem even more relevant here than they were in the case of Eisner.

The other major issue we shall raise about Gitlin *et al.*'s argument relates to their claim that research should be directly concerned with the pursuit of political goals. Most educational research is not so committed, even though all researchers have political preferences (preferences that could bias their findings) and even though research may sometimes have significant political consequences. None of the arguments put forward in support of this redefinition of the purpose of research is

[7] For criticism of the idea of a distinct feminist methodology, see Hammersley (1992c). For responses, see Gelsthorpe (1992), Ramazanoglu (1992), and Williams (1993).

entirely convincing, in our view. That interventionist research of the kind recommended by Gitlin *et al.* will have more impact upon the people studied than conventional forms of ethnographic research is very probable, but whether the effects will be 'emancipatory' is another matter. The authors themselves note that the sort of research they are recommending cannot by itself achieve 'emancipatory change at a societal level' (p. 192). Even beyond this, though, we might want to question the political values on which 'educative research' is based. What is the emancipation promised an emancipation from? From all forms of oppression simultaneously? How could this be achieved? What about differences in view about what constitutes oppression, equality and democracy? Also, we might reasonably ask what concept of education is involved in the idea of educative research. Apparently, it amounts to learning what is necessary to overcome inequality. Many would agree that this is important, but it does not exhaust the meaning of education. Given this, we should ask what other aspects of education ought to be taken into account in educative research. Furthermore, the authors seem to have an excessive confidence that disagreements about such issues can be resolved; and resolved in a just fashion, via dialogue. From a more traditional research point of view, what is proposed by Gitlin *et al.* seems to be a transformation of research into a political campaign and perhaps one directed towards goals that are questionable in terms of both desirability and feasibility.

In discussing Gitlin *et al.*'s argument, as with our earlier discussion of the work of Eisner and Phillips, we have tried to give you a sense of the sort of debate that is currently going on in the field of educational research; in this case about its ethical and political dimensions.

As with critical ethnography, so too in the field of educational evaluation, criticism of quantitative research was, from the beginning, as much concerned with ethical and political issues as it was with the issue of validity. In particular, what was rejected was the hierarchical relationship built into traditional forms of evaluation, with the evaluator claiming to stand above the teachers involved in curricular projects and to assess their work. This concern is exemplified in MacDonald's 'A political classification of evaluation studies in education'. He identifies three kinds of evaluation study:

> *Bureaucratic evaluation*
>
> Bureaucratic evaluation is an unconditional service to those government agencies which have major control over the allocation of educational resources. The evaluator accepts the values of those who hold office, and offers information which will help them to accomplish their policy objectives. He acts as a management consultant, and his criterion of success is client satisfaction. His techniques of study must be credible to the policy-makers and not lay them open to public criticism. He has no independence, no control over the use that is made of his information and no court of appeal. The report is owned by the bureaucracy and lodged in its files. The key concepts of bureaucratic evaluation are 'service', 'utility' and 'efficiency'. Its key justificatory concept is 'the reality of power'.
>
> *Autocratic evaluation*
>
> Autocratic evaluation is a conditional service to those government agencies which have major control over the allocation of educational resources. It offers external validation of policy in exchange for compliance with its recommendations. Its values are derived from the evaluator's perception of the constitutional and moral obligations of the bureaucracy. He focuses upon issues of educational merit, and acts as external adviser. His techniques of study must yield scientific proofs, because his power base is the academic research community. His contractual arrangements guarantee non-interference by the client, and he retains ownership of the study. His report is lodged in the files of the bureaucracy, but is also published in the academic journals. If his

> recommendations are rejected, policy is not validated. His court of appeal is the research community, and higher levels of the bureaucracy. The key concepts of the autocratic evaluator are 'principle' and 'objectivity'. Its key justificatory concept is 'the responsibility of office'.
>
> *Democratic evaluation*
>
> Democratic evaluation is an information service to the community about the characteristics of an educational programme. It recognises value-pluralism and seeks to represent a range of interests in its issue-formulation. The basic value is an informed citizenry, and the evaluator acts as broker in exchanges of information between differing groups. His techniques of data-gathering and presentation must be accessible to non-specialist audiences. His main activity is the collection of definitions of, and reactions to, the programme. He offers confidentiality to informants and gives them control over his use of the information. The report is non-recommendatory, and the evaluator has no concept of information misuse. The evaluator engages in periodic negotiation of his relationships with sponsors and programme participants. The criterion of success is the range of audiences served. The report aspires to 'bestseller' status. The key concepts of democratic evaluation are 'confidentiality', 'negotiation', and 'accessibility'. The key justificatory concept is 'the right to know'.
>
> (MacDonald, 1977, pp. 226–7)

It is not difficult to detect MacDonald's commitment to democratic evaluation here, a commitment that he makes explicit elsewhere in the article.

From a slightly different angle, but still within the field of evaluation, Walker (1978) has criticized both quantitative research and traditional forms of ethnographic research for failing to recognize the rights of informants to have control over the data they produce during interviews, as well as for what he regards as the lack of practical relevance of their findings. It was partly on the basis of arguments like these that it came to be proposed that teachers in schools should become their own researchers, rather than being subjected to research by outsiders, an argument we shall examine in Section 3.

2.3 CONCLUSION

In this section we have looked at some of the debates about the nature of educational research. We examined the influence of the natural sciences as a methodological model and the reactions against it. We saw that for much of the history of educational research the scientific approach was very influential, but that in recent decades criticism has grown, both of quantitative educational research and of the scientific approach itself. Criticisms of quantitative research have taken two forms: arguments about the validity of its findings and about its political and ethical aspects. The growing influence of these criticisms was accompanied by a great increase in the amount of qualitative research, initially in the fields of the sociology of education and evaluation studies, but later across all fields of educational study. At the same time, we saw how the continuing commitment of more traditional forms of qualitative research to key elements of the scientific method has come under increasing challenge. One result of this is that there is now a great diversity of approaches to educational research, many of them at odds with one another.

3 RESEARCH, THEORY AND EDUCATIONAL PRACTICE

In this section we shall look at the role of research in relation to educational practice. This relationship is an issue about which there has been, and continues to be, much disagreement; both among researchers as well as between them and educational practitioners of various kinds. Sometimes practitioners are criticized for ignoring the results of educational research, for persisting with discredited teaching or management techniques, for failing to reflect sufficiently on what they do, etc. On the other hand, the results of educational research are often dismissed by practitioners as trivial, as too theoretical, or as just plain wrong.

As we saw in the previous section, in the first half of the twentieth century, indeed well into its second half, there was great confidence in the potential contribution to education of scientific research. What was impressive about the natural sciences for the pioneers of educational research was not just the understanding of the natural world that they provided, but also the technologies produced on the basis of science and the benefits of these technologies. Many early educational researchers saw their task as to produce educational and administrative technologies that would improve the quality of education in much the same way that other forms of technology were believed to have improved other aspects of modern life.

In recent years, however, confidence in the contribution to educational practice of scientific educational research has waned considerably. This reflects in part a more widespread disillusionment with the natural sciences following from recognition of the negative aspects of the technologies that science has generated: from nuclear weapons to industrial pollution. Equally important, ironically, has been the failure of educational research to produce technologies that work with anything like the same degree of success as those developed on the basis of the natural sciences. Various explanations for this have been put forward, often involving a questioning of whether human behaviour can be understood in the same manner as phenomena in the natural world. As we saw earlier, this criticism was one of the major reasons for the development of qualitative approaches to educational research.

At the centre of many of the debates about the relationship between educational research and practice has been the concept of theory. The provision of sound educational theory has often been seen as the distinctive contribution that research can make to educational practice. On the other hand, the results of research have sometimes been dismissed as 'merely theoretical'. There can be few words used in such diverse, and frequently vague, ways as 'theory'. As a result, before we can make much headway in understanding the role of theory in relation to educational research and practice we need to clarify its meaning.

3.1 THE NATURE OF EDUCATIONAL THEORY AND PRACTICE

We can start by distinguishing between normative and factual senses of 'theory'. In the former and older sense the term refers to abstract principles that guide action, indicating what should and should not be done in particular sorts of practical circumstances, and why. These principles include general moral precepts as well as ideas about the goals of particular activities, such as teaching. There have been many attempts to spell out what are the main principles of education in this sense; and it has been one of the concerns of much philosophy of education. Such principles and such thinking about them are, however, not restricted to philosophers: all educational practices are premised on some such principles. Moreover, most teachers reflect on educational principles at some time or other. Indeed, these principles are often at the heart of debates about education. Discussions about 'traditional' and 'progressive' teaching are an example. Each of these terms is associated with distinctive clusters of educational principles, and these are widely seen as having little overlap with one another. In our view, though, it is misleading to think that people can be neatly divided into adherents of one or other of these educational ideologies (or indeed of any others). In practice, we all share many educational principles, although we may give these different emphasis in particular cases.

Over the course of the twentieth century this normative conception of theory was in large part eclipsed by a second, quite different, notion; one which treats educational theory as factual, as referring to how things *are* rather than to how they *should be*. This interpretation of 'theory' derives in large part from the influence of what we referred to earlier as the scientific approach. From this point of view, theory is often conceived of as a system of laws that explain the occurrence of particular types of event in particular types of circumstance. It was believed that these laws would provide the basis for improved educational practice by replacing the folk knowledge on which practice had hitherto been based. This view is still influential in some quarters today. Indeed, while qualitative researchers often deny the possibility of laws of human behaviour, even many of them retain the idea that their research produces theory that is factual in character, provides explanations for social events, and constitutes a basis for improved educational practice. This is true, for example, of much ethnographic research on schools (see, for example, the arguments promoting the practical value of sociological work in Woods and Pollard, 1988).

A useful contribution to thinking about this issue is Paul H. Hirst's book about the nature of educational theory and its relationship to the foundation disciplines, (Hirst, 1983). At one point, Hirst outlines a dispute with another philosopher of education, D. J. O'Connor. Whereas O'Connor regards educational theory as consisting of scientific laws produced by researchers, Hirst sees it as consisting of normative principles, to a large extent generated in the course of practice itself. He goes on to outline what he thinks is the character of those principles, as well as the role of educational research and philosophical inquiry in relationship to them. He sees educational theory as guiding practice, though not as completely determining it. Furthermore, while the work of psychologists, sociologists and others can inform that theory, it cannot in any sense replace or predetermine it. He argues that, unlike practical educational theory, the theories produced by educational research are not directed towards the improvement of practice, but rather towards the cumulation of knowledge about particular aspects of human behaviour. The focus of such research is necessarily very narrow, by contrast with the need for educational theory to cover the whole range of considerations taken into account by educators.

In the course of his discussion, Hirst mentions the work of the German social theorist Jurgen Habermas, but he does not elaborate much on the tradition in which Habermas works, which is very different from his own. That tradition, often referred to as 'critical theory', represents a third position contrasting with those represented by O'Connor and Hirst as well as with the assumptions of much qualitative research. It is one which is closely related to the tradition of critical sociological research which we mentioned in Section 2.[8]

This critical tradition seeks to combine the normative and factual forms of theory, indeed its adherents regard the distinction between the two as misconceived. They believe that what *ought to be done* arises directly out of an understanding of what *is*. Most versions of this view today are influenced by Marxism, so that Marx's critique of capitalism represents the paradigm. He sought not only to display the inequalities of that social system, but also to show that it was a necessary phase in the historical development of humanity, one which could be overcome in such a way as to realize the true potential of human beings. Indeed,

[8] For an account of educational theory and inquiry from this point of view, see Carr 1995.

he claimed that capitalism contained the seeds of its own destruction and of the future communist society within it. He saw his own research as playing a crucial role in enlightening people, and the working class in particular, thereby laying the basis for the political mobilization of anti-capitalist forces that would be necessary to achieve the social transformation required for further societal development.

More recent versions of critical theory have differed from Marx in various respects, while retaining the overall form of the argument. For example, many no longer see the working class in Western societies as the most oppressed group or as the one that is most likely to be able to rise up and overthrow capitalism. Other possible groups include ethnic minorities, women, and the poor of the Third World. Some do not see capitalism as the root of the problem, but only as a symptom, regarding the whole ethos and structure of Western society as the problem. Others question the influential role that Marx ascribed to theory and thereby to intellectuals, arguing that the understanding of the world necessary for its transformation can only be generated by those engaged in political struggle.

We raised questions about the values implicit in the critical tradition earlier, in discussing the article by Gitlin *et al.*

3.2 THE RELATIONSHIP BETWEEN EDUCATIONAL THEORY, RESEARCH AND PRACTICE

In thinking about the relationship between theory and practice, let us begin with theory in the normative sense. A tempting interpretation of this relationship, especially for the theoretician perhaps, is to see practice as the acting out of a theory. Sometimes the advocates of progressivism or traditionalism seem to see things in this way, seeking to spell out their educational principles in such a way as to provide a clear and detailed guide for action. The same idea is built into some versions of critical theory: what is required, it is suggested, is a comprehensive world view that will counter the dominant ideology and guide people to emancipation.

Even more common is to find this attitude in relation to factual theory. What is involved here is what is often referred to as the engineering model of the relationship between research and practice. Advocates of this view take the goals of education to be relatively unproblematic and widely agreed. The problem in their view is how to achieve those goals and they believe that this task is ideally suited to resolution by scientific research. In these terms, the aim of such research is to find the most effective and efficient means of achieving educational goals. Some curricular packages follow this model, perhaps even specifying the behaviour of teachers down to the very words they should use when addressing their pupils.

The converse of the treatment of theory as properly controlling practice is, of course, the rejection of theory and research on the grounds that they fail to tell practitioners what to do in the most problematic situations, that they often proffer conflicting advice, and/or that the advice they give does not work. Theory is rejected in these terms as useless; we must rely instead, it is suggested, on practical experience.

The history of the education of teachers and of professional education in other fields seems to have oscillated between these two poles. It seems to us, however, that neither of these views is satisfactory. The first tends to lead to dogmatism, to the attempt to reduce all situations to the categories of a theory and to try to resolve practical problems by standard means. Such dogmatism usually leads to failure, frustration and the search for scapegoats. The danger with the rejection of theory, on the other hand, is that the theoretical principles (of both normative and factual kinds) that are built into the strategies and tactics routinely used by practitioners are overlooked. They may no longer be recognized for what they are and therefore may become largely immune to criticism, even when they require scrutiny and re-thinking. In the absence of theoretical reflection, practice may also become governed to an excessive degree by expediency and convenience. Indeed, discussion or thought about any other values than these may come to be treated by practitioners as idealistic or pompous. This is likely to have undesirable educational consequences.

What is the appropriate relationship between theory and practice? One of the most striking intellectual trends of recent years has been a revival of the influence of Aristotle's ideas about theory and practice. This has occurred in many fields: in discussions of ethics, in political philosophy, and in the field of education itself. Indeed, the conception of educational practice advanced by Hirst in the book referred to earlier bears strong similarities to Aristotle's account of practice. What is of central importance here is Aristotle's emphasis on the essential role of judgement in all practical activities. For him, wise practical conduct cannot take the form of the mere application of principles, but nor can it ignore principles. Particular situations must be assessed in terms of goals and values, but goals and values must also be interpreted in the light of the experience of particular situations, including the one in which action must take place. Only then will reasonable conclusions be reached about what it is appropriate to do. Practical judgement may be improved, then, both by clarification of what abstract normative principles should guide action of particular types and of the meaning of those principles, as well as by reflection on practical experience.

Much the same model can be applied to the case of factual theory. Even if a theory of this kind is true, whether it applies to the particular situation a practitioner faces and what its implications are for what should be done, are matters of judgement. Furthermore, of course, ideas about educational goals are not as consensual as the engineering model implies, nor should the selection of means be based solely on considerations of effectiveness and efficiency. These arguments have led many of those thinking about the relationship between research and practice to reject the engineering model in favour of what is usually referred to as the enlightenment model. Here the knowledge produced by research provides ideas that are intended to be a useful resource for practitioners, rather than consisting of ready-made solutions to their problems.

A rather different view of the proper relationship between theory and practice, departing in important respects from both the engineering and enlightenment models, is represented by action research. This is often put forward as a solution to the problem of the relation between research and practice because it involves practitioners in theorizing that is directly related to their work. Typically, educational researchers have been located in institutions of higher education, but rather than doing research on that sector of the educational system they have mostly carried out research in secondary and primary schools. While many of these researchers are ex-teachers in such schools, the institutional separation of researchers and teachers has increasingly come to be challenged by advocates of action research on methodological and political grounds. They emphasize the similarities between research and professional activities like teaching. Indeed, sometimes it is suggested that teaching should become a form of action research (on this argument, see Hammersley, 1993). However, action research can take a wide variety of forms (see Carr and Kemmis, 1986 and Kemmis, 1988).

3.3 CONCLUSION

In this section we have looked at the contentious relationship that exists between educational research and practice. We noted how after an initial period of confidence in the potential contribution of scientific research to educational practice, that confidence began to wane. We examined the effects of this on thinking about educational theory, comparing various conceptualizations of it. These also carry implications about the nature of educational practice, and we argued for an Aristotelian emphasis on the importance of practical judgement, with theory informing rather than replacing this. We also noted how action research is sometimes put forward as a solution to the problem of the relationship between research and practice.

The next section of this Part of the Handbook looks in a little more detail at the relationship between qualitative and quantitative approaches, and at the process of assessing educational research.

4 APPROACHES TO EDUCATIONAL RESEARCH AND ITS ASSESSMENT

The range of strategies that can be used to pursue educational research is very wide. It includes: laboratory and classroom experiments; large-scale surveys of the behaviour, attitudes, aptitudes, etc., of teachers, pupils and others; secondary analysis of available information; small-scale investigations of particular schools or classrooms, etc. The data may be the product of direct observation on the part of the researcher or it may be produced by others, and can take a variety of forms: ticks in boxes on interview or observational schedules, numbers as recorded in published statistics, text from published or unpublished documents or from field-notes written by the researcher during the course of observations or interviews, audio- or video-recordings and transcripts of these, etc.

As we saw earlier, a common way of conceptualizing this diversity is the distinction between quantitative and qualitative approaches. This is a distinction we shall use in the remainder of this Handbook. It is necessary, however, to emphasize that it is a very crude distinction and one that is potentially misleading. It obscures as much as it reveals.

4.1 DISTINGUISHING BETWEEN QUANTITATIVE AND QUALITATIVE RESEARCH

What do we mean by the terms 'quantitative' and 'qualitative'? The most obvious distinction between the two sorts of research is that the former deals with numbers and usually employs statistical techniques, whereas the latter does not, or does so only to a minor degree. Various other features of the research process tend to be associated with each side of this division. For instance, if one is to count, calculate percentages and use statistical analysis, one must have data that are amenable to these procedures. As a result, quantitative research typically employs what are usually referred to as structured forms of data, consisting of frequency counts or measurements of other kinds.

By contrast, the data that qualitative researchers typically deal with are verbal accounts in natural language, produced by them or by informants, and full or edited transcripts from audio- or video-recordings of events. As they stand, such data cannot be subjected to counting or measurement and therefore are not susceptible to quantitative analysis; though they can subsequently be structured so as to become amenable to such analysis.

Although there are constraints on what methods can be combined, it is easy to exaggerate the degree to which different forms of research design, data collection, and data analysis belong exclusively together. Much educational research combines qualitative and quantitative methods in various ways and to varying degrees; and there is probably even more scope for doing so than is currently exploited. At the same time, there are those who argue that qualitative and quantitative approaches represent contrasting forms of educational research, and that they should not be combined. For example, Smith and Heshusius (1986) claim that the history of educational research, and of social research generally, must be seen as involving the development of these two competing paradigms of research. They further claim that quantitative and qualitative approaches are fundamentally at odds with one another, since they are based on conflicting assumptions about the nature of the phenomena studied and about how those phenomena can be understood. This contrasts with the view that we have adopted in this Handbook, which is that the difference between quantitative and qualitative educational research is neither so clear-cut nor so deep. (For further discussion of this view see Hammersley, 1992a, chapter 9.)

There is, of course, a wide range of ideas about how educational research should be done, how its products should be assessed, and even about what its purpose is; but these cannot be reduced to two contrasting positions without distortion. Furthermore, much of this diversity stems from the fact that different studies are designed to serve different purposes, and their character is shaped by those purposes. It must also be remembered that research is very much a practical activity carried out in particular contexts under varying constraints.

One of the areas where disagreements about quantitative and qualitative approaches have been most significant is the assessment of research. On the one hand, some have argued that the standards of assessment typically employed in quantitative research – such as internal and external validity, and reliability – should be applied to qualitative work as well. On the other hand, many qualitative researchers argue that distinctive standards are appropriate to qualitative studies. We adopt neither of these approaches. We argue that the same standards should be applied across the qualitative–quantitative divide, but at the same time these are not identical with those conventionally applied to quantitative research.

4.2 STANDARDS OF ASSESSMENT

We suggest that there are just two overarching criteria in terms of which educational research, both quantitative and qualitative, should be assessed: validity and relevance. We shall discuss each in turn.

VALIDITY

By 'validity' we mean truth: the extent to which an account accurately represents the phenomena to which it refers. There are few concepts that have led to more controversy among philosophers than truth. Indeed, there are many educational researchers who reject this concept as inapplicable to the assessment of their work. One reason for this is that they believe that use of the term 'truth' implies the possession of knowledge whose validity is *absolutely certain*, proven beyond all possible doubt; yet knowledge can never be certain in this sense.

These critics point out that in deciding the validity or otherwise of some claim we always rely on presuppositions whose own validity we must take for granted. If we seek to test any of those presuppositions, we shall be forced to rely on further ones. For instance, even in simple measurements of physical objects with a ruler we take for granted certain properties of rigid bodies, in this case the ruler and the object. We assume, for example, that small changes in temperature will not have any significant effect on our measurements. Testing these presuppositions would involve us in measuring temperature, which itself involves presuppositions about the operation of thermometers, and so on.

Now, the second half of this argument is sound, but the first – that use of the concept of truth implies knowledge that is certain beyond all possible doubt – is not. To claim that some statement is true is not incompatible with a recognition that our judgements about it may be wrong. In fact, we can *never* be absolutely certain about the truth of anything, not even in the natural sciences or in our personal lives. There are, however, many things about whose truth we are very confident, and about which we are justifiably confident. In other words, there can be good reasons for believing that some statement is true or false without our ever being absolutely certain about the validity of the claim. We rely on a whole host of presuppositions about the world in our everyday lives and, while many of them are probably approximately true, we can never be confident beyond all possible doubt about the truth of any of them. Yet, this ever-present uncertainty does not undermine our use of the concept of truth in that context, and there is no reason why it should do so in the research situation either.

A second source of problems with 'truth' arises from beliefs about the nature of human social life. There are those who hold that in the case of social phenomena there is no single reality to which claims made in research reports correspond. It is argued that it is characteristic of human beings that they create multiple social worlds or realities, that all perception and cognition involves the *construction* of phenomena rather than their mere discovery. It may be concluded from this that contradictory views of the 'same' phenomena by different cultural groups are equally 'true' in their own terms. Of course, if we apply this argument to educational research itself, as we should if we are to be consistent, we see the latter as also creating a world (or, given the dissension among social scientists, multiple worlds). This is the sort of extreme relativism that we discussed in Section 2, from which point of view research reports do not provide an account of independent phenomena, but *create* the social reality they purport to describe, for instance through textual strategies of various kinds. Effectively, the argument here is not just that we can never be sure of the truth or falsity of our claims about reality, but that we have no grounds for believing that there are phenomena that are independent of our knowledge of them, since all the knowledge we can ever have is formed by our culture and that culture is only one of many.

While this argument makes an important point about the limits and difficulties of understanding that result from cultural diversity, the conclusion that there are no phenomena independent of researchers for them to document does not follow from it. All social phenomena are human products and are therefore, in some senses, not independent of humanity as a whole. Much social life, however, *is* independent of any particular researcher or group of researchers. Furthermore, we are able to learn other cultures to one degree or another and, thereby, to understand human behaviour that is framed in terms of them. This implies some commonalities among cultures on which knowledge may be built. It is also worth pointing out that to claim that there are other cultures, or even that one's own views represent a culture, itself implies the claim that there is a larger world within which those cultures are to be found and which is not relative. In this way, and others, relativism is self-contradictory.

Of course, even if we accept that validity is a feasible and legitimate criterion in terms of which to assess educational research, the question remains: on what basis can assessment of it be carried out, given that there is no foundation of evidence whose validity is absolutely certain and by which researchers can validate their accounts? The only basis available, it seems to us, is judgements of the likelihood of error. From this point of view, there are three steps in assessing the validity of research claims:

1. The first question that we must ask about a claim is how 'plausible' it is: that is, whether we judge it as very likely to be true given our existing knowledge. In the case of some claims, they will be so plausible that we can reasonably accept them at face value without needing to know anything about how researchers came to formulate them or what evidence is offered in support of them. The first test, then, is plausibility.
2. A second question we may need to ask is whether it seems likely that the researcher's judgement of matters relating to the claim is accurate, given the nature of the phenomena concerned, the circumstances of the research, the characteristics of the researcher, etc. We shall call this 'credibility'. In assessing credibility we make a judgement about the likely threats to validity involved in the production of a claim, and the likely size and direction of their effect. As with plausibility, there are claims

whose credibility is such that we can reasonably accept them without further ado (albeit always recognizing that we *could* be mistaken).

3 Of course, where we conclude that a claim is neither sufficiently plausible nor sufficiently credible to be accepted at face value, to be convinced of its validity we shall require evidence. When we examine the evidence, however, we shall have to employ much the same means to assess its validity as we applied to the claim itself: we will judge *its* plausibility and credibility. Of course, in turn we may require further evidence to support the evidence, which we shall again judge in terms of plausibility and credibility.

In many respects, this seems to us to be the sort of basis on which we judge claims, our own and those of others, in everyday life. It is important to point out, though, that we do not do it on a purely individual basis. As co-participants in various communal activities we compare our judgements with those of others; and where there are disagreements these may need to be resolved. In a research situation, moreover, there is an obligation to try to resolve disagreements and to do so through rational discussion. Such discussion may reveal to us that what we have been disposed to accept as adequately plausible or credible should not be accepted (or it may reveal errors in the presuppositions on which others' judgements were made). It is the function of the research community to act as a corrective to the beliefs of individual researchers in this way.

Needless to say, plausibility and credibility are a relatively weak basis for judging the validity of claims, compared to the idea that we can assess claims directly according to their correspondence with reality, or by relying on some body of evidence whose validity is absolutely certain. The approach we are suggesting provides no guarantee that our judgements will be correct, nor any way of knowing for certain whether they are correct. Neither will judgements always be consensual, since there are very likely to be different views about what is plausible and credible; and rational discussion carries no guarantee of reaching agreement. In our view, however, this is the only viable basis for assessing the truth of knowledge claims that we have.

Truth or validity is the first criterion, then, in terms of which we believe that research accounts should be judged. Also important is 'relevance'.

RELEVANCE

To be of value, research findings must not only be valid, but must also be relevant to issues of public concern. This second criterion is curiously neglected in many treatments of educational research methodology. It is rarely mentioned explicitly in discussions of standards of assessment, whether those appealing to the quantitative tradition or those offering distinctive qualitative criteria.

Our interest in facts, in everyday life as much as in educational research, is selective. All descriptions are for some purpose and the nature of the purpose will crucially shape the character of the description. If, say, we are describing a classroom lesson, it will make a considerable difference whether our interest is in the extent to which there is balanced participation between girls and boys, in whether the teacher seems to discriminate against black students, in how the knowledge that forms part of the syllabus is presented, or in something else. The descriptions produced on the basis of these various interests may overlap, but equally they may be so different as to be not recognizably referring to the same lesson (although if we believe that they are all true they should not contradict one another). Just as there is always a large number of points of view from which we could *describe* a phenomenon, so, too, with *explanations*. These will not only be concerned with accounting for some aspects of a phenomenon rather than others, but will also involve the selection of explanatory factors partly according to the purpose that the explanation is to serve.

It is also of significance in this context that research reports are communications addressed to an audience. When we communicate with people they assume that we are telling them something that is likely to be of significance to them. If it turns out that we merely communicate facts, any facts, we shall soon find that we have few listeners. In the case of most educational research, the aim is to communicate with a relatively large audience (otherwise, what would be the point of publication?). It follows that what is communicated should be relevant in some way to such an audience. The obvious questions that follow from this are: who are the appropriate audiences and what sort of relevance should educational research reports have for them?

Intended audiences for research reports vary of course. Sometimes reports are directed primarily towards other researchers; sometimes they are addressed to a particular practitioner audience; sometimes they are directed at a general audience. Whatever the intended audience, though, there are two aspects of relevance that need to be distinguished:

- *The importance of the topic*. The research topic must relate (however remotely) to an issue of importance to the intended audience.
- *The contribution of the conclusions to existing knowledge*. The research findings must add something to our knowledge of the issue to which they relate. Research that merely confirms what is already beyond reasonable doubt makes no contribution.

In these terms research findings may connect with an important topic, but still not be relevant since they do not tell us anything new about it. Conversely, research may add new knowledge, but this may relate to no topic of any significance and so still lack relevance. Importance and contribution are necessary and jointly sufficient conditions for relevance, and we must assess any set of findings in terms of both; though, of course, there may be disagreement about these matters.

Later in this section we shall look at what is involved in applying the standard of validity to examples of educational research.[9] Before we can do this, though, we must look at the sort of reading of research reports that is necessary to lay the basis for such assessment.

4.3 READING FOR UNDERSTANDING

The first task in reading a research report is to try to understand what it focuses on and the arguments it contains. This means that we need to look for information of the following kinds: about the research focus; about the cases studied; about the methods of data collection and analysis; about the major claims and the evidence provided for them; and, finally, about the conclusions drawn concerning the research focus. While research reports are not always organized in these terms, information relevant to all of these matters can usually be found and it is useful to organize one's notes in terms of these headings. We shall spell out in a little more detail what we mean by each of them.

THE RESEARCH FOCUS

We use the term 'research focus' to refer to the most general set of phenomena (one or more) about which a study draws conclusions, and the aspects of those phenomena that are of concern. Equally, we can think of the research focus as the general set of questions that the study addresses. There are, of course, different sorts of question that can be addressed. The research may be primarily designed to answer descriptive, explanatory, predictive, evaluative or prescriptive questions. The distinctions among these types of question are not always made by researchers and, thus, may not be clearly marked in research texts. These different

[9] Applying the standard of relevance is something that only individual readers can do, since judgements of the importance of the topic, and perhaps even of whether the conclusions of the research contribute to existing knowledge, are likely to vary considerably across audiences.

types of question, however, place different requirements on the researcher, in terms of the sort of evidence that is required to support answers to them. They therefore have implications for what evidence the reader should expect.

Besides the focus itself, we must also look out for any rationale that the author offers as to why the focus is important and thus why the conclusions might be of interest to us. Most research reports provide some explicit statement of their focus and of its assumed significance, but this is not always the case. Here, for example, is the opening paragraph of an article on 'Gender imbalances in the primary classroom':

> It is now well established that in mixed sex classrooms male pupils receive more teacher attention than do females. Brophy and Good, for example, have observed that 'boys have more interactions with the teacher than girls and appear to be generally more salient in the teacher's perceptual field' (1970, p. 373). Stanworth (1983) and Spender (1982) have also noted an imbalance in this respect and, although their formulation is more tentative, Galton, Simon and Croll's conclusion is in essence the same: 'There does appear to be a slight tendency for ... boys to receive more contact than girls' (1980, p. 66).
>
> The present study reveals imbalances in teacher–pupil contact which, in broad terms, are compatible with these observations. However, rather than simply reporting the occurrence of the imbalances ... the principal aim of this study is to provide the basis for ... an explanation ... .
>
> (French and French, 1984, p. 127)

Activity 2

On the basis of this brief extract, what do you take to be the focus of French and French's research?

French and French give a clear account here of the focus of the research and of its relationship to other literature. The aim is to provide an explanation for gender imbalances in the distribution of teachers' attention and of pupils' participation in classroom interactions. They give no indication, however, of why they believe this focus to be important; nor do they provide this elsewhere in the article. Where a rationale for the focus is absent, we need to think about what the rationale might be.

Activity 3

Why do you think the authors believed this topic to be important?

There are various possibilities, but it seems to us that French and French probably regarded gender imbalance in classroom interaction as important because it might have effects on the relative achievement levels of girls and boys later in their school careers, which in turn might affect their job prospects.

Where there is a discussion of the focus of the study, and of a rationale for this, this usually occurs at the beginning of the account, though relevant material may be found in any part of it. In book-length studies, the rationale for the research focus may amount to one or more chapters, including reviews of the literature that identify the gap that the study is intended to fill.

THE CASES INVESTIGATED

There is a need for care in distinguishing the focus of the research from the case or cases studied. We defined the focus as the most general set of phenomena about which the study makes claims. Usually, this will be a *type* of phenomenon or some feature of a large *aggregate* of cases. Examples include 'school bullying', 'learning algebra', 'the pedagogical styles of secondary-school teachers in the United Kingdom', 'the curricular organization of primary schools in England and Wales', etc. By 'the case studied', on the other hand, we mean the phenomena specifically located in place and time to which the data analysed relate.

Educational research can vary considerably in the number of cases investigated. Quantitative research typically, but not always, studies quite large numbers: fifty or more, perhaps even thousands of cases. Qualitative research, on the other hand, usually deals with a small number of cases, perhaps even just one.

Sometimes the focus of the research is restricted to the cases studied, where these are of general interest in themselves. Sometimes the stated focus is the case studied even when this does not seem to be of obvious general interest. For example, in a study of classroom interaction, Hammersley explicitly limits his conclusions to what occurred in the particular inner-city secondary modern school he studied at the time he studied it (Hammersley, 1974). Such a cautious limitation of focus is surely misleading, however. After all, why would this study warrant publication if it did not have implications for some more widely relevant focus? Where this happens, we should probably conclude that the focus is different from the case studied, but is left implicit; and we must try to identify what seems likely to have been the intended focus.

Most accounts provide at least some information about the cases selected and the reasons for their selection. Of course, the information that could be provided is virtually endless. What we need is information that allows us to judge how confidently we can draw conclusions about the focus of the research from findings about the cases studied. This is necessarily a matter of judgement. Here, for instance, is what French and French provide in their article on gender imbalances in classroom interaction:

> The data to be considered comprise a verbatim transcription of a fourth-year junior school lesson (pupils aged 10 and 11 years). The lesson is one from an extended series that one of us (JF) observed and recorded as part of an ethnographic study of gender differentiation in primary classrooms. ... The lesson is organized as a teacher-class discussion of the topic 'What I do on Mondays and what I would like to do on Mondays'. In an earlier lesson pupils had addressed this topic in writing, but their essay answers proved unsatisfactory to the teacher. The present lesson therefore covers a number of points which, the teacher explains, he would like to have seen included. After the lesson, pupils make a second attempt at the essay. The class contained 29 pupils, 16 girls and 13 boys. The teacher was male.
>
> (French and French, 1984, p. 128)

In addition to information about the cases studied, we must also look out for any indication of why the cases are believed to be of relevance to the research focus, or at least the basis on which they were selected. This may involve the claim that the cases are typical of some category or population of cases. In the case of quantitative research the cases studied may be a systematically selected sample from the aggregate that is the focus of the research. Indeed, sometimes the selection will have been made on a random basis, in such a way as to maximize the chances that the cases studied are representative. Often, though, there will be an element of convenience built into the sampling strategy, and this sometimes makes generalization problematic. For example, in a well-known study of teaching styles and pupils' performance in primary schools, Bennett studied a large sample of teachers, but they all worked in schools in the North West of

England, within easy access of Bennett's base at the University of Lancaster (Bennett, 1976). This means that, in some respects at least, these teachers were probably unrepresentative of larger populations, such as primary teachers in England and Wales. In the case of qualitative research, where a relatively small number of cases is usually studied, generalization to a larger population is often even more problematic. Here, though, as with Bennett's work, judgements of the wider significance of the findings can usually be made on the basis of information about the sample itself, on the one hand, and whatever information is available about the wider population to which generalization is to be made, on the other.

IDENTIFYING THE MAIN ARGUMENTS AND EVIDENCE

The most central task in understanding a study is to identify its main findings, and the evidence presented in support of them. Above, we drew a distinction between the research focus and the case or cases studied. Corresponding to this, we shall also make a distinction between the conclusions of a study, which relate to its focus, and the major claims, which relate to the cases. In looking for the major claims of a study we are therefore looking for those findings that refer specifically to the cases investigated, leaving any that refer beyond them for later consideration as conclusions. Of course, there will often be considerable overlap in content between the major claims and the conclusions; that which is found in the cases studied frequently being generalized to other cases. The distinction between claims and conclusions is important because assessing the validity of such generalizations is an extra task over and above assessment of the claims themselves.

Within any research report there will be a host of claims made and the task of identifying the main ones involves detecting the argumentative structure of the account so as to see which are superordinate and which subordinate. Usually this is not too difficult: authors will indicate to one degree or another which are the most important points they are making, and how the others relate to these. Sometimes, of course, authors provide summaries of their claims. These may occur in the conclusions at the end of an article, or in concluding chapters of books, or they may come earlier. Here, for example, is the author's summary, provided quite near the beginning of his article, of an account of the effects of variations in teachers' expectations on pupils' performance in the kindergarten and early grades of an inner-city school in a predominantly black urban community in the United States (we have introduced paragraphs into this extract for the purpose of clarification).

> The argument may be succinctly stated in five propositions.
>
> First, the kindergarten teacher possessed a roughly constructed 'ideal type' as to what characteristics were necessary for any given student to achieve 'success' both in the public school and in the larger society. These characteristics appeared to be, in significant part, related to social class criteria.
>
> Secondly, upon first meeting her students at the beginning of the school year subjective evaluations were made of the students as to possession or absence of the desired traits necessary for anticipated 'success'. On the basis of the evaluation, the class was divided into groups expected to succeed (termed by the teacher 'fast learners') and those anticipated to fail (termed 'slow learners').
>
> Third, differential treatment was accorded to the two groups in the classroom, with the group designated as 'fast learners' receiving the majority of the teaching time, reward-directed behaviour, and attention from the teacher. Those designated as 'slow-learners' were taught infrequently, subjected to more frequent control-oriented behaviour, and received little if any supportive behaviour from the teacher.

> Fourth, the interactional patterns between the teacher and the various groups in her class became rigidified, taking on caste-like characteristics during the course of the school year, with the gap in completion of academic material between the two groups widening as the school year progressed.
>
> Fifth, a similar process occurred in later years of schooling, but the teachers no longer relied on subjectively interpreted data as the basis for ascertaining differences in students. Rather, they were able to utilize a variety of informational sources related to past performance as the basis for classroom grouping.
>
> (Rist, 1970, pp. 413–4)

Such summaries are extremely useful in giving us a sense of the overall argument of a study, but we should not rely on them entirely. Sometimes, we shall find that, in our own judgement at least, they are not entirely accurate or complete. For example, *our* summary of Rist's main claims would include one that he omitted: that the pupils themselves responded differentially to the teacher's behaviour towards them, in ways that reinforced the teacher's expectations. Also, where Rist refers to two groups of children in the summary (fast and slow learners), the teachers he studied divided their classes into three groups, though still ranging from 'fast' to 'slow'.

Although summaries of the main claims provided by the author are useful, then, they are no substitute for one's own careful reading of the whole text. At the very least, one may find differences of emphasis between the summary and the actual account, and sometimes there can be important discrepancies. Finally, it is worth noting that authors may mix what we have distinguished as claims and conclusions.

Once we have identified the main claims, we need to think about what *sorts* of claims they are. There are several types of claim to be found in educational research reports, and it is worth distinguishing among these because they require different sorts of evidence. They can be listed under three headings, as follows:

1 Definitions

2 Factual claims
   - (a) descriptions
   - (b) explanations
   - (c) predictions

3 Value claims
   - (a) evaluations
   - (b) prescriptions

Definitions

Definitions tell us how a particular term is being used in an account. For instance, in introducing a distinction between teaching and survival strategies on the part of secondary school teachers, Woods provides the following definition of 'survival':

> It is, in short, a *survival* problem. What is at risk is not only [the teacher's] physical, mental and nervous safety and well-being, but also his continuance in professional life, his future prospects, his professional identity, his way of life, his status, his self-esteem ... .
>
> (Woods, 1979, p. 145)

Woods is spelling out here what he means when he claims that teachers are concerned with 'survival'. This is essential information if we are to be able to assess his argument that survival was a predominant concern among the secondary-school teachers he studied.

It is unlikely that the central claims of a study would be definitional. As in the example of Woods' work, however, definitions may well form an important part of the substructure of the argument.

Factual claims

By factual claims we mean those that document features of the cases studied by the researcher, and their causes and consequences. These claims may take several forms: descriptions, explanations, or predictions.

Descriptions Descriptions are one of the most important sorts of argument to be found in research texts, since all of the other types, apart from definitions, depend on them. We cannot explain, predict, evaluate, or prescribe about something without describing it, or at least assuming some description of it.

What we mean by a description is a verbal or numerical representation of some feature of an object: for example, of a person or a situation. Often, descriptions will be quite complex, relating to multiple features of many objects. Here is some of the descriptive information about the participation of boys and girls that French and French provide in the research on gender imbalance in primary classrooms referred to earlier:

> *(i) Distribution of interaction turns between boys and girls*
>
> We begin the analysis with a numerical breakdown of the interaction turns that occurred during the lesson.
>
> **Table 1**
>
> | | |
> |---|---|
> | Turns taken by teachers | 81 |
> | Turns taken by pupils as 'chorus' | 33 |
> | Turns taken by unidentified pupils | 8 |
> | Turns taken by boys (13 out of 29 pupils) | 50 |
> | Turns taken by girls (16 out of 29 pupils) | 16 |
> | Total | 188 |
>
> Table 1 indicates that, when taken as categories, 'boys' took more turns than did 'girls': 50 instances of turn-taking are clearly attributable to boys as against only 16 to girls. When one considers that girls are in a (16:13) majority in the class, the proportions of the imbalance become all the more apparent.
>
> [...]

(ii) Detailed breakdown of interaction turns

Table 2

Male speakers	*Turns*	*Female speakers*	*Turns*
Tom	17	Marie	5
Matthew	10	Rachel	3
Andrew	10	Angela	2
Simon	5	Sharon	2
Peter	3	Anne	1
Wayne	1	Claire	1
Jason	1	Laura	1
Warren	0	Rowena	1
Thomas	0	Anna	0
Andrew C.	0	Debbie	0
Allan	0	Gina	0
Martin	0	Helen	0
Paul	0	Jenny	0
		Joanne	0
		Linda	0
		Lorraine	0

It is clear from Table 2 that it is not the boys generally who monopolize the interactional space of the lesson. Indeed, some boys take fewer or no more turns than most girls. The distributional imbalance between boys and girls is manifestly due to a particular, small subset of boys taking a disproportionately higher number of turns (Tom 17, Matthew 10, Andrew 10, and Simon 5).

(French and French, 1984, pp. 127–8)

In this extract we have a mixture of numerically and verbally presented information that describes some aspects of the pattern of interactions between the teacher and pupils in the lesson studied, in particular as regards gender differences.

It is worth noting that descriptions are always selective, they never include all the information that could, in principle, have been provided about the phenomena studied. Thus, French and French do not tell us about the amount of time the children spent on and off a task, what their relative levels of ability were, what proportions came from working-class and middle-class homes, etc. What is selected should, of course, relate to the focus of the research, as indeed it does in this case. And all of the information relevant to that focus needs to be presented.

Explanations Where descriptions provide an account of features of some phenomenon, explanations are concerned with *why* one or more of those features occurred; and seek to show that they are the product of particular factors, operating directly or indirectly. We can illustrate this in relation to Rist's study of teacher-pupil interactions in the early years of schooling. It is the central claim of his account that the different levels of achievement of the children are largely a product of the teachers' expectations of them, based on social class. Therefore, besides providing descriptions of the teachers' procedures for allocating children to groups, and of their interactions with members of these groups, Rist also makes an explanatory claim. Indeed, the descriptive claims are subordinated to the task of explanation.

Explanations, like descriptions, are selective. For any phenomenon, we can identify a potentially infinite number of causes. There may be one or more immediate causes and each of these can in turn be explained in terms of other more remote causes – and so on, *ad infinitum*. For instance, we may explain the differential performance of the children that Rist studied in terms of differences in academic ability, or in their attitude to school. Each of these variables, along with Rist's own preferred explanatory factor (the teachers' expectations), could be explained on the basis of more remote factors, for example differences in the children's home background. Furthermore, home background could, in turn, be explained by appeal to family histories, or to the nature of the local communities from which the children come. These, again, may be accounted for on the basis of various features of the character and history of American society, notably its racial and social-class structure (as indeed Rist seeks to do later in his article). The implication of this is that where explanations are presented we must look out for any indication of the criteria that have guided the selection of explanatory factors.

Predictions By 'predictions' we mean claims that if particular conditions are met certain other events will occur. Predictions are symmetrical with explanations. In explaining something we start with what happens and look for significant causes; in predicting we start with some actual or possible state of affairs and pick out likely effects that are significant. Once again, relevance to the focus underlies the process of analysis here. There is an infinite number of potential consequences, immediate and more remote, that may follow from any given conditions. Not all will be judged relevant.

Predictions do not often form part of the major claims in educational research. They do occur as part of the substructure of the argument, however. Indeed, as we shall see in Section 6, they play an important part in much quantitative analysis, where what actually happened is compared with what would have been expected to happen given particular theoretical assumptions. As with explanations, when we identify predictive claims we must look out for the theoretical claims implicit in them, and for the relevances that have structured them.

Value claims

By value claims we mean those which not only describe, explain and/or make predictions about a feature but also express some view about it in terms of one or more values. There are good arguments for suggesting that research reports should not include value claims, since the primary task of research is to produce factual knowledge and, as we have seen, value judgements cannot be based solely on such knowledge. However, research reports do sometimes include such judgements.

Evaluations Evaluations involve descriptions of phenomena and perhaps explanation of them. In addition, they also give some indication of whether the things described or explained are good or bad, or in what respects they are good or bad. Some educational research openly shuns evaluative intent, being exclusively concerned with describing or explaining what *is* rather than what *ought to be*. As we saw in Section 2, however, there is a considerable amount of such research that is explicitly devoted to evaluation. Moreover, it is not uncommon to find evaluative claims embedded in many other educational research reports, too. For example, in Peter Woods' description of the process of choosing a course at the secondary school he studied, he contests the teachers' claim that 'the advice and guidance offered is given in the best interests of the pupil' (Woods, 1979, p. 51). Here he is moving beyond description and explanation to an evaluation of the teachers' actions (Hammersley, 1990a).

Of course, evaluations necessarily imply some set of values and we need to look out for information about what these are.

Prescriptions Occasionally, on the basis of their research, researchers outline some recommendations about what changes ought to be made in the phenomena that they have studied. In the conclusion to an account of the coping strategies that teachers use to deal with the constraints imposed upon them by the British educational system, Andy Hargreaves offers the following:

> The crucial axis which might provide the possibility for radical alteration and humanisation of our educational and social structures would seem to be that which connects teacher 'experience' to structural constraints. Change of such a magnitude demands the active involvement of teachers in particular, and men and women in general, in the collective criticism of existing practices, structural arrangements and institutional goals. Furthermore, the possibility of change is contingent upon the provision of institutional conditions under which such collective criticism could take place and be reflexively integrated with ongoing practice. Paradoxically, this requires the fulfilment of 'gradualist' policies such as small class-sizes and the creation of more 'free-time' so that a meaningful integration between theory and practice might arise and thus produce a reconstruction of teacher 'experience' on radical lines, infusing it with the power of transformation.
>
> (Hargreaves, 1978, pp. 81–3)

What is being suggested here is not very clearly specified and it is worth noting that Hargreaves does not explicitly recommend the possible 'radical alteration and humanisation' or the gradualist policies he mentions, but it seems obvious that he is nonetheless to be read as prescribing them.

The reader needs to watch carefully for evaluations and prescriptions that seem to take the form of descriptions, explanations or predictions. As with evaluations, in trying to understand prescriptions we must try to identify the values underlying them.

IDENTIFYING CONCLUSIONS

Earlier, we drew a distinction between major claims and conclusions, the former applying to the case or cases studied, the latter going beyond these to deal with the focus of the study. Therefore, as the final step in trying to understand a research report, we need to identify the conclusions of the report. Sometimes there will be a section labelled 'Conclusions', but as we noted earlier authors do not always distinguish between major claims and conclusions. It is therefore not unusual to find major claims as well as conclusions summarized in closing sections. As an example, here is the final section from the article by French and French:

> *(iii) Policy implications*
>
> Our suggestion here has been that gender imbalances in teacher attention and turn distribution among pupils may be in part attributable to subsets of boys engaging in strategies to secure that attention. Rather than attempting an exhaustive account of these strategies, we have provided only a broad outline of some of the more obvious exemplars. The analysis should be received, then, as a beginning, not as an end to investigation of this area. Even at this early stage, however, we would see the sort of approach adopted here as bearing relevance to those who are concerned about the remediation of gender imbalances at the level of classroom practice.
>
> Feminist work in pursuit of this goal has already pointed, though in general rather than detailed terms, to the tendency for boys to demand more of the teacher and hence receive more than their share of attention (Spender, 1982). Whilst existing analyses have therefore

> acknowledged that pupils may play a part in the shaping of classroom events, rather more emphasis has, in our view, been placed upon teachers being socially and psychologically predisposed to favour boys. As we have already noted, we do not oppose this claim. However, we would suggest that the redress of imbalances in teacher attention does not necessarily follow from the remediation of male-biased attitudes in teachers, unless they also become sensitive to the interactional methods used by pupils in securing attention and conversational engagement. Although there is occasionally evidence that teachers are aware of pupils' behaviour in this respect ... it may well be that in a great many instances pupil strategies remain invisible to them. Teachers' immersion in the immediate concerns of 'getting through' lessons may leave them unaware of the activities performed by boys in monopolizing the interaction.
>
> This view finds support in a recent report by Spender. Even though she consciously tried to distribute her attention evenly between boys and girls when teaching a class, she nevertheless found that 'out of 10 taped lessons (in secondary school and college) the maximum time I spent interacting with girls was 42% and on average 38%, and the minimum time with boys was 58%. It is nothing short of a substantial shock to appreciate the discrepancy between what I *thought* I was doing and what I actually *was* doing' (Spender 1982, p. 56; original emphasis). We think that one would be safe in assuming that Spender's lack of success could not be attributed to her having a male-biased outlook. It seems clear to us that much would be gained from developing, in the context of teacher education programmes, an interaction-based approach to this issue which sought to increase teachers' knowledge and awareness of what may be involved through the use of classroom recordings.
>
> (French and French, 1984, pp. 133–4)

Here, on the basis of their claim that there was an imbalance in participation in the lesson they studied in favour of the boys, and that this was produced by attention-seeking strategies used by a small number of them, French and French conclude that such strategies may also be responsible for gender imbalance in other contexts. On this basis they recommend that teachers need to be aware of this if they are to avoid distributing their attention unequally.

As this example indicates, conclusions, like main claims, can be both factual and value-based. We will focus here on factual conclusions. There are two ways in which researchers may draw such a conclusion. One is by means of what we shall call 'theoretical inference' and the other is by generalizing the findings in the case studied to a larger number of cases, which we shall refer to as 'empirical generalization'.

Theoretical inference

In the sense in which we are using the term here, theories are concerned with why one type of phenomenon tends to produce another, other things being equal, *wherever* instances of that first type occur. While studies concerned with drawing theoretical conclusions do, of course, have an interest in particular phenomena occurring in particular places at particular times, that interest is limited to the relevance of those phenomena for developing and testing theoretical claims.

Most experimental research relies on theoretical inference in drawing conclusions. For example, in the case of Piaget's research on children's cognition, mentioned in Section 2, he sought to create situations that would provide evidence from which he could draw conclusions about the validity or otherwise of his theoretical ideas. His critics have done the same. Thus, Donaldson and others have carried out experiments designed to test his theory against competing hypotheses, such as that the children in his experiments simply did not understand properly what they were being asked to do.

Non-experimental research may also rely on theoretical inferences, but often the distinction between theoretical inference and empirical generalization is not drawn explicitly, so that sometimes it is not easy to identify the basis on which conclusions have been reached.

Empirical generalization

Instead of using the cases studied as a basis for theoretical conclusions, researchers may alternatively seek to generalize from them to a finite aggregate of cases that is of general interest. For example, Woods claims that the secondary school he studied was:

> ... ultra-typical in a sense. Pressure was put on the teachers to prosecute their professional task with extra zeal; both the task, and the strategies which supported or cushioned it, were, I believe, highlighted in consequence. In turn, the pressures on the pupils being greater, their resources in coping were stretched to great limits and appeared in sharper relief. Thus, though the school could be said to be going through a transitional phase, it was one in which, I believe, typical processes and interrelationships were revealed, often in particularly vivid form.
>
> (Woods, 1979, pp. 8–9)

Woods does not tell us which larger population of schools he believes this school to be typical of, but we can guess that it was probably secondary schools in England and Wales in, say, the 1970s and 1980s.

In examining the conclusions drawn in research studies, we therefore need to consider whether theoretical inference or empirical generalization, or both, are involved. As far as theoretical conclusions are concerned, we need to be clear about the theory that the cases have been used to develop or test, and about why those case studies are believed to provide the basis for theoretical inference. Where empirical generalization is involved, we must look out for indications of the larger whole about which conclusions are being drawn, and for the reasons why such generalization is believed to be sound.

4.4 READING FOR ASSESSMENT

Understanding the argument of a research report is usually only the first task in reading it. Often, we also wish to assess how well the conclusions are supported by the evidence. In Section 4.2 we introduced the concept of validity as a standard to be used in assessing research reports and explained how we thought the validity of claims and conclusions could be assessed. We suggested that this assessment had to rely on judgements of plausibility and credibility.

It is rare for the major claims in research reports to be so plausible that they need no evidential support. It is unlikely that any such claims would be judged to have much relevance. Faced with a claim that is not sufficiently plausible to be accepted, the second step is to assess its credibility. Here the task is to decide whether the claim is of such a kind that a researcher, given what is known of the circumstances of the research, could have made a judgement about the matter with a reasonably low chance of error. Here, we must use what knowledge we have, or what we can reasonably assume, about how the research was carried out. For instance, we must look at whether the research involved the researcher's own observations or reliance on the accounts of others, or both; and whether the claims are of a kind that would seem unlikely to be subject to misinterpretation or bias. Again, it is rare for major claims to be sufficiently credible to be accepted at face value.

As an illustration of judgements about credibility, let us consider again the research of Ray Rist into the effects of teachers' expectations of pupils' school performance (Rist, 1970). In the course of his study, Rist makes claims about which pupils were allocated to which classroom groups by the kindergarten teacher he studied. It seems to us that we can conclude that his judgement of this distribution is unlikely to be wrong, given that it involves a relatively simple matter of observation, that he observed the class regularly over a relatively long period, and that on this issue he seems unlikely to have been affected by bias. However, Rist also makes the claim that the three groups of children received differential treatment by the teacher. In our view, the validity of this second claim should not be accepted simply on the basis of his presence as an observer in the situation. This is because multiple and uncertain judgements are involved: for example, judgements about amounts and types of attention given to pupils by the teacher over a lengthy period of time. Thus, while we might reasonably accept Rist's first claim as credible on the basis of what we know about his research, we should not accept his second claim on the same basis.

If we find a claim very plausible or highly credible, then we should be prepared to accept it without evidence. If we judge a claim to be neither sufficiently plausible nor credible, however, then we must look to see whether the author has provided any evidence to support it. If not, then our conclusion should be that judgement must be suspended. If evidence *is* provided we must assess the validity of that evidence in terms of *its* plausibility and credibility. Where that evidence is itself supported by further evidence, we may need to assess the latter too.

As we saw earlier, claims can be of several types, and different sorts of evidence are appropriate to each. Let us look at each type of claim and the sort of evidence required to support it.

DEFINITIONS

Definitions are not empirical claims about the world, but statements about how an author is going to use a term, about what meaning is to be associated with it. As such, they are not open to assessment in the same manner as factual claims, but this does not mean that they are open to no assessment at all.

One obvious assessment we can make of a definition is whether it has sufficient clarity for the purposes being pursued. Where there is a standard usage of a term that is clear enough for the purposes at hand, no definition is required. Many concepts used in educational research, however, are ambiguous or uncertain in meaning and yet they are often used without definition. A notorious example is 'social class', which can have very different definitions, based on discrepant theoretical assumptions; usage is often vague. Many other concepts raise similar problems.

Faced with uncertainty about the meaning of key concepts, whether or not definitions are provided, we must give attention to two aspects of that meaning: intension (the concept's relationship to other concepts) and extension (its relationship to instances).

To clarify the intension of a concept we must identify other elements of the network to which it belongs. Concepts get some of their meaning by forming part of a set of distinctions that is hierarchically organized. We can illustrate this by looking at Woods' contrast between teaching and survival strategies on the part of secondary school teachers, mentioned earlier (Woods, 1979, chapter 7). We can note that despite their differences, these are sub-types of a higher-level category – teachers' strategies. This opens up the question of what other types of action teachers use in the classroom, besides strategies. Similarly, at the other end of this conceptual network, Woods himself identifies a variety of different sorts of survival strategy. Putting these two points together, we can see how the distinction between teaching and survival strategies forms part of a larger conceptual structure which can be represented diagrammatically as shown in Figure 1.

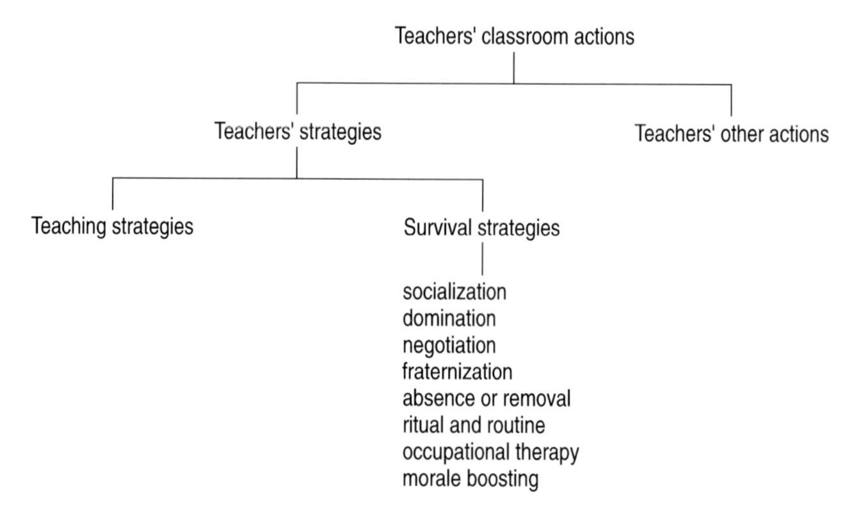

Figure 1

By mapping out conceptual networks of this kind we may be able to see weaknesses in the formulation of key terms. In the case of Woods' study, it seems that the distinction between strategies and other forms of classroom action on the part of teachers might need clarification.

The second aspect of meaning, extension, concerns what would and would not count as instances of a category. Sometimes the problem of identifying instances may be quite difficult. Staying with the example from Woods, he argues that survival strategies:

> ... expand into teaching and around it, like some parasitic plant, and eventually in some cases the host might be completely killed off. However, like parasites, if they kill off the host, they are a failure and they must die too, for they stand starkly revealed for what they are. The best strategies are those that allow a modicum of education to seep through. Alternatively, they will appear as teaching, their survival value having a higher premium than their educational value.
>
> (Woods, 1979, pp. 146–7)

Although the definition of survival is reasonably clear in its intension, its extension is problematic. Given that the concern with survival may masquerade as teaching and that survival strategies may have educational value, how are we to distinguish instances of the two? This issue may be of considerable importance if we are to assess the validity of Woods' claims.

Another basis on which we may criticize definitions is that they fail to make distinctions that we believe are important, given the goal of the research. An example arises in Jean Anyon's report of a study of teacher–pupil relations in five elementary schools in the United States. Discussing her findings in two of the schools, catering primarily for working-class pupils, she writes the following:

> A dominant theme that emerged in these two schools was student *resistance*. Although some amount of resistance appeared in every school in this study, in the working-class schools it was a dominant characteristic of student–teacher interaction. In the fifth grades there was both active and passive resistance to teachers' attempts to impose the curriculum. Active sabotage sometimes took place: someone put a bug in one student's desk; boys fell out of their chairs; they misplaced books; or forgot them; they engaged in minor theft from each other; sometimes they rudely interrupted the teacher. When I asked the children during interviews why they did these things they said, 'To get

> the teacher mad'; 'Because he don't teach us nothin'; 'They give us too many punishments'. When I asked them what the teachers *should* do, they said, 'Teach us some more'; 'Take us alone and help us'; 'Help us learn'.
>
> The children also engaged in a good deal of resistance that was more passive. They often resisted by withholding their enthusiasm or attention on occasions when the teacher attempted to do something special. ... Passive resistance can also be seen on some occasions when the children do not respond to the teacher's questions. For example, they sit just staring at the board or the teacher while the teacher tries to get them to say the answer, any answer. One such occasion, the teacher shouted sarcastically across the room to me, 'Just *look* at the motivation on their faces'. On occasions when teachers finally explode with impatience because nobody 'knows' the answer, one can see fleeting smiles flicker across some of the students' faces: they are pleased to see the teacher get angry, upset.
>
> (Anyon, 1981, pp. 11–12)

It has been argued, with some justification, that the concept of resistance used by Anyon is insufficiently discriminating. As Hargreaves comments: 'the mistake Anyon makes is to assume that acts of overt social protest are of the same nature as more minor transgressions, pranks and absences of enthusiasm ... . Almost all pupils' actions that fall short of absolute and willing compliance to teachers' demands are counted as resistance by her' (Open University, 1984, pp. 31–2). He contrasts this usage with the more restricted one found among other writers on pupils' orientations to school. They often distinguish a wide range of pupils' adaptations and recognize that not all of pupils' actions in the classroom are oriented primarily towards the teacher (see for example Furlong, 1976; Woods, 1979; Hammersley and Turner, 1980).

Definitions may be an important part of research accounts and, even where they are absent, they may need to be reconstructed by the reader (as far as that is possible). While they cannot be judged in empirical terms, we can assess their clarity; and whether they make what seem to be necessary distinctions given the purposes of the research.

DESCRIPTIONS

There are two main considerations we must bear in mind in looking at evidence for descriptions. First, how plausible and how credible are the evidential claims themselves? Secondly, how convincing is the relationship between them and the descriptive claim they have been presented to support.

Validity of evidential claims

Assessment of the validity of evidence must proceed in much the same fashion as we recommended in assessing the validity of major claims. To start with, we must assess its plausibility in terms of our existing knowledge. If it is very plausible, then we may simply accept it at face value. If not, we must assess its credibility.

In assessing credibility, we must take account of the process by which the evidential claims have been produced. The two basic sorts of evidence to be found in educational research reports are extracts from observational reports by the researcher and information provided by others, whether via interviews, responses to postal questionnaires, documents (including published statistics), etc. Let us look at the sorts of threat to validity associated with each of these sources of evidence.

The researcher's own observations These may take the form of tallies of the responses of experimental subjects, or of answers by interviewees to survey questions, or they may consist of field-notes or transcriptions of audio- or video-recordings, etc.

There are three general sources of error in observational reports that we need to consider.

First, we must think about the potential effect of the research process and of the researcher on the behaviour observed. This is often referred to as the problem of reactivity. Thus where people know that they are being observed they may change their behaviour: for instance, they may act in the way they believe they are supposed to, rather than the way they usually do. Equally important are the possible effects of the personal and social characteristics of the researcher on the behaviour observed. Thus, the age, gender, social class, 'race', professional identity, etc., of the researcher, or the participants' perceptions of them, may affect what people do and say when being observed.

Clearly, reactivity can be a significant source of error in researchers' observations. It is important, however, to remember what is at issue here. It is not whether the research process or the characteristics of the researcher have affected the behaviour that was observed, but rather whether they have affected it in respects that are relevant to the claims made (and to a significant degree). Often, reactive effects may be judged likely to have occurred, but unlikely to have had a significant effect on the validity of the findings.

A second source of error lies in the nature of what is being observed. Some features (e.g. which pupils are allocated to which group) are less likely to be misperceived than others (e.g. the similarities or differences in treatment of groups). This is not a matter of some features being directly observable in a way that guarantees the validity of observational reports, while other features are merely inferred. All observations involve inferences, but some are much less likely to be erroneous than others.

Thirdly, and equally important, we must consider features of the researcher and of the circumstances in which the research was carried out, in so far as these might have affected the validity of the researcher's observational reports. We need to think about the sorts of constraints under which observation occurred, and the resulting danger of misperceiving what took place (especially when simultaneously trying to record it).

There are two main strategies that researchers may use to record their observations of events, often referred to as 'structured' (or 'systematic') and 'unstructured' observation. The former involves the recording of events of predefined types occurring at particular points in time, or within particular intervals. A very simple example is the categorization of a pupil's behaviour as 'working' or 'not working' on a task, as judged, say, every twenty-five seconds. The aim of this would be to produce a summary of the proportion of time spent by the pupil on a task. As this example illustrates, 'structured' observation typically produces quantitative data (information about the frequency of different sorts of event or of the proportion of time spent on different types of activity). 'Unstructured' observation, by contrast, does not produce data that are immediately amenable to quantitative analysis. This form of observation involves the researcher in writing field-notes, using whatever natural language terms seem appropriate to capture what is observed, the aim being to provide a description that is relatively concrete in character, minimizing the role of potentially controversial interpretations.

These two forms of observation typically involve different threats to validity. Among the dangers with structured observation is that the predefined categories used will turn out to be not clearly enough distinguished, so that there is uncertainty in particular instances about which category is appropriate. There may also be relevant events that do not seem to fit into any of the categories. Unstructured observation generally avoids these problems because the language available for use in the description is open-ended. This, however, is only gained at the cost of the information being collected on different cases or at different times often not being comparable.

Increasingly, observational research uses audio- or video-recording, which usually provides a more accurate and detailed record than either 'structured' or 'unstructured' observation. These techniques, however, still do not record everything: for instance, audio-recordings omit non-verbal behaviour that can be very significant in understanding what is happening. Furthermore, audio- and video-records need to be transcribed and errors can be introduced here. Even transcription involves inference.

Besides features of the research process, we must also take account of what we know about the researcher, and the resulting potential for bias of various kinds. For example, we must bear in mind that Rist may have been unconsciously looking out for examples of what he took to be differential treatment of the 'slow learners', interpreting these as negative, and neglecting the respects in which all the children were treated the same. This is not a matter of dismissing what is claimed on the grounds that the researcher is probably biased, but rather of taking the possibility of bias into account in our assessment.

Information from others Information from others may take the form of responses to interview questions or to a postal questionnaire, documents of various kinds and even accounts given by one participant to another that were overheard by the researcher. They may be handled by the researcher in raw form, extracts being quoted in the research report, or they may be processed in various ways: for example, by means of descriptive statistics.

All three sources of error that we identified as operating on observers' reports must also be considered in relation to information from others. Thus, where they are reports from witnesses of events, we must consider the possible effects of the witness's presence and role on what was observed. Second, we must assess the nature of the phenomenon being described and the implications of this for the likelihood of error. The third source of error, the reporting process itself, is more complex in the case of information from others. We must note whether the account is a first-hand report, or a report of what others have told someone about what *they* saw or heard. Evidence of the latter kind is especially problematic, since we will not know what distortions may have occurred in the passage of information from one person to another. It should also be borne in mind that those who supply information are likely to rely on memory rather than field-notes or audio-recording, so that there is more scope for error.

In addition to assessing the threats to validity operating on the information available to the people supplying the information, we must also consider those that relate to the transmission of information from them to the researcher. For example, in the case of data obtained by interview we must assess the effects of the context in which the interview took place: for what audience, in response to what stimulus, with what purposes in mind, under what constraints, etc., did the person provide information to the researcher? Also, what threats to validity may there have been to the researcher's recording and interpretation of the information? Of course, it must be remembered that what are made available in research reports are selections from or summaries of the information provided, not the full body of information.

These, then, are the sorts of consideration we need to bear in mind when assessing the validity of evidence. Equally important, though, is the question of the strength of the inferences from the evidence to the main descriptive claim.

The relationship between evidence and claim

Evidence may seem quite plausible or credible in itself, and yet the support it offers for the claim can be questionable. Evidence sometimes gives only partial support, at best, for the set of claims that the author is presenting. Sometimes, too, one finds that there are other plausible interpretations of the evidence that would not support the claim. For example, French and French provide information about the number of turns taken by girls and boys in the lesson they studied. When they draw conclusions from this about the differential distribution of the teacher's attention, we might reasonably ask whether the inference from evidence to claim is sound. Does the number of turns at talking provide a good measure of the distribution of the teacher's attention? If it does, does the fact that the researchers were only concerned with discussions involving the whole class create any problems? Could it be that if they had taken account of informal contacts between the teacher and pupils their conclusions would have been different? The answer is that it is difficult to know on the evidence provided, and we probably should suspend judgement about their conclusions as a result (Hammersley, 1990b).

In this section we have looked at the assessment of descriptions, suggesting that this requires examination of the plausibility and credibility of the claims and of any evidence provided in their support. In the case of evidence, we must look at both the likely validity of the evidential claims themselves and of the inferences made on the basis of them. We have spent quite a lot of time looking at the assessment of descriptions because these are the foundation of almost all research. We shall deal with the other sorts of claim more briefly.

EXPLANATIONS AND PREDICTIONS

As we noted earlier, all types of claim (except definitions) include a descriptive component. Given this, the first step in assessing the validity of explanatory, and predictive, claims is to identify and assess their component descriptions, explicit or implicit. This is done in precisely the same way as one assesses any other description. Over and above this, though, we must look at how well the evidence supports the specifically explanatory or predictive element of the claim. There are two steps in this process. First, all explanations and predictions involve theoretical assumptions, and it is necessary to assess the validity of these. Second, it must be shown that the explanation or prediction fits the case at least as well as any competing alternative.

As an illustration, let us return again to Rist's study of early schooling. He argues that the differential achievement of the children after three years of schooling is significantly affected by the differential expectations of the teachers. The first question we must ask, then, is whether the theoretical idea he is relying on is plausible. The idea that teachers' expectations can affect children's learning has stimulated a great deal of research and certainly seems plausible at face value, though the evidence is mixed (see Rogers, 1982). We have no reason to rule it out of account.

The next question is whether Rist successfully shows that this factor is the most plausible cause in the cases he studied. The answer to this, in our view, is that he does not. This is because he does not deal effectively with the possibility that the differences were produced by other factors: for example, by differences in ability among the children before they entered school.

A similar sort of approach is required in assessing predictions. It is necessary, of course, to begin by assessing the description of the situation or causal factor from which the predicted event is believed likely to stem. If the period over which the prediction should have been fulfilled has expired, we must also examine any account of what actually occurred and its relationship to what was predicted. The next concern, as with explanations, is the validity of the theoretical assumptions on which the prediction is based. Can we accept them as plausible? Finally, we must consider the possibility that the predicted event would have occurred even if the factor that is claimed to have produced it had not been present, or that some other factor explains both of them. Here, again, we must rely on thought experiments to assess the likelihood of different outcomes under varying conditions; though we may subsequently be able to test out different interpretations in our own research.

The assessment of explanations and predictions, then, involves all the considerations that we outlined in discussing descriptions, plus distinctive issues concerning the specifically explanatory or predictive element. The latter, like the former, requires us to make judgements about what is plausible and credible, judgements that can be reasonable or unreasonable but whose validity or invalidity we can never know with absolute certainty.

EVALUATIONS AND PRESCRIPTIONS

In assessing evidence for value claims, once again we begin with their descriptive components. Is the phenomenon evaluated, or the situation to be rectified by the prescribed policy, accurately represented? In addition to this, in the case of prescriptions a predictive assumption is involved: that if such and such a course of action was to be taken a particular type of situation would result. The validity of these various assumptions must be assessed.

The distinctively evaluative or prescriptive element of claims concerns whether the phenomenon described, or the situation the policy prescribes, is good or bad. We must decide whether evidence is required to support this component (that is whether it is insufficiently plausible) and, if so, what evidence is necessary. What we are looking for here are arguments that appeal in a convincing way to generally accepted value and factual assumptions. On this basis, we must consider both what values have and have not been, should and should not have been, taken into account in the value judgement. We must also consider how those values have been interpreted in their applications to the particular phenomena concerned.

ASSESSING CONCLUSIONS

When it comes to assessing the conclusions of a study we have to look at the relationship between the information provided about the cases studied and what is claimed about the focus of the research on the basis of this evidence. Earlier, we identified two strategies by which researchers seek to draw such inferences: theoretical inference and empirical generalization. We need to look at how to assess examples of each of these types of inference.

Theoretical inference

Theoretical claims are distinctive in that they are universal in scope. They refer to a range of possible cases, those where the conditions mentioned in the theory are met, rather than specifically to a finite set of actual cases. What we must assess in the case of theoretical conclusions is the extent to which evidence about the case or cases studied can provide a basis for such universal claims.

We should begin by recognizing that there is one sense in which no basis for universal claims can be made: evidence about a finite number of particular cases can never allow us to draw conclusions on a strictly logical basis (i.e. with complete certainty) about a universal claim. This is known as the problem of induction. Various attempts have been made to find some logical basis for induction, but it is widely agreed that none of these has been successful (Popper, 1959; Newton-Smith, 1981). However, once we abandon the idea that a claim to validity must be certain beyond all possible doubt before we can call it knowledge, and accept that we can distinguish between claims that are more or less likely to be true, the problem of induction becomes less severe; though it is still not easy to deal with.

What we need to ask is: does the evidence from the cases studied provide strong enough support for the theory proposed to be accepted? Some cases will by their nature provide stronger evidence than others. Take the example of testing the theory that streaming and banding in schools produces a polarization in attitude on the part of students, with those in top streams or bands becoming more pro-school and those in bottom streams or bands becoming more anti-school. Hargreaves (1967) investigated this in a secondary modern school, where we might expect to find a polarization in attitude towards school resulting from the effects of different types of home background and school experience. Lacey (1970) tested the theory in a grammar school where most, if not all, of the students had been successful and probably pro-school in attitude before they entered the school. The fact that Lacey discovered polarization at Hightown Grammar constitutes much stronger evidence than any that Hargreaves' study could provide, in this respect, because in the case he investigated a key alternative factor (differences in attitude among pupils before they entered secondary school) had been controlled.

Empirical generalization

The other way in which researchers may seek to draw conclusions about their research focus from their findings about the cases studied is through empirical generalization. Here the aim is to generalize from the cases studied to some larger whole or aggregate of cases of which they form a part. A first requirement in assessing such generalizations is to know the identity of the larger aggregate. The second step is to make a judgement about whether that generalization seems likely to be sound. We can be reasonably confident about such judgements where statistical sampling techniques have been used effectively. Indeed, in such cases we can make precise predictions about the likelihood of the generalization being false. It is important, however, not to see statistical sampling techniques as the only basis for empirical generalizations. It may be possible to draw on relevant information in published statistics about the aggregate to which generalization is being made, and to compare this with what we know of the cases investigated. This at least may tell us if those cases are atypical in some key respect.

4.5 CONCLUSION

In this section we looked initially at the relationship between qualitative and quantitative approaches to educational research, and then at how we should set about assessing educational research reports. As is probably very clear from what we have written, our view is that 'quantitative' and 'qualitative' are simply labels that are useful in making sense of the variety of strategies used in educational research. They do not mark a fundamental divide in approaches to educational research.

To adopt this position is not to deny that there is considerable diversity in the philosophical and political assumptions that motivate or are implicit in educational research, as well as in the techniques of research design, data collection, and analysis that are used by educational researchers. Quite the reverse, we have tried to stress this diversity. What we deny is that it can be reduced to just two contrasting approaches.

We also question how much a commitment to particular philosophical and political assumptions determines what educational researchers do or should do, or how research reports should be evaluated. There is undoubtedly some influence in this direction, but it is less than might be imagined. In particular, it is very important to remember that research is a practical activity and, like other practical activities, it is heavily influenced by the particular purposes being pursued, by the context in which it has to be carried out (including the resources available), and by the particular audiences to be addressed. In other words, the approach one adopts depends at least as much on the sort of research in which one is engaged as on one's political or philosophical assumptions. The latter will shape how one goes about research, but will not determine it. Hence, one finds people doing research in similar ways whose philosophical and political assumptions are quite different. Equally, those who share the same assumptions often engage in very different kinds of research. In short, just as teaching is a practical activity that involves judgement and the taking into account of local circumstances, so too research is not simply the application of methodological principles. Those principles are important, but they are not all-important. This is essential to remember whether one is assessing research or engaged in it oneself.

Up to now we have only provided rather superficial information about the methods used by educational researchers to obtain and analyse data. In the next two sections of this Part we shall look in more detail at some of the principles and techniques involved in both qualitative and quantitative research.

5 QUALITATIVE RESEARCH

There are many types of qualitative educational research, influenced by different disciplines (mainly sociology and anthropology) and by different sorts of theoretical approach (symbolic interactionism, Marxism, etc.). Moreover, some qualitative work is aimed at developing disciplinary knowledge, while other work has a much more applied orientation (e.g. in the field of educational evaluation) and may even take the form of action research.

We shall concentrate here for the most part on the approach that has had the most general influence in the UK in recent years – ethnographic work deriving from symbolic interactionism. Studying one approach in some detail gives us an opportunity to follow through the interconnections between initial conceptualizations, data collection techniques, analysis, and theory generation and development. At the same time, though, many of the principles and techniques involved are shared in common with other forms of qualitative work.

5.1 MAIN FEATURES OF QUALITATIVE RESEARCH

Most forms of qualitative research have the following main features:

- A focus on natural settings.
- An interest in meanings, perspectives and understandings.
- An emphasis on process.
- Inductive analysis and grounded theory.

Let us consider each in turn.

A FOCUS ON NATURAL SETTINGS

Qualitative research is concerned with life as it is lived, things as they happen, situations as they are constructed in the day-to-day, moment-to-moment course of events. This might be contrasted with the setting up of artificial experiments. Qualitative researchers seek lived experiences in real situations. In general, they try not to disturb the scene and aim to be unobtrusive in their methods. This is to attempt to ensure that data and analysis will closely reflect what is happening.

At the same time, qualitative researchers welcome *natural* experiments. When ordinary processes are disrupted, basic rules and norms are thrown into relief. Usually, these rules and norms are tacit. They are understood, perhaps subconsciously, by people in a particular situation and may be difficult to discover by a researcher. The 1988 Education Reform Act set off a whole chain of 'natural experiments' as it challenged a number of basic assumptions. The introduction of material for the new curriculum, new teaching methods, institutional change, such as school amalgamations, or reforms in school organization, such as changing from streamed to mixed-ability groups, are all examples of natural experiments. They allow one to study 'what would happen if ... ' as it really happens.

A corollary of a commitment to naturalism is that the researcher makes as few assumptions in advance of the study as possible. Seeley (1966) drew the distinction between the 'making' and 'taking' of research problems. Sociologists, he argued, must make their own problems rather than 'taking' those defined by others. Mac an Ghaill (1989) describes how he changed from one to the other during the course of his research on the schooling of black youths. He started by 'taking a problem', accepting 'the white norm': that is, viewing black youths themselves as being the 'problem'. Placing students at the centre of his research and using qualitative methods to explore their perspectives brought him to a view that this norm was 'distorted, de-racialized and de-gendered' (p. 186). Through the process of research he 'made' a problem generated by what he discovered: namely, that students' behaviour was a response to a 'wider framework of sexism and racism'.

It helps if the researcher 'makes the familiar strange', not taking things for granted, questioning the bases of actions. The problems of studying the familiar are well illustrated by the sociologist Howard S. Becker:

> We may have understated a little the difficulty of observing contemporary classrooms. It is not just the survey method of educational testing or any of those things that keeps people from seeing what is going on. I think, instead, that it is first and foremost a matter of it all being so familiar that it becomes impossible to single out events that occur in the classroom as things that have occurred, even when they happen right in front of you. I have not had the experience of observing in elementary and high school classrooms myself, but I have in college classrooms and it takes a tremendous effort of will and imagination to stop seeing the things that are conventionally 'there' to be seen. I have talked to a couple of teams of research people who have sat around in classrooms trying to observe and it is like pulling teeth to get them to see or write anything beyond what 'everyone' knows.
>
> (Becker, 1971, p. 10)

Situations are deemed to be important because they influence behaviour. For example, Lacey (1976, p. 60) noted that many of the teachers in the school of his research were 'sincere in their desire to help and encourage their pupils to learn'. On occasions, however, these 'reasonable, kindly men' turned into 'bellowing, spiteful adversaries. They left the staffroom in good order; it was in the classroom that things went wrong'. Keddie (1971) also noted this change in teachers and advanced an explanation based on the difference between two contexts. In the 'educationist' context, which prevailed outside the classroom, teachers employed definitions derived from theory. For example, they saw streaming by ability as an institutional reinforcement of social-class inequalities. In the 'teacher' context of the classroom, however, their knowledge of pupils derived from streaming and prevailing definitions of 'ability'. Keddie argues that: 'This knowledge of what pupils are like is often at odds with the image of pupils the same teachers may hold as educationists since it derives from streaming, whose validity the educationist denies' (p. 139). Thus, it is argued, teachers are constrained by the circumstances of their work – large classes, examination pressures, mandated curriculum – which might exert a profound influence on their views, attitudes and behaviour. Clearly the research methods need to sample across these contexts to observe their effects.

For this reason, some qualitative researchers prefer fairly lengthy and deep involvement in the natural setting. Social life is complex in its range and variability. It also operates at different levels. Berger (1966, p. 34) talks of social reality having 'many layers of meaning. The discovery of each new layer changes the perception of the whole'. Blumer (1976, p. 15) talks of 'lifting veils'. A school, for example, typically presents a 'public face' to outsiders. A researcher who stays for one or two weeks might discover more than a casual visitor about how the school really works, for public facades cannot be maintained for long. A longer stay is needed and much work is necessary, however, to develop the knowledge, skills and trust that will permit entry into innermost arenas and confidences. This may not be necessary, of course, if the researcher is already an insider.

Methodologically, a focus on natural settings means, firstly, maintaining a certain openness of mind, not pre-judging the matter, nor necessarily settling for first or even second appearances. As in all research, curiosity should be fostered, in this case to see beneath the various layers. What is presented is carefully noted, but the status to be attached to it is temporarily suspended. Guesses might be made, tested along the way and abandoned, changed or revised in the light of later discoveries. Secondly, in its purest form, this kind of investigation is conducted in the actual situation of the object of study and over a period of time. Depending on the area under investigation, it can take months or years working 'in the field'. This is not to say that smaller-scale studies, say of a classroom, or an interview with a teacher or pupil, are without their uses. These will, however, have more limited objectives and be more exploratory. Thirdly, this mode of study has implications for the relationships the researcher fosters with subjects in the research. People are unlikely to allow total strangers into their private and confidential gatherings, or to tell them their innermost thoughts and secrets without certain guarantees. They must be backed by a certain trust in the researcher, reflected in the 'rapport' traditionally developed between researcher and subjects.

Activity 4

The advocacy of naturalism is not without its problems. In line with the major focus, it is common for qualitative research reports to try to re-create some part of the reality they have been studying by such techniques as finely detailed description, evocative language and liberal use of participants' own speech. Do you see any problems with such attempts to be naturalistic? Make brief notes on problems over the researcher (a) studying and (b) representing natural events.

You might well have asked how it is possible for one researcher to know what is happening or has happened in a certain situation – he or she has only one set of eyes and ears. A classic problem in qualitative research is the 'elsewhere syndrome' – a constant feeling that the important business is happening somewhere other than where the researcher is. Even in the situation where one is, one has to choose a focus. The basis for this selection is not always made clear. Would different researchers choose different foci? Would they *see* different things in the same foci? Representations of reality in these matters always involve some kind of selection and interpretation. One can guard against abuse of this fact by:

- being aware of it, and making one's selection a principled one, as far as that is possible (e.g. by appropriate sampling – discussed later);
- making reasonable claims in the research report;
- making the bases of one's selections and methods clear, and including some biographical information about the researcher. Seen like this, the researcher is not some faultless, detached recorder of an absolute truth, but a participant in the research process.

AN INTEREST IN MEANINGS, PERSPECTIVES AND UNDERSTANDINGS

The qualitative researcher seeks to discover the meanings that participants attach to their behaviour, how they interpret situations and what their perspectives are on particular issues. Just as situations can influence perspectives, as discussed above, so perspectives can help determine situations. Thus Denscombe (1980) shows how teachers, faced with an unpopular new policy of 'open' classrooms and team teaching, subtly 'closed' them again by, for example, breaking down the larger group of pupils into three sub-groups and individual members of the teaching team taking responsibility for them. Equally, some pupils' understanding of the school situation can be vastly different from teachers'. For example, they may see it not as a 'place of learning', but as an 'arena for socializing', for which learning may be counter-productive. Several studies have shown how pupils transform situations to be more in line with their own interests. Turner (1983) gives an example of a pupil who conformed in some lessons, but was disruptive in others. Turner argues that this was because the school did not always meet the pupil's own ideal of wanting to do well by providing good teachers. Bad teachers did not give 'proper lessons', therefore, but such lessons were functional in providing the pupil with an opportunity to respond to peer group pressure and 'mess about a bit'. A similar example arose in the research of Measor and Woods (1984) into the transfer of pupils between schools. The secondary school studied in this research was attempting to dissolve some gender boundaries by having a common curriculum, but pupils noticeably 'regendered' them. Boys used cakes as weapons and a sewing machine as a train. Girls protested about nasty smells and unisex goggles in physical science. In other words, these lessons were very useful to boys and girls in developing their gender identities. They also became very skilled in the practice of what the authors called 'knife-edging': that is, making the most of their options by delicately balancing some of them in opposition to each other – like in the example from Turner above where 'doing well' was counterpoised by 'mucking around'. They could define situations at will, switching between them with polished ease.

Activity 5

Study the following scenario. Place yourself in the position of (a) the pupils and (b) the teachers, and contrast their points of view. How might different understandings of the situation be at the bottom of the dispute?

> The 'blazer-ripping' incident
>
> At one secondary school the school blazer was a prime symbol of teachers' authority and pupils' subordination. The rules for school uniform were enforced with vigour in the interests of maintaining order. On the last day of term, it was traditional for there to be a certain amount of 'blazer-ripping' – symbolic of pupils gaining their freedom. One year, however, a boy's blazer was ripped to shreds early in the week of departure. This precipitated a crisis that disrupted the whole of the week for both teachers and pupils. The teachers launched a major offensive to apprehend and punish the culprits. The boys simply could not understand what all the fuss was about. 'They'd been writing all over blazers, writing their names on them, it's a traditional activity at the end of your school days'.
>
> (Woods, 1979, pp. 118–9)

The school uniform, the 'ideal' pupil's appearance, with its associated 'ideal' behaviour, is clearly an important symbol. Unsurprisingly, at the end of compulsory schooling, the desecration of these symbols by pupils is a prominent part of the celebrations, part of the rites of passage that mark transition into adulthood. Such desecration seems to be recognized as a legitimate activity by teachers, too, but only at the proper point of the passage – at the end of the week. The beginning of the week was still 'school', requiring business as usual, governed by school rules. Hence competing definitions of the situation between teachers and pupils were at the root of the problem.

Clearly the methods employed have to be sensitive to the perspectives of all participants. In addition, the research methods must pick up the interaction between perspectives and situation to see how they bear on each other. Researchers must also sample across time, since the same items or activities may mean different things on different occasions. If the researcher took the teachers' perspective the pupils would be blamed for the disorder; if the pupils' perspective were taken, the teachers would appear unreasonable.

Researchers therefore work to obtain 'inside' knowledge of the social life under study. If they are to understand people's outlooks and experiences, researchers must be close to groups, live with them, look at the world from their viewpoints, see them in various situations and in various moods, appreciate the inconsistencies, ambiguities and contradictions in their behaviour, explore the nature and extent of their interests, understand their relationships among themselves and with other groups. In short, researchers should, if possible, adopt the roles of the people being studied. To these ends, researchers have at times joined such groups as delinquent gangs, the teaching staff of a school, a group of hippies, bikers, or pupils.

The researcher tries to appreciate the culture of these groups. The task is to try to capture the meanings that permeate the culture as understood by the participants. The consequences of not doing so have been occasionally illustrated in teacher-pupil studies. Dumont and Wax (1971), for example, showed how a teacher of many years' experience took her pupils' silence and docility as indicating respectful conformity, when in fact it had the opposite meaning within the culture of the Cherokee community to which the pupils belonged. What she was doing was interpreting the pupils' behaviour solely through her own perspective and not theirs. Moore (1992) similarly suggests how a teacher, avowedly working to an anti-racist policy, was operating within an ethnocentric framework in evaluating a pupil's essay.

Close monitoring of scenes is required if we are to identify their inner mysteries. Understandings among pupils and teacher can become extremely recondite, triggered by the briefest of signals among them, which are inaccessible to outsiders. For example, Delamont and Galton (1986) refer to a 'Horace' joke. A child had spelt horse as 'h o r a c e' and it had been taken up by another child calling out 'Look! There's a Horace outside the window eating the grass'. Thereafter mis-spellers were referred to as 'Horace' or described as 'doing a Horace'. This may seem unremarkable – simply a joking aside – but basically it is a reminder both of group identity and of underlying rules, very important ones concerning correct spelling, which are both dramatized and made more acceptable by being displaced in humour and by being deeply embedded within the classroom culture. The group collectively thus 'owns' the mystery. It is something they have generated and which belongs to them and them alone as a group. The more impenetrable it is to outsiders the more successful it is in these respects.

The interrelationship between behaviour and language, and its embeddedness within the social structure of the classroom, is well illustrated by Werthman (1963) in describing how 'looking cool' emerges from interaction wherein teachers transgress certain unwritten but tacitly agreed rules. The heavy but ingenious symbolism of the behaviour is expressed here:

> Of all the techniques used by gang members to communicate rejection of authority, by far the most subtle and most annoying to teachers is demeanour. Both White and Negro gang members have developed a uniform and highly stylized complex of body movements that communicate a casual and disdainful aloofness to anyone making normative claims on their behaviour. The complex is referred to by a gang member as 'looking cool', and it is part of a repertoire of stances that include 'looking bad' and 'looking tore down'. The essential ingredients of 'looking cool' are a walking pace that is a little too slow for the occasion, a straight back, shoulders slightly stooped, hands in pockets, and eyes that carefully avert any party to the interaction. There are also clothing aides which enhance the effect such as boot and shoe taps and a hat if the scene takes place indoors.
>
> (Werthman, 1963, p. 221)

This behaviour is distinctive for its superb efficacy. Its message is clear, unmistakable and hurtful, but giving little purchase for counter-attack. Werthman's point of entry was the boys' references to 'looking cool', which the researcher then 'unpacked' by observations. Subjects' own references cue one in to important aspects of their culture, whether it is 'dossing or swotting', 'blagging or wagging', 'having a laugh', or 'bunking off'.

Distinctive terminology is not the only clue, however. Subjects may use the same words as the researcher, but intend very different meanings. Cues indicating a term of special significance might be frequency of use, emphasis and generality. Thus pupils' references to 'work' have been shown to vary among different groups. Furthermore, what various pupils understand by 'work' may be considerably different from the researcher. The words themselves are not enough, even though they may be the same as the researcher's. They have to be interpreted. The researcher aims for 'shared meanings, when one feels part of the culture and can interpret words and gestures as they do' (Wax, 1971).

Similarly, we need to know what meaning is attributed to actions by participants and beware of attributing our own.

Activity 6

Consider the following examples of classroom behaviour. In each case, if we were using pre-constructed categories, as in systematic observation, all observed instances of the action would have to be included. These actions could, however, have vastly different meanings to the participants. Note down some of the possibilities in each case.

(a) Student hits other student.

(b) Teacher asks a question.

(c) Student works.

We shall limit our comments to the first example, which comes from Wilson (1977), leaving you to consider the second and third examples. The qualitative researcher would want to know how the action was understood by those involved:

> How do the various participants (the hitter, person being hit, onlookers, teacher) perceive the event?
>
> Do they even see it as aggression?
>
> Do the hitter and person being hit concur on the meaning?
>
> (Wilson, 1977, p. 252)

Wilson goes on to point out that it may not even be an act of aggression. It could, in fact, be the reverse – an act of affection, or part of subcultural norms that indicate 'playful demonstration of strength'. Even if it is aggression, there are many subtleties involved. For example,

> The event could be an initiatory first act, or it could be a retribution for previous acts of aggression not necessarily linked immediately in space, time, or kind. The event could be part of a personal relationship between the two students involved, or it could be part of a larger interpersonal network of relations – for example, inter-group hostility.
>
> (Wilson, 1977, p. 252)

There are many other possible meanings to such an act, not all of them readily explainable by the participants. Though it may be impossible to comprehend them all, the researcher aims to uncover as many as possible through long-term observation and close discussion with the actors.

AN EMPHASIS ON PROCESS

As you saw in Section 2, educational research in the 1950s and early 1960s was strongly interested in input and output factors, such as parental social class and academic achievement, and in measuring the relationship between the two. Qualitative researchers, by contrast, are concerned with what goes on in between the input and output, that is, with processes. They are interested in how understandings are formed, how meanings are negotiated, how roles are developed, how a curriculum works out, how a policy is formulated and implemented, how a pupil becomes deviant. The researcher attempts to penetrate the layers of meaning and to uncover and identify the range and depth of situations and perspectives that apply in the area under study. This has been called 'thick description', which Denzin (1989) describes thus:

> It goes beyond mere fact and surface appearances. It presents detail, context, emotion and the webs of social relationships that join persons to one another. Thick description evokes emotionality and self-feelings. It inserts history into experience. It establishes the significance of an experience, or the sequence of events, for the person or persons in question. In thick description, the voices, feelings, actions, and meanings of interacting individuals are heard.
>
> (Denzin, 1989, p. 83)

Quantitative and qualitative methods can work well together here. For example, quantitative methods can show, by before and after tests, that change has occurred and, by surveys, how generally and frequently it occurred. On the other hand, qualitative methods reveal in fine detail just how change occurred in day-to-day activities, negotiations and decisions. Sometimes, however, quantitative and qualitative methods may appear to work against each other. This is well illustrated by studies of pupils' inter-ethnic association. The great majority of work in this area, using predominantly sociometric techniques, had previously found pupils preferring their own ethnic group and not forming many inter-ethnic friendships. Denscombe *et al.* (1986), however, state that this finding was contrary to many teachers' observations in the schools of their research.

Activity 7

On the basis of what has already been said about natural settings, meanings, perspectives, and process, how would you set about the qualitative study of pupils' inter-ethnic relationships? Consider what you would look for, how you would do it, how long for, where, and what part would be played by the pupils and by teachers, if any.

Let us take the study by Denscombe *et al.* as an example. They studied two multi-ethnic classes, using a range of methods, including extended observation of free association in the classrooms and in the playground. They indeed found a high degree of ethnic integration, which supported the teachers' own observations. This, of course, may be a product of those particular schools, but it is also quite likely that the quantitative techniques of the earlier studies failed to capture the complexity of the situation. There could have been many forms of interaction, both conflictual and consensual, both between and within ethnic groups, varying with situations, time, and in the nature and the degree of 'friendship'. In the quest for statistically significant results over a larger sample, a great deal of this significant interaction is missed. Furthermore, though the earlier work was about 'friendship', what this actually meant to the participants was not explored.

Qualitative methods, on the other hand, are designed to grasp the complexity and flux of social life. They may reveal that some forms of behaviour are fairly stable, others variable, others emergent and developmental. Some forms of interaction proceed in stages, and the research methods need to encompass each stage and its place in the whole. Consider, for example, the process of 'labelling' deviants.

Labelling may begin with some comparatively insignificant deviation from one's customary law-abiding role, which in itself is easily normalized. This is primary deviance. Secondary deviance arises out of the social reaction to primary deviance. As Hargreaves *et al.* (1975) put it:

> The labelling creates, under certain conditions, problems for the person who committed the deviant act which can be resolved by the commission of yet further deviant acts and by a self-designation as a deviant person. The paradox is that the social reaction which was intended to control, punish or eliminate the deviant act has come to shape, stabilize and exacerbate the deviance.
>
> (Hargreaves, 1975, pp. 5–6)

Consider the stages of the labelling process in the following hypothetical example:

1. A girl in a class of schoolchildren likes socializing with her peers during lessons and often talks to her neighbours.
2. She is perceived by the teacher as a chatterbox, a bit of a nuisance, a low achiever and, on occasions, a little 'sly' in her perpetration of misdeeds.
3. She is disciplined, perhaps through sarcasm. The sarcasm stings and promotes feelings of revenge and antagonism, which encourage her to increase her deviant behaviour.
4. The teacher meanwhile discusses the girl with colleagues, some of whom may have noted similar tendencies. There develops a consensual view of her deviance and she is treated as such by all her teachers.
5. The girl responds with more persistent deviant behaviour which becomes habitual. Eventually, the role becomes internalized and the girl acts out her teachers' expectations. This role may also be reinforced by her own peers' reactions to her.

The initial reaction by the teachers might have been crucial in this development. The 'primary' deviance, if treated in a different way, might have remained at a low level, marginal to the girl's otherwise completely acceptable behaviour. Clearly, it is necessary for the research methods to encompass the whole of this process, and to delineate each part of it and their interconnections. If only one part is sampled, the wrong conclusions might be drawn.

INDUCTIVE ANALYSIS AND GROUNDED THEORY

Qualitative researchers do not, on the whole, start with a theory which they aim to test and prove or disprove, though there is no reason why they should not do that if they wished. They mainly work the other way round, seeking to generate theory from data. The theory is then said to be grounded in the social activity it purports to explain (Glaser and Strauss, 1967).

The debate on differentiation and polarization, mentioned in Sections 2 and 4, is a good example of both the generation and testing of theory. The initial work of Hargreaves (1967) and Lacey (1970) in a secondary modern school and a grammar school, respectively, produced a theory that claimed that where pupils were differentiated by ability, as in streaming or tracking, then a polarization of attitudes into pro- and anti-school would occur among them. Ball (1981) examined this theory in a comprehensive school, finding the process still held under 'banding' (broad streaming arrangements), but was very much modified when mixed-ability classes were introduced. Abraham (1989) set out to explore the extent to which the theory was applicable to a setted comprehensive school in the south of England. He discovered a similar syndrome, but with variations, which led him to conclude that there were other factors helping to modify and promote polarization (such as examination and career pressure and the onset of subject options). Others have used and developed the theory in different settings:

Burke (1985) in a sixth-form college; Foster (1990) in a multi-ethnic comprehensive school. This, then, is an example of how qualitative researchers can build on each other's work in a theoretically productive way.

By no means all qualitative researchers are concerned to generate or test theory of this kind in this way. The 'thick' description typically produced is often termed 'theoretical description'. It might involve the generation of an idea or concept that offers to cast new light on the activity under study, such as 'labelling', as discussed earlier. Once an activity or process has been identified in this way, one can study the conditions that give rise to the activity, the context in which it is embedded and how it is managed. Of course, predictive theories can be developed from this kind of analysis and they can then be tested. Another popular form of analysis is the construction of models and typologies. We shall discuss this later in Section 5.3, but the important point to note here is the typically inductive nature of qualitative studies.

SUMMARY

We have considered the chief features of a popular approach to qualitative research. Firstly, it involves: a focus on natural settings; 'making', rather than 'taking' problems; making the familiar strange; recognizing the importance of situations; recognizing that there are different levels of activity in social life. Secondly, there is an interest in meanings, perspectives and understandings. This involves appreciating different definitions of situations, working to obtain inside knowledge and learning group culture. There is, thirdly, an emphasis on process, on complexity, flux and emergence. Consequently, there is an emphasis on covering whole processes and on producing a 'thick description' that will encompass this richness. Quantitative methods can work well here with qualitative ones, though there are dangers. Fourthly, the approach is characterized mainly by inductive analysis and grounded theory, (i.e. generating theory from data), though one line of development has seen the testing of theory in differentiation-polarization studies. In Section 5.2 we shall go on to consider the research methods that follow from this approach.

5.2 THE METHODS OF QUALITATIVE RESEARCH

The discussion of methods is organized around (a) the researcher's self (the main research instrument) and (b) validity. In the final section, the strengths and weaknesses of qualitative research are reviewed.

THE RESEARCHER'S SELF

Skills of the researcher

The qualitative researcher works to 'fine-tune' the self. So much depends on what one sees and hears that much rests on one's powers of observation and listening. The kinds of skills that are involved are those of social management – interpersonal skills that facilitate the negotiation of access both into private places and private thoughts, that develop the kind of trust and rapport that encourage people to relax, be 'natural', go about their everyday business in the researcher's presence in their usual way, to hold nothing back in an interview. Good social management helps to ensure that there are worthwhile things to be seen and heard. To this end some researchers have cultivated the 'good guy' image, one sympathetic to the group under study. Where there are two or more groups in conflict under study, considerable personal skills are required to handle the role conflict engendered in the researcher and to steer a way through the ethical issues that might be raised.

Though 'naturalism' may be a keynote, things do not just happen and unfold before one's eyes. One's right to witness and take part in other people's lives has to be worked for and earned. Though just 'hanging around' is a not uncommon activity in qualitative research and quite appropriate in some circumstances, at other times one has to make things happen in the sense of effecting entry to an important event or meeting, arranging interviews, approaching people with a view to conversing with them. For this, one needs inter-personal skills and fine judgement as to when to bring them into play and when to leave things alone. The inclination is to be as unobtrusive as possible, but sometimes important situations are not immediately revealed or access offered.

If entry is achieved, one then needs observational skills. These involve, in the first place, vision – the ability to see and take in a wide range of activity over a period of time. Vision consists of a cultivated power of scanning which ensures that as wide a portion of activity as possible is covered. Scanning will include the less as well as the more obvious places, people and activities. At the same time, the researcher needs powers of discernment – selecting specific aspects for more concentrated scrutiny and greater definition. This inevitably means letting other aspects go by. Two kinds of indicator – strange behaviour and the subjects' own distinctive terms – were mentioned in Section 5.1; others will be discussed in Section 5.3. Once these are detected, how to record material has to be considered. Filming and taping are useful aids where they do not intrude, but in many situations this is neither possible nor appropriate. The researcher therefore cultivates the art of mentally photographing and logging for commitment to written record as soon as possible, noting key aspects or comments on scraps of paper, or even a sleeve, summarizing incidents with key words that will recall whole incidents, speaking into a dictaphone, punctuating the period of observation with 'recording slots', to insure against 'drowning' in the data, and performing all these activities smoothly in a seamless web both for efficiency and so as not to intrude on the action.

Similarly, skills are needed for interviewing, at their centre a certain persona showing understanding of and empathy with the interviewee. Such a disposition would appear to be necessary if we are to penetrate 'fronts', achieve access to people's self and share in their innermost confidences. Once started, other skills are brought into play: notably *active listening*, which shows the other person that you hear and react, essaying interpretations occasionally, both with a view to maintaining the interpretative frame and keeping the other 'warmed up'; *focusing*, that is, keeping the interviewee to the subject and, in an unobtrusive way, not allowing rambling; *infilling* and *explicating* where material is incomplete, unclear or ambiguous; *checking* for accuracy by pressing points, seeking evidence, rephrasing, summarizing, playing devil's advocate, seeking contrary instances; *identifying* clues and indicators. There are few straight answers, there is always more to be said, people are of almost infinite depth. In some instances, such as life histories, the discussion may be a voyage of discovery for the subject as well. They may find out new things about themselves, or come to new realizations, which in a curious way, empower them. One ex-teacher, who was constructing his life-history with a researcher over a series of ten conversations, each lasting two to three hours, said:

> Now the more we talk about it, the more the uncertain things become, you know, fixed. The minute I put it into *my* words, my words, I've got it. Now the only other way is for me to go away and write it all down, longhand. When I've written it, again it's mine. So that's what I believe about this discussion thing. If you don't write copious notes, if you're not that sort of person, then you must sit down and talk about it.
>
> (Woods and Sikes, 1986, p. 176)

The interview, therefore, is not just a device for gathering information. It is a process of constructing reality to which both parties contribute and by which both are affected. Interviewers put something of themselves into an interview. It may be some contrasting or complementary experiences, perhaps, or some indications of their own personae, or at the very least they act as a sounding board. They come out reflecting on how the interview has affected their thoughts, ideas, viewpoints, theories. The researcher is, however, already looking to the next chain in the construction of the research, be it another interview in a different place, or at a different time, or with a different person; or be it observation, study of documents, questionnaire or whatever.

The researcher as a person

Thus the researcher is a finely tuned instrument with considerable skills, but is a person no less, with values, beliefs and a self. Since these are all bound up with the research, it is a very personal business. It frequently has as much to do with the understanding of oneself as of the world. For this reason, research diaries are often kept, containing reflexive observations. Thus the report may include some of these observations in a research biography, which acknowledges that the researcher is part of the research process and does not somehow stand outside it.

The researcher's own background, interests and values will be influential in selecting a topic for research. There are, however, other criteria used in selecting subjects for study. These include balance, which will direct one to areas and subjects as yet uncovered; refinement and development, where previous studies have not exhausted the topic; relevance, where the research is deemed to be directed toward some social good.

The research subject is thus identified partly by personal interests and values, as are some choices within the study, such as what to concentrate on, whom to see and talk to, what one sees and notices. The conduct of the research, however, is subject to checks and balances. One of these is representative sampling, or what Ball calls 'naturalistic sampling' (Ball, 1990, p. 102). This covers places, times, and persons. Thus, if we were studying teachers' or pupils' perspectives, or the culture of a group, we would need to consider them in different settings, since it is well known that behaviour can differ markedly in different situations, as noted in Section 5.1. This goes for interviewing as well as for observation. The character of a discussion and the quality of material can show a marked contrast between an interview held in the formal circumstances of a teacher's office and one held in the informal ambience of a pub. The same point applies to time. Weekly and yearly cycles, for example, are critical in schools. If our research sampled at just the beginnings and ends of terms, weeks, or days, we should end up with a distorted study if we were to claim our results applied more generally. Again, if we are seeking to represent a group in our findings, we should ensure that we have sampled across that group according to some appropriate criteria, which might be, for example, age, gender, ethnicity, or subject specialization.

Systematic sampling on this scale is not always possible, but at least the basis of one's sampling as far as it goes should be made clear. Sampling biases easily creep into qualitative work. Ball, for example, describes how he concentrated upon the academic teaching in the school and saw little of the 'non-academic' curriculum. He gave little attention to pastoral work or extra-curricular activities and observed those lessons to which he could gain access. He admitted that his 'account of the school is as a result profoundly distorted' (Ball, 1984, p. 77). Hammersley also reflects on how, in his research, he made *ad hoc* decisions about which lessons to record, concentrated on oral aspects of classroom work, made irregular visits to the staffroom, and indulged in uneven interaction with teachers. All of this raises questions about 'the representativeness of my data to which the lack of systematic sampling gave rise' (Hammersley, 1984, p. 51). In general, it is necessary to aim for 'intentional, systematic and theoretically guided' sampling (Hammersley, 1984, p. 53).

This cannot always be fully achieved in qualitative work because of (a) its initially largely unsystematic, exploratory nature; (b) problems of negotiating access; (c) problems of gathering and processing data using only one set of ears and eyes. Some unrepresentativeness is almost inevitable, therefore. Often, one has to make do with an 'opportunity sample' in those areas where access is offered; or a 'snowball sample', where the sample is developed through personal contact and recommendation. In all these cases the biases should be recognized and no inappropriate claims made.

However rigorous the methods used, the research is always a construction. This is because researchers must put their own selves into the research and interpret what they see or hear. This is so however much one tries to disguise one's presence. King (1978) took refuge in the 'play house' in an infants' classroom so that he could better observe activity unaffected by his presence. Everyone knew he was there, however, and he had to make sense of what was happening. He would do this by observing, taking notes, talking to the teachers involved, writing up field-notes after the event, reflecting on them and doing some initial analysis, which might then guide further investigations, and so on. The research is thus gradually constructed over time. The people concerned, the researcher included, are continually making indications to each other, attributing meanings, interpreting symbols. How researchers do this depends, again, on the kind of self they bring to the interpretation – experiences undergone, interests and values, personal reference groups, affective disposition toward those studied, commitment to causes involved in the research.

This is most clearly illustrated in life histories. The subjects' memories, thoughts, perceptions are of unknown scope and depth, even to themselves. Accounts are built up through successive discussions over a period of time, as the life history is reconstructed. A first discussion reveals some parameters and sparks off ideas that are pursued in more detail in the next, and so on, until no new material emerges. Previous conversations are reviewed for accuracy and completeness. Subject and researcher might work between meetings reflecting on the material, refining points, discovering new slants, spotting apparent inconsistencies and contradictions, attempting some preliminary analysis. Again the researcher does not stand above or outside this activity, but shares in it – not just as a trigger to release the other's thoughts, but as a participant in a particular kind of situation, where both parties project part of their selves into the interaction and both construct meanings from it.

How the subjects interpret situations depends on similar factors to those influencing the researcher to some degree, but of key importance is how they perceive the researcher. Delamont shows, by the different appearances she chose when first meeting different groups, how self-presentation might affect access:

> When I saw heads I always wore a conservative outfit and real leather gloves. I had a special grey dress and coat, for days when I expected to see the head and some pupils. The coat was knee-length and very conservative-looking, while the dress was mini-length to show the pupils I knew what the fashion was. I would keep the coat on in the head's office, and take if off before I first met the pupils. When observing I tried to dress like the student teachers who were common in all the schools; no trousers, unladdered tights, and no make-up.
>
> (Delamont, 1984, p. 25)

Similarly, it is necessary to know something about how subjects construct the situation with the researcher in it. For example, in interviewing pupils, it is possible they may interpret the situation as a counselling session, or as a spying manoeuvre (in the interests, perhaps, of the teaching staff, inspectorate or parents), or as an opportunity to promote various interests of their own (e.g. to wreak revenge, or to secure favours).

VALIDITY

The validity of qualitative research commonly rests upon three main features: (a) unobtrusive measures to ensure data reflect the scene studied; (b) respondent validation; (c) triangulation.

Unobtrusive measures

Some research methods (such as questionnaires) require subjects to react to a stimulus. Unobtrusive measures are non-reactive. It would be difficult for a researcher to be completely unobtrusive, but the less the natural scene is disturbed, the less the danger of people reacting to the researcher's presence. This is one of the reasons why participant observation is a favoured approach among some qualitative researchers. Here, the researcher adopts a recognized role within the institution, such as a teacher in a school, and follows all the normal processes required of that role. This has several advantages. It makes the researcher a member of the institution under study and thus reduces the distance between researcher and subjects. It gives the researcher access to the same places, people and events as the subjects, a key concern in qualitative research; it gives access to documents relevant to the institutional role, perhaps confidential reports and records, children's schoolwork; it permits the use of a number of mechanical aids, such as tape recorders and cameras, to help 'capture' events that can be analysed at leisure later; it provides personal first-hand experience of that role and a strong basis for understanding the perspectives of incumbents of that role. It might also meet an ethical point, in that one might feel, whatever the purposes and results of the research, a worthwhile contribution is being made to the life of the institution.

The researcher might already be a member of the institution before starting the research. In this case, a great deal will already be known about the institution, but it will be known mainly as an insider. Such knowledge will be invaluable for its authenticity, but might take a number of things for granted that others might consider problematic. It is therefore necessary to achieve an analytical distance and to render the situation 'anthropologically strange' for, as noted earlier, strangers' perceptions are often sharper than those of inmates. Reflectivity and personal diaries assist here. Collaboration work, involving perhaps colleagues observing one's teaching, have brought new insights.

Where one cannot gain direct access oneself, one might have the aid of key informants. These are people within the institution under study with whom the researcher comes to form an especially close relationship. They identify with the researcher and the research objectives to such an extent that they almost become research assistants. The classic example, 'Doc' in Whyte's *Street Corner Society,* told the researcher:

> That's right. You tell me what you want to see, and we'll arrange it. When you want some information, I'll ask for it, and you listen. When you want to find out their philosophy of life, I'll start an argument and get it for you. If there's something else you want to get, I'll stage an act for you. Not a scrap you know, but just tell me what you want, and I'll get it for you.
>
> (Whyte, 1955, p. 292)

Clearly key informants can provide vast amounts of information. They provide access to hidden inside places, offer another set of eyes and ears, present an historical dimension. The danger is that one selects or acquires key informants in one's own image, thus compounding one's own biases. Either this should be recognized or one should deliberately try to cultivate a cross-section covering the population in question.

Key informants, of course, might also be available to the non-participant observer. Here, the researcher has only the role of researcher and observes situations of interest in that capacity. For example, a lesson may be observed from the back of a classroom, a school assembly from the back of the hall, a staff meeting or a playground from behind the sidelines. The researcher is, ideally, not part of these proceedings and adopts 'fly on the wall' techniques (e.g. King's use of 'play house') to observe things as they happen naturally, as undisturbed by the presence of the researcher as possible.

It is not difficult to see why some prefer non-participant observation, which today is the more common mode. Qualitative research makes great demands on the researcher's energies and time and frequently presents a mass of confusing and intricate data which the researcher has to analyse. Whatever advantages participating brings, it adds to those demands. In the first place, it takes up valuable time. Secondly, it adds to one's responsibilities. One must meet the requirements of the role and must meet them regularly, on the prescribed terms and at stipulated times. Thirdly, it increases the possibilities of conflict between the two roles – one's objectives as a teacher and those as a researcher may occasionally clash.

Hargreaves (1967) found he had to give up a large part of his 'carefully nurtured teacher-role' through a different result of role conflict; for, while participation aided his relationships with the teachers and his appreciation of their concerns, it affected his rapport with some of the pupils, which it was necessary in his project for him to have. He therefore stopped teaching and 'from that point my relations with the boys improved to a remarkable extent'. Some tested him out with cheekiness, which he would 'immediately have crushed as a teacher', but when he 'failed to respond as they expected, these attempts at provocation ceased'. It was replaced, gradually, by a form of collusion. 'When they discovered I would not report them for offences against the school rules which I had observed, the teacher-role began to diminish, and was replaced by a new form of respect and trust.' How did Hargreaves handle the role-infractions he observed or to which he was made privy? 'A convenient attack of blindness or deafness proved to be invaluable in resolving such problems' (Hargreaves, 1967, pp. 203–4).

Clearly, participating as a teacher may be counter productive to an investigation into pupils. Participation as a *pupil* would appear to be ideally indicated here, but is not a practical proposition for most weathered researchers. As one would-be youth notes:

> Another important personal failure which changes the research techniques a lot is the fact that I am 6 feet 4 inches tall and that most fourteen-year-olds in Sunderland are considerably smaller than that. This means that the sort of unobtrusive participant observation by hanging around on a corner with them was simply impossible. Rather it would have consisted of a totally different situation where [they] had suddenly picked up this large ally to use in street fights: the existence of this large ally would have grossly changed their actions.
>
> (Corrigan, 1979, p. 14)

Some, though, have managed to do it to advantage and some have been awarded a status of 'honorary pupil' (Fuller, 1984). More usually one has to manufacture a special role.

Refraining from fully participant observation is also a defence against 'going native', an over-identification with people's views so that one's perspective as a researcher is submerged beneath them. In ethnographic work, strong ties are made with the subjects of study. Indeed, we have seen that it is an indispensable requirement if we are to understand their ways of life in any depth. It is necessary, too, to empathize with people's views, to see and feel things as they do. The danger is clear. The empathy may take over and we may find ourselves according primacy to the views of a particular group, interpreting all other material through those views and romanticizing the activities and beliefs of the privileged group. This is less likely to happen with non-participant observation. Not only does it keep the researcher from real involvement in a role, but by the same token it encourages the cultivation of a detachment necessary for the appraisal of material discovered and presented. This is one of the abiding dilemmas of the approach – to become involved to the extent of being able to appreciate life as a native, yet to be able to become detached at will in order to be able to represent that life in its proper context. An awareness of the problem aids its resolution, but again, non-participant observation is a precaution for those who find their sympathies easily aroused to the extent where it colours their judgement.

Non-participation does not completely avoid these problems, of course, and it lacks the benefits of aiding ease of access, penetrating to the heart of the group, the satisfaction of contributing toward the function of the group or institution and its use as a bargaining counter enjoyed by participation. Whichever approach one adopts depends entirely on the kind of project and the character and personal disposition of the researcher.

There is a sense, as we have seen, in which one is always participating. In the first place, it is difficult *not* to have an effect on the situation under observation, particularly in sensitive areas such as classrooms. Hargreaves, for example, describes how, as soon as he began classroom observation, the teachers' perceptions of his role changed and hence their behaviour changed. He was no longer seen as a teacher, but more of an inspector. One teacher 'made the boys work quietly out of textbooks, talked in a whisper to boys at his desk [another] usually set the form some written work and then joined me at the back of the room, where he chatted with me or told me jokes' (Hargreaves, 1967, p. 196). After one lesson, one teacher commented: 'They've got a bit noisy, haven't they? I think I'll cane a few when you've gone' (p. 17). However much one tries to reduce this effect, there is almost bound to be some influence, which then has to be taken into consideration. The non-participating observer, though not sharing in any of the roles under observation, is nonetheless part of the scene.

Secondly, one is always participating in the sense that, in any long-term research, it is difficult to avoid becoming involved in some way in the life of the group or institution. There are a number of problems associated with this. By appearing to be 'all things to all people' one runs the risk of being seen as insincere, two-faced and underhand. For example, in situations where deep conflict exists between teachers and pupils, empathizing with both sides in an attempt to understand their perspectives (as in the earlier example of blazer-ripping) can be mistaken for sympathizing and lead to trouble. In certain situations, empathizing with a group can be taken as legitimizing, or at least condoning, a group's behaviour. Where this involves rule- or law-breaking, there can be severe problems. Patrick (1973), for example, gave up his research on a criminal gang when his association with them threatened to involve him in criminal activity. In general, adopting a covert role in order to get as close as possible to the group under observation is regarded as ethically suspect. Most researchers work to a principle of 'informed consent': that is to say, the people being studied know something of what the research is about (by the very nature of qualitative work, it is impossible for them to know all), and agree to it taking place in the manner specified.

Respondent validation

Lincoln and Guba (1985) argue that the standard for qualitative research, where the objective is to reconstruct events and the perspectives of those being studied, is the demonstration that the findings and the researcher's interpretations are credible to those who were involved. Who better to judge whether their views, understandings, feelings and experiences were being accurately represented? Thus Willis showed various drafts of his book to the 'lads' who were the subject of his research and included their reactions as an appendix. Here is one extract, which has the lads testifying to how closely Willis had represented their perspectives:

> JOEY: ... you were someone to pour our hearts out to. You were obviously as old as most of the staff, and yet ... they were so far apart from us. They used to sit with us at dinner table but you couldn't really talk to them just 'cos of the fact that they were staff.
>
> JOHN: You could understand what they was sayin' and doin' like. Anything that happened you'd understand, like, if they'd done something wrong the night before, you'd just listen, understand, whereas

teachers ... you know, they'd say, 'That's wrong' anyway, and you'd think, 'Don't say anymore about it.'

BILL: The main difference is, you listen to us, you want to know what we've got to say, they don't none of them.

(Willis, 1977, p. 197)

Similarly, Mac an Ghaill showed his manuscript to the students featuring in his research. There is nothing more heartening for a researcher to hear than:

JOANNE: It's really good. I've read through most of it. I think that you have really captured what it's like for black kids at school.

(Mac an Ghaill, 1988, p. 142)

Consider, however, the purport of the following two comments:

JUDITH: I mean it's bound to be biased, you being for black people but it was because of that, that we really talked to you as we really felt. You knew what you thought about us, you were more aware, but for most white people they hide it and pretend they see us just the same as them but at the same time they treat us differently. As long as you make it clear in your study where you stand then it's OK.

(Mac an Ghaill, 1988, p. 143)

JUDITH: In a way you see our lives as being worse than we do because you have an alternative to measure it against. But in another way it's worse for us because you can get on with your life. Tomorrow you can leave Kilby and go to your white areas. But we are always black living in a racist society. You can't really know, feel, what it's like for a black woman. That's why I think that although what you have done is good, I think black women should carry out their own studies.

(Mac an Ghaill, 1988, p. 144)

This is a reminder that we can never get into another's mind to see exactly how it is working, but these researchers have come as close as any to empathizing with their subjects, although, as Judith astutely observes, any 'bias' should be declared.

Respondent validation, however, may not always be appropriate or desirable. For example, where the subject of study is school processes rather than perspectives, the subjects' view of the research may be strongly influenced, if not completely dominated, by their role within the institution. Scarth reports the response of a 'working party' of seven of the teachers in the school of his research to two draft chapters on timetabling and examinations:

> The first discussion which focused on timetabling was reduced to the Deputy Head responsible for timetabling defining the arrangements and trying to identify staff members from their reported comments. The teachers, for their part, were put in the position of being either 'for' the school timetable or 'against' it. This polarisation of viewpoints was even more marked during the second seminar on examinations, and discussion frequently centred on personalities rather than issues. As a result, I was put in the position of, on the one hand, being asked to name the respondents, and on the other, defending staff members' criticisms of the Head and Deputy Head. I did not feel in a position to do either; I couldn't reveal confidential data and I wished to avoid being personally associated with teachers' comments cited in the text. I tried to direct discussion away from simply focusing on personalities by highlighting some of the general patterns across both departments

> and subjects. Unfortunately the general feeling at the end of the second seminar was such that future meetings were cancelled.
>
> (Scarth, 1985, pp. 78–9)

Thus one may risk, on occasions, giving offence, being misinterpreted, or having one's material used for different purposes. It would never do, of course, to betray any confidences. Some respondent validation, however, is useful. Again it is a matter of judgement when, how and with whom it is used.

Triangulation

The major means of validating accounts and observations and, indeed, anything else in qualitative work is through 'triangulation'. The use of several methods to explore an issue greatly increases the chances of accuracy. For example, we might interview a head teacher with regard to policy concerning new intakes of pupils. The head's view of that policy would be interesting. It would be far more interesting, though, if we had the benefit of other vantage points: for example, the various meetings that are held with parents, pupils and teachers, the views of people in these groups, as well as observing aspects of the policy in action. We should then have a much better idea of the accuracy of the account by the headteacher, its comprehensiveness, strengths and weaknesses, and the actual effect of the policy.

When one wishes to study a teacher's performance in a particular lesson, another form of triangulation would be to:

- discuss with the teacher, beforehand, what was planned for the lesson;
- observe the lesson as it happened;
- discuss with the teacher afterwards what had happened and why, if aims had been modified and how far achieved, etc.

One form of this was practised by Hargreaves *et al.* in their study of how teachers and pupils think about rules in school. Since most of these rules are implicit, rarely articulated, or even thought about, the researchers had to take care not to 'impose a structure that would misrepresent and distort common-sense thinking rather than explicate it' (Hargreaves *et al.*, 1975, p. 45). They accordingly used a variety of methods over a lengthy period of participation, including asking teachers and pupils about rules and observing lessons. Teachers were also asked to comment on events that had occurred during the lesson or things that were said in the lesson. These commentaries were then, in turn, analysed.

In yet another form of triangulation, Elliott and Adelman (Open University, 1975) propose that role-partners, such as teachers, pupils and researchers, should cross-check each others' accounts to expose discrepancies and inconsistencies.

Lynda Measor gives another illustration.

> What is happening is that I'm getting data back about Teacher A from Teacher B or from other person C. This then informs my next set of questions at the next interview. For example, I interviewed D.R. Then I got information about him via the Labour Party and from another teacher. This changed my view of the man somewhat, or to be more accurate, it led me to consider another view of the man, and it led me into a different sort of question with him to get more data on those areas of his personality and attitudes. It also leads into theoretical issues, like the fact that he must have exceptional role distance qualities. The man in the interview was so very different from the man I've been told about.
>
> (Personal communication)

One of the commonest forms of triangulation is to combine interviews with observation. Observation will test and fill out accounts given in interviews and vice versa. For example, during observations of a games period, Woods (1979) noticed that one of the main principles that structure pupils' experience appeared to be the fear of being 'shown up'. Accounts of being 'shown up' were repeated, voluntarily, and explained at greater length in interviews, where researcher and pupils were able to explore the nature of the experience, when it occurred and whom it concerned. Woods also observed lessons and other areas of the pupils' day and made particular note of any such incidents. This put him in a stronger position, not only to delineate these incidents accurately, but also to assess the pupils' accounts for bias, exaggeration and misrepresentation. In other words, it gave him a vantage point from which to view those accounts and to consider what they were 'doing' for the pupils – how far, for example, the pupils were 'letting off steam' or 'getting back at the teachers', or even, perhaps, just 'trying it on' with the researcher.

The combination of interviews with observation also permits a fuller participation. During discussions with pupils, for example, another dominant experience the researcher was made aware of was 'being bored'. Time and again, pupils described their boredom, putting great feeling, at times, into their expressions: 'It's so *boring*, here!'; 'Those lessons were such a drag, what a bore!'. Such expressions brought the realization that the term is actually onomatopoeic: 'It's so bo-or-ing!' delivered with all the pent-up pain and frustration accumulated over a lengthy period. Even so, the point would not have been fully appreciated without the researcher actually observing some of the circumstances particularly conducive to the experience. In these lessons, with the teacher talking for hour-long stretches in a dull monotone, with very little participation by the pupils, some would occasionally turn to the researcher (sitting at the back of the class) with the same pained expression on their faces as when describing their experience of boredom. He knew exactly how they felt. Observation, then, grounds the related experience in a real-life event.

QUALITATIVE RESEARCH ASSESSED

What potential strengths and weaknesses of qualitative research have you noted? On the credit side is the attention to detail, the ability to embrace both verbal and non-verbal behaviour, to penetrate fronts, uncover meanings and reveal the subtlety and complexity of cases or issues. These might reveal conflicts, discrepancies, inconsistencies, contradictions, but these things are typical of everyday life. A multidimensional picture is built up. Qualitative research is strong in portraying perspectives and conveying feelings and experiences. It encompasses processes, natural environments and tends to be less reactive than other forms of research. Actions are contextualized within situations and theory is generated from the empirical data. Although qualitative studies individually might be concerned with single cases, collectively they might form an archive that then becomes available for reinterpretation. Hargreaves (1988), for example, working from a number of existing qualitative studies, developed a different explanation of teaching quality from 'official' ones, which placed emphasis on the personal qualities of teachers. He was interested in why teachers adopted transmission patterns of teaching and suggested that the reasons lay in the social circumstances that attended teaching (such as large cohorts of pupils, low levels of resources, a mandated curriculum) and that lay beyond teachers' control. The different implications for policy of the two theories should be clear.

As for difficulties and weaknesses, it has been argued that qualitative studies singly cannot provide grounds for generalizing across cases, though collectively they can be used in this respect. Also, a single case can be the beginning of a general argument, or develop concepts that can be applied to other studies, or have serious repercussions for one claiming universality. Another critique is that immersion in the depths of a qualitative study might lead to 'macro-blindness'. That is to say, the researcher might offer explanations in terms of the situation itself and be unaware of possibly more powerful forces operating externally. Equally, the researcher might be so successful in penetrating the culture of a group that he or she 'goes native' and sees everything from the perspective of the group.

Qualitative research can be a high-risk, low-yield enterprise. Negotiating access, attending to sampling, working out whom to interview and what to observe, continuously refining one's research design, can all bring worries. A big concern is 'what sense to make of it all'. Without benefit of sufficient time, one might drown in the maelstrom. Qualitative studies are often accused of being impressionistic, subjective, biased, idiosyncratic and lacking in precision. Although this is a charge that might be made of particular studies, there are rigorous procedures available to withstand the charge, such as triangulation, due attention to sampling, documentation, appropriate claims, reflectivity, tightness of fit between data collection, analysis and theory. Standards vary widely in these respects among published work. Many overclaim, seeking perhaps to prove a general case by a single instance, even in some instances by a single quotation. They might engage in 'selective perception': that is, seeing what they want to see, turning a blind eye, albeit unconsciously, to other material that might challenge that line of enquiry. They might not make their sampling or selection procedures clear. They might build up a case, typically, interweaving different kinds of evidence, which collectively sound convincing, but on closer examination reveal weaknesses. The researchers might tell you nothing of themselves, either as an oversight, or perhaps because the research has been non-reflexive. Clearly, therefore, we need to compile and examine research reports carefully.

SUMMARY

In this section we discussed the researcher's self as the main research instrument and how the qualitative researcher works to fine tune the self. Researchers' skills include: social management skills, important for negotiating access and establishing and maintaining rapport; the ability to be unobtrusive, but to 'make things happen' if and when required; observational skills of scanning and discernment; the skill of active listening; the skill of recording, by mind as well as machine. The researcher's self has its own values and background and these are influential in selecting topics for study. There are, however, other criteria, such as the need for balance. The research is also subject to rigorous scrutiny, including saturation, sampling and reflectivity. Yet the research is always a construction, part of the rigour being how explicit this construction is made by the researcher. Another consideration is that the researcher may be perceived differently by subjects. It is vital to know their perspectives in this matter in order to interpret their contributions to the research.

Secondly, we considered validity. The first of the three main groups of strategies is to take unobtrusive measures to preserve, as far as possible, the natural setting. This includes adopting measures to make the situation anthropologically strange. We discussed the advantages and disadvantages of participant and non-participant observation and how respondent validation has its uses, though it is not always appropriate. Finally, there is the strategy of 'triangulation', the combining of methods, researchers, situations or times for added strength.

The potential strengths and weakness of qualitative research were reviewed. In Section 5.3, we shall go on to consider the analysis of data produced by these methods.

5.3 ANALYSIS OF QUALITATIVE DATA

In qualitative research, analysis frequently takes place at the same time and in interaction with data collection. Many consider it a mistake to go on accumulating data without examining it from time to time to see if any major themes, issues or categories are emerging. These, in turn, will then direct future data collection in the process known as 'progressive focusing'. If this is not done, the researcher risks becoming swamped in data that are difficult to analyse because of their bulk and all-inclusiveness. Many data may have to be jettisoned and all that is left may be low-level description. Principled analysis helps to organize the data and to generate insights that aid understanding. In turn, this may lead to new or reformulated theory.

We have organized this section in three parts:

(a) preliminary and primary analysis;

(b) category and concept formation;

(c) the generation of theory.

PRELIMINARY AND PRIMARY ANALYSIS

As interview transcripts are made, or field-notes of observation compiled, or documents assembled, the researcher continuously examines the data, perhaps highlighting certain points in the text or making comments in the margins. These may be identifying what seem to be important points, noting contradictions and inconsistencies, any common themes that seem to be emerging, references to related literature, comparisons and contrasts with other data and so on. The researcher is not just collecting data, but *thinking* about them and interacting with them. Much of these first attempts at speculative analysis will probably be discarded, but some ideas will no doubt take shape as data collection and analysis proceed. Much of this early activity may appear chaotic and uncoordinated, but such 'chaos' is a prolific seed-bed for ideas.

Sometimes, because of pressure of time, the notes one makes may be little more than a scribbled comment, or a one-word 'indicator'; at other times, particularly as the research goes on, one might write longer notes or memos, summarizing parts of data that go together, but have come from different sources, or rehearsing ideas at greater length. The following three examples illustrate the range of these preliminary reflections.

The first example is illustrated in Figure 2, a marked-up page of an interview, showing the researcher's first reactions on things to note. You should examine this now.

The following extract from an interview with a teacher about the members of his form gives another example of a researcher's initial analysis. The researcher took notes at the interview (this one was not taped) and wrote them up the same evening. A few days later, when time permitted, he reflected on his comments and added some notes.

> Teacher
>
> Tim Brown – very disappointing. I noted a decline last year and I spoke to him about it; and he's a right lout isn't he? Always shuffling around with his hands in his pockets, instead of being a nice young man, as he was, but he's far from ... .
>
> Researcher
>
> Immediately he reveals his conception of the ideal pupil, at least the behavioural one. Note the importance of appearance and the choice of terminology – a 'right lout' is counterpoised to a 'nice young man' – and a great deal seems to be inferred from his appearance and demeanour. There is a great deal of this among the staff ... he could be subscribing to my double standard hypothesis and assuming that kids may well be different at school from what they are at home; it is what he expects that is important, and the very fact that he sees fit to divide his comment into 'academic' and 'behaviour'. So I conclude, tentatively, that JG is subscribing to the prevailing image of the ideal pupil and that his choice of words and unqualified use of them is an indication of his commitment to that ideal.

i.e. Teacher as 'chief clown'

Martin Glass (Chief Clown)

Humorous start to discussion, establishing rapport

M: Yes, some people said type-casting again.

Note - pressures on decision point below

P: Type-casting again – member of staff, yes, and the only member of staff actually in the production.

M: Yes, it was very interesting.

Open quetion, but aligned to teacher role.

P: Well, I think yes, that's what I'd like to ask you about. I mean what was it like being a member of staff amongst all these young people?

Surprise, part of the 'magic'

M: Well I think really that one of the amazing things of the whole thing was that there weren't any barriers of any sort. I think there must have been originally, right at the very beginning, although its very difficult to remember exactly what it was like then because things have moved on so much from there, but I can remember right at the very beginning, before – when the chief toys were selected, after all the auditions – we had about two sessions together in a distant room which were sort of breaking down barriers sessions and it was some of the techniques that Sally's learnt at, you know, college and so on, but there were sort of I suppose like games in a way where you had to react to each other and report back to everyone else – for example, one of the techniques was – think of something which is important to you that's happened in the recent past, or something in your life and tell it to someone else – and you know I could either have opted out totally or joined it totally, which – I chose the latter course as it happens. And then we had things like – choose one of the people here, in the group, and pick out a quality that you admire and a quality that you dislike about that person and tell everyone else about it. Little things like that and before we actually started, amongst the chief toys there was already working a sort of a group identity, a sense of togetherness, and virtually from the beginning I think – specifically with the chief toys but even later on gradually with all the other toys – there were no us and them barriers at all, it wasn't me, a member of staff, plus the pupils – we were just other different actors, that was it, and really they referred to me by my Christian name and so on and there were no barriers.

No barriers (one aspect of Communitas?)

Teacher strategies to induce 'togetherness' & 'break barriers'

plenty of evidence

Communitas

Equal status roles – no hierarchy, symbolised by

P; So, you noticed a change in their attitude towards you, as the thing went on?

Development

M: Yes, particularly those who were in I suppose the group I was working with

easing into new roles, and developing the culture of the group

Figure 2 Page of an interview marked up by the researcher.

These, then, are the first tentative steps in analysis. They may have a certain untidiness about them, their object being to suggest lines of analysis, to point the way to connections with other data and with the literature, to indicate the direction of future enquiries, rather than to round off in neat, considered packages.

Our third example is a more considered note or memo, seeking to launch and develop an idea across a range of data. It is a communication from Lynda Measor, prepared during the course of her work for *Teacher Careers* (Sikes, Measor and Woods, 1985). It is presented as it was written in order to illustrate the emergence of a new theme, carrying with it a sense of excitement at a new discovery, speculation at the possibilities, but also hesitancy in case, after further consideration, it is not such a good idea after all!

> 4.1.83
>
> A new idea, and as yet not very well thought out, but here goes. Also I'm not certain if it has been used and talked about by interactionists as I'll try and indicate later. I know the 'bibliography' in other fields – mainly political theory actually. I'm working towards a notion of 'special events' in the individual's life. This would connect into the theme B we have discussed, that of 'critical periods'.
>
> Methodology
>
> How did I come across the idea? As I'm building up numbers of interviews, that is I interview the same person lots of times. I've noticed that they repeat their account of certain incidents, usually fairly important ones in their lives. The other salient factor is that the account is given in the same words each time, with remarkably little variation. In addition this kind of repeating of tales is elicited most often when there has been a gap in my interviewing of a few weeks, so the narrative has gone cold. They cannot immediately recall exactly what they told me before. Then I get the repetition of incidents, and the repetition of phrases, e.g.
>
> 1 Matt Bruce on being the leader of the invasion force into Jersey and the way that got him introduced into schools on Jersey.
> 2 Maggie Corbin on the picture in her portfolio of her father; he had a C.P. badge of the Soviet hammer and sickle in his lapel and as a result the headmistress of Varndean, who was interviewing her, found out she was a Communist Party member herself.
> 3 There actually are quite a number in R.C. Clarke, and in Reeves.
>
> Explanations and ideas
>
> It might simply be that the repetition of incidents is due to lapses in memory, especially as people are getting older, that would not be surprising. But there is a problem there, because it fails to explain why these incidents should be repeated in exactly the same phraseology. Why doesn't the lapse of memory extend to that too? Why also is it that it is only certain things, certain incidents, that get repeated?
>
> So maybe we can work towards a notion of 'special events' in people's lives, 'key incidents' yes, around which pivotal decisions revolve, incidents which lead to major decisions or directions being taken.
>
> *But* it seems to me that there is something else of interest too, and that is what people make of these incidents. A range of devices seem to be employed to make these incidents 'special' or more accurately 'more special'. I'm afraid I delve back into folk loric stuff again, people seem to make a kind of mystique hang around these incidents and events, they make them out of the ordinary, they bestow special 'meaning' and special 'status' upon them. They seem to do this by a variety of oral

> devices, storytelling, ornate tale-making devices, which have the effect of drawing the listener's attention to them. Humour is used too, or more accurately 'wit', humorous short phrases surround the telling of the event, again these act as a signal flag, what Lewis called an 'alerting factor'. I'm also reminded of Sykes' material you found in the article on tale-telling in the factory, some of those devices seem to be at work.
>
> The device seems at a theoretical level to be involved with putting meaning, organisation, shape to a life, trying to understand a career? I picked up the idea of 'special event' however from political theory (again I'm afraid it's my thesis material). It comes from people like Sorel and Edelman. They discuss it in terms of the political life of a nation, and point to the way that particular events in that nation's history become special. Bastille Day to the French, and the taking of the Winter Palace to the Russians, it's a bit harder to do for England but maybe the Battle of Britain, or Dunkirk, as an example. These events do get a lot of attention anyway, they are meant to have meaning for the citizens of a nation, in that sense they are 'special'. But for political theorists it is the secondary devices which describe them which are equally significant. It is the film, a TV repetitious coverage, and the telling the tale again and again by many media means, which helps build up the mystique. Telling the tale, reciting events, helps make the thing 'remade', 'different' and special. In fact there is more to this from classical theorists, especially those on Greece, with a whole lot of stuff about 'Kerygma' which might I suppose be relevant, it's all about events – real events, being seen as revealing underlying purposes and directions. In a people like the British, who have been very affected by Judaic-Christian and then Darwinian notions of onward progress and purpose underlying it, we might be able to see something of that socialisation. Anyway that may be getting too fanciful. You may think the whole thing is too fanciful.
>
> (Measor, 1983, personal communication)

The research team did not consider the idea fanciful. In fact Pat Sikes was able to provide further substantiation from her own data and the theme was written up as one of the key features of a teacher's career. Discovery of the theme was made possible by certain clues – repetition of the incident, use of the same words. There is also something special about the words used, which put one on the alert.

Other clues might be irregularities that one observes, strange events, certain things that people say and the way they say them, things that get people excited, angry, surprised. In the researcher is the recognition that 'something is up', prompting the use of a 'detective's nose' for putting the available pieces of the jigsaw together to form a larger, more meaningful picture. For example, Measor and Woods were cued in to the importance of the myths that surrounded school transfer because a number of pupils prefaced their comments with remarks such as: 'I have heard that ... '; 'They tell me that ... '; 'There is this story that ... '. Clearly, these accounts were connected and there was a special quality to them (Measor and Woods, 1984).

In *The Divided School*, Woods's (1979) examination of 'teacher survival' led to the theory that, in situations where constraints on action exceeded the expectations of strong commitment, a struggle for survival would result. It was initiated by some observations of what appeared to be very strange behaviour. One of these was a chemistry lesson where the teacher taught for seventy minutes, complete with experiment and blackboard work, while the pupils manifestly ignored him. They were clearly doing other things. Only in the last ten minutes of the lesson did they dutifully record the results in their exercise books at his dictation. In another instance, a teacher showed a class a film, even though it was the wrong film that had been delivered and had nothing remotely to do with the subject. Such events seemed to cry out for explanation. Why did people behave in these strange ways?

Inconsistencies and contrasts are other matters that arouse interest. Why, for example, should teachers change character so completely between staffroom and classroom, as Lacey noted? Why do they lay claim to certain values and beliefs in the one situation and act out values and beliefs of strong contrast in another? Why do they behave with such irrationality and such pettiness on occasions? Why do pupils 'work' with one teacher and 'raise hell' with another, as Turner (1983) noted? From this latter observation, Turner came to certain conclusions about pupils' interests and school resources and important refinements to notions of 'conformity' and 'deviance'. The investigation of key words, as discussed in Section 5.1, is another common method for unpacking meanings.

CATEGORY AND CONCEPT FOUNDATION

There comes a time when the mass of data embodied in field-notes, transcripts, documents, has to be ordered in some kind of systematic way, usually by classifying and categorizing. At an elementary level, this simply applies to the data one has. There may be no concept formation, importation or discovery of theory, creation of new thoughts at this stage. The object is to render one's material in a form conducive to those pursuits. This means ordering data in some kind of integrated, exhaustive, logical, succinct way.

The first step is to identify the major categories, which, in turn, may fall into groups. The data can then be marshalled behind these. What the categories are depends on the kind of study and one's interests. They may be to do with perspectives on a particular issue, certain activities or events, relationships between people, situations and contexts, behaviours and so forth.

The test of the appropriateness of such a scheme is to see whether most of the material can be firmly accommodated within one of the categories and, as far as is possible, within one category alone. Also, the categories should be at the same level of analysis, as should any subcategories. One usually has to have several shots at this before coming to the most appropriate arrangement, reading and re-reading notes and transcripts and experimenting with a number of formulations. It may be helpful to summarize data, tabulate them on a chart, or construct figures and diagrams. Such distillation helps one to encapsulate more of the material in a glance as it were and thus aids the formulation of categories.

The following are some fairly typical examples of categorization.

Example 1

Paul Willis (1977), 'Elements of a culture' from *Learning to Labour.* These were the major features of 'the lads'' culture:

- Opposition to authority and rejection of the conformist.
- The informal group.
- Dossing, blagging and wagging.
- Having a 'laff'.
- Boredom and excitement.
- Sexism.
- Racism.

Under these headings, Willis reconstructed the lads' outlook on life, using liberal portions of transcript to build up a graphic and evocative picture. Notice that the categories include a mixture of the lads' own terms, which alerted the researcher to major areas of activity, and Willis' own summarizing features.

Example 2

John Beynon (1984), ' "Sussing out" teachers: pupils as data gatherers'. Beynon observed a class of boys during all their lessons in the first half-term of their first year at comprehensive school. The general interest at first was in 'initial encounters' between boys and teachers. He became interested in 'the strategies the boys employed to find out about classrooms and type teachers; the specific nature of the 'knowledge' they required; and the means they employed to (in their words) 'suss-out' teachers' (p. 121). He found there was a main group of boys who used a wide variety of 'sussing' strategies. One of his first tasks, therefore, was to organize his data and identify the kinds of strategy. He found six major groups:

1 Group formation and communication.
2 Joking.
3 Challenging actions (verbal).
4 Challenges (non-verbal).
5 Interventions.
6 Play.

Within these, he put forward sub-groups of activities. For example:

Joking

- Open joking.
- Jokes based on pupils' names.
- Risqué joking.
- Lavatorial humour.
- Repartee and wit.
- Set pieces.
- Covert joking.
- 'Backchat' and 'lip'.
- Closed joking.
- Michelle: a private joke.

This, then, shows an organization of data using categories and subcategories, each being graphically described by classroom observations, notes and recorded dialogue and interaction. The effect is to re-create 'what it was like' for these pupils and their teachers and to show the considerable depth and range of their 'sussing' activities.

Example 3

Howard Gannaway (1976) 'Making sense of school'. One of the questions raised in the construction of categories is the interconnections between them. There had been a number of studies of pupils' views of teachers which simply identified certain prominent features. Gannaway was concerned to identify priorities and inter-relationships among his categories. He summarized his conclusions in Figure 3 (overleaf).

THE GENERATION OF THEORY

Some qualitative studies do not proceed beyond the construction of models and typologies. Even so, this is a useful exercise, since it ensures that notions like 'sussing-out' have substance and delineates their major forms. We should want to go on from there, however, if we had the time and resources, to consider why 'sussing-out' occurs and why it takes this particular form. The research becomes more theoretical as it moves from 'how' to 'why' questions. To answer these questions we should need to consider three things.

Firstly, we need to seek to understand events from the point of view of the participants and try to discover the pupils' intentions. The second factor is incidence. One would want to know when and where this kind of activity took place and with whom. Is it limited to initial encounters between teachers and pupils? If it is occurring at other times, another explanation is required. Under what sort of circumstances does it occur, with what kinds of teachers and what kinds of pupils? Are all pupils involved, or only some? What proportion of the pupils' behaviour is taken up with this kind of activity? This is the contextual aspect. Comparisons need to be made with other sections of activity. Theory and methodology interact, the emerging theory guiding the next part of the investigation. If there is similar activity elsewhere then the theory may have to be revised, though there may be another explanation for that activity.

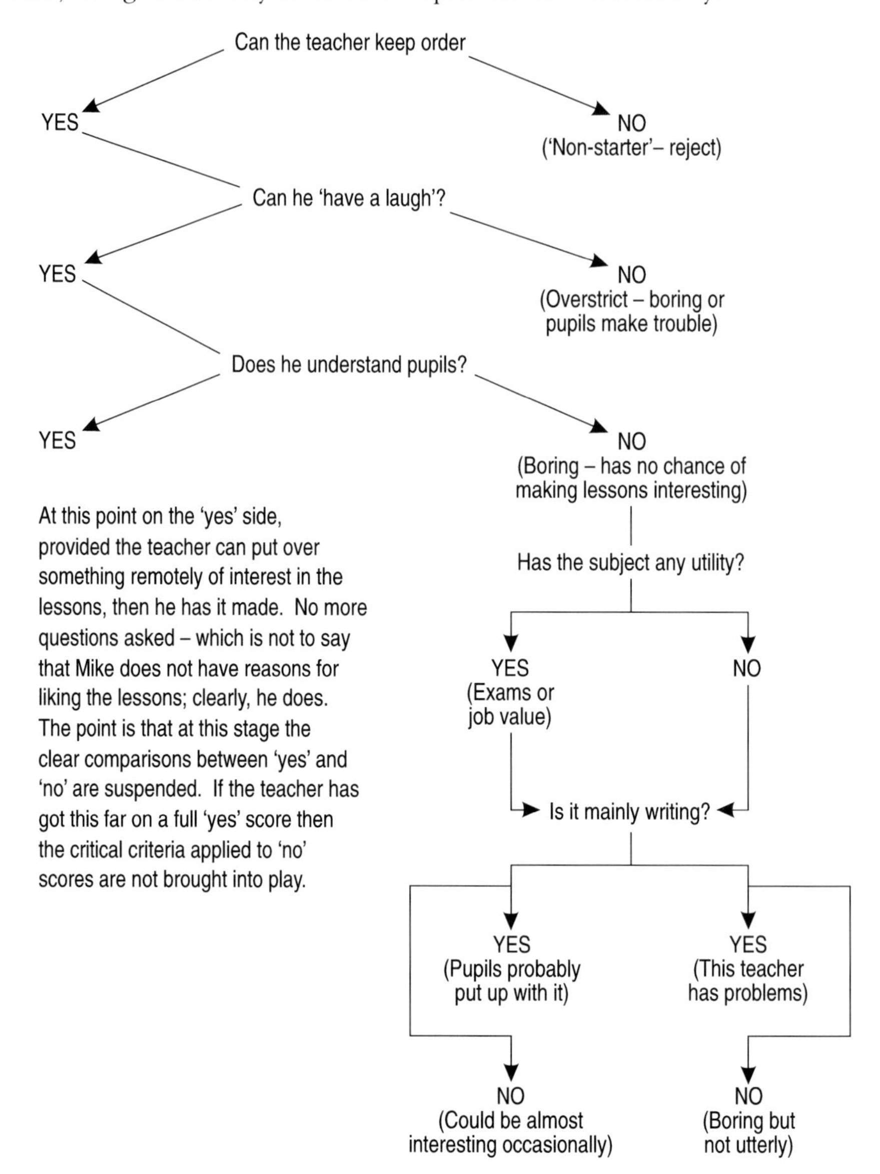

Figure 3 An evaluation scheme for teachers.

Thirdly, what are the consequences of sussing-out? The theory would lead us to expect that where the required knowledge was ascertained, where teachers justified their claims to being able to teach and to control, different, more 'settled' behaviour would ensue. Where it was not, the behaviour would presumably continue and perhaps intensify since the boundaries of tolerance would be being seen as lying further and further back. If this is not the case, again the theory may have to be revised.

It is also necessary to explore alternative theories. In the case of 'sussing-out' one would need to consider the possibility that the behaviour was a cultural product (e.g. of male, working-class or ethnic culture) or an institutional product (i.e. a function of a particular kind of school organization). Some of these, of course, may also be involved: that is, the behaviour may be and probably is multi-functional.

Comparative analysis

The development of the theory proceeds typically through comparative analysis. Instances are compared across a range of situations, over a period of time, among a number of people and through a variety of methods. Attention to sampling is important if the theory being formulated concerns a particular population. Thus comparisons are made among a representative set. Negative cases are sought for these might perhaps invalidate the argument, or suggest contrary explanations. These comparisons may be made both inside and outside the study. These kinds of comparisons, however, can also be used for other purposes – establishing accurate evidence, establishing empirical generalizations, specifying a concept (bringing out the distinctive elements or nature of the case) and verifying theory.

Theorizing begins from the first day of fieldwork with the identification of possible significant events or words, as we have seen earlier, leading eventually to identification of categories. As categories and concepts are suggested by the data, so they prefigure the direction of the research in a process known as 'theoretical sampling'. This is to ensure that all categories are identified and filled or groups fully researched. Thus Mac an Ghaill (1988) followed the identification by observation of an anti-school group, the 'Warriors', with the collection of material from school reports and questionnaires on their attitudes to school, which enabled him to build case histories. This is another good illustration of how theory and methodology interrelate, leading to an 'escalation of insights' (Lacey, 1976).

To aid this process the researcher becomes steeped in the data, but at the same time employs devices to ensure breadth and depth of vision. These include the compilation of a field diary, a running commentary on the research with reflections on one's personal involvement; further marginal comments on field-notes, as thoughts occur on re-reading them; comparisons and contrasts with other material; further light cast by later discoveries; relevance to other literature; notes concerning validity and reliability; more *aides-mémoire*, memos and notes, committing thoughts to paper on interconnections among the data, and some possible concepts and theories. Consulting the literature is an integral part of theory development. It helps to stimulate ideas and to give shape to the emerging theory, thus providing both commentary on, and a stimulus to, study.

Consulting colleagues, for their funds of knowledge and as academic 'sounding-boards', is also helpful. The 'sounding-board' is an important device for helping to articulate and give shape to ideas. What may seem to be brilliant insights to the researcher may be false promises to others. The critical scrutiny of one's peers at this formative stage is very helpful. It may be obtained by discussion (the mere fact of trying to articulate an idea helps give it shape), by circulating papers, by giving seminars.

Another important factor is time. The deeper the involvement, the longer the association, the wider the field of contacts and knowledge, the more intense the reflection, the stronger the promise of 'groundedness'. As Nias remarks:

> The fact that I have worked for so long on the material has enabled my ideas to grow slowly, albeit painfully. They have emerged, separated, recombined, been tested against one another and against those of other people, been rejected, refined, re-shaped. I have had the opportunity to *think* a great deal over 15 years, about the lives and professional biographies of primary teachers and about their experience of teaching as work. My conclusions, though they are in the last resort those of an outsider, are both truly 'grounded' and have had the benefit of slow ripening in a challenging professional climate.
>
> (Nias, 1988)

Nias reminds us that a great deal of *thinking* has to go into this process and that this is frequently *painful,* though ultimately highly rewarding. Wrestling with mounds of accumulating material, searching for themes and indicators that will make some sense of it all, taking some apparently promising routes only to find they are blind alleys, writing more and more notes and memos, re-reading notes and literature for signs and clues, doing more fieldwork to fill in holes or in the hope of discovering some beacon of light, presenting tentative papers that receive well-formulated and devastating criticisms – all these are part and parcel of the generation of theory.

Grounded theory has not been without its critics. Brown, for example, has argued that Glaser and Strauss are not clear about the nature of grounded theory, nor about the link between such theory and data. They refer to categories and their properties and to hypotheses as 'theory'. Their examples are of a particular kind of data – classificatory, processual – amenable to that kind of analysis, but 'some phenomena involve much greater discontinuity in either time or space or in the level of the systems studied' (Brown, 1973, p. 6). Greater immersion in the field is unlikely to yield useful theories here. Equally plausible alternative explanations from elsewhere may be available, so questions of how one decides among them (i.e. methodological issues) must be considered at an early stage. We need a balance, therefore, between verification and exploration and formulation. Bulmer (1979) raises doubts about Glaser and Strauss' *tabula rasa* view of enquiry in urging concentration, and a pure line of research, on the matter in hand, discounting existing concepts (in case of contamination) until grounded categories have emerged. This must be very difficult to do in well-researched areas. More characteristic is the interplay of data and conceptualization. Also, he wonders, when should the process of category development come to an end? Possibly the method is more suited to the generation of concepts than of testable hypotheses.

In fairness, Glaser and Strauss do acknowledge the construction of theory on existing knowledge, where that already has claims to being well grounded. They also recognize the importance of testing. Their complaint is about testing theory inadequately related to the material it seeks to explain. As for the confusion over theory, the identification of categories and their properties, the emergence of concepts and the formulation of hypotheses represent a clear and well-tried route. The fact is that many qualitative studies do not cover all these stages. This does not mean that they are without worth. Detailed ethnographic description and theory-testing (of reasonably grounded theories) are equally legitimate pursuits for the qualitative researcher.

5.4 SUMMARY

In this section we have considered the various stages of analysis, from the first tentative efforts to theory formation. Preliminary and primary analysis begins by highlighting features in field-notes or transcripts and making brief marginal notes on important points, suggested issues, interconnections, etc. It proceeds to more extended notes on emerging themes and possible patterns and then to more fully fledged memos, which may be half-way to the draft of a paper or at least a section of one.

At this stage, the researcher is studying the data and seeking clues to categories, themes and issues, looking for key words, other interesting forms of language, irregularities, strange events, and so on. This, in turn, leads to the formation of categories and concepts. We discussed the main methods and principles involved and considered examples of some typical attempts at forming categories and subcategories. One study had gone further and sought to establish the relative importance of the categories identified and their interconnections.

From here we considered the further generation of theory. This could involve the further elaboration of categories and concepts, investigating the conditions that attend them, the context and the consequences.

Theoretical sampling also takes place, ensuring coverage and depth in the emerging pattern. Comparative analysis plays a large part in this process, the researcher constantly comparing within and between cases and seeking negative cases as a rigorous test of the developing theory. In another kind of comparison or testing there is consultation with the literature and among one's peers.

Having sufficient time for this whole process is vital, as is the recognition that it involves a great deal of thought, frequently painful and sometimes apparently chaotic. We concluded with a review of the strengths and weaknesses of 'grounded theorizing'.

6 QUANTITATIVE RESEARCH

In this section we turn from qualitative to quantitative methods. As we explained earlier, the distinction between these two sorts of approach to educational research is not clear-cut. Indeed, in beginning our exploration of quantitative research we shall examine part of a study that is generally regarded as qualitative in character, but which, in fact, also employs a good deal of quantitative data.

The term 'quantitative research' is subject to different definitions. For the purposes of this section we shall proceed as if it referred to:

(a) The search for causal relationships conceptualized in terms of the interaction of 'variables', some of which (independent variables) are seen as the cause of other (dependent) variables.

(b) The design and use of standardized research instruments (tests, attitude scales, questionnaires, observation schedules) to collect numerical data.

(c) The manipulation of data using statistical techniques.

Our emphasis will be very much on the forms of analysis used by quantitative researchers, rather than on the data collection techniques they employ. Selectivity is unavoidable given the time available and we decided that this focus would give you the best sense of the character of quantitative research. We do need to begin, however, by outlining the main sources and types of data that quantitative researchers use. These are constrained to a considerable degree by the requirements of quantitative analysis. Most obviously, the data need to be in numerical form – measurements of the intensity and/or frequency of various phenomena. Some of this type of data is readily available in the form of published or unpublished statistics: for example, school examination results, figures for absenteeism, etc. Often, though, researchers have to produce the data themselves. This may be done in various ways. For example, via a laboratory experiment, in which responses to some stimulus, such as a particular method of teaching, are measured. Here the interest might be in the effectiveness of the method in bringing about students' learning. Alternatively, quantitative data may also come from structured questionnaires administered to relatively large samples of respondents, say teachers or pupils. If unstructured interviews can be coded into elements that can be counted they may also be a source of quantitative data. Another source is data produced by an observer or a team of observers using an observational schedule, which identifies various different sorts of action or event whose frequency is to be recorded.

Phenomena vary, of course, according to how easily and accurately they can be measured. It is one thing to document the number of A levels obtained by each member of the sixth form in a school in a particular year. It is quite another to document the proportion of sixth formers from working-class and from middle-class homes. There are troublesome conceptual issues involved in identifying membership of social classes and collecting accurate information on which to base assignment to social classes is much more difficult than finding out how many A levels were obtained. Although we shall concentrate primarily on techniques of analysis, the threats to validity involved in the process of collecting data must not be ignored. We shall have occasion to discuss them at several places in this section.

We shall look firstly at the kind of causal logic that underpins quantitative methods and then at various ways in which numerical material can be analysed in quantitative research. We have two main objectives in this. The first and major purpose is to put you in a position where you can read the results of quantitative research knowledgeably and critically. This is an objective that runs from beginning to end of the section. The second objective is to show you how relatively simple quantitative methods can be used in school-based research. The first half of this section will serve this purpose since the major example chosen is, indeed, relatively simple and the techniques discussed are usable by a researcher with limited time and resources.

INTRODUCING BEACHSIDE

Early in the section we shall make extensive use of a relatively simple example of quantitative work drawn from Stephen Ball's *Beachside Comprehensive,* a book whose main approach is qualitative rather than quantitative (Ball, 1981). In his book, Ball is primarily concerned with finding out whether, or how far, the principles of comprehensive education have been implemented at a particular school, to which he gives the pseudonym Beachside. One of the main criticisms of the selective educational system in Britain of the 1950s and the early 1960s was that it disadvantaged working-class children because selection for different kinds of education occurred so early. The move to comprehensive schools was intended, in part, to overcome this problem. In carrying out this research in the late 1970s, Ball was particularly interested in how far it was the case that working-class and middle-class children had an equal chance of educational success at schools like Beachside Comprehensive. We shall look at only a very small part of his work, where he examines whether the distribution of working-class and middle-class children to bands on their entry to the school shows signs of inequality.

Activity 8

You should now read the extract from Stephen Ball's *Beachside Comprehensive* which is printed in an appendix at the end of Part 1. As you do so, make a list of the main claims he puts forward and of the types of evidence he presents. You do not need to go into much detail at this point. Do not worry about statistical terminology that you do not understand, your aim should be simply to get a general sense of the structure of Ball's argument. This *will* take careful reading, however.

In the extract Ball argues that there is evidence of bias against working-class pupils in their allocation to bands at Beachside. He supports this by comparing the distribution of middle-class and working-class children across Bands 1 and 2 with their scores on the NFER tests of reading comprehension and mathematics. We shall be considering this evidence in some detail later, but first we need to give some attention to the nature of the claim he is making.

6.1 CAUSAL THINKING

Ball's argument can be represented in the causal-network diagram shown in Figure 4.

While this causal model captures the main lines of Ball's argument, of course it represents only a small proportion of the factors that might interact to cause pupils to be allocated to bands at Beachside.

It is worth noting that the diagram presupposes a temporal sequence in that all the arrows go one way, from left to right. The one solid fact about causality is that something can only be caused by something that precedes it. Thus, the left-hand side of the diagram must refer to earlier events and the right-hand side to later events. In our case 'social class' must mean something about pupils' home background which existed prior to their allocation to bands. Only in this sense can 'social class' be said to have a causal relationship to allocation to bands. Of course, the causal network could be extended almost indefinitely backwards or forwards in time.

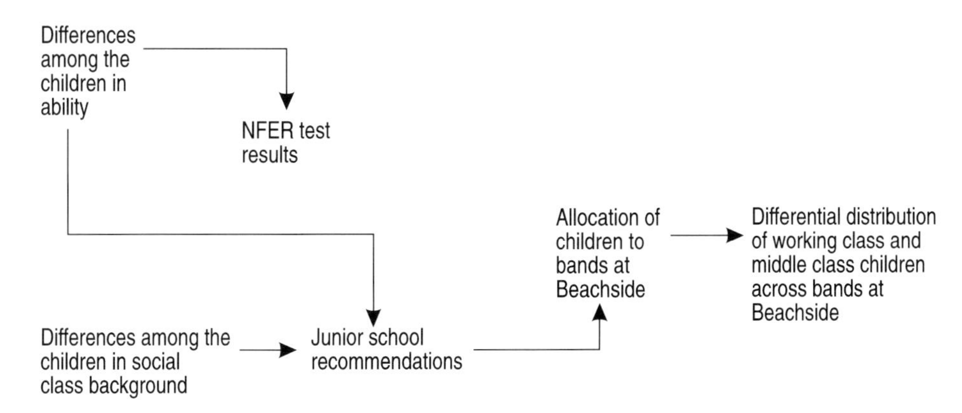

Figure 4 A causal-network diagram of Stephen Ball's argument.

In quantitative analysis the terms 'dependent' and 'independent' variables are frequently used. The causes and effects identified in Figure 4 are variables. The dependent variable is the effect we are interested in explaining and the independent variables are what are held to cause it. In Figure 4, the allocation to bands is the dependent variable, while social class and pupil's ability (and junior teachers' recommendations) are independent variables.

The 'time rule' for causal analysis means that changes in independent variables must occur before the changes in the dependent variables they are held to cause. Beyond this, the way the terms are used relates to the explanatory task at hand. Thus we could move back a step and see differences in pupils' ability as the dependent variable, in which case differences in social background (and other things) would be the independent variable. On the other hand, we could treat social-class differences in upbringing as the dependent variable and look for factors that explain this, treating these as independent variables. The meaning of the terms 'independent' and 'dependent' variables, then, derives from the explanatory task being pursued.

Another point to notice is that we could go on adding to our independent variables, perhaps for ever. In setting up an explanatory model, a causal network, we are selective about what we include among the independent variables. The decision about what to include is based on the theory that we want to test.

Activity 9

What theory was Ball trying to test in the extract you read earlier?

Ball was concerned with the extent to which the allocation of pupils to bands at Beachside was affected independently by social class, rather than being based solely on pupils' ability. He was looking to see if middle-class children were more likely than working-class children to be allocated to Band 1 over and above any differences in ability. This research problem determined his selection of independent variables: social-class background and pupils' ability.

In our diagram, we have also included the junior schools' recommendations as a factor mediating the effects of those two other variables. The teachers from Beachside who carried out the initial allocation to bands had no knowledge of the children other than what was available to them via the junior schools' records and recommendations. If they had had such knowledge then we should have needed to include direct causal relationships both between ability and band allocation and between social class and band allocation.

It is worth thinking a little about the nature of Ball's hypothesis. As we indicated earlier, his concern is with the extent to which there is inequality (or, more strictly speaking, inequity) in allocation to bands in terms of social class. This is quite a complex issue, not least because it relies on assumptions about what we believe to be equitable and, more generally, about what is a reasonable basis for allocation of pupils to bands within the context of a school. It suggests that what is partly at issue in Ball's argument is a question about the basis on which band allocation *should* be made, not just about how it is actually carried out. In our discussion here, however, we shall treat Ball's hypothesis as factual; as concerned with whether or not social class has an effect on allocation to bands over and above the effects of differences in ability.

OPERATIONALIZATION

In order to test his hypothesis, of course, Ball had to find measures for his variables. This is sometimes referred to as the process of 'operationalization'. Thus, in the extract you read, he is not directly comparing the effect on band allocation of social class and the ability of children. Rather, he compares the band allocation of children who obtained scores in the same range on the NFER tests for reading and mathematics, whose fathers are manual and non-manual workers. He has 'operationalized' social class in terms of the difference between households whose head has a manual as opposed to a non-manual occupation and has 'operationalized' ability in terms of scores on NFER achievement tests. This, obviously, raises questions about whether the variables have been measured accurately.

How well does the occupation of the head of household (categorized as manual or non-manual) measure social class? This is by no means an uncontroversial question.

Activity 10

What potential problems can you see with this operationalization?

There are several problems. For one thing, there are conceptual issues surrounding what we mean by social class. Furthermore, what this operationalization typically means is that allocation of children to social classes is based on their father's occupation. Yet, of course, many mothers have paid employment and this may have a substantial impact on households. There has been much debate about this (see Marshall *et al.*, 1988). A second question that needs to be asked is whether the distinction between non-manual and manual occupations accurately captures the difference between working class and middle class. This too raises problems about which there has long been and continues to be much discussion. We might also raise questions about the accuracy of the occupational information that was supplied by the pupils and on which Ball relied.

Activity 11

Can you see any likely threats to validity in Ball's operationalization of ability? Note down any that you can think of before you read on.

To answer this question, we need to think about what the term 'ability' means in this context. It is worth looking at how Ball introduces it. He appeals to the work of Ford, arguing that controlling for measured intelligence is the most obvious way of testing for the presence of equality of opportunity. If the impact of social class on educational attainment is greater than can be explained by the co-variation of social class and IQ, then the existence of equality of opportunity must be called into question, he implies.

One point that must be made in the light of this about Ball's operationalization of ability is that he relies on achievement tests in reading and mathematics, not on the results of intelligence tests (these were not available). We must consider what the implications of this are for the validity of the operationalization. We need to think about what is being controlled. Effectively, Ball is asking whether the allocations to bands were fair, as between children from different social classes, and takes a 'fair allocation' to be one that reflects differences in intelligence. What this seems to amount to is placing those who were more likely to benefit from being placed in Band 1 in that band and those who were more likely to benefit from being placed in Band 2 in that band. In other words, the allocations are to be made on the basis of predictions of likely outcomes. If this is so, it seems to us that teachers operating in this way are unlikely to rely only on the results of achievement tests. They will use those scores, but also any other information that is available, such as their own and other teachers' experience with the children. Furthermore, they are likely to be interested not just in intelligence and achievement, but also in motivation to do academic work, since that too seems likely to have an effect on future academic success. In fact, you may remember that Ball notes that Beachside School allocated children to bands on the basis of the primary school's recommendations and that 'test scores were not the sole basis upon which recommendations were made. Teachers' reports were also taken into account' (see Section 2 of the Appendix). What this indicates is that the primary schools did not regard test scores as in themselves sufficient basis for judgments about the band into which pupils should be placed. Given this, it would not be too surprising if Ball were to find some discrepancy between band allocation and test score, although this discrepancy would not necessarily be related to social class.

Over and above these conceptual issues, all tests involve potential error. Ball himself notes the problem, commenting that 'to some extent at least, findings concerning the relationships between test-performance and social class must be regarded as an artefact of the nature of the tests employed' (see Section 2 of the Appendix). These are not grounds for rejecting the data, but they are grounds for caution.

There are some serious questions to be raised about the operationalization of both social class and of ability in Ball's article. For the purposes of our discussion, however, let us assume that the measurements represented by Ball's figures are accurate and that ability is the appropriate criterion for band allocation.

6.2 CO-VARIATION

In quantitative research the evidence used to demonstrate a causal relationship is usually 'co-variation'. Things that vary together can usually be relied upon to be linked together in some network of relationships between cause and effect, although the relationships may not be simple or direct.

Activity 12

Look again at Table 2.5 in the extract from Ball in the Appendix. Does this table display co-variation between social class (in Ball's terms) and allocations to the two forms that he studied?

The answer is that it does. We can see this just by looking at the columns labelled 'Total non-manual' and 'Total manual'. Form 2CU contains 20 pupils from homes of non-manual workers and 12 from those of manual workers, whereas the corresponding figures for Form 2TA are 7 and 26. This pattern is also to be found if we look at the two top bands as a whole, rather than just the individual forms (Table 3).

Table 3 Distribution of social classes by ability bands

Band	*Non-manual*	*Manual*	*Unclassified*
top band	40	54	15
middle band	29	83	19
bottom band	10	20	6

Source: Table N2, p. 293, Ball (1981)

Notice how we produced Table 3 by extracting just a small portion of the information that is available in Ball's Table N2 (See Appendix, endnote 3). Doing so enables us to see patterns much more clearly. At the same time, of course, it involves losing, temporarily at least, quite a lot of other information: for example, the differences between the social classes that make up the manual and non-manual categories. Having noted the general relationship, let us now include this extra information.

Table 4 Distribution of social classes across the second-year cohort at Beachside 1973–74

Band	*I*	*II*	*IIIn*	*Total non–manual*	*IIIm*	*IV*	*V*	*Total manual*	*Unclassified*	*Band total*
Band 1	11	26	23	60	49	5	0	54	15	129
Band 2	5	11	13	29	55	23	5	83	19	131
Band 3	2	4	4	10	11	9	0	20	6	36
Total	18	41	40	99	115	37	5	157	40	296

Source: Table N2, p. 293, Ball (1981)

Table 4 is much more difficult to read at a glance than Table 3. We need a strategy to make it easier to compare the various cells produced by the two co-ordinates, social class and band allocation.

Ball is quite right to give us the actual number of pupils in each cell, but we are trying to make a comparison between different kinds of pupil. The fact that there are different numbers of the various kinds of pupil makes this difficult. When making comparisons between groups of different sizes it usually helps to use one of the devices that standardizes for group size. These are rates, ratios, proportions and percentages. Percentages will almost certainly be the most familiar of these to you. The formula for percentages is

$$percentage = \frac{f}{N} \times 100$$

where f = frequency in each cell and N equals, well what?

There are three possibilities in the case of Table 4. It could be the total of all pupils, or the total of pupils of a particular social class, or the total of pupils in a particular band.

Activity 13

People so often misinterpret tables of percentages that it is worth doing this exercise to check your understanding. Think of each of the fragments (a), (b) and (c) below as parts of a new percentage table based on Table 4. Write a verbal description for each.

(a)	Band 1	social-class I 3.7%	(*N* = 296)
(b)	Band 1	social-class I 61.1%	(*N* = total of social-class 1 pupils = 18)
(c)	Band 1	social-class I 8.5%	(*N* = total in Band 1 =129)

When you have done this think about which of the three possibilities outlined above is most useful in making comparisons between pupils of different social classes in terms of their allocation to bands.

Here are our answers:

Item (a) can be described as the percentage of all pupils who are *both* classified as social-class I *and* allocated to Band 1.

Item (b) is the percentage of all pupils classified as social-class I who are allocated to Band 1.

Item (c) is the percentage of Band 1 places taken by social-class I pupils. (c)

For our current purposes (b) is the most useful percentage since it tells us something about the relative frequency with which pupils from a particular social class are allocated to a particular band. Item (c) might be interesting if you were concerned with the composition of bands, rather than with the chances of pupils gaining allocation to a band.

Table 5 is an expansion of item (b).

Table 5 Percentage of pupils from each social class allocated to particular bands

Band	*I*	*II*	*IIIn*	*Total non-manual*	*IIIm*	*IV*	*V*	*Total manual*	*Unclassified*
Band 1	61	64	57	61	43	14	–	34	38
Band 2	28	27	33	29	48	63	100	53	48
Band 3	11	10	10	10	10	24	–	13	15
	100	101	100	100	101	101	100	100	101
Total	(18)	(41)	(40)	(99)	(115)	(37)	(5)	(157)	(40) 296

Source: Table N2, p. 293, Ball (1981)

Now the data are converted into percentages we can, once again, see at a glance some co-variation between social class and band allocation. You could say, for example, that each pupil from social-class I has six chances in ten of being allocated to Band 1, while each pupil in social-class IV has under 1.5 chances in ten; the chances of a pupil from social-class I being in Band 1 is four times that of the chances of a pupil from social-class IV.

There are two problems with percentages, however. First, once you have converted numbers into percentages, there are strict limits to what you can do with them mathematically. Percentages are mainly for display purposes. Secondly, once a number is converted into a percentage it is easy to forget the size of the original number. For example, look at the entries under social-class V. One hundred per cent of these pupils are in Band 2, but 100% is only five pupils. If just one of these five pupils had been allocated to Band 1, then there would have been 20% of pupils from social-class V in Band 1 and only 80% in Band 2. Then, a higher percentage of pupils from social-class V than from social-class IV would have been in Band 1. Again, one extra pupil from social-class I in Band 1 would raise their percentage to 66%. Where *N* is small, small differences appear as dramatically large percentages. For this reason it is good practice in constructing tables of percentages to give the real totals (or base figures) to indicate what constitutes 100%. The misleading effects of converting small numbers to percentages can then be detected and anyone who is interested can recreate the original figures for themselves.

Activity 14

The information provided in Tables 3 or 5 shows you that there is an association between social class (measured in the way that Ball measured it) and allocation to bands. What conclusions can you draw from this co-variation?

There are several ways in which this association could have been produced. First, it may be that teachers made allocations on the basis of their judgments of the social class of children or, more likely, on criteria that favoured middle-class children. A second possibility is that the teachers allocated children on the basis of their ability, but that this is determined by, or co-varies strongly with, social class. There is also the third possibility that both social class and allocation to bands are caused by some other factor: in other words, that the association is spurious. We can illustrate these possibilities by use of causal-network diagrams (Figures 5 and 6).

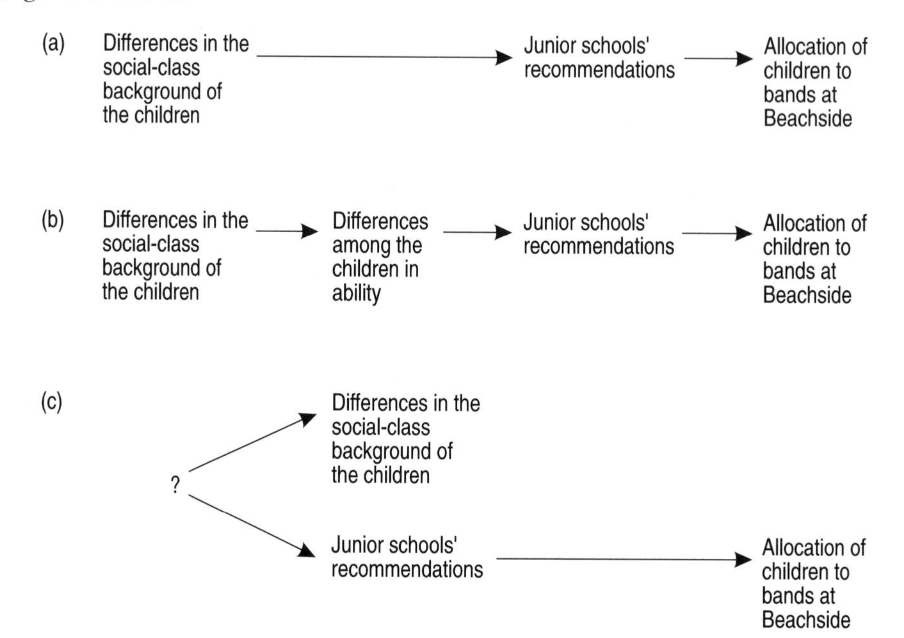

Figure 5 Models of the relationship between social class and allocation to bands.

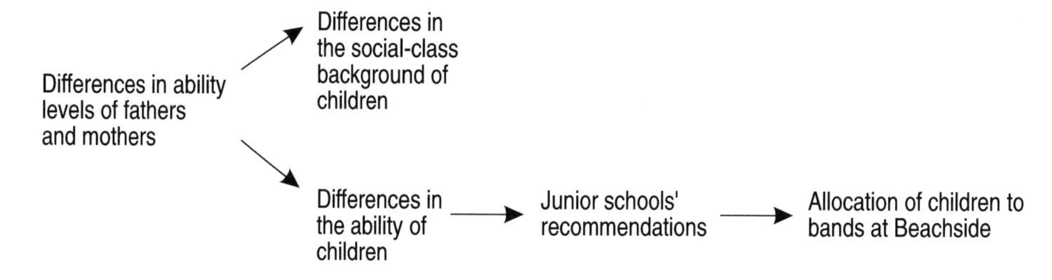

Figure 6 A model assuming the inheritance of ability.

It might be difficult to see what the mystery factor could be in Figure 5(c). It is worth noting, however, that some commentators have argued that ability is for the most part genetically determined and that ability to a large extent determines social class. On this view, we might get the causal network shown in Figure 6.

A demonstration of co-variation between banding and social class, therefore, leaves room for different interpretations. This is generally true in social research. Here we are dealing with causal networks in which each item in the network may have a number of different possible relationships with the others. A crucial element in the art of planning a research study is to find ways of manipulating situations or data so that the independent effect of each possible causal factor becomes clear. The general terms for this kind of manoeuvre are 'controlling a variable' or 'holding a variable constant'.

6.3 CONTROLLING VARIABLES: EXPERIMENTATION

The scientific experiment is the classic example of a strategy for controlling variables. It is often said to involve physical control of variables, since it entails actual alteration of the independent variable of interest and the holding constant or minimizing of other factors likely to affect the dependent variable.

Suppose, as experimenters, we are interested in how *teachers' judgements of pupils' ability* and *pupils' ability as measured independently of teachers' judgements* each affect the position of pupils in some ability-banding system. Furthermore, we are interested in how far either or both create a pattern of distribution so that position in ability bands co-varies with social class, a pattern like that shown in Tables 3 or 5 in Section 6.2. As we have seen, social class may have a causative effect on allocation to ability bands through different routes because:

- Ability varies with social class and teachers recognize the differences in ability between pupils, which are then manifest in decisions about allocating pupils to bands.
- Teachers make assumptions about the ability of pupils of different social classes (which are not reflections of their ability) and implement these in decisions about allocating pupils to bands.

Our first problem in designing an experimental strategy is ethical. Even if people would agree to co-operate, it would be quite wrong to subject pupils to an experiment that was likely to have a real effect on their educational chances. We shall avoid this problem by conducting an experiment with fictional pupils who exist only on paper. The subjects for the experiment will be a group of teachers who have actually been involved in allocating pupils to bands. In the experiment we are going to ask them to make pencil and paper decisions about the allocation of fictional pupils to three ability bands: top, middle and bottom. For the purpose of the experiment we shall divide the teachers into three groups, either at random or by matching. In other words, we shall try to ensure a similar balance in each group for age and gender, at least, and preferably also for other relevant variables, such as kind of subject taught. Either way, the aim is to make each group of teachers as similar as possible so as to rule out the effects of their personal characteristics.

The two important features of our fictional pupils will be their ability, as measured by some standardized test, and their social class, as designated, say, by the occupation of the head of their households. For a real experiment we might want a more elaborate system of classification, but for demonstration purposes let us say that the pupils will be designated as of high, middle or low ability and as coming from manual or non-manual backgrounds. We shall also make sure that there will be exactly the same number of pupils in each ability band for each social class.

As it stands, the object of our experiment is likely to be transparently obvious to the teachers involved, so we shall need to dissimulate a little. To do this we shall provide the pupils with genders, heights, weights and other details, but ensuring that the same characteristics always occur with the same frequency for each cell of a table that tabulates social class by ability. In other words, if there are twenty-five girls in the category 'high ability/non-manual background' then there must be twenty-five girls in every other category.

The task we are going to ask our experimental subjects to perform is to allocate the pupils to ability bands, but under three different sets of conditions:

Condition A

There will be as many positions in the high-ability *band* as there are pupils in the high-ability *group,* with a similar match for the middle- and low-ability bands and groups.

Condition B

There will be fewer positions in the high-ability *band* than there are pupils in the high-ability *group* and more positions in the middle-ability band. There will be as many positions in the bottom band as there are pupils in the bottom-ability group.

Condition C

There will be fewer positions in the bottom-ability *band* than there are pupils in the bottom-ability *group,* more in the middle band and equivalence in the top-ability band.

Condition A gives teachers the opportunity to use measured ability alone to distribute pupils between ability bands. Condition B forces teachers to use criteria other than measured ability to 'save' certain pupils (and not others) from the middle band. Condition C forces teachers to use criteria other than measured ability to place in a higher band pupils who might otherwise be placed in the bottom-ability band.

Our hypothesis for this experiment might be that if teachers use evidence of social class to place pupils in ability bands then:

(a) There will be no exact correspondence between measured ability and band position for Condition A and the discrepancies will be shown in a co-variation between social class and placement in ability bands.

and/or

(b) For Condition B, teachers will show a stronger tendency to place one social class of pupil in a lower band than pupils of another social class. There will be a co-variation of social class and placement in Bands 1 and 2.

and/or

(c) For Condition C, teachers will show a greater tendency to place one social class of pupil in a higher band than pupils of another social class. There will be a co-variation of social class and placement in Bands 2 and 3.

It is worth considering the way in which this structure controls the variables. It controls for differences in ability by ensuring that for each condition teachers have exactly the same distribution of abilities within their set of pupils. In this way, different outcomes for Conditions A, B and C cannot be due to differences in the ability distribution. The structure also controls for any correlation between social class and measured ability (which occurs in real life), because each social class in the experiment contains the same ability distribution and vice versa. Differences between teachers are also controlled by making sure that each group of teachers is similar, as far as is possible. This is obviously less amenable to experimental control and is a case for running the experiment several times with different groups of teachers to check the results.

In addition, for Condition B, ability was controlled by making it impossible for teachers to use the criterion of ability alone to decide on Band 1 placements. Thus, whichever high-ability pupils they allocated to Band 2, they must have used some criterion other than ability to do so, or to have used a random allocation. Given this, we should be able to see the independent effect of this other criterion (or of other criteria) in their decisions. Much the same is true of Condition C. By having a Condition B and a Condition C we have controlled for any differences there might be in the teachers' behaviour with regard to placing pupils in higher or lower bands. By juxtaposing Condition A with Conditions B and C we can control for the effects of unforced, as against forced, choice. Our interest was in social class rather than in gender or pupils' other characteristics, but even if it turned out that teachers were basing decisions on gender or some other characteristic we have already controlled for these.

There are obviously possibilities for other confounding variables to spoil our experiment. We might, for example, inadvertently allocate more teachers vehemently opposed to streaming to one of the groups than to the others, or a disproportionate distribution of teachers with different social origins might confound our results. Such problems can never be entirely overcome.

Activity 15

Suppose we ran this experiment as described and found that for all three groups there was no co-variation between social class and ability band placement: that is, no tendency for teachers to use social class as a criterion of ability band placement. What conclusions might we reasonably draw?

We might conclude that these teachers showed no social-class bias in this regard and perhaps that, insofar as they were representative of other teachers, social-class bias of this kind is uncommon. We certainly should consider two other possibilities, though. One is that the experiment was so transparent that the teachers saw through it. Knowing that social-class bias is bad practice, perhaps they did everything possible to avoid showing it. This is a common problem with experiments and one of the reasons why experimenters frequently engage in deception of their subjects. The second consideration is that while the teachers in this experiment behaved as they did, the experimental situation was so unrealistic that what happened may have no bearing on what actually happens in schools.

Both of these problems reflect threats to what is often referred to as ecological or naturalistic validity: the justification with which we can generalize the findings of the experiment to other apparently similar and, in particular, 'real-life' situations. It is a common criticism of experimental research made by qualitative researchers and others that its findings have low ecological validity. If you think back to Section 5 you will recall the great emphasis placed by qualitative researchers on 'naturalism'. It can be said that experimental control is often purchased at the expense of naturalistic validity.

True experiments, which involve setting up artificial situations to test hypotheses by controlling variables, are rare in educational research. A large range of possible experiments is ruled out by ethical considerations or by the difficulty of getting subjects to co-operate. Others are ruled out by considerations of ecological or naturalistic validity.

6.4 CORRELATIONAL RESEARCH

Our discussion of experimental method has not been wasted, however, because it illustrates what quantitative researchers in education are often trying to do by other means. Rather than trying to control variables by manipulating situations, most educational researchers engaged in quantitative research utilize ready-made, naturally occurring situations and attempt to control variables by collecting and manipulating data statistically. If the experimental researcher gains control at the expense of ecological validity, then correlational research gains what ecological validity it does at the expense of physical control. Furthermore, naturally occurring situations are very rarely shaped so as to lend themselves easily to research. If you look back at the passage that described how we would control variables in our proposed experiment, you will see how difficult it would be to control for variables in a situation where we studied teachers who were allocating pupils to ability groups under real circumstances.

We shall illustrate the strategy used in correlational research by looking at how Stephen Ball used Beachside Comprehensive as a site for a natural experiment on ability banding. While in his Table 2.5 Ball simply displays the co-variation between social class and allocation to Band 1 or Band 2, he does not conclude from this that the allocation is biased against working-class children. He recognizes that this co-variation may be the product of co-variation between social class and ability. In order to test the hypothesis that there is social-class bias in the banding allocations, he sets out to control for ability. He does this, as we have seen, by relying on the NFER tests for reading comprehension and mathematics, which had been administered to most of the entrants to Beachside in their primary schools. He employs statistical tests to assess the relationship between social class and allocation to bands. The results of those tests are reported at the bottom of two of his tables. In this section we shall explain how he obtained his results and what they mean.

A great deal of quantitative analysis involves speculating what the data would look like if some causal connection existed between variables (or if no causal connection existed between variables) and comparing the actual data with these predictions. This kind of speculation is, of course, a device to compensate for the fact that under naturally occurring situations variables cannot be physically controlled. The researcher is saying in effect: 'What would it look like if we had been able to control the situation in the way desired?'

We might therefore ask: 'What would data on banding and social class look like if there were no relationship at all between banding and social class: that is, if there were a *null* relationship?'

Table 6 provides the answer to this question. We have collapsed the data into three categories: 'non-manual', 'manual' and 'unclassified'.

Table 6 Numbers of pupils of different social classes to be expected in each ability band, if there were no relationship between banding and social class (E figures), compared with the observed figures (O figures)

Band	*Non-manual*		*Manual*		*Unclassified*		*Total*
	E	O	E	O	E	O	
Band 1	43	60	69	54	17	15	129
Band 2	44	29	70	83	18	19	131
Band 3	12	10	19	20	5	6	36
Total	99		157		40		296

To create this picture we assumed that a null relationship between social class and banding would mean that pupils from different social classes would appear in each band in the same proportion as they appear in the year group as a whole. In the year group as a whole non-manual, manual and unclassified pupils appear roughly in the proportions 10:16:4 (99:157:40). In Band 1 there are 129 places and sharing them out in these proportions gives us our expected figures.

For the first cell of the table, the calculation was done by dividing the total number of places, 296, by the column total, 99, and dividing the row total, 129, by the result.

Comparing the E (expected) and the O (observed) figures by eye in Table 6 should show you, once again, that social class does have some role to play in the real distribution. For example, if social class were irrelevant there would be 17 fewer non-manual children in Band 1 (60 – 43) and 15 more manual children in that band (69 – 54).

As we noted earlier, this in itself does not mean that teachers are making biased decisions against working-class pupils, or in favour of middle-class pupils, in allocating pupils to bands. It remains possible that there are proportionately more middle-class pupils in Band 1 because there are proportionately more middle-class pupils of high ability. This means that the co-variation between social class and ability banding reflects a co-variation between social class and ability. We do find such co-variation in Ball's data as shown in Table 7.

Table 7 Social class and scores on NFER reading comprehension test (percentages and numbers)

Score	*Middle-class pupils*		*Working-class pupils*	
115 and over	26%	(7)	7%	(4)
100–114	53%	(14)	45%	(26)
1–99	22%	(6)	49%	(29)
	101%	(27)	101%	(59)

Source: Table 2.6, p. 33, Ball (1981)

Table 7 relates only to the test of reading comprehension. You might like to check whether the same is true of the mathematics scores. Note that these scores are for a sample of 86 pupils only. We shall be commenting further on this later.

Activity 16

Now try your hand at constructing a table to show what distribution of test scores would be expected if there were *no* relationship between social class and scores on the test for reading comprehension. Follow the procedures we adopted to construct Table 6.

When you have done this, comment on the comparison between your results and the data in Table 7, which you should have used to obtain 'Observed' columns.

Your result should be similar to Table 8.

Table 8 Distribution of test scores to be expected if there were no relationship between test score and social class (E) and actual distribution (O)

Score	*Middle-class pupils*		*Working-class pupils*		*Total*
	E	O	E	O	
115+	3	7	8	4	11
100–114	13	14	27	26	40
1–99	11	6	24	29	35
Total	27	27	59	59	86

There is no reason why you should not have given the results in percentages, but if you wanted to make further calculations you would have to convert them back into numbers.

Comparing the observed and the expected figures by eye shows you there is co-variation between social class and test score. For example, if there were no relationship between social class and test score then there would be four fewer middle-class children and four more working-class children scoring 115 and above.

Assuming that these scores and teachers' judgements are based on ability, the distribution of children in bands should co-vary with test results. Of course, they should also co-vary with social class, since social class also co-varies with test results.

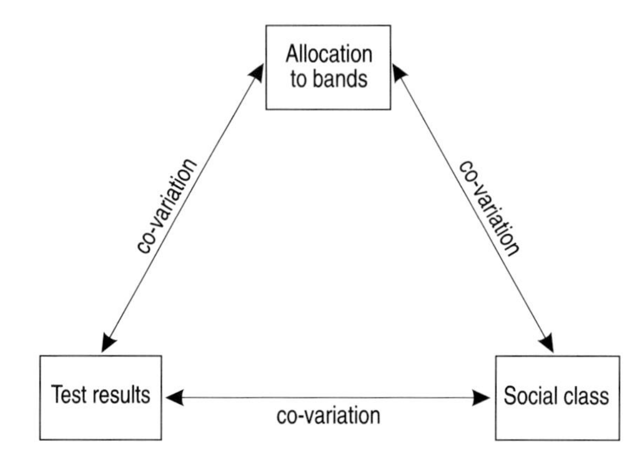

Figure 7 Co-variation among test scores, allocation to bands and social class.

When everything varies together, it is difficult to judge the contribution of any particular factor. As things stand, we cannot see whether the co-variation between social class and allocation to bands is simply due to the fact that middle-class children have higher ability, as indicated by a test, or whether other social-class-related factors not associated with ability are playing a part. It is highly likely that both social-class-related ability and social-class-related 'non-ability' factors are at work.

As with an experimental approach, in order to tease out the relative contribution of different factors it is necessary to control variables. In correlational research, however, we do this through manipulating the data rather than the situation. What this means is that we compare cases where the variable we wish to control is at the same level or varies only within a small range.

Activity 17

Look again at the article by Ball in the Appendix to this Part. How does he attempt to control for the co-variation of ability with social class? What conclusion does he draw?

Ball takes pupils with the *same* range of test scores, but from *different* social classes, and investigates how they are distributed in the ability bands. This is an attempt to break out of the co-variation triangle (Figure 7 above) by holding one of its corners fixed. Thus, it can be argued that, where the test ability of the pupils is the same, any differences in band allocation that co-vary with social class must be due to the effects of social class over and above the linkage between social class and test score (see Figure 8).

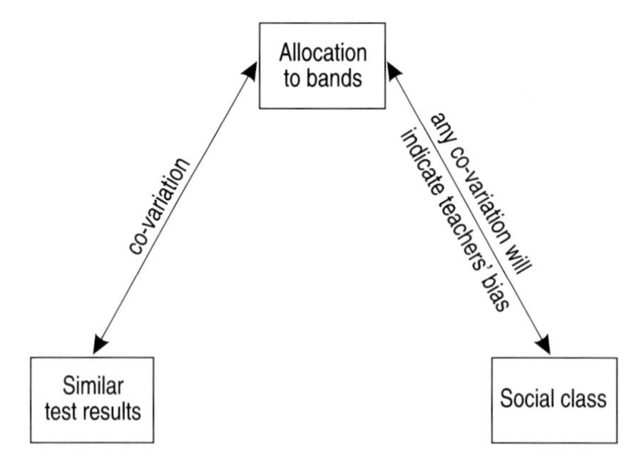

Figure 8 Controlling for test results.

Ball used a statistical test to investigate the strength of the relationships amongst these factors. We shall look at the test he used later, but here we will mirror his procedures in a way that is now familiar to you.

Table 9 Distribution of pupils in ability bands expected if social class played no part in the distribution, E, compared with actual distribution, O (all children scoring 100–114)

Band	*Working-class pupils*		*Middle-class pupils*		*Total*
	O	E	O	E	
Band 1	10	14	12	8	22
Band 2	16	12	2	6	18
Total	26	26	14	14	40

Activity 18

Looking at Table 9, how far would you say that it supports Ball's argument that even when test ability is held constant social class affects the distribution of pupils to ability bands?

So long as we take Ball's data at face value, the data in Table 9 support his claim. For example, if social class did not enter causally into the distribution of pupils between ability bands then there should be four (or five) fewer middle-class pupils with test scores of 100–114 in Band 1. Similarly, there should be five (or four) more working-class pupils with this kind of score in Band 1.

In our discussion of Ball's data up to now, we have often asked you to draw conclusions by visual inspection. Much more reliable conclusions can be drawn by subjecting the data to a statistical test. Of course, statistics is a highly specialist field of knowledge and, if they are going to use statistical methods, most wise researchers ask the advice of a professional statistician. It is not our purpose in this section to turn you into a statistician, but it is important for you to know enough about statistics to be able to read the results of statistical tests when they are presented in educational research.

Statistical testing derives from knowledge about the laws of chance and we actually know a great deal more about chance than we know about non-chance occurrences. Paradoxically, perhaps, statistics applies certain knowledge about chance to the uncertainties of everything else.

We can illustrate this by simulating the allocation of pupils to ability bands at Beachside.

Activity 19

Take a standard pack of cards. Shuffle and select twenty cards, ten red and ten black. Let the red cards be the children of manual workers and the black cards the children of non-manual workers. Shuffle and deal the cards into two piles. Call one pile Ability Band 1 and the other Ability Band 2. Count the number of red cards and the number of black cards in the Band 1 pile (you can ignore the other pile because it will be the exact mirror image in terms of the number of red and black cards). You know two things intuitively: firstly, that the pile is more likely to contain a roughly equal number of black cards and red cards than to contain only one colour; secondly, that it is also rather unlikely to contain exactly five red cards and five black cards. Put another way, you know that a sample of ten cards selected by chance (a random sample) will reflect the proportions of red and black cards in the population of twenty, but that chance factors will make it unlikely that it will reflect this distribution exactly.

In fact the chances of these two unlikely events occurring can be calculated precisely assuming random allocation. Of course, shuffling cards does not give us a perfectly random distribution of the cards, but it does approximate to such a distribution. The probability of you dealing ten red cards into one pile would be one chance in 184,756. This is because there are 184,756 ways of selecting ten cards from twenty and only one of these ways would result in a selection of ten reds. On the other hand, the probability of your ending up with two piles each containing no more than six of one colour would be about 82 in 100, since there are nearly 82,000 ways of selecting no more than six of one colour.

Now you ask someone else to allocate the same twenty cards to the two piles, any way they like, but according to a principle unknown to you. Suppose the result is a Band 1 pile entirely composed of black cards. This raises the suspicion that in allocating cards to piles they showed a bias for putting black cards in the Band 1 pile and red cards in the Band 2 pile. Knowing what you know about the distributions likely to occur by chance, you can put a figure to the strength of your suspicion about their bias. You could argue as follows. If a set of ten red and ten black cards are shuffled and divided into two piles at random, then the chances of an all-black (or an all-red) pile are around 0.001% (actually 1 in 92,378). Therefore it is very unlikely that this pile resulted from an unbiased (random) distribution.

If the result was a pile of six black and four red cards then you could have argued that distributions with no more than six of one colour could have occurred by chance 82% of the time. The actual distribution might have been due to a small bias in favour of putting red cards in the Band 1 pile, but the most sensible conclusion for you to reach would be that there is insufficient evidence for you to decide whether this was a biased distribution or an unbiased, random distribution.

The situation faced by Ball was very similar to this example of card sorting. He was suspicious that pupils (our cards) were being sorted into ability bands (our piles) in a way that showed bias against working-class pupils (red cards) and in favour of middle-class pupils (black cards). To check out this suspicion he used a statistical test that compares the actual distribution (the distribution in our experiment obtained by unknown principles) with a distribution that might have occurred by chance. The result of using the test is a figure which will show how reasonably he can hold to his initial suspicion.

You have already encountered the way in which the figures were set up for statistical test by Ball in our Table 9. We suggest that you now look at this table again. Remember that for this test Ball has selected pupils from within the same range of measured ability, so that he can argue that any differences in allocation to bands are likely to be due to social-class bias, or chance: in other words, he has controlled for ability. The statistical test will help to control for the effects of chance. Therefore, logically, to the extent to which the actual figures depart from what might have occurred by chance, this is likely to be due to social-class bias. You can now regard the 'expected' figures as the figures most likely to have occurred by chance. They are the equivalent of our 5:5 ratio of black to red cards in the example above and, in this case, are just the distribution that would be expected if working-class children and middle-class children had been allocated to bands in the same proportions as they appeared in a total 'pack' of forty.

6.5 THE CHI-SQUARED TEST

The statistical test Ball used is the chi-squared test, pronounced 'ki-squared test'. (You will often see this written simply as 'the χ^2 test', using the Greek letter chi.) What the test does mathematically is to compare the actual or observed figures (O) with the figures expected by chance (E). The comparison is done by subtraction.

There are four sets of O and E figures in Table 9 and so there are four sets of subtractions. These are squared and divided by the relevant E figure. The results are then added together. This figure is looked up in a ready reckoner called a 'Table of critical values for χ^2'. It tells us how often a particular deviation from what *might* have occurred by chance, *would* have occurred by chance. Note the double use of chance in this sentence. Like our 5:5 ratio in the card-sorting simulation, the E figures are the single most likely chance figures, but other chance combinations may occur. We want to know how often.

One feature of the chi-squared calculations makes them look more complicated than they are and tends to obscure what is going on. This is that the differences between O and E figures are squared. Doing this avoids the problem that arises from the fact that if you add up all the differences they would total to zero, cancelling each other out. Squaring them converts negatives to positives and leaves you with all positive numbers which express the amount of variety (variance) in the data.

Statistical calculations are full of squarings and the taking of square roots mainly for this reason. It is probably one reason why non-mathematicians find statistics so threatening. In fact, though, what is being done is quite simple.

Table 10

Band	*Working-class pupils*		*Middle-class pupils*		*Total*
	O	E	O	E	
Band 1	10	14.3	12	7.7	22
Band 2	16	11.7	2	6.3	18
Total	26		14		

The calculation of chi squared for Table 10, in broadly the way Ball calculated it, is as follows:

$$\chi^2 = \frac{(10-14.3)^2}{14.3} + \frac{(12-7.7)^2}{7.7} + \frac{(16-11.7)^2}{11.7} + \frac{(2-6.3)^2}{6.3}$$

$$= \frac{18.49}{14.3} + \frac{18.49}{7.7} + \frac{18.49}{11.7} + \frac{18.49}{6.3}$$

$$= 1.29 + 2.40 + 1.58 + 2.93$$

$$\chi^2 = 8.2$$

Before you can look this figure up in a table of critical values it is necessary to work out what are called 'degrees of freedom'. These express the amount of free play in the data. In our card sorting exercise cards could only be black or red and could only be sorted into one pile or the other. If you imagine sorting the cards such that ten cards were allocated to the first pile, then by the time this was complete everything about the second pile was decided. There is only one degree of freedom here. If there are more degrees of freedom then there is more free play for chance and this has to be taken into consideration. The usual way of calculating degrees of freedom is by the formula

$$\text{df} = (\text{number of columns} - 1) \times (\text{number of rows} - 1)$$

In the simulation and in Table 10, there are two rows and two columns, thus

$$\text{df} = (C - 1) \times (R - 1) = 1 \times 1 = 1$$

Table 11 Part of the table of critical values for χ^2

Degrees of freedom	*Levels of significance (probability, p)*					
	0.2	0.10	0.05	0.02	0.01	0.001
df = 1	1.64	2.71	3.84	5.41	6.64	10.83
df = 2	3.22	4.60	5.99	7.82	9.21	13.82

Ball's analysis had one degree of freedom and the value of chi squared was 8.2. This value exceeds 6.64, but falls below 10.83. Therefore, from Table 11, the level of significance (the level of probability p), is 0.01.

It is perhaps more meaningful to multiply 0.01 by 100 and then to say: only once in 100 times would this result occur by chance. Remember how the question was posed in setting up the chi-squared test. Ball asked how often would a distribution like the one in his table occur by chance. Once in a 100 is rather unlikely.[10] Thus if all the other procedures followed by Ball, and repeated by us, are correct, we can be fairly confident that the observed figures in the table were not the product of chance and were the product of social-class bias.

A small annoyance with regard to the chi-squared test is something called 'Yates correction' which entails reducing by 0.5 each observed figure that is greater than expected and increasing by 0.5 each observed figure that is less than expected. This should be used whenever there is only one degree of freedom. Ball should have done this in his calculation, but did not, and we followed his procedures here. If we apply Yates' correction, the first two calculations for Table 10 should have been

$$\frac{(10+0.5-14.3)^2}{14.3} \quad and \quad \frac{(12-0.5-7.7)^2}{7.7}$$

and the resulting figure for chi squared should have been χ^2=6.4.

Activity 20

Try your hand at using the table of critical values (Table 11) to establish the level of significance for a value of chi squared of 6.4. There is still of course only one degree of freedom.

On this basis, how many times out of 100 would a distribution like the one in Ball's table occur by chance?

You should conclude that it is still rather unlikely. The figure is 0.02, or twice in a hundred.

Activity 21

If you are unsure about the workings of chi squared, do your own calculations for the card sorting simulation where the observed figures were Band 1, 10 black cards, and Band 2, 10 red cards. Remember to take away Yates' correction, since there is only one degree of freedom here.

Our answer to Activity 21 is calculated from Table 12.

Table 12

Band	*Black*		*Red*	
	O	E	O	E
Band 1	10	5	0	5
Band 2	0	5	10	5

$$\chi^2 = \frac{(10-0.5-5)^2}{5} + \frac{(0+0.5-5)^2}{5} + \frac{(0+0.5-5)^2}{5} + \frac{(10-0.5-5)^2}{5}$$

$$\chi^2 = 16.2$$

Reading from Table 11, since the degree of freedom is one, $p < 0.001$. In other words, less than once in 1000 times would this result occur by chance and you can be fairly certain that the way the cards were actually distributed was not randomly.

[10] Conventionally, statisticians do not take seriously any level of probability greater than 0.05, where only 5 times in 100 would you expect the observed pattern to occur by chance.

6.6 RELATIVE CONTRIBUTIONS: MEASURES OF THE STRENGTH OF ASSOCIATION

Both ability, as measured by a test score, and social class, as measured by whether the occupation of the head of a household was manual or non-manual, seem to have some independent effect on the way in which pupils are distributed to ability bands in Ball's data. As yet, we have not established which has the strongest influence. To estimate this there are various statistical techniques available that go under the general heading of 'correlation co-efficients'.

We shall demonstrate the use of a measure called phi, represented by Ø, which is easily calculated from the value of chi squared. The minimum value of phi is 0 and the maximum value (for 2 × 2 tables) is 1. Ball used the co-efficient *C*, which is also easy to calculate, but is difficult to interpret because its maximum value is less than 1 and varies from one data set to another.

Unlike Ball, who used only a part of the data available to him, we shall use all the data available. You will see that below we have made separate calculations of chi squared for:

Social class and banding, irrespective of ability (Table 13).

Ability (test score) and banding, irrespective of social class (Table 14).

Social class and ability (test score) (Table 15).

From this we shall be able to see which are the strongest relationships in the causal network.

Table 13 Social class and banding

Band	*Working-class pupils*		*Middle-class pupils*		*Total*
	O	E	O	E	
Band 1	18	26	20	12	38
Band 2	41	33	7	15	48
Total	59		27		86

chi squared = 12.3, df = 1, $p < 0.001$

Table 14 Test score and banding

Band	*100+*		*1–99*		*Total*
	O	E	O	E	
Band 1	32	22.5	6	15.5	38
Band 2	19	28.5	29	19.5	48
Total	51		35		86

chi squared = 15.82, df = 1, $p < 0.001$

Table 15 Test score and social class

Test score	*Working-class pupils*		*Middle-class pupils*		*Total*
	O	E	O	E	
100+	30	35	21	16	51
1–99	29	24	6	11	35
Total	59		27		86

chi squared = 4.53, df = 1, $p < 0.02$

Tables 13 and 14 show you what you already suspected from working with the data earlier. They show that there is a significant relationship between social class and banding and between ability (test score) and banding. The chi-squared test tells you that these patterns are most unlikely to have occurred by chance. In both cases the probability of this happening is under 1 in 1000 ($p < 0.001$). You will note that chi squared for Table 14 is higher than that in Table 13. This is an indication that allocation to bands shows a stronger relationship with test scores than it shows with social class.

Comparing the figures for chi squared can be misleading, however. A better measure of the relative strength of the relationship is derived from calculating phi, ϕ. The formula for this is

$$\phi = \sqrt{\frac{\chi^2}{N}}$$

This means that we must divide chi squared by the number in the sample and take the square root of the result.

To read phi or any other correlation co-efficient as a measure of the strength of a relationship, it is conventional to square it and multiply by 100 to produce a percentage figure. Thus

Phi for social class and ability banding (Table 13) is 0.378 or 14% ($0.378^2 \times 100 = 14.288$)

Phi for test score and ability banding (Table 14) is 0.429 or 18%

Phi for social class and test score (Table 15) is 0.230 or 5%

One way of looking at this is in terms of Figure 9.

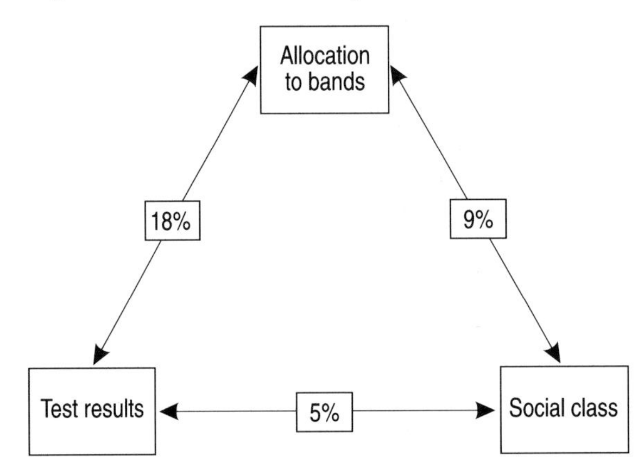

Figure 9 Strength of association between tested ability, social class and banding in a causal network.

In Figure 9 we have subtracted the 5% for the correlation between ability and social class from the 14% for the correlation between social class and allocation to bands. This is a way of separating the influence of social class itself from the influence of social-class-related ability. We do not have to add that 5% to the influence of ability alone because it is already included within the 18%.

It is important to be clear about what the percentages in Figure 9 mean. It might be tempting to look at Figure 9 and say that 18% of the pattern in banding is *caused* by ability, as measured by test scores. Statisticians often come close to this kind of statement by using phrases such as 'explained by' or 'accounted for by'. This is slightly misleading. You already know that test scores do not cause banding in any simple way, although you might suspect that some underlying ability of pupils causes their test score *and* causes teachers to do what they do to allocate pupils to ability bands.

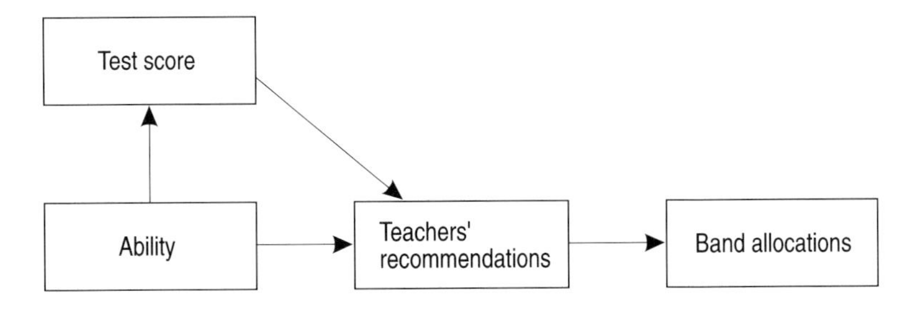

Figure 10 The possible role of ability in the causal network.

Correlations may or may not indicate causes, but what they always do represent are predictions. Thus when we say that '18% of the distribution of pupils in the banding system can be accounted for by the distribution of test scores', what we actually mean is that knowing the distribution of test scores improves our ability to predict the distribution within ability bands, and it does this by 18%. This can be demonstrated quite easily.

Suppose all you knew about the distribution of pupils within bands was that there were 38 in Band 1 and 48 in Band 2 (Table 16). The best prediction you could make for any particular pupils would be that they would be in Band 2. This is simply because there are more pupils in Band 2 than in Band 1. If you guessed that all the pupils were in Band 2 you would in fact be right 48 times out of 86 – a success rate of 56%.

Table 16 Test score and banding

Band	*100+*	*1–99*	*Total*
Band 1	32	6	38
Band 2	19	29	48
Total	51	35	86

If you were told the distribution of pupils across bands according to their test score, you could improve your prediction. Now your best bet would be that all pupils with test scores above 100 would be in Band 1 and all pupils with test scores from 1 to 99 would be in Band 2. You would be correct on 61 occasions (32 + 29) out of 86 and your success rate would have increased to 71%.

Thus, knowing the test scores improves your ability to predict by 15%: it reduces the error in guessing by 15%. (In the first instance the percentage error is 100–56=44%, in the second it is 100–71=29% and 44–29=15%.)

What phi and other correlation co-efficients do is to provide a more exact measurement of the extent to which the distribution of one variable (say, allocation to bands) can be predicted from knowledge of the distribution of another (say, test score). The 18% in Figure 9 says that knowing the distribution of test scores we can improve our ability to guess the distribution into bands by about 18%. (This is not quite the same estimate as the 15% we gained by guessing. Different methods produce different estimates.) The fact that we can improve our predictions in this way is prima-facie evidence that the two variables are linked together in some causal network. Exactly what is the relationship between them is something which has to be inferred.

6.7 REPRESENTATIVE SAMPLES AND STATISTICAL TESTING

As we noted earlier, Ball used data on 86 pupils to examine or illustrate what was happening to all pupils. So the question arises of how representative the allocation of the sample to bands is of the allocation of the *whole year group* to bands. The chi-squared test does not inform us directly about this. It tells us that if the teachers had allocated an infinite number of working-class and middle-class children to the bands on the basis of their measured ability, the likelihood of drawing a sample of 86 children from this population which showed the inequalities in distribution Ball found, is very small. As it stands, then, this is evidence to suggest that the teachers did not allocate these children to bands on the basis of measured ability alone. However, in using any test we need to know the conditions the data must meet for it to work properly. In the case of the chi-squared test there are two of these: the samples drawn of working-class and middle-class children must be both independent and random. Ball's use of chi-squared meets the first of these conditions (the composition of each social-class sample did not have any effect on that of the other), but it clearly does not meet the second. Ball's sample was determined by the test result data he could obtain. While it was not selected systematically, neither was it selected randomly. Therefore, there is a risk that the difference between observed and expected allocations is a product of factors involved in the way in which Ball's sample was drawn from the year group.

This leads us on to a further point. Since we are interested in whether allocation was biased in the year group as a whole, rather than just in the sample, it is important to note that the latter is not very representative of the year group as regards the allocation of working-class and middle-class students to bands (taking no account of ability). If we compare the data for the sample with that in Table N2 in endnote 3 of Ball's article, we find that by comparison with the whole year group both middle-class pupils in Band 1 and working-class pupils in Band 2 are over-represented in the sample. As a result, there is a smaller percentage of middle-class pupils in Band 2 and of working-class pupils in Band 1 in the sample than in the school year. Ball's argument is that teachers are biased in favour of middle-class pupils and place more of them in Band 1, and therefore place more working-class pupils in Band 2. His sample is, however, already biased in this direction. The extent of the bias is more easily seen if we calculate the figures for a precisely representative sample and compare them with the actual sample, as in Table 17.

Table 17 Comparing Ball's sample with the numbers expected in a representative sample

Band	*Working-class pupils*		*Middle-class pupils*		*Total*
	actual	representative	actual	representative	
Band 1	18	21	20	23	38
Band 2	41	32	7	11	48
Total	59	53	27	34	86

chi squared = 3.92, df = 1, $p < 0.05$

From the chi-squared test you can see that a sample that deviated from the representative sample to the same degree as Ball's might be drawn at random less than 5 times out of a 100. Put the other way, around 95 samples out of 100 drawn at random would be more representative than Ball's sample. Clearly, Ball's is not a very representative sample in these terms. And we also know that the direction in which it deviates from being representative is precisely the direction which Ball takes as evidence of bias in the allocation process. Of course this could be because the distribution of higher and lower ability pupils across the social classes in Ball's sample is very different from that in the year group; but we have no way of gauging this. This does not disprove the validity of Ball's chi-squared result, but it should make us rather cautious about accepting it as evidence that there was bias in the teachers' allocation of pupils to bands in the year group as a whole.

6.8 STATISTICAL SIGNIFICANCE AND SUBSTANTIVE SIGNIFICANCE

This is not the end of the story. It is quite possible and, indeed, quite common to work out statistical tests correctly and to obtain statistically significant results, but to demonstrate nothing of any importance in a theoretical or practical sense. Worse still, it is possible to produce results that are misleading!

Even if Ball's sample had been representative, there is an important substantive matter that he neglects, which could have threatened the validity of his findings. To recapitulate, Ball's main claim was that social-class bias was at play in allocating pupils to ability bands. To demonstrate this bias he performed a chi-squared test, which compared the actual distribution of pupils of different social classes into ability bands with the distribution that would have occurred if the two classes had been allocated to ability bands proportionately (i.e. if pupils of the same ability had been allocated to bands randomly without taking their social class into consideration). Deviation from a proportional distribution is how Ball has operationalized 'social-class bias'. The question we should ask is whether this is a sensible way of operationalizing social-class bias.

For his demonstration Ball only used the figures for pupils with test scores of 100–114. What he did not take into consideration was the fact that, in reality, the decisions on band allocation for these particular pupils are influenced by the allocation of pupils with test scores of over 114. This is because allocations are usually made in a situation where the number of places in bands is more or less fixed.

Let us use the cards again to simulate the situation. We shall still have ten red cards and ten black cards and once again ten cards will have to be placed in each pile. This time, however, there will be four black kings and one red king. We shall introduce the rule that all kings must be allocated to the Band 1 pile first and then the other cards divided into the two piles at random. You will see immediately that this considerably reduces the chances of red cards appearing in the pile representing Band 1. Whether it does so 'unfairly' depends on our judgement about the rights of kings to a place in that pile.

At Beachside 'kings' are the pupils scoring 115 and above. Within the framework within which Ball is operating, achievement-test scores are taken to represent the ability to benefit from placement in different bands. There really seems to be no objection to assuming that those pupils with high abilities should have priority claims to places in Band 1. In Ball's sample, there are more middle-class pupils with high ability than working-class pupils. By giving high-ability pupils priority for Band 1 placement, we automatically give priority to middle-class pupils.

Taking this into consideration, we can work out a 'fair' distribution for ability banding assuming that the number of places in each band is fixed. In terms of the reading comprehension test (see Table 2.6 in the extract from Ball), there are eleven pupils of the highest ability, four working-class and seven middle-class pupils. Give them Band 1 positions. Since there are thirty-eight Band 1 positions there are now only twenty-seven places left. There are forty pupils with test scores of 100–114 with an equal claim to Band 1 positions. To avoid social-class bias we shall distribute them in proportion to the number of working-class and middle-class pupils. Since there are twenty-six working-class and fourteen middle-class pupils, we shall give Band 1 positions to 17.5 working-class pupils and 9.5 middle-class pupils (you can do things with statistics which you could never do in reality!). Now there are 4 + 17.5 working-class pupils and 7 + 9.5 middle-class pupils in Band 1. The remainder of the pupils are now allocated to Band 2. These procedures provide us with the expected figures given in Table 18.

Table 18 Distribution of pupils of different social classes in ability bands. Observed distribution compared with distribution expected from 'fair' allocation taking highest ability pupils into consideration

Band	*Working-class pupils*		*Middle-class pupils*		*Total*
	O	E	O	E	
Band 1	18	21.5	20	16.5	38
Band 2	41	37.5	7	10.5	48
Total	59		27		86

chi squared = 2.06, df = 1, $p < 0.10$

From the figures in Table 13, the extent to which the actual figures departed from a simple proportional distribution was calculated. Chi-squared was then 12.3, with a very high level of statistical significance. Our new calculation compares the actual distribution with a distribution that might have occurred had pupils been allocated to bands by giving those of the highest ability priority to Band 1 and then distributing the remainder proportionately between pupils of different social classes. We think this is a better model of a 'fair' distribution than the one adopted by Ball. Now chi squared is only 2.06. It is statistically significant only at the 10% level. This means that had teachers at Beachside really been distributing pupils to bands on the same basis as our model, then 10% of representative samples of 86 drawn from the whole year population would show this degree of 'social-class bias', simply because of the chancy nature of samples. As we noted earlier, the convention in statistics is not to take seriously any level of significance greater than 0.05, or 5%.

Put more formally, our null hypothesis was that there was no statistically significant relationship between social class and allocation to bands when ability was controlled. Following statistical convention, we would want $p < 0.05$ to reject the hypothesis. In our calculations p did not reach the 5% level, hence our null hypothesis is not rejected and we have no good grounds for saying that social-class bias influences decisions on band allocation. For this reason, over and above the fact that he may have been working with an unrepresentative sample, Ball does not provide convincing evidence that social-class bias is an important influence on the distribution of pupils to bands in the cohort of pupils he studied at Beachside. It is worth emphasizing that this does not necessarily mean that there was no social-class bias, merely that Ball gives no strong evidence for it.

6.9 UNDERLYING ASSUMPTIONS

It is important to be as critical of our own procedures as we have been of Ball's. There is the question of how reasonable our model is of a fair distribution. We think that it is an improvement on Ball's model, for two reasons. First, it takes into consideration the claims of those with high test scores to be placed in the top band and, secondly, the fact that the number of places in the top band is likely to be restricted. Our application of the model, however, does give rise to some problems. We adopted the model on the assumption that the placement of any one pupil is likely to result from all the decisions about all the pupils. Unfortunately, we only know about the test scores of the pupils in Ball's sample and, as we know, Ball's sample is unrepresentative. Our application of the model to Ball's data relies on the assumption that in the cohort as a whole the ratio of high to middle to low test scores is 11:40:35. In other words, it is similar to that in the sample. It also relies on the assumption that test scores and social class in the cohort covary in the same way as in the sample. If, in fact, there were just as many working-class pupils as middle-class pupils with test scores of 115 and above then our procedures would be severely awry. All we can say about this is that when NFER tests are administered to large groups of pupils, middle-class pupils do usually score more highly on average.

It is also worth remembering at this point an issue that we raised earlier about Ball's operationalization of ability. We can ask: 'Why should we regard NFER achievement test scores as a better measure of a pupil's ability than the estimates of junior-school teachers?'. After all, the bands group pupils for all subjects, whereas the tests measure achievement in specific areas. While there are very few ways of getting a high score on a test, there is a large number of ways of getting a low score, many of which would not be indicative of underlying inability. We should rightly complain if junior-school teachers did not take this possibility into consideration in making recommendations about the allocation of pupils to bands in secondary school. For what it is worth, Ball's data do show more pupils being 'over-allocated' than 'under-allocated'. Ball's argument was constructed on the basis that test scores represented 'true ability', so decisions on band allocation that departed from what might be predicted by a test score could be seen as social-class bias. Our argument has been that Ball has demonstrated no social-class bias, but in order to pursue it we have had to assume with him that test scores provide a sufficient indication of the way in which pupils should be banded by ability. This is not an assumption we should like to defend.

6.10 REGRESSION ANALYSIS

Up to now we have concentrated on the underlying logic of quantitative data analysis, introducing a small number of techniques as and when they became appropriate for the analysis of the data from Ball's study. You will find in the literature quite a lot of research that relies primarily on the techniques we have discussed so far. However, they represent only a very small range of the statistical techniques that are available and that have been used by educational researchers. We cannot hope to cover all the others, but what we shall do in the remainder of this section is to introduce one of the most frequently used of the more advanced techniques, 'regression analysis'. As you will see, regression analysis is a development of the techniques to which you have already been introduced. Before we discuss it fully, however, we need to cover one or two other issues.

TYPES OF DATA

The kinds of statistical tests that can be employed in educational research depend on the kinds of data that are used. So far we have been using data as if they were *nominal* or *categorical* in character. This is the form of data that is least amenable to statistical use. For regression analysis, higher levels of data are required. Below we outline the standard classification of different types of quantitative data.

- *Nominal-level data*
  Examples: classifications of gender and ethnicity. These are just categories. You *cannot* add together the number of males and the number of females, divide by the total and come up with an 'average gender'. You cannot multiply ethnic groups together and come up with something different. Within the bounds of common sense, however, you can collapse nominal categories together. For example, Ball collapses the Registrar General's classes into the two-category system, of manual and non-manual.
- *Ordinal-level data*
  Examples: ability bands or the rank order of pupils in a form. These are ordinal-level data in the sense that they can be ranked from highest to lowest. You cannot, however, give a measurement for how much higher Band 1 is than Band 2. In other words, ordinal data can be ranked, but the intervals between the ranks cannot be specified.
- *Interval-level data*
  Interval data have a standard and known interval between points on the scale. Thus, in the case of SATs scores, if we were justified in assuming that the difference between a Grade 2 and a Grade 6 is the same as that

between a Grade 6 and a Grade 10, then we could say with justification that SATs scores are interval data.

- *Ratio-level data*
  Chronological age, parental income, height, distance travelled to school, would all be ratio-level data. This is because there is a standard scale of measurement that can be used that has equal intervals and a true zero point. With ratio-level data we know that a score is a specified number of equidistant units away from zero. Although this is not precisely true of GCSE grades or IQ scores, many educational researchers behave as if it is.

Activity 22

What level of data are the following:

(a) Pupils classified into the social-class groupings in Ball's Table 2N.
(b) NFER test scores grouped into three categories.
(c) NFER test scores showing the actual score per pupil.
(d) Examination marks.
(e) Position of a pupil in the banding system.
(f) Social class in two categories: working class and middle class.

Here are our answers:

(a) Ordinal-level data, if you ignore the problem of the unclassified pupils, but more safely regarded as nominal.

(b) Technically this is interval- or ratio-level data, but clumped together in this way it is not much of an improvement on ordinal-level data.

(c) There is some debate about whether test scores are interval- or ratio-level data. In most educational research they would be treated as ratio-level data.

(d) The answer will depend on the way in which the examinations are marked, but it would be safe to assume no higher than interval-level data.

(e) Ordinal-level data.

(f) Nominal-level data.

These answers indicate what is the highest level at which you can use each kind of data, since you can always use data of a higher level as if it were of a lower level.

DIVERSITY AND SIZE OF SAMPLE

If you remember that in quantitative work we are usually looking for co-variation, you will understand that co-variation is most easily seen where data can be scaled precisely, as with interval-level and ratio-level data. We can illustrate this speculatively by thinking about Ball's data on the allocation to ability bands of the group of pupils with test scores of 100–114 (Table 9). As his data stand, pupils with a very wide range of test scores are grouped together in a single category. This lumping together seems to make it reasonable to assume that all these pupils should be treated similarly, but what if we knew their individual scores; what if we had interval- or ratio-level data for these pupils? Table 19 shows two possible distributions of the pupils' scores.

Table 19 Two possible distributions of NFER test scores among those scoring 100–114: by social class

Distribution 1			*Distribution 2*		
Scores	*Working-class pupils*	*Middle-class pupils*	*Score*	*Working-class pupils*	*Middle-class pupils*
114	1	2	114	3	2
113	1	1	113	4	1
112	1	3	112	2	0
111	1	0	111	1	0
110	1	3	110	2	0
109	1	1	109	1	0
108	1	1	108	2	0
107	3	1	107	2	0
106	2	0	106	1	1
105	3	0	105	1	2
104	2	0	104	1	2
103	3	0	103	2	0
102	2	0	102	1	1
101	3	1	101	1	2
100	1	1	100	0	3

Activity 23

What important difference is there between these two distributions from the point of view of Ball's analysis?

On the first hypothetical distribution, placing all pupils with scores of 100–114 in Band 1 would give the actual social-class differences shown in Table 9. This is quite 'fair', too, because middle-class pupils are, on average, scoring higher marks than working-class pupils. In the case of the second hypothetical distribution, however, what is shown in Ball's data cannot be consistent with an even-handed treatment of pupils from different social classes because, on average, working-class pupils are scoring higher. What the actual situation was we cannot know because of the way in which differences within the groups have been submerged by treating all those scoring 100–114 as the same.

Given that the more data can be differentiated the better chance there is of accurately displaying co-variation, why do authors often work with data that are grouped into very crude categories? There are two main reasons for this. Firstly, highly differentiated data are often not available. This is frequently the case when a researcher relies on second-hand data. For example, we might guess that the only test data Ball could obtain was clumped into three test-score categories. The second common reason relates to the size of the set of data. Again, a pack of cards provides a convenient demonstration.

As you saw, a random sample of ten cards drawn from a pack of ten reds and ten black cards gave you a fairish chance of getting a sample which represented the colour distribution of the cards in the pack. That is, on 82 occasions out of 100 you might have dealt ten cards with no more than six cards of any colour. Suppose now that the 'population' of twenty cards had five hearts, five diamonds, five clubs and five spades. You should realize intuitively that the chance of a deal of ten accurately representing suits is much less than the chance of it accurately representing colours. In turn, the chance of a deal of ten accurately representing the denominations of the cards is even less than the chance of accurately representing the suits.

An adequate size for a sample is determined by the amount of the diversity you want to represent. By the same token, the smaller the sample the less diversity you can represent. Let us think of this in terms of two of Ball's important variables: social class and test scores. Ball had data that would enable him to subdivide pupils into social classes in the six categories of the Registrar General's scheme plus an 'unclassified category' (see Ball's Table N2).

Let us imagine that he had test-score data enabling him to divide pupils into groups that each represented an interval of ten test-score points (e.g. 1–10, 11–20 ... 121–130). This results in thirteen categories, producing a table with seven columns (for social class) and thirteen rows (for scores). This gives a table with ninety-one cells: in fact, a table of around the same size as Table N2. Given that Ball only had test-score data for eighty-six pupils, had he subdivided as above, many of the cells in his table would have remained empty. It is probable that many of the others would have contained only one or two entries. In addition, Ball was interested in how pupils with particular scores from particular social classes were allocated to the *three* ability bands. This in effect makes a table with 91 × 3 = 273 cells. Even if Ball had had test-score data for the entire 296 pupils in the year group (a 100% sample) it would have been too small to display adequately the relationships between social class, test score and ability banding at this level of detail.

Under these circumstances it is necessary to collapse data into cruder categories. The payoff is that patterns can be seen in the collapsed data which are not visible in highly differentiated data. On the other hand, the costs of degrading data are that important differences may become invisible and that patterns may emerge that are largely the result of the way the data have been collapsed.

THE TECHNIQUE OF REGRESSION ANALYSIS

Much sophisticated quantitative work in educational research uses the technique of regression analysis. This requires data to be of at least interval level. To illustrate what is involved in regression analysis we have invented a set of data that might apply to a class in a top-ability band in a school like Beachside. Imagine an NFER test in English conducted in the last year of junior school. The examination mark is the mark received by the pupils in their end-of-third-year examination. Social class is collapsed into the two categories, middle and working class, as with Ball's data.

We are going to use the data in Table 20 to investigate whether social-class differences in achievement in English increase, decrease or stay the same over the first three years of secondary schooling. Ability in English at the beginning of the period is measured by the NFER test and, at the end, by the score in the school's English examination. For the time being ignore the column headed 'residual'.

Before we do anything more sophisticated with these figures it is worth manipulating them to see what patterns can be made visible. Since we can treat the test scores and the examination results as interval-level data, we can calculate averages for the two social classes of pupils.

Table 20 Fictional data set showing NFER test scores and examination results for working-class (W) and middle-class (M) pupils

Pupil	*Social class*	*NFER test score*	*Examination mark*	*Residual*
1	M	127	80	2.97
2	M	128	79	0.66
3	M	116	76	13.38
4	M	114	75	15.01
5	M	125	74	-0.41
6	W	130	68	-12.96
7	M	111	67	10.94
8	M	114	65	5.01
9	W	100	64	22.35
10	M	110	60	5.25
11	W	106	58	8.49
12	M	105	57	8.80
13	M	110	56	1.25
14	M	113	55	-3.68
15	M	104	54	7.11
16	W	101	53	10.04
17	W	105	50	1.80
18	M	100	48	6.35
19	M	100	46	4.35
20	W	103	44	-1.58
21	M	102	42	-2.27
22	W	112	41	-16.37
23	W	107	38	-12.82
24	W	100	36	-5.65
25	W	94	34	0.22
26	W	100	33	-8.65
27	W	110	32	-22.75
28	M	92	30	-1.16
29	W	87	28	3.39
30	M	100	24	-17.65
31	M	96	15	-21.40

AVERAGES

There are three kinds of average: the 'mode', the 'mean' and the 'median'. They all express a central point around which the scores cluster and, hence, are called measures of the central tendency.

The mode is the most frequently occurring score for a group. In our data there are no modes for examination results, since each pupil has a different score, but the mode for the test scores for all pupils is 100, which appears six times. The mode is not a particularly useful measure statistically; it corresponds roughly with what we mean verbally by 'typical'. In the case of our data it is not very useful as an indication of the central tendency, since twenty-one out of thirty-one pupils scored more than the mode. You should realize that if we treat data at the nominal level, the mode is the only kind of 'average' available.

The mean, or mathematical average, is a more familiar measure. It is calculated by adding together all the scores and dividing by the number of scores.

Table 21 Means for NFER test scores and examination results: working-class and middle-class pupils: derived from Table 20

	Test scores	*Examination results*
middle-class pupils	109.28	55.72
all pupils	107.16	51.03
working-class pupils	104.23	44.54

We shall not be using the third type of average, the median, in the calculations to follow, so we shall leave discussion of it until later.

MEASURES OF DISPERSION

The mean by itself can be misleading, because it does not take into consideration the way in which the scores are distributed over their range. Thus two sets of very different scores can have very similar means. For example, the mean of (2,2,4,4,6,6) and (2,2,2,2,2,14) is 4 in both cases.

In effect, you have already encountered the problem of using mean scores for statistical calculations. The problem we noted as arising from lumping together all pupils scoring 100–114 is of much the same kind.

In our data, the range of examination scores for working-class children is 40 and for middle-class pupils it is 65. Moreover, the way in which the scores are distributed across the range is very different. This can be made visible by collapsing the examination scores from Table 20 into intervals of ten (Figure 11).

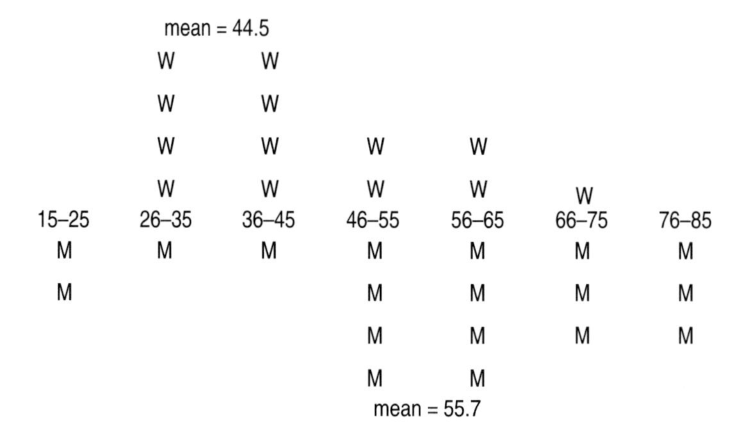

Figure 11 A comparison of the two distributions for working-class (W) and middle-class (M) pupils.

You can see from Figure 11 that the scores for working-class children are clustered much more towards their mean, while the scores for middle-class children are much more dispersed. It shows that the mean for working-class pupils is a rather better measure of the central tendency of the scores for them than the mean for middle-class children. Simply comparing mean scores for both groups would ignore this.

Standard deviation

You probably realize that the range of scores also does not capture the dispersion of data very effectively. It tells us the difference between the end points of the distribution, but nothing about how the data are distributed between those points. More effective is the 'standard deviation'. To understand the idea of standard deviation you may find the following analogy useful.

In the game of bowls the best player is decided by whosoever manages to place a single wood closest to the jack. Imagine that we want a more stringent test of which of two players is the better, taking into consideration the position of all woods in relation to the jack. Thus, for the first bowler we measure the distance between the jack and each of that player's woods and divide by the number of woods. We now have a single measure of the extent to which all the first player's woods deviated from the position of the jack: an average deviation. If we do the same for the other player, then whoever has the smaller average deviation can be said to be the more accurate bowler. Accuracy in this case equals ability to cluster woods closely around the jack.

In statistics, the smaller the average deviation the more closely the data are clustered around the mean. You should also realize that our test of bowling accuracy does not require that each player bowls the same number of woods and in statistics standard deviations can be compared irrespective of the number of scores in different groups. (Though the accuracy of our estimates of bowling accuracy will increase the greater the number of woods.)

Our bowling example was in fact a statistic called the 'mean deviation'. The standard deviation itself is more complicated to calculate because it involves squaring deviations from the mean at one stage and unsquaring them again at another by taking a square root. If, however, you keep the bowling example in mind you will understand the principle which underlies it.

In terms of our examination scores the standard deviation for working-class pupils is 12.96 and for middle-class pupils is 17.4. This is what you could see in Figure 11, but is difficult to express in words. If we had much bigger samples of pupils with the same standard deviations their scores would make graphs like those in Figure 12.

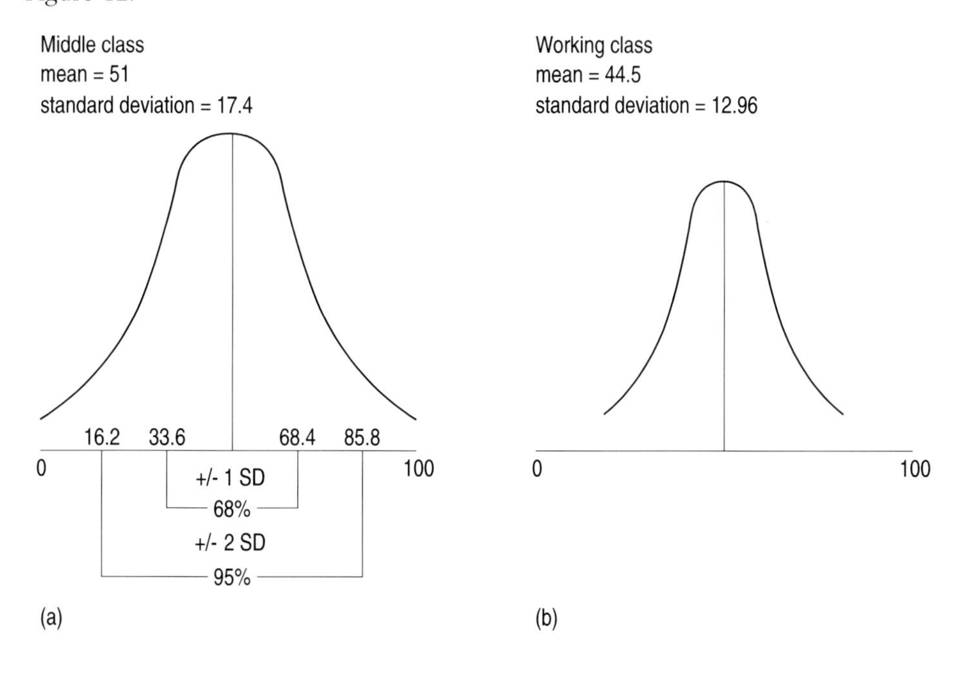

Figure 12 Distribution of scores (a) for middle-class pupils and (b) for working-class pupils.

You will see from the annotations in Figure 12 that if we know the standard deviation of a set of figures we know what percentage of the scores will lie within so many standard deviations of the mean, although in this case the number of pupils in the class is too small for this to work out exactly. You should be familiar with this principle because it is exactly the same as that which underlay our card-dealing simulation. Unfortunately, this principle only applies when the distribution is symmetrical or 'normal', as shown in Figure 12. Ability and achievement tests are usually designed to give results which are normally distributed, as are national examinations such as GCSE and GCE A level.

We are not giving you the formula for working out standard deviations statistically because this is usually incorporated into the formulae for particular statistical tests, which you can find in standard statistical texts and which can be followed 'recipe-book style' without bothering too much about why the recipe is as it is. Furthermore, many of the more sophisticated pocket calculators have a function for standard deviations.

Scattergrams

Having introduced means and standard deviations, let us return to regression analysis. The first step is usually to draw a scattergram. The scattergram for our test scores and examination scores is shown in Figure 13.

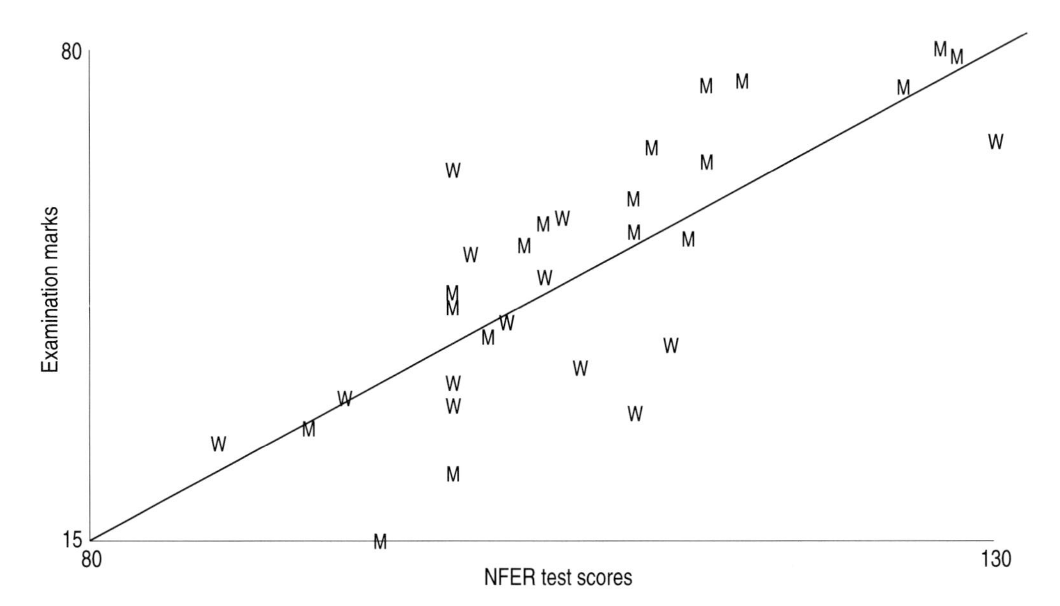

Figure 13 Scattergram for the whole data set.

You will see that the bottom or x axis is the scale for the NFER test scores and the vertical or y axis is the scale for the examination results. It is conventional to put the dependent variable on the y axis and the independent variable on the x axis. In this case, since the examination results cannot have caused the test scores, the test scores must be the independent variable. You will see also that we have differentiated working-class and middle-class pupils on the scattergram as W or M.

The pattern shown in the scattergram is one of positive correlation because, in a rough and ready sort of way, pupils who score more highly on the NFER test are more likely to score highly in the examination. The scores can be visualized as distributed around a line from bottom left to top right.

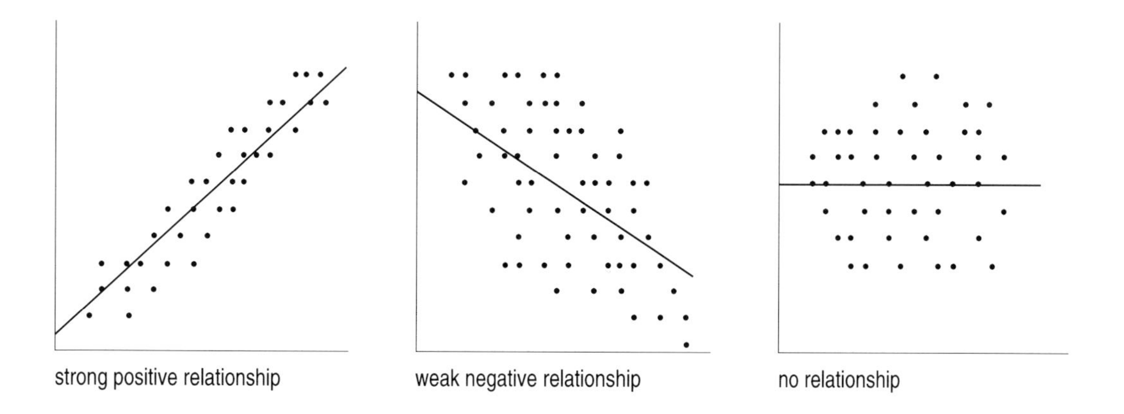

Figure 14 Scattergrams illustrating different relationships.

The next step in regression analysis is called fitting a line, producing what is called the regression line. (In simple regression analysis this is always a straight line). We have already fitted the line to the scattergram. It represents a kind of moving average against which the deviations of the actual scores can be measured. If you remember our bowling example it is as if the bowlers had to place their bowls in relation to a moving jack.

The calculations for fitting the line take all the data and work out the average relationship between scores on the NFER tests and scores on the examination. The result is a statement, such as, on average x number of points on the x scale equate with y number of points on the y scale. This average is calculated from the performances of all pupils, not just those scoring 100 on the test. Suppose, for example, the result is that on average pupils scoring 100 on the NFER scale score 41.65 in the examination. Now we have a way of dividing pupils scoring 100 on the NFER scale into those who actually score above and those who actually score below this average.

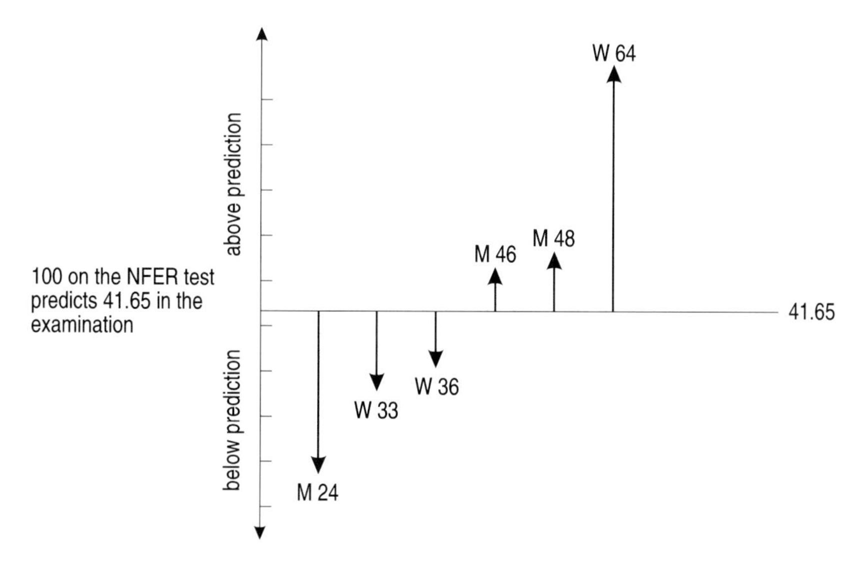

Figure 15 Identifying those pupils who scored 100 on the NFER test who score above and below the identified average.

You can now see what is meant by the 'residuals' in the table of NFER and examination scores (Table 20). A residual is the figure produced by subtracting the actual score (on the examination here) from the score predicted (by the relationship, on average, between the NFER test score and the examination score). In principle, it is exactly the same as the result of subtracting expected figures from observed figures in a chi-squared test. Indeed, in a chi-squared test these are also called residuals. The regression line functions in the same way as the expected figures in a chi-squared test.

Remember that in this particular case we are interested in whether the gap between working-class pupils and middle-class pupils increases in the first three years of secondary school. If it does, we should expect to find more working-class pupils scoring below the regression line and more middle-class pupils scoring above. What we have done in effect is to control for ability (as measured by NFER test score) so that we can measure differences in examination achievement for pupils of the *same* ability from *different* social classes.

We could follow our bowling example and actually use the graph to measure this, physically measuring the distances above and below the line for each pupil of each social class and calculating a standard deviation for each social class of pupil. Physically measuring the residuals in this way, however, would be a very tedious procedure. Instead we can use any one of a number of statistical 'recipes' to reach the same result.

Demonstrating how to calculate a statistical regression goes beyond our objectives here. We only want you to understand what authors are writing about when they say they have conducted a regression analysis. We shall, however, show you visually what this means. First, look at the original scattergram (Figure 13). You should be able to see that more middle-class pupils have scored more in the examination than might have been predicted from their NFER score and fewer have scored less. The reverse is true for working-class pupils. We have in the scattergram a visual display of a gap opening up between working-class and middle-class pupils, when previously measured ability is held constant.

Activity 24

How would you interpret this 'gap' under the following two conditions:

(a) If the examination were criterion referenced: that is, marked according to who had and had not reached a particular absolute standard.

(b) If the examination were norm referenced: that is, marked so that each pupil's performance was judged according to its relation to the performance of the others.

Assuming we can treat the NFER test as a criterion-referenced test then:

(a) The interpretation for a criterion-referenced examination would have to be that the performance of middle-class pupils had improved and the performance of working-class pupils had declined relative to expectations.

(b) The interpretation for a norm-referenced examination might be that middle-class pupils had improved relative to working-class pupils.

CHANCE AND SIGNIFICANCE

Any interpretation of our data as suggesting that social-class differences are involved stands or falls on the assumption that the differences between working-class and middle-class pupils are not simply due to the chance combination of particular pupils and particular happenings in this particular school class. Statistically speaking, there are no grounds for generalizing our findings for this school class to the ability band as a whole, the school as a whole, or to the whole age group in the country, because it is very unlikely that any single school class is statistically representative even of its own school and highly improbable that any school class is representative of the national age group. This is not a problem that is confined to quantitative research. It is one associated with the study of any naturally occurring group, such as a school class, whether by quantitative or qualitative methods. Had our data been drawn from a real school class we would have regarded the findings as interesting and worth following up by studying other school classes, but we would have had to have been circumspect about how far the findings could be generalized.

Chance factors might even undermine the validity of our findings as they relate to the pupils we are studying. That is to say, while it might appear that differences in examination scores are related to social class, they may instead be caused by chance. If you think of real examinations you will realize that many factors are each likely to have some small effect on examination performance: a cold, a broken love affair, a misread question, a cancelled bus, an absence from a critical lesson, the fortuitous viewing of a useful television documentary, the lucky choice of topics for revision – plus the vagaries of examination marking. Sometimes, of course, all these chance factors will cancel each other out, but occasionally they may fall, by chance, in such a way as to depress the performance of one particular group of pupils relative to another. Thus factors that are actually unrelated to social class might, by chance, add to the scores of one social class and subtract from the scores of another.

What we need is some way of estimating the likely play of chance factors that might skew the results in this way. This, of course, is the purpose of testing for statistical significance. The question in this case is whether or not the scores of the thirteen working-class pupils (and hence the eighteen middle-class pupils) are significantly different from those of the whole class. We might ask this question in relation to differences in terms of how well NFER test scores predicted examination scores, or more simply in terms of whether there is a statistically significant difference in examination scores between the two groups. The second logically precedes the first, since if there is no significant difference in examination scores between pupils from the two social classes then there is nothing to explain.

If we said that the examination scores are not significantly different it would mean that we could often draw random samples of thirteen pupils from the thirty-one, with scores departing from the profile of the whole class to the same extent as the scores of the thirteen working-class pupils differ from those of the whole class.

To put this into more concrete terms, imagine our class of pupils as a pack of thirty-one cards, each with an examination result written on it. Think of shuffling the pack and dealing out thirteen cards in order to produce two decks of thirteen and eighteen. Think of doing this again and again and again; each time recording the mean examination score of each pack. Intuitively you will know that the chance of dealing the thirteen lowest scoring cards into a single deck and the highest scoring eighteen cards into the other deck is very low. Similarly, so is the chance of dealing the thirteen highest scoring cards into a single deck very low. The vast majority of deals will result in something in between.

With this in mind, imagine asking someone else to divide the pack into a deck of thirteen and a deck of eighteen, by some unknown criterion. Again, intuitively, you know that if the mean score of one pack is very different from the mean score of the other it is much less likely that your collaborator used a random technique for the deal. In the same way, if the aggregate examination scores of our working-class pupils are very different from those of our middle-class pupils it is less likely that chance alone determined them and likely that there is some factor related to social class at play.

That is the logic of statistical testing. The question that remains is that of how much difference between the groups would allow us safely to conclude that our working-class pupils were a special group, rather than randomly allocated.

Given the kind of data available to us here, which is at least of ordinal level, we would normally use more powerful statistical tests to establish this than a chi-squared test. A t-test would be a common choice, but since you are familiar with chi-squared tests, it is the one we shall use. To do this we shall degrade the data to convert it to the nominal level, by grouping pupils into two achievement categories: those scoring above the mean for the class and those scoring below the mean. We can then conduct a chi-squared test in the way that should be now familiar to you. For this operation the expected figures are those deriving from calculating what should happen if there were no difference in the distribution of working-class and middle-class pupils between the high- and low-scoring categories (i.e. if high and low scores were distributed proportionately).

Table 22 Observed distribution of examination scores for working-class and middle-class pupils (O) compared with those expected if scores were distributed proportionately (E): pupils scoring above and below the school-class mean of 51.03

	Middle-class pupils		*Working-class pupils*		*Total*
	O	E	O	E	
above mean	12	9.3	4	6.7	16
below mean	6	8.7	9	6.3	15
Total	18	18	13	13	31

chi squared = 2.57, df = 1, $p < 0.2$ (20%)

From this calculation you will see that significance does not reach the 5% level and this means that if we kept on dealing out thirteen cards at random then we would quite often come up with results which departed from a proportional distribution of scores to this degree: in fact, about 20% of samples would be expected to deviate from a proportional distribution to this extent.

INCONCLUSIVE RESULTS

People are often very disappointed when they achieve inconclusive results and it is worth considering why the results are inconclusive in our case. On the one hand, there are the possibilities that the set of data contained too few cases to give a significant result, or that the particular school class chosen for research was odd in some way. These considerations suggest that we should expand our data set and try again, because so far we do not have enough evidence to accept or reject the idea that something about social class, other than ability, affects performance in secondary school. On the other hand, if we did investigate a larger set of data and still came up with the same kind of results, we should have to conclude that the results were not really 'inconclusive'. They would be conclusive in the sense that as we achieved the same findings from bigger and bigger sets of data, so we should become more confident that social class is *not* an important factor determining examination results, once prior ability is held constant. This unlikely conclusion, of course, would be a very important finding theoretically and in terms of educational policy – it would run against the findings of many previous studies.

Activity 25

Suppose well-conducted large-scale research on educational achievement and social class showed that pupils aged 16+ and from different social backgrounds were performing, on average, much as might be predicted from tests of educational achievement at aged 11+. What interpretations might you make of these findings?

One possible interpretation would be that secondary schooling had much the same average effect on all pupils irrespective of social class. In other words, the differences already present at aged eleven persisted without much change to aged 16+. In this case you would be interested in whether social-class differences in educational achievement were to be found in primary school, or whether differences in achievement were produced by factors that were uninfluenced by pupils' schooling at all, such as innate ability or parental support. How one would translate this kind of finding into policy terms would depend on whether you believed that secondary schools ought to level up (or level down) educational achievement between pupils of different social classes, in terms of predictions made at aged eleven for performance at aged 16.

6.11 CONCLUSION

Quantitative studies often use large samples, which are either chosen to be representative or are chosen to span a range of different educational institutions. By contrast with these kinds of study, an ethnographic investigation of a school, which usually boils down to a detailed study of a few school classes or less, has no comparable claim to be representative. Generalizing from ethnographic (or indeed from experimental) studies to the educational system as a whole is extremely problematic. Small-scale studies may well provide inspiration as to what mechanisms actually create the causal links demonstrated in large-scale quantitative research, but without the latter we can never know how important observations at school level are.

At the same time, we must remember that large-scale quantitative studies buy representativeness at a cost. There are respects in which the validity of small-scale qualitative studies is likely to be greater.

Activity 26

Drawing on your reading of Sections 5 and 6, what would you say are the strengths and weaknesses of both qualitative research and quantitative research?

When reading the results of quantitative research and engaging in the sort of manipulation of figures in which we have been engaged in Section 6, it is easy to forget that the validity of conclusions based on quantitative data hinges on the extent to which the data actually measure accurately what we are interested in. Early on in Section 6 we noted how the operationalization of concepts in quantitative research often raises questions about whether the phenomena of concern to us are being measured, or at least how accurately they are being measured. This problem is not absent in the case of qualitative research, but in the latter we are not forced to rely on what numerical data are already available or can be easily obtained from a large sample of cases. Particularly in assessing any quantitative study then, we must always ask ourselves about the validity of the measurements involved.

In public discussions and policy making, there is often a tendency for these problems to be forgotten. Worse still, sometimes the use of quantitative data comes to structure our thinking about education in such a way that we start to believe, in effect, that the sole purpose of schools is, for example, to produce good examination results. In this way we may treat these as satisfactorily measuring academic achievement when they do not. We may thereby ignore other sorts of effect that we might hope schools would have on their pupils which cannot be measured so easily. Quantitative analysis provides a useful set of techniques, but like all techniques they can be misused.

7 PLANNING RESEARCH

Up until now in this Handbook we have been primarily concerned with providing some of the background knowledge and skills that are necessary to understand and assess published examples of educational research. That, indeed, is the major purpose of the Part, but you may well also be interested in carrying out research of your own, now or in the future. In this final section, therefore, we shall sketch what is involved in planning a piece of research. At the same time you will find that in doing this we provide an overall view of many of the issues we have dealt with earlier in this Part, but from a different angle.

We can distinguish five broad aspects of the research process: problem formulation, case selection, data production, data analysis, and writing the research report. It would be wrong to think of these as distinct temporal phases of the research process because, although each may assume priority at particular stages, there is no standard sequence. To one degree or another, all aspects have to be considered at all stages. Indeed, how each aspect is dealt with has implications for the others.

We shall look briefly at what is involved in each of these aspects of the research process.

7.1 PROBLEM FORMULATION

What we mean by problem formulation is the determination of the focus of the research: the type of phenomenon or population of phenomena that is of concern and the aspect that is of interest. It is tempting to see problem formulation as something that has to be done right at the beginning of research, since everything else clearly depends on it. This is true up to a point. Obviously it is important to think about exactly what one is investigating at the start. Research, however, is often exploratory in character and in this case it is best not to try to specify the research problem too closely early on, otherwise important directions of possible investigation may be closed off. Even when research is not exploratory, for example when it is concerned with testing some theoretical idea, there is still a sense in which what is being researched is discovered in the course of researching it. The research problem usually becomes much clearer and our understanding of it more detailed by the end of the research than it was at the beginning. Indeed, it is not unknown for a research problem to be modified or completely transformed during the course of research. This may result from initial expectations about the behaviour to be studied proving unfounded, the original research plan proving over-ambitious, changes taking place in the field investigated, etc.

Research problems may vary in all sorts of ways, but one important set of distinctions concerns the sort of end-product that is intended from the research. In Section 4 we distinguished among the various kinds of argument that are to be found in research reports and these give us an indication of the range of products that are possible. We can identify six: descriptions, explanations, predictions, evaluations, prescriptions, and theories. Of course, whichever of these is intended, other sorts of argument are likely to be involved in supporting it. Which sort of end-product is the goal will, however, make a considerable difference to the planning of the research. It will shape decisions about how many cases are to be investigated and how these are to be selected, what sorts of data would be most useful, etc.

7.2 CASE SELECTION

Case selection is a problem that all research faces. What we mean by the term 'case' here is the specific phenomena about which data are collected or analysed, or both. Examples of cases can range all the way from individual people or particular events, through social situations, organizations or institutions, to national societies or international social systems.

In educational and social research, we can identify three contrasting strategies for selecting cases. These do not exhaust the full range of strategies used by researchers, but they mark the outer limits. They are experiment, survey and case study.

What is distinctive about an *experiment* is that the researcher constructs the cases to be studied. This is achieved by establishing a research situation in which it is possible to manipulate the variables that are the focus of the research and to control at least some of the relevant extraneous variables.

The distinctiveness of *surveys*, on the other hand, is that they involve the simultaneous selection for study of a relatively large number of naturally occurring cases, rather than experimentally created cases. These cases are usually selected, in part, by using a random procedure. Survey data, whether produced by questionnaire or observational schedule, provide the basis for the sorts of correlational analysis discussed in Section 6.

Finally, what we shall call *case study* combines some features of these other two strategies. It involves the investigation of a relatively small number of naturally occurring cases, rather than researcher-created cases. These are often selected consecutively rather than simultaneously, so that analysis of data from earlier cases influences the selection of subsequent cases. Most qualitative research adopts a case study approach.

The three strategies differ, then, in two respects: in how many cases are studied and in how these are selected.

Each of the case-selection strategies may be usable to investigate any particular research topic, though their strengths and weaknesses will have varying significance, depending on the purposes and circumstances of the research. In selecting one case-selection strategy rather than another, we are usually faced with trade-offs. We can never have everything we want and usually we can only get more of one thing at the expense of getting less of something else. In other words, a researcher can usually only gain the benefits of one strategy at the expense of what could be avoided by using another strategy, but whose use would carry other costs. The choice of case-selection strategy ought to be determined, then, by judgement of the likely resulting gains and losses in the light of the particular goals and circumstances of the research, including the resources available.

We can sketch the methodological advantages and disadvantages of these three case-selection strategies in broad terms as follows. Comparing the survey with the case study, other things being equal, the first will provide us with a sounder basis for empirical generalization, whereas the second will provide more (and more detailed) data on each case studied, as well as allowing more scope for checking the validity of those data. These advantages follow from the logistics of the research process. Usually, the more cases studied the more confident we can be in generalizing our findings, but (given fixed time and resources) the more cases studied the less detailed the data that can be collected on each and the less time is available for checking the validity of those data.

If we compare the experiment and the case study, we find that the former allows for more rigorous testing of theories than does the latter. On the other hand, experiments typically involve a high level of reactivity, in that subjects will usually be aware that they are taking part in an experiment and may therefore act in a different way from normal; as a result, the findings may be defective in terms of our ability to draw inferences about what happens in non-experimental situations. Conversely, case study typically involves a lower level of reactivity, but even where comparison of several cases is carried out it is not usually possible to come to judgements about what caused what with as high a level of justifiable confidence as in experimental research.

As we said earlier, these three case selection strategies simply mark the outer bounds of variation, they are not the only options. Obviously, the number of cases studied can vary from one to a very large number, with many mid-way points. Similarly, the amount of control exerted over variables can vary considerably. There are mid-points between the laboratory experiment, on the one hand, in which maximal physical control over variables is exercised, and the survey and case study, on the other, where no physical control is exerted. Field experiments and quasi-experiments fall between these extremes. Finally, even where the aim is empirical generalization, it is not simply a matter of selecting cases randomly or not, there is a variety of sampling strategies available.

7.3 DATA PRODUCTION

Not all research involves the collection of new data. It may rely on data collected by others – this is sometimes referred to as analysis of secondary data. Both primary and secondary data can take a wide variety of forms: published and unpublished documents or statistics; audio- or video-recordings or transcripts of these; notes written by the researcher on the basis of direct observation or of interviewing; tallies produced by the use of an observational schedule or questionnaire, etc. What sorts of data and how much of each sort should be selected will depend, of course, on the focus of the research and on the circumstances in which it is being carried out, particularly the time available. It is very common for researchers to collect too much data, and then to be unable to analyse it all. On the other hand, to find that one has insufficient, or the wrong sort of, data for one's purpose can be an even more serious problem. Some optimal way between these two extremes needs to be found. Sometimes this problem can be overcome by carrying out more than one phase of data production, so that the second or subsequent phases can take account of what has been discovered in analysing the first batch of data. This is quite common in case study and experimental research, less so in survey research because of the scale and cost of the data collection process.

Besides taking a variety of forms, primary data can also be produced in diverse ways. The most important distinction here is between the researcher producing the data her or himself, on the one hand, and, on the other hand, using information from others. In Section 4, in discussing description, we looked at the various threats to validity associated with these two sources. We must take these into account in carrying out research, though sometimes we will not have much choice about which data sources to use.

Another important issue in data production concerns the degree to which the data are structured. In quantitative research data are very often collected in the form in which they will subsequently be analysed; in other words, they will conform to the structure of categories that is to be employed in the analysis. This is true of closed questionnaires where the different possible answers to each question are specified by the researcher, and the respondent has simply to choose amongst them. It is also true of observational schedules, where the observer must indicate to which of various pre-specified categories an observed event belongs. At the other extreme are so called 'unstructured' data, for example field-notes written by the researcher or audio- or video-recordings. (These sorts of data are, of course, characteristic of qualitative research.) Where the data are unstructured there will usually need to be much more data processing before analysis can begin. Jotted field-notes made during observation will have to be filled out and written up more clearly, recordings will have to be transcribed or indexed, etc.

All sources and types of data can be valuable, but each also has its drawbacks; and in selecting amongst them their strengths and weaknesses must be borne in mind. Of course, data sources and types can be combined, whether to provide information on different aspects of the phenomena being studied or to provide comparable information on the same aspect. (Indeed, they often are combined; as we noted at several places in this course, there are few examples of 'pure' qualitative or quantitative research.) But the more forms of data used, other things being equal, the more time and other resources will be required for data production and analysis.

7.4 DATA ANALYSIS

The form that data analysis takes will depend, of course, both on the focus and intended end-product of the research and on the sorts of data that are being employed. Where the data are numerical in kind the statistical techniques introduced in Section 6 may be applicable. Which of these techniques are or are not appropriate will depend on the precise character of the data, for example the level of measurement involved. It may be necessary to seek expert advice about the most effective strategies, or at least to consult statistical texts.

Where the data are qualitative, an even wider range of options may be available. On the one hand, it may be possible to process these data to produce numerical results to which statistical techniques can be applied. This is most obviously the case with video- and audio-recordings, which one may be able to code using a schedule of some kind. Where this is not possible, or where the decision is taken against such quantitative processing, qualitative data analysis will be required. This can take a variety of forms. One of the most common of these, that characteristic of much ethnographic work, was illustrated in Section 5. Here the aim is to develop a set of categories relevant to the focus of the research on the basis of careful scrutiny of the data. Once this has been done, further data are then coded and allocated to the categories. This produces a set of themes or features, each of which can be illustrated by data extracts. Examples include a concern with survival on the part of teachers, and various strategies arising from that concern (Woods, 1979); or, alternatively, resistance to teachers and others on the part of pupils and the various ways in which this is expressed (Anyon, 1981). This is not the only sort of qualitative data analysis that can be carried out, however; and, once again, advice or recourse to the methodological literature may be necessary in order to find the most appropriate form of analysis for a particular piece of research.

7.5 WRITING RESEARCH REPORTS

A key element of the research process, but one that has until recently received rather less attention than it deserves, is the writing of research reports. The reason for this relative neglect is probably that reports are very often seen as transparent representations of the findings of research, so that it is assumed that once data production and analysis have been done, the process of writing up is straightforward, or should be. Another way of putting the same point is to say that research reports should be written in a plain and honest manner, without rhetoric.

As you might expect, this is too simplistic a view. All writing employs rhetorical devices, so it is not a matter of rhetoric versus no rhetoric but rather of what are appropriate and inappropriate forms of rhetoric for research reports. As we saw in Section 2, some educational researchers have concluded from the fact that all research reports are constructions that what they purport to represent are themselves constructed by the researcher in the process of writing the report. In our view this is an overreaction, and what we shall outline here is an approach to the writing of research reports that continues to emphasize the values of clarity and plain writing, without forgetting that reports are constructions. In our view, the primary task of the writer is to present her or his research in a way that best facilitates the sort of understanding and assessment that we outlined in Section 4.

Educational research reports can take a variety of forms, and these differ somewhat between quantitative and qualitative approaches. There is a conventional format that is sometimes used in the former. In this, the research problem and hypotheses are presented first, then the methods by which the problem was investigated, there follows an account of the findings, and the report ends with a discussion of the implications of these findings. Qualitative research reports, on the other hand, rarely take this form, and there is no single model that guides them. All we can say is that in general they consist of realistic descriptions or explanations (or both) of particular perspectives, cultures, situations, or patterns of events; though in recent years there have even been calls for this realistic mode of writing to be abandoned in favour of less conventional modes like dialogues and other sorts of multi-vocal text (Clifford and Marcus, 1986).

One of the most difficult tasks in writing research reports, as with writing anything of an extended length, is to decide on an overall structure. This is a particular problem in the case of qualitative research, given that there is no standard format. However, it is our view that a structure organized in terms of the major elements of research reports that we identified in the Section 4 is of advantage, both to readers and to the writer. It makes it easier for the reader to locate the information that they need; at the same time it makes clear to the writer the various sorts of information that should be provided.

Following this pattern, then, there should be an opening section that spells out the focus of the research and the reasons why that focus is believed to be important. There should be information about the case(s) studied and about the methods used to investigate them. There should be a clear presentation of the main claims and the evidence supporting them. The conclusions should be highlighted, and an indication given of why they are believed to be justifiable inferences from the claims.

Of course, this by no means completely resolves the problems one faces as a writer. In each part of the report one will be faced with difficult decisions in which one has to try to balance competing considerations. For instance, in deciding on the focus of one's report and what conclusions can be drawn about it, one must balance the requirement to address issues that have relevance and yet not to draw conclusions that simply cannot be sustained on the basis of one's work. With much small-scale research (and with some large-scale work, too) this can be quite difficult to resolve. However, it can be eased by drawing conclusions in an explicitly tentative manner, and by indicating what further research would be needed to test the validity of those conclusions. Honesty about the weaknesses of one's study can usefully accompany a judicious assessment of its strengths. It is perhaps also worth pointing out that negative findings can be as important as positive ones, even though they may often not seem as dramatic or as directly useful.

A similar problem of balance arises with the presentation of evidence for claims. In discussing the reading of research reports in Section 4 we outlined the sorts of threats to validity that can undermine claims and evidence. As writers we have to anticipate that readers will have these in mind and will want, where possible, to be shown that serious error is not involved in the claims and evidence we present. Of course, there is a limit to how much evidence we can provide; we can rarely include all our data in a research report. Judgements have to be made about what it is necessary to provide at any particular point in the text, and a balance struck between the danger of not providing sufficient evidence, on the one hand, and, on the other hand, of providing so much that the reader gets lost in it. This problem can often be partly alleviated by providing fuller information about the data in appendices, for example by including transcripts, field-notes, additional tables, etc., there.

It is particularly important not to present data in the body of the text that are not directly relevant to the points being made. Extracts from field-notes or transcripts, tables, graphs etc. should be specially tailored to fit the point in the text where they are placed. Also, it is necessary to think about what is the best way to present information for it to be intelligible to a reader. For example, in a table it will often be best to present percentages rather than raw figures; though marginal figures should always be provided to allow the reader to calculate raw scores. (Sometimes, of course, the numbers will be so small as to make percentages misleading.) Similarly, in presenting extracts from interview data it may be necessary to indicate the question that the informant was responding to; but this will not always be essential. Judgement is required in each case.

We noted in Section 4 that authors often provide a summary of their main claims. This is something that we recommend that you do as a writer, not just to make life easier for your readers but because producing it will probably clarify your own sense of the structure of your account and thereby make writing easier. Having said that, you may need to work quite hard to produce something that effectively summarizes what you are saying in a way that stands at least partially independent of the rest of the text. Still, the effort is almost always valuable.

Finally, it is worth noting that how we should resolve the various problems involved in writing research reports depends in large part on our intended audience. Different audiences will probably have different sorts of background knowledge, so that what can be referred to briefly for one audience may have to be spelt out in greater detail for another. Similarly, audiences will differ in their levels of interest in the various aspects of the research. It may be necessary to give different aspects of the research salience according to the intended audience. Equally, some audiences may need more evidence to convince them of the importance of a research topic or of the validity of a particular finding than others. The intended audience may therefore affect what sorts of supporting argument need to be included in a report. Of course, often researchers do not have a single, relatively well-defined audience in mind for their research. In this situation it may be worthwhile to produce more than one report, each directed at different audiences.

7.6 CONCLUSION

In this final section of the first part of the Handbook we have looked briefly at some of the issues involved in the design of research. We identified five aspects of the research process in relation to which a variety of decisions have to be made. We stressed that these aspects are not fixed stages through which all research passes. Indeed, given that the decisions one makes in relation to one aspect often have implications for what would be the most appropriate decisions in relation to others, all have to be borne in mind at all stages; though their salience will certainly vary over the course of research.

Research is an exciting and productive enterprise, but it is also one that is not always easy, and sometimes requires esoteric knowledge and difficult skills. In this Part of the *Research Methods in Education Handbook* we have tried to give you a sense of the diverse forms that research may take and to provide some of the background knowledge and skills that are necessary both to understand and assess it, and to do research yourself. We hope you found this interesting and useful, and wish you well with any research you do in the future.

REFERENCES

ABRAHAM, J. (1989) 'Testing Hargreaves' and Lacey's differentiation–polarisation theory in a setted comprehensive', *British Journal of Sociology*, vol. 40, no. 1, pp. 46–81.

ALEXANDER, R. (1992) *Policy and Practice in Primary Education*, London, Routledge and Kegan Paul.

ANYON, J. (1981) 'Social class and school knowledge', *Curriculum Inquiry*, vol. 11, no. 1, pp. 3–42.

ARNOT, M. and WEINER, G. (eds) (1987) *Gender and the Politics of Schooling*, London, Hutchinson.

BALL, S.J. (1981) *Beachside Comprehensive*, Cambridge, Cambridge University Press.

BALL, S.J. (1984) 'Beachside reconsidered: reflections on a methodological apprenticeship' in Burgess, R.G. (ed.) *The Research Process in Educational Settings: ten case studies*, Lewes, Falmer Press.

BALL, S.J. (1987) *The Micro-politics of the School: towards a theory of school organization*, London, Methuen.

BALL, S.J. (1990) 'Self-doubt and soft data: social and technical trajectories in ethnographic fieldwork', *International Journal of Qualitative Studies in Education*, vol. 3, no. 2, pp. 157–72.

BARONE, T. (1990) 'On the demise of subjectivity in educational inquiry', *Curriculum Inquiry*, vol. 22, no. 1, pp. 25–38.

BECKER, H.S. (1971) Footnote added to the paper by Wax, M. and Wax, R. 'Great tradition, little tradition and formal education' in Wax, M. *et al.* (eds) *Anthropological Perspectives on Education*, New York, Basic Books.

BENNETT, S.N. (1976) *Teaching Styles and Pupil Progress*, London, Open Books.

BERGER, P.L. (1966) *Invitation to Sociology*, Harmondsworth, Penguin.

BEYNON, J. (1984) '"Sussing-out" teachers: pupils as data gatherers' in Hammersley, M. and Woods, P. (eds) *Life in School: the sociology of pupil culture*, Milton Keynes, Open University Press.

BLUMER, H. (1976) 'The methodological position of symbolic interactionism' in Hammersley, M. and Woods, P. (eds) *The Process of Schooling*, London, Routledge and Kegan Paul.

BROPHY, J. and GOOD, T. (1970) 'Teachers' communications of differential expectations for children's classroom performance: some behavioral data', *Journal of Educational Psychology*, vol. 61, no. 5, pp. 365–74.

BROWN, G.W. (1973) 'Some thoughts on grounded theory', *Sociology*, vol. 7, no. 1, pp. 1–16.

BRYMAN, A. (1988) *Quantity and Quality in Social Research*, London, Unwin Hyman.

BULMER, M. (1979) 'Concepts in the analysis of qualitative data', *Sociological Review*, vol. 27, no. 4, pp. 651–77.

BURKE, J. (1985) 'Concord sixth-form college: the possibility of school without conflict' in Ball, S.J. and Goodson, I.F. (eds) *Teachers' Lives and Careers*, Lewes, Falmer Press.

CARR, W. and KEMMIS, S. (1986) *Becoming Critical*, Lewes, Falmer.

CARR, W. (1995) *For Education: towards critical educational inquiry*, Buckingham, Open University Press.

CLIFFORD, J. and MARCUS, G. (1986) *Writing Culture: the poetics and politics of ethnography*, Berkeley, University of California Press.

COLEMAN, J. (1966) *Equality of Educational Opportunity*, Washington DC, US Government Printing Office.

COMMUNITY RELATIONS COMMISSION (1976) *Between Two Cultures: a study of relationships between generations in the Asian Community in Britain*, London, Community Relations Commission.

CORRIGAN, P. (1979) *Schooling the Smash Street Kids*, London, Macmillan.

CUTTANCE, P. (1988) 'Intra-system variation in the effectiveness of schools', *Research Papers in Education*, vol. 2, no. 3, pp. 180–216.

DEAN, J.P. and WHYTE, W.F. (1958) 'How do you know if the informant is telling the truth?' *Human Organisation*, vol. 17, no. 2, pp. 34–8.

DEEM, R. (ed.) (1980) *Schooling for Women's Work*, London, Routledge and Kegan Paul.

DELAMONT, S. (1984) 'The old girl network: reflections on the fieldwork at St. Lukes" in Burgess, R.G. (ed.) *The Research Process in Educational Settings: ten case studies,* Lewes, Falmer Press.

DELAMONT, S. and GALTON, M. (1986) *Inside the Secondary Classroom,* London, Routledge and Kegan Paul.

DENSCOMBE, M. (1980) 'Pupil strategies and the open classroom' in Woods, P. (ed.) *Pupil Strategies*, London, Croom Helm.

DENSCOMBE, M., SZALE, H., PATRICK, C. and WOOD, A. (1986) 'Ethnicity and friendship: the contrast between sociometric research and fieldwork observation in primary school classrooms', *British Educational Research Journal*, vol. 12, no. 3, pp. 221–35.

DENZIN, N.K. (1989) *Interpretive Interactionism,* London, Sage.

DONALDSON, M. (1978) *Children's Minds*, London, Fontana.

DUMONT, R.V. and WAX, M.L. (1971) 'Cherokee school society and the intercultural classroom' in Cosin, B.R., Dale, I.R., Esland, G.M. and Swift, D.F. (1971) (eds) *School and Society*, London, Routledge and Kegan Paul.

EGAN, K. (1983) *Education and Psychology: Plato, Piaget, & Scientific Psychology*, London, Methuen.

EGGLESTON, S.J., DUNN, D. and ANJALI, M. (1986) *Education for Some: the educational and vocational experiences of 15–18 year old members of minority ethnic groups*, Stoke on Trent, Trentham Books.

EISNER, E. (1991) *The Enlightened Eye: qualitative enquiry and the enhancement of educational practice,* New York, Macmillan.

EISNER, E. (1992) 'Objectivity in educational research', *Curriculum Inquiry*, vol. 22, no. 1, pp. 9–15.

FINK, A.H. and HYDE, D.R. (1985) 'Behavioural disorders: social' in Husen, T. and Postlethwaite, K.(eds) *The International Encyclopaedia of Education*, Oxford, Pergamon.

FOSTER, P.M. (1990) *Policy and Practice in Multicultural and Anti-racist Education: a case study of a multi-ethnic comprehensive school*, London, Routledge and Kegan Paul.

FRENCH, J. and FRENCH, P. (1984) 'Gender imbalances in the primary classroom', *Educational Research*, vol. 26, no. 2, pp. 127–36.

FULLER, M. (1984) 'Dimensions of gender in a school: reinventing the wheel?' in Burgess, R.G. (ed.) *The Research Process in Educational Settings: ten case studies*, Lewes, Falmer Press.

FURLONG, V.J. (1976) 'Interaction sets in the classroom' in Stubbs, M. and Delamont, S. (eds) *Explorations in Classroom Observation*, Chichester, Wiley.

GALTON, M., SIMON, B. and CROLL, P. (1980) *Inside the Primary Classroom*, London, Routledge and Kegan Paul.

GANNAWAY, H. (1976) 'Making sense of school' in Stubbs, M. and Delamont, S. (eds) *Explorations in Classroom Observation*, Chichester, Wiley.

GEERTZ, C. (1973) *The Interpretation of Cultures*, New York, Basic Books.

GELSTHORPE, L. (1992) 'Response to Martyn Hammersley's paper "On feminist methodology"', *Sociology*, vol. 26, no. 2, pp. 213–8.

GILLBORN, D. (1990) *Race, Ethnicity and Education: teaching and learning in multi-ethnic schools,* London, Unwin Hyman.

GITLIN, A., SIEGEL, M. and BORU, K. (1989) 'The politics of method: from leftist ethnography to educative research', *Qualitative Studies in Education*, vol. 2, no. 3, pp. 237–53.

GLASER, B.G and STRAUSS, A.L. (1967) *The Discovery of Grounded Theory*, London, Weidenfeld and Nicolson.

GRAY, J., JESSON, D. and SIME, N. (1990) 'Estimating differences in the examination performances of secondary schools in six LEAs: a multilevel approach to school effectiveness', *Oxford Review of Education*, vol. 16, no. 2, pp. 137–58.

GRIFFIN, C. (1985) *Typical Girls?*, London, Routledge and Kegan Paul.

HAMILTON, D., JENKINS, D., KING, C., MACDONALD, B. and PARLETT, M. (eds) (1977) *Beyond the Numbers Game: a reader in educational evaluation*, London, Macmillan.

HAMMERSLEY, M. (1974) 'The organization of pupil participation', *Sociological Review*, vol. 22, no. 3, pp. 355–69.

HAMMERSLEY, M. (1984) 'The researcher exposed: a natural history' in Burgess, R.G. (ed.) *The Research Process in Educational Settings: ten case studies*, Lewes, Falmer Press.

HAMMERSLEY, M. (1990a) 'A myth of a myth? An assessment of two studies of option choice in secondary schools', *British Journal of Sociology,* vol. 41, no. 2, pp. 61–94.

HAMMERSLEY, M. (1990b) 'An assessment of two studies of gender imbalance in primary classrooms', *British Educational Research Journal,* vol. 16, no. 2, pp. 125–43.

HAMMERSLEY, M. (1992a) *What's Wrong with Ethnography*, London, Routledge and Kegan Paul.

HAMMERSLEY, M. (1992b) 'A response to Barry Troyna's "Children, Race and Racism: the limits of research and policy"', *British Journal of Educational Studies*, vol. XXXX, no. 2, pp. 174–7.

HAMMERSLEY, M. (1992c) 'On feminist methodology', *Sociology*, vol. 26, no. 2, pp. 187–206.

HAMMERSLEY, M. (1993) 'On the teacher as researcher' in Hammersley, M. (ed.) *Educational Research: current issues*, London, Paul Chapman.

HAMMERSLEY, M. and TURNER, G. (1980) 'Conformist pupils' in Woods, P. (ed.) *Pupil Strategies*, London, Croom Helm.

HARGREAVES, A. (1978) 'The significance of classroom coping strategies' in Barton, L. and Meighan, R. (eds) *Sociological Interpretations of Schooling and Classrooms*, Driffield, Nafferton Books.

HARGREAVES, A. (1988) 'Teaching quality: a sociological analysis', *Journal of Curriculum Studies,* vol. 20, no. 3, pp. 211–31.

HARGREAVES, D.H. (1967) *Social Relations in a Secondary School,* London, Routledge and Kegan Paul.

HARGREAVES, D.H., HESTER, S.K. and MELLOR, F.J. (1975) *Deviance in Classrooms,* London, Routledge and Kegan Paul.

HIRST, P.H. (1983) *Educational Theory and its Foundation Disciplines*, London, Routledge and Kegan Paul.

JENCKS, C. *ET AL.* (1972) *Inequality: a reassessment of the effect of family and schooling in America*, New York, Basic Books.

KEDDIE, N. (1971) 'Classroom knowledge' in Young, M.F.D. (ed.) *Knowledge and Control,* London, Collier-Macmillan.

KEMMIS, S. (1988) 'Action research' in Keeves, J.P. (ed.) *Educational Research Methodology and Measurement,* Oxford, Pergamon.

KING, R.A. (1978) *All Things Bright and Beautiful,* Chichester, Wiley.

KUHN, T.S. (1970) *The Structure of Scientific Revolutions,* Chicago, University of Chicago Press.

LACEY, C. (1966) 'Some sociological concomitants of academic streaming in a grammar school', *British Journal of Sociology,* vol. 17, pp. 243–62.

LACEY, C. (1970) *Hightown Grammar,* Manchester, Manchester University Press.

LACEY, C. (1976) 'Problems of sociological fieldwork: a review of the methodology of "Hightown Grammar"' in Hammersley, M. and Woods, P. (eds) *The Process of Schooling,* London, Routledge and Kegan Paul.

LAMBART, A. (1976) 'The sisterhood' in Hammersley, M. and Woods, P. (eds) *The Process of Schooling,* London, Routledge.

LAMBART, A. (1982) 'Expulsion in context: a school as a system in action' in Frankenberg R. (ed.) *Custom and Conflict in British Society,* Manchester, Manchester University Press.

LAMBART, A. (1997) 'Mereside: a grammar school for girls in the 1960s' *Gender and Education,* vol.9, pp. 441–56.

LINCOLN, Y.S. and GUBA, E.G. (1985) *Naturalistic Inquiry,* Newbury Park, CA, Sage Publications.

MAC AN GHAILL, M. (1988) *Young, Gifted and Black,* Milton Keynes, Open University Press.

MAC AN GHAILL, M. (1989) 'Beyond the white norm: the use of qualitative methods in the study of black youths' schooling in England', *International Journal of Qualitative Studies in Education,* vol. 2, no. 3, pp. 175–89.

MACDONALD, B. (1977) 'A political classification of evaluation studies in education' in Hamilton, D., Jenkins, D., King, C., MacDonald, B. and Parlett, M. (eds) *Beyond the Numbers Game,* London, Macmillan.

MARSHALL, G., ROSE, D., NEWBY, H. and VOGLER, C. (1988) *Social Class in Modern Britain,* London, Unwin Hyman.

MEASOR, L. and WOODS, P. (1984) *Changing Schools: pupil perspectives on transfer to a comprehensive,* Milton Keynes, Open University Press.

MEHAN, H. (1973) 'Assessing children's school performance' in Dreitzel, H.P. (ed.) *Recent Sociology vol.5, Childhood and Socialization,* London, Collier Macmillan.

MOORE, A. (1992) 'Genre, ethnocentricity and bilingualism in the English classroom' in Woods, P. and Hammersley, M. (eds) *Gender and Ethnicity: ethnographic perspectives,* London, Routledge and Kegan Paul.

NEWTON-SMITH, W. (1981) *The Rationality of Science,* Boston, Routledge and Kegan Paul.

NIAS, J. (1998) 'Introduction' in Nias, J. and Groundwater-Smith, S. (eds) *The Enquiring Teacher: supporting and sustaining teacher research*, Lewes, Falmer Press.

OPEN UNIVERSITY (1975) E203, 'Innovation at the classroom level' (Case study of the Ford teaching project), Unit 28, Milton Keynes, The Open University.

OPEN UNIVERSITY (1984) E205 *Conflict and Change in Education*, Unit 22, *Marxism and Relative Autonomy*, Milton Keynes, The Open University.

PATRICK, J. (1973) *A Glasgow Gang Observed*, London, Eyre Methuen.

PHILLIPS, D.C. (1990) 'Subjectivity and objectivity: an objective inquiry' in Eisner, E.W. and Peshkin, A. (eds) *Qualitative Inquiry in Education: the continuing debate*, New York, Teachers College Press.

PHILLIPS, D.C. (1992) *The Social Scientist's Bestiary: a guide to fabled threats to, and defences of, naturalistic social science*, Oxford, Pergamon.

POPPER, K.R. (1959) *The Logic of Scientific Discovery*, London, Routledge and Kegan Paul.

RAMAZANOGLU, C. (1992) 'On feminist methodology: male reason versus female empowerment', *Sociology*, vol. 26, no. 2, pp. 207–12.

RIST, R. (1970) 'Student social class and teacher expectations', *Harvard Educational Review*, vol. 40, no. 3, pp. 411–51.

RIST, R. (1984) 'On the application of qualitative research to the policy process: an emergent linkage' in Barton, L. and Walker, S. (eds) *Social Crisis and Educational Research*, London, Croom Helm.

ROGERS, C. (1982) *The Psychology of Schooling*, London, Routledge and Kegan Paul.

RUTTER, M., MAUGHAN, B., MORTIMORE, P. and OUSTON, J. (1979) *Fifteen Thousand Hours: secondary schools and their effects on children*, London, Open Books.

SCARTH, J. (1985) 'The influence of examinations on curriculum decision-making: a sociological case-study'. PhD thesis, Department of Educational Research, University of Lancaster.

SEBORG, L.M. and HOSFORD, R.E. (1985) 'Behaviour modification' in Husey, T. and Postlethwaite, T.N. (eds) (1985) *The International Encyclopædia of Education*, vol. 1, Oxford, Pergamon.

SEELEY, J. (1966) 'The "making" and "taking" of problems', *Social Problems*, vol. 14, pp. 382–9.

SIKES, P., MEASOR, L. and WOODS, P. (1985) *Teacher Careers: crises and continuities*, Lewes, Falmer Press.

SMITH, D.J. and TOMLINSON, S. (1989) *The School Effect: a study of multi-racial comprehensives*, London, Policy Studies Institute.

SMITH, J.K. and HESHUSIUS, L. (1986) 'Closing down the conversation: the end of the quantitative-qualitative debate among educational inquirers', *Educational Researcher*, vol. 15, no. 1, pp. 4–12.

SPENDER, D. (1982) *Invisible Women: the schooling scandal*, London, Writers and Readers Publishing Co-operative with Chameleon Editorial Group.

STANWORTH, M. (1983) *Gender and Schooling*, London, Hutchinson.

THOMAS, S., NUTTALL, D. and GOLDSTEIN, H. (1992) 'In a league of their own', *Guardian Education*, 20 October, page II.

TROYNA, B. (1991) 'Children, race and racism: the limitations of research and policy', *British Journal of Educational Studies*, vol. 39, no. 4, pp. 425–36.

TROYNA, B. and CARRINGTON, B. (1989) 'Whose side are we on? Ethical dilemmas in research on "race" and education' in Burgess, R.G. (ed.) *The Ethics of Educational Research*, Lewes, Falmer Press.

TURNER, G. (1983) *The Social World of the Comprehensive School,* London, Croom Helm.

WALKER, R. (1978) 'The conduct of educational case studies: ethics, theory and procedures' in Dockrell, B. and Hamilton, D. (1978) (eds) *Rethinking Educational Research*, London, Hodder and Stoughton.

WAX, R.H. (1971) *Doing Fieldwork*, University of Chicago Press, Chicago.

WEINER, G. (ed.) (1985) *Just a Bunch of Girls*, Milton Keynes, Open University Press.

WEINER, G. and ARNOT, M. (eds) (1987) *Gender Under Scrutiny*, London, Hutchinson.

WERTHMAN, C. (1963) 'Delinquents in schools: a test for the legitimacy of authority', *Berkeley Journal of Sociology*, vol. 8, no. 1, pp. 39–60. Also in Hammersley, M. and Woods, P. (eds) (1984) *Life in School: the sociology of pupil culture,* Milton Keynes, Open University Press.

WHYTE, W.F. (1955) *Street Corner Society*, Chicago, University of Chicago Press.

WILLIAMS, M. (1993) 'Diversity and agreement in feminist ethnography', *Sociology*, vol. 27, no. 4, pp. 575–89.

WILLIS, P. (1977) *Learning to Labour*, Farnborough, Saxon House.

WILMS, J.D. (1987) 'Differences between Scottish education authorities in their examination results', *Oxford Review of Education,* vol. 13, no. 2, pp. 211–32.

WILSON, S. (1977) 'The use of ethnographic techniques in educational research', *Review of Educational Research,* vol. 47, no. 1, pp. 245–65.

WOODS, P. (1979) *The Divided School,* London, Routledge and Kegan Paul.

WOODS, P. and POLLARD, A. (eds) (1988) *Sociology and Teaching: a new challenge for the sociology of education*, London, Croom Helm.

WOODS, P. and SIKES, P. J. (1986) 'The use of teacher biographies in professional self-development' in Todd, F. (ed.) *Planning Continuing Practitioner Education*, London, Croom Helm.

WRIGHT, C. (1986) 'School processes – an ethnographic study' in Eggleston, J., Dunn, D. and Anjali, M. (eds) *Education for Some: the educational and vocational experiences of 15–18 year old members of minority ethnic groups,* Stoke-on-Trent, Trentham Books.

APPENDIX: STEPHEN BALL ON BANDING AND SOCIAL CLASS AT BEACHSIDE COMPREHENSIVE

1 INTRODUCTION

Below we have reprinted an extract from Stephen Ball's book, *Beachside Comprehensive*. By way of a preface to this, the following is Ball's account of the focus of his research, which he provided in the introduction to the book:

> This is a detailed study of a single co-educational comprehensive school, referred to under the pseudonym of Beachside Comprehensive. The overall aim of the study is to examine the processes of comprehensive schooling; that is to say, I am concerned with the dynamics of selection, socialization and change within the school as these processes are experienced and dealt with by the pupils and their teachers. The stress is upon the emergent nature of social interaction as well as the playing out of social structural and cultural forces in the school. Several specific aspects of the school are addressed: the impact of selective grouping upon the pupils' experience of schooling, focusing in particular on the different school careers of the pupils allocated to different ability groups; the introduction of mixed-ability grouping into the school; and the impact of this on the pupils' experiences of schooling.
>
> In general terms the book takes up the central question of the works of Lacey (1970) and Hargreaves (1967), that is, how one can study the social mechanisms operating within a school and employ such knowledge to explain the disappointing performance of working-class pupils. Social class emerges as a major discriminating factor in the distribution of success and failure within the school examined here. Social class differences are important in terms of allocation to ability groups, the achievement of minor success roles, entry into O-level courses, examination results, early leaving, and entry into the sixth form and A-level courses. However, this study is not concerned simply with the way in which these differences are manifested in terms of rates of achievement or levels of access to high-status courses, but rather with the processes through which they emerge in the school.
>
> (Ball, S.J., 1981, *Beachside Comprehensive: a case study of secondary schooling*, Cambridge, Cambridge University Press, p. xv)

2 EXTRACT FROM *BEACHSIDE COMPREHENSIVE*

The extract from Ball's book reprinted below deals with a very small part of the topic with which the book is concerned: the allocation of children to ability bands on entry to Beachside.

> It is important [...] to look at the way in which the pupils are allocated to their bands in the first year. This takes place on the basis of the reports and recommendations of the primary school teachers and headmasters of the four schools that provide Beachside with pupils. Almost all of the pupils who enter the first year at Beachside come from the four 'feeder' primary schools within the community: North Beachside, South Beachside, Iron Road and Sortham. In the cohort with which we are concerned here, the original distribution by school and allocation to bands is presented in Table 2.4 below.

Table 2.4 Allocation of pupils to bands according to primary school

	S.Beachside	*N.Beachside*	*Iron Road*	*Sortham*	*Others*	*Total*
Band 1	33	36	37	11	4	121
Band 2	32	16	52	13	4	117
Band 3	17	7	15	4	4	47
Total	82 (29%)	59 (21%)	104 (36%)	28 (10%)	12 (4%)	285 (100%)

There is no significant relationship between primary school of origin and the allocation to bands. The process of negotiation of recommendations and allocation to bands was done by the senior mistress at Beachside. Where the numbers of pupils recommended for band 1 was too large, the primary headmasters were asked to revise their recommendations until an acceptable distribution of pupils in each band was obtained. When they arrived at the secondary school, the pupils went immediately into their banded classes.

> The primary school heads sent us lists with their recommendations for band 1, band 2 and band 3; it was up to us to try and fit them into classes. If there were too many in one band, then we had to go back to the primary heads to ask if all the list was really band 1 material and that way the bands were allocated and then they were broken into classes alphabetically. There was a lot of movement between the classes at the end of the first term, but very little movement between bands.
>
> (Senior mistress)

Thus Beachside carried out no tests of its own; the primary schools acted as selecting institutions, and Beachside, initially at least, as the passive implementer of selection. Three of the four primary schools did make use of test scores in the decision to recommend pupils for bands, and these were passed on to Beachside on the pupils' record cards, but these test scores were not the sole basis upon which recommendations were made. Teachers' reports were also taken into account.

[...]

The possibility of biases in teachers' recommendations as a means of allocating pupils to secondary school has been demonstrated in several studies. For instance, both Floud and Halsey (1957) and Douglas (1964) have shown that social class can be an influential factor in teachers' estimates of the abilities of their pupils. The co-variation of social class and 'tested ability' in this case is examined below.

The practice adopted by the majority of social researchers has been followed here, in taking the occupation of the father (or head of household) as the principal indicator of pupils' social class background. Although this is not an entirely satisfactory way of measuring social class, the bulk of previous research seems to indicate that, in the majority of cases, the broad classification of occupations into manual and non-manual does correspond to the conventional categories – middle-class and working-class. For the sake of convenience, I have adopted these social class categories when describing the data of this study[1].

[...]

Beachside was a streamed school until 1969, and was banded at least to some extent until 1975. It was not surprising, then, to find that, as analysis in other schools has shown, there is a significant relationship between banding and social class. If the Registrar General's Classification of Occupations is reduced to a straightforward manual/ non-manual social class dichotomy for the occupations of the parents of the pupils, then the distribution of social classes in 2TA [a Band 1 group] and 2CU [a Band 2 group], the case-study forms, is as shown in Table 2.5.

Table 2.5 Distribution of social classes across the case-study forms 2TA and 2CU

Form	*I*	*II*	*IIIN*	*Total non-manual*	*IIIM*	*IV*	*V*	*Total manual*	*Unclassified*
2CU	5	10	5	20	12	-	-	12	-
2TA	2	3	2	7	15	8	3	26	-

There are 20 children from non-manual families in 2CU compared with 7 in 2TA, and 12 from manual families in 2CU compared with 26 in 2TA. This is a considerable over-representation of non-manual children in 2CU; a similar over-representation was found in all the Band 1 classes across this cohort and in previously banded cohorts[2]. Thus on the basis of reports from junior schools, the tendency is for the children of middle-class non-manual families to be allocated to Band 1 forms, whereas children from manual working-class homes are more likely to be allocated to Bands 2 or 3.

[...]

One of the main platforms of comprehensive reorganisation has been that the comprehensive school will provide greater equality of opportunity for those with equal talent. Ford (1969) suggests that the most obvious way of testing whether this is true is 'by analysis of the interaction of social class and measured intelligence as determinants of academic attainment'. If the impact of social class on educational attainment is greater than can be explained by the co-variation of class and IQ, then the notion of an equality of opportunity must be called into question.

There were no standard IQ tests available for the pupils at Beachside[3], but, as noted above, three of the four 'feeder' primary schools did test their pupils. There was a great variety of tests used, for reading age, reading comprehension, arithmetic and mathematics. Each pupil's record card noted a selection of these test-scores, but only in a few cases were results available for the whole range of tests.

The clearest picture of the interaction between social class, test-scores and band allocation were obtained by comparing pupils who scored at different levels. Taking N.F.E.R. Reading Comprehension and N.F.E.R. Mathematics, the co-variation of social class and test-scores within Band 1 and Band 2 is shown in Tables 2.6 and 2.7. By extracting the 100–114 test-score groups, the relationship between social class and band allocation may be tested. This suggests a relationship between banding and social class at levels of similar ability. Taking the mathematics test-scores, there is also a significant relationship. Altogether, the evidence of these test-scores concerning selection for banding was far from conclusive; the result is to some extent dependent upon which test is used. It is clear, however, that social class is significant, and that ability measured by test-score does not totally explain the allocation to bands. This falls into line with the findings of Ford (1969) and others that selection on the basis of streaming in the comprehensive school, like selection under the tripartite system, tends to underline social class differentials in educational opportunity. However, my work with these results also suggests that, to some extent at least, findings concerning the relationships between test-performance and social class must be regarded as an artefact of the nature of the tests employed, and thus the researcher must be careful what he makes of them.

Table 2.6 Banding allocation and social class, using the N.F.E.R. Reading Comprehension Test

Test-score	*Band 1*		*Band 2*	
	Working-class	*Middle-class*	*Working-class*	*Middle-class*
115 and over	3	7	1	0
100–114	10	12	16	2
1–99	5	1	24	5
	18	20	41	7

Table 2.7 Banding allocation and social class, using the N.F.E.R. Mathematics Test

Test-score	*Band 1*		*Band 2*	
	Working-class	*Middle-class*	*Working-class*	*Middle-class*
115 and over	5	8	0	0
100–114	15	13	15	3
1–99	1	0	25	1
	21	21	40	4

N.F.E.R. Reading Comprehension Test (scores 100–114)

	Working-class	*Middle-class*
Band 1	10	12
Band 2	16	2

$\chi^2 = 8.2$, d.f. = 1, $p < 0.01$ $C = 0.41$

N.F.E.R. Mathematics Test (scores 100–114)

	Working-class	*Middle-class*
Band 1	15	13
Band 2	15	3

$\chi^2 = 4.28$, d.f. = 1, $p < 0.05$ $C = 0.29$

Notes:

1 All responses that could not be straightforwardly fitted into the Registrar General's classifications - e.g. 'engineer', 'he works at Smith's factory' – were consigned to the Unclassified category, as were the responses 'deceased', 'unemployed', 'I haven't got a father', etc.

2 The distribution of social class across the whole cohort is presented in Table N2.

Table N2. Distribution of social classes across the second-year cohort, 1973–4

	I	*II*	*IIIN*	*Total non-manual*	*IIIM*	*IV*	*V*	*Total manual*	*Unclassified*
2CU	5	10	5	20	12	-	-	12	-
2GD	4	8	5	17	12	-	-	12	4
2ST	-	2	32	5	14	3	-	17	8
2FT	2	6	10	18	11	2	-	13	3
Band 1	11	26	23	40	49	5	0	54	15
2LF	-	4	1	5	13	6	1	20	8
2BH	2	2	6	10	12	4	-	16	8
2WX	1	2	4	7	15	5	1	21	3
2TA	2	3	2	7	15	8	3	26	-
Band 2	5	11	13	29	55	23	5	83	19
2UD	-	2	4	6	6	5	-	11	4
2MA	2	2	-	4	5	4	-	9	2
Band 3	2	4	4	10	11	9	-	20	6

The questionnaire on which this table is based was not completed by nine pupils in the cohort. The relationship between banding and social class is significant $\chi^2 = 20$, d.f. = 2, $p < 0.001$.

3 IQ testing was abandoned by the Local Authority in 1972.

BIBLIOGRAPHY

DOUGLAS, J.W.B. (1964) *The Home and the School: a study of ability and attainment in the primary school*, London, MacGibbon and Kee.

FLOUD, J. and HALSEY, A. H. (1957) 'Social class, intelligence tests and selection for secondary schools', *British Journal of Sociology*, vol. 8, no. 1, pp. 33–9.

FORD, J. (1969) *Social Class and the Comprehensive School*, London, Routledge and Kegan Paul.

HARGREAVES, D.H. (1967) *Social Relations in a Secondary School*, London, Routledge and Kegan Paul.

LACEY, C. (1970) *Hightown Grammar*, Manchester, Manchester University Press.

(Ball, S.J. (1981) *Beachside Comprehensive: a case study of secondary schooling*, Cambridge, Cambridge University Press, pp. 29–34)

PART 2 PRACTICAL GUIDELINES FOR PRACTITIONER RESEARCH

CONTENTS

INTRODUCTION

The first four sections of this Part provide guidance on research design and appropriate ways of collecting evidence. Section 1 introduces you to the various research traditions in education and discusses some factors that need to be taken into account when designing practitioner research. Section 2 is about documentary analysis and the use of written documents as evidence. Section 3 contains advice about interviewing techniques and questionnaire design. Section 4 examines how you can collect evidence by watching and recording what people do and say. It offers advice on observation, recording and analysing classroom talk, and using children's work as a source of evidence. Section 5 offers advice on the interpretation, analysis and presentation of evidence.

As well as providing advice on collecting and analysing evidence, the various sections contain many examples of practitioner research. Some of these have been drawn from the work of the teachers who helped develop the material, while others come from published accounts of practitioner research in books and journals.

1 ABOUT PRACTITIONER RESEARCH

1.1 INTRODUCTION

This section provides a brief introduction to practitioner research and offers general advice on how to design an inquiry which is ethically sound and which will provide reliable and valid information. You will probably find it most useful to skim through the whole section first before going on to reread sub-sections which you find particularly interesting or challenging.

1.2 WHY PRACTITIONER RESEARCH?

Practitioner research is a relatively new recruit to the many traditions of educational research. As its name implies, practitioner research is conducted by teachers in their own classrooms and schools. It is carried out 'on-the-job', unlike more traditional forms of educational and classroom research where outside researchers come into schools, stay for the duration of the research project and then leave. As David Hopkins comments, 'Often the phrase "classroom research" brings to mind images of researchers undertaking research in a sample of schools or classrooms and using as subjects the teachers and students who live out their educational lives within them' (Hopkins, 1985, p. 6). Similarly, Rob Walker maintains that much of what passes for educational research, 'is more accurately described as research on education' rather than research 'conducted primarily in the pursuit of educational issues and concerns' (Walker, 1989, pp. 4–5).

When it comes to the kind of 'classroom research' described by Hopkins and Walker, the teacher or school has little or no control over the research process. The subject, scope and scale of the investigation are set by the outside agency to which the researchers belong, and although the research findings themselves may be communicated to participating schools, often they are of little relevance or direct benefit to the people teaching and learning in those schools. By contrast, practitioner research is controlled by the teacher, its focus is on teaching and learning or on policies which affect these, and one of its main purposes is to improve practice. It also has another important purpose: it can help develop teachers' professional judgement and expertise. Hopkins expresses this aspect of practitioner research in the following words:

> Teachers are too often the servants of heads, advisers, researchers, text books, curriculum developers, examination boards, or the Department of Education and Science among others. By adopting a research stance, teachers are liberating themselves from the control position they so often find themselves in ... By taking a research stance, the teacher is engaged not only in a meaningful professional development activity but [is] also engaged in a process of refining, and becoming more autonomous in, professional judgement.
>
> (Hopkins, 1985, p. 3)

'Practitioner research' has its origins in the teacher researcher movement of the early 1970s, which focused on curriculum research and development, and the critical appraisal of classroom practice through 'action research' (e.g. The Open University, 1976; Stenhouse, 1975). A key feature of action research then and now is that it requires a commitment by teachers to investigate and reflect on their own practice. As Nixon notes, 'action research is an intellectually demanding mode of enquiry, which prompts serious and often uncomfortable questions about classroom practice' (1981, p. 5). To engage in action research you need to become aware of your own values, preconceptions and tacit pedagogic theories. You also need to make a genuine attempt to reflect honestly and critically on your behaviour and actions, and to share these reflections with sympathetic colleagues. Trying to be objective about one's own practice is not at all easy. As Gates (1989) has shown, however, developing habits of critical self-reflection makes an enormous contribution to teachers' confidence and professional expertise.

Like other forms of research, action research involves identification of problems, collection of evidence, analysis and diagnosis, interpretation using theory, and the communication of findings to audiences outside the researcher's immediate working context. It is unlike more conventional research in that most problems usually arise directly from practice rather than from published theory. Its main purpose is to identify appropriate forms of action or intervention which may help solve those problems. Once an appropriate form of action is identified, it must be implemented, and its effectiveness closely monitored. If the intervention is successful, it might necessitate a change in practice. This in turn may raise new problems which must be solved and so on. These recursive processes make up what is know as the 'action-research cycle'. Figure 1 gives an example of an action-research cycle.

1.3 RESEARCH GROUND RULES

In the first of a recent series of articles examining the nature of research in education, Michael Bassey states that:

> In carrying out research the purpose is to try to make some claim to knowledge; to try to show something that was not known before. However small, however modest the hoped for claim to knowledge is, provided it is carried out systematically, critically and self-critically, the search for knowledge is research.
>
> (Bassey, 1990, p. 35)

While Bassey's definition of research as 'the search for knowledge' is a very loose one, he qualifies this definition by insisting that all research must be systematic and critical, and by claiming that it must conform to the following set of rules:

1. Any research inquiry must be conducted for some clearly defined purpose.
   It should not be a random amassing of data but must entail a planned attempt to arrive at answers to specific questions, problems or hypotheses.
2. When conducting an inquiry data should be collected and recorded systematically, so that, if necessary, it can be checked by others.

3 There should be a clear rationale or theory informing the way the data is analysed.

4 Researchers must critically examine their evidence to make sure that it is accurate, representative and reliable.

5 Researchers must be self-critical and should scrutinize their own assumptions, methods of inquiry and analysis, and ways of presenting their findings.

6 As the purpose of research is 'to tell someone something that they didn't know before', then researchers should aim to communicate their findings to a wider audience so that they can also benefit from the new knowledge.

7 Researchers should attempt to relate any new knowledge or understanding they gain to both their own personal theories and to published theories so that the former can be evaluated in terms of its wider conceptual and theoretical context.
(adapted from Bassey, 1990, p. 35)

Like Bassey, we believe that this set of ground rules is fundamental to any kind of inquiry.

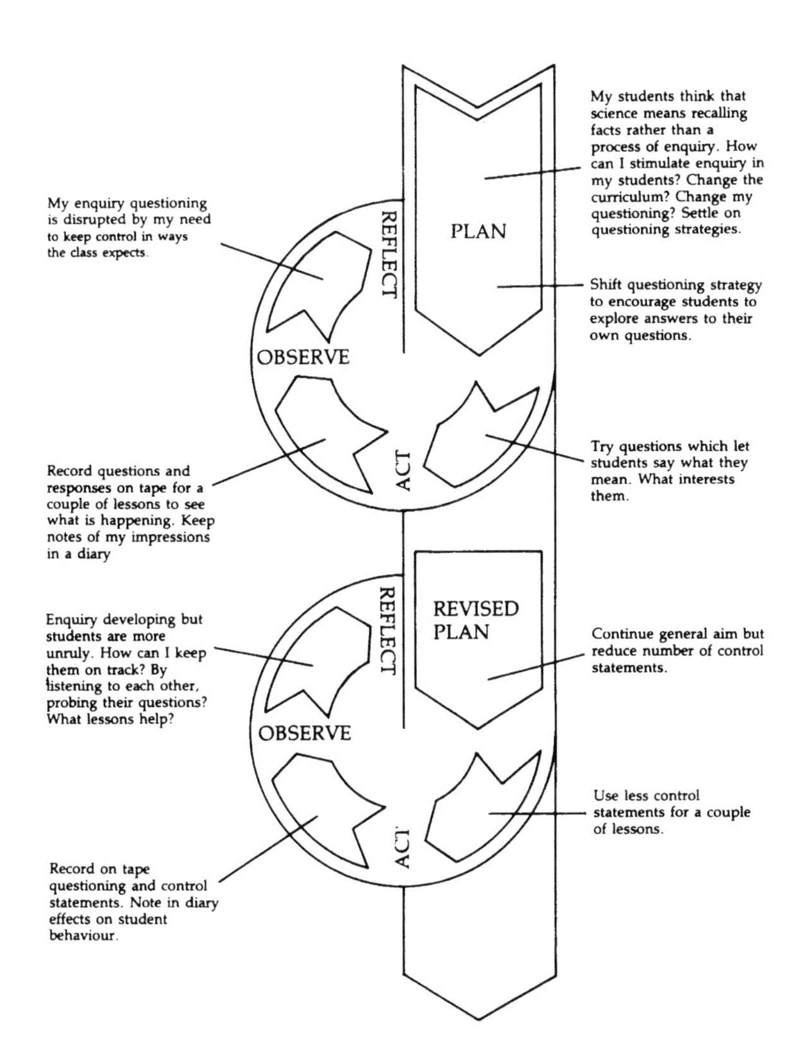

Figure 1 Action research in action (Kemmis and McTaggart, 1981, p. 14, reprinted in Hopkins, 1985, p. 55).

1.4 ETHICS AND PRACTITIONER RESEARCH

Strangely enough, Bassey does not mention taking ethical considerations into account, although these are of paramount importance. As Nias points out:

> ... Enquiry-based courses ... have far-reaching implications for teachers, schools and providing institutions and for the relationships between them. For a student, to subject professional practice (be it one's own or that of others) to systematic enquiry and to share the results of this scrutiny with a wider audience than simply a course tutor is to open oneself and one's colleagues to self-doubt and criticism. ... Schools too may be opened up to more examination than many of their members want and, as a result, internal differences and divisions may be exacerbated.
>
> (Nias, 1988, p. 10)

Sound ethical practices should be observed whatever kind of research one is engaged in. As Nias points out, many sensitive issues can arise as a result of practitioners carrying out research into their own institutional context. Making sure that ethical procedures are carefully followed may not completely resolve problems, but will certainly show others that you are aware of your responsibilities and the potential consequences of your enquiry. Each of the sections which follow contains advice on ethical procedures which are specific to the methods they describe. The following is a more general list.

> *Ethics for practitioner research*
>
> **Observe protocol**: Take care to ensure that the relevant persons, committees and authorities have been consulted, informed and that the necessary permission and approval have been obtained.
>
> **Involve participants:** Encourage others who have a stake in the improvement you envisage to shape the form of the work.
>
> **Negotiate with those affected:** Not everyone will want to be directly involved; your work should take account of the responsibilities and wishes of others.
>
> **Report progress:** Keep the work visible and remain open to suggestions so that unforeseen and unseen ramifications can be taken account of; colleagues must have the opportunity to lodge a protest with you.
>
> **Obtain explicit authorization before you observe**: For the purposes of recording the activities of professional colleagues or others (the observation of your own students falls outside this imperative provided that your aim is the improvement of teaching and learning).
>
> **Obtain explicit authorization before you examine files, correspondence or other documentation**: Take copies only if specific authority to do this is obtained.
>
> **Negotiate descriptions of people's work:** Always allow those described to challenge your accounts on the grounds of fairness, relevance and accuracy.
>
> **Negotiate accounts of others' points of view (e.g., in accounts of communication):** Always allow those involved in interviews, meetings and written exchanges to require amendments which enhance fairness, relevance and accuracy.
>
> **Obtain explicit authorization before using quotations:** Verbatim transcripts, attributed observations, excerpts of audio- and video-recordings, judgements, conclusions or recommendations in reports (written or to meetings) [for advice on quotations from published materials, see Section 6].

Negotiate reports for various levels of release: Remember that different audiences demand different kinds of reports; what is appropriate for an informal verbal report to a [staff] meeting may not be appropriate for a ... report to council, a journal article, a newspaper, a newsletter to parents; be conservative if you cannot control distribution.

Accept responsibility for maintaining confidentiality.

Retain the right to report your work: Provided that those involved are satisfied with the fairness, accuracy and relevance of accounts which pertain to them; and that the accounts do not unnecessarily expose or embarrass those involved; then accounts should not be subject to veto or be sheltered by prohibitions of confidentiality.

Make your principles of procedure binding and known: All of the people involved in your ... research project must agree to the principles before the work begins; others must be aware of their rights in the process.

(Kemmis and McTaggart, 1981, pp. 43–4, reprinted in Hopkins, 1985, pp. 135–6)

1.5 THEORY AND EVIDENCE IN PRACTITIONER RESEARCH

Now that we have established a set of ground rules and a set of ethical principles it is time to go on to consider the relationship between theory and evidence in practitioner research. Bassey mentions the importance of relating research to theory in his rules 3 and 7, where he makes the distinction between 'personal' and 'published' theories.

THEORIES

There is nothing mysterious about a theory. People devise theories to explain observable relationships between events or sets of events. Traditional scientific theories offer explanations in terms of causal relationships between events and/or behaviours. Once a theory has been formulated it can be used to predict the likely outcome when similar sets of circumstances occur. Testing whether these predictions are correct or not is one way of testing the theory itself. A theory is, then, a coherent set of assumptions which attempts to explain or predict something about the behaviour of things and events in the world. A physicist might have a theory which can predict the behaviour of subatomic particles under certain conditions; an historian might have a theory about the causes of the Industrial Revolution; and an educational psychologist a theory about the causes of underachievement in inner-city schools. In all these cases, the theories held by the physicist, historian and psychologist are likely to have been derived from published accounts of previous research. They might also have personal theories, based on their own experiences, beliefs and observations. Often what attracts people to one published theory rather than another is its close match with their own personal ideas and assumptions.

For example, take the commonly held idea that practical experiences enhance and consolidate children's learning. This idea (or hypothesis) stems from the published theories of the Swiss psychologist Jean Piaget. Piaget's ideas became popular through documents such as the Plowden Report (Central Advisory Council for Education, 1967) and the Cockcroft Report (DES, 1982) and are reflected today in recommendations put forward in various national curriculum documents. For example, attainment target 1 – exploration of science – reads as follows:

> Pupils should develop the intellectual and practical skills that allow them to explore the world of science and to develop a fuller understanding of scientific phenomena and the procedures of scientific exploration and investigation.
>
> (DES, 1989, p. 3)

In a published account of her work, Virgina Winter explains how this idea, coupled with her own belief that science teaching should emphasize 'practical, investigative and problem-solving activities', led her to undertake a systematic appraisal of the science work offered in her school (Winter, 1990, p. 155). She was particularly interested in the ways in which her pupils acquired 'process skills', that is the practical skills necessary for them to carry out controlled scientific experiments. She also wanted to find out about children's perceptions of science, and whether they understood the way scientists worked. In this example, you can see how public and personal theories can come together to act as a stimulus for a piece of research.

EVIDENCE AND DATA

In order to compare two rival theories, one needs to gather evidence. It is worth remembering that showing a theory is incorrect is more important than simply confirming it. In science, falsifying theories and setting up and testing alternative theories is the principal means of advancing knowledge and understanding. This is also the case in educational research. As an example of this, let's take a closer look at Virginia Winter's research.

Winter used a 'multiple strategy' approach (Winter, 1990) to collect evidence about 11- and 12-year-olds' perceptions of science and their developing process skills. She observed the children at work in her science classes and wrote accounts of her lessons in a research diary. She carried out semi-structured, tape-recorded interviews with children, and kept samples of their work on scientific topics. In addition, she asked some children to keep diaries in which they made notes of their comments and impressions about their science lessons. Winter's methods were participant observation, interviewing, and analysis of children's work. Her data were her written diary record of her observations; transcripts of the interviews; samples of children's work; and the diaries they kept. This was the evidence she used to support her arguments and recommendations. You will find all of these methods of gathering evidence discussed in subsequent sections of this Handbook.

Winter found that children's practical work benefited most when they were allowed to work in friendship groups, and when they were encouraged to take responsibility for managing their own group work. On the basis of her evidence Winter demonstrated that, for her children, the original assumption that practical experiences enhance and consolidate children's learning needed to be modified. She found that children make more progress when they are encouraged to take control of their own learning, and when they are allowed to work in friendship groups. Contrary to her original assumption, simply giving them practical experience was not enough. Very often in educational research new theories and hypotheses arise in the course of collecting information to answer a particular research question. Where this happens we talk about theories being 'grounded in the data', to describe the way in which some theories can arise directly from practical experiences and observations. You will find more on 'grounded theory' in sub-section 5.3.

THE QUALITATIVE/QUANTITATIVE DISTINCTION

So far we have only talked about 'theories', 'evidence', and 'data' in very general terms. It is customary, however, to make a distinction between methods of collecting evidence that give rise to qualitative data and those which give rise to quantitative data.

Hugh Coolican explains the difference between qualitative and quantitative approaches as follows:

> 'Quantification' means to measure on some numerical basis ... Whenever we count or categorise we quantify. ... A qualitative approach, by contrast, emphasises meanings, experiences ... descriptions and so on. Raw data will be exactly what people have said (in interview or recorded conversation) or a description of what has been observed.
>
> (Coolican, 1990, pp. 36–7)

Traditional experimental approaches to educational research use quantification and measurement to examine the contributions of different factors to the behaviours studied. So suppose you were interested in comparing the effects on children's reading performance of two different reading schemes, one based on a phonic approach, and one based on a visual word-recognition approach. In an experimental study, it would be essential to choose a reliable and unbiased measure of reading performance, such as scores from a standardized reading test, which could be used with both schemes. The measure should either provide a numerical score for each child, or tell you how many children fall within each of a set of defined categories. Data of this sort can be interpreted with the aid of statistics to allow you to make a quantitative comparison between the two schemes.

The use of quantitative techniques is not restricted to experimental studies. Data from observations, interviews and questionnaires can also be quantified provided that it is structured appropriately. Examples of this type of study are discussed in Section 5.

We do not deal with the statistical analysis of quantitative data in this Part. However, the further reading lists at the end of this section and at the end of Section 5 contain a selection of books about quantitative experimental techniques and statistical analysis.

Quantitative techniques are extremely useful if you want to compare things like people's test scores or measures of performance under different conditions, or how people behave under different conditions. Quantitative experimental techniques have the disadvantage that, to make the resulting data statistically meaningful and generalizable to a wider sample than the one you are testing, you will need to test large numbers of people. Also, if you want to be confident of getting the same pattern of results again when you test a different sample of people, your first sample must be representative of the population to which both samples belong.

Critics of this experimental approach argue that in order to make quantitative measurements, the behaviours you are interested in have to be reduced to their very simplest form, and therefore you do not get a true picture of the way people behave. For example, they would argue that assessing children's reading competence requires a more complex approach than simply comparing reading scores on a standard test.

To carry on the reading theme, let's compare an example of a qualitative approach with the experimental one discussed above. Hilary Minns, a head teacher from Warwickshire, carried out a long-term investigation of the development of five children's reading and literacy skills using qualitative techniques. She wanted to understand the contribution of home background to children's initial competency, and later progress in reading and writing. She also wanted to study the part played by literacy in the lives of her sample of children and their families (Minns, 1990).

Using a biographical, case-study approach, Minns built up detailed pictures of the lives of the five children. She arranged a series of home visits, carried out informal interviews with parents and teachers, and made observations of the children at home and in their classrooms. She collected tape-recordings of parents reading to their children, and asked them to provide her with lists of books and other written materials they used in their homes. Finally, she collected samples of the children's drawings and early writing.

As a result of this study, Minns gained great insight into what literacy meant in the lives of the children and their families. She also learned more about the processes which the family and school used to support these children's early attempts to read and write. She was able to reappraise her own school's language policy and reading methods and to recommend that 'knowledge of the cultural beliefs and values of families and their effect on children as readers has to be made a professional concern' (Minns, 1990, p. 113).

While this qualitative approach may seem to offer more insight than the experimental approach, it is not without its difficulties. Minns only studied five children, too small a sample to allow her to make generalizations which could apply to all young children. Also, the methods she used meant that she had to spend a lot of time with the children and their families to understand their views on literacy and get a feel for their lives. As Woods points out, studies like this one are like a 'snapshot frozen in time' (Woods, 1988, p. 102). They may give a more complete picture, but it is a picture limited to one set of people and circumstances over a particular period of time. So while qualitative techniques can yield extremely rich data, they are frequently time consuming; they may present problems of sampling; and they do not allow one to make generalizations about large samples of people.

You will find when you look at other people's research reports that qualitative and quantitative techniques are frequently combined. Much qualitative data can be quantified for purposes of analysis (see Section 5), and in practitioner research the two approaches tend to complement each other.

1.6 SAMPLING, RELIABILITY, VALIDITY AND BIAS

We quoted Bassey earlier as saying that research is only worth doing if it tells you something you didn't know before. This is why confirming a theory is not as valuable as proving it to be false or in need of modification. Another of Bassey's ground rules is that researchers have a duty to make sure that their data are accurate and reliable. No matter how interesting new knowledge is, it is only really valuable if you have guarded against various sources of error which can affect the way you collect and analyse your data. Sampling, or the way you go about selecting people to take part in your inquiry, is a frequent source of error.

SAMPLING

The notion of 'sampling' has already been introduced. Researchers are often interested in finding out something about, or seeking information from, particular categories of people, such as parents, school leavers, probationary teachers, or pupils with special learning needs. A 'population' consists of all possible people who fall into a particular category. Populations can be large (for example, all 18-year-olds in sixth-form colleges in England and Wales), or they can be small (for example, all pupils attending Montrose Academy, or even all 16-year-olds attending Montrose Academy). A 'sample' is a smaller number of individuals drawn from the total population which can be taken as representative of that population. Whether the population is large or small it is important to make sure that the sample you select is truly representative in some relevant way of the population of interest, unless the population is so small that you can include all its members in the study.

For example, suppose you wanted to find out parents' views on setting up an after-school club in your school. You decide to send a questionnaire to all parents and 40 per cent respond. Of this 40 per cent it appears that the majority support the idea of an after-school club. Checking the questionnaire returns against school records, however, you find that most returns were from single-parent families and those families where both parents are out at work. In this case you have a self-selected sample whose views may not represent those of the population of parents as a whole.

A better strategy might have been to subdivide the population of parents into the following categories: single-parent families with parent at home; single-parent families with parent at work; two-parent families with both parents at home; two-parent families with both parents at work; two-parent families with one parent at work. You could then send questionnaires to a sample of parents in each of these categories. This way you would be more likely to sample parental opinion across the board. But remember that you need to balance the desire to make your research as reliable as possible against ethical considerations. In this example the use of school records might be seen as a breach of confidentiality.

Inquiries which draw on fairly small, local populations and samples are more feasible for practitioner research than inquiries which involve gathering large amounts of data from samples drawn from wider populations.

It is also possible to carry out an in-depth study of an individual case or small number of cases (as Hilary Minns did). Even here, however, you are not necessarily free from sampling error. Although she only studied five families, Minns was very careful to select children whom she felt represented the ethnic and socio-economic balance of pupils in her school.

BIAS

What do we mean by bias? Very generally, bias can be taken to mean unfairly favouring one thing at the expense of another. Bias is error which arises when we allow our own values and expectations to colour the way we conduct our research. It can exert its effect at a number of different stages of an inquiry. For example, bias can enter into the initial stages of designing questionnaires or interview and observation schedules. Suppose that, as science INSET co-ordinator in an English primary school, you are interested in assessing colleagues' perceptions of the national curriculum attainment targets. You decide to carry out informal interviews with staff. One of your questions might be, 'Some of the attainment targets for key stage 1 look like posing problems for us. Our pupils might find them difficult to achieve. What do you think?' Not only does this question reveal your own value judgements, it also puts interviewees in the difficult position of having to decide whether or not to agree with your assessment of the situation, particularly if their perceptions are different. It would be better to ask, 'What is you impression of the attainment targets for key stage 1? How do you think our pupils will fare on these?'

Bias can influence the selection of children you chose to observe or test and it can affect the choice of people you decide to interview. Do you interview all staff, or only those known to be sympathetic to your research? At the data collection stage, you can fall prey to bias by failing to report on all the relevant data. For example, keeping field-notes can be highly selective and people sometimes fall into the trap of recording facts and incidents which confirm their own ideas and interpretations rather than others. Similarly, when carrying out documentary analysis, one can select arguments and evidence which favour one viewpoint and ignore contradictory evidence.

When recording interviews or taking notes at a meeting, again it is easy (and only human) to give more weight to some arguments and opinions than others. It is easier to remember information that matches our own expectations and values. Also, observations, assessments or interviews can be subject to 'halo' effects. These arise from involuntary reactions to how people are dressed, how clean they are, the sort of language style they use, how influential they are and so on, and can affect judgement.

Once the data have been collected, bias can enter into analysis and interpretation, again through selective reporting of aspects of the research which support particular beliefs. Also, people can be highly partisan about their choice of evidence from published studies, choosing only that which supports their own findings.

There are a number of things you can do to guard against bias. Simply being aware of it is a first step. Bassey's ground rule 5 which states that 'researchers must be self-critical and should scrutinize their own assumptions, methods of inquiry and analysis, and ways of presenting their findings' is obviously important here. Both Burgess (1981) and Hutchinson (1988) recommend using a diary or journal to record personal feelings and reflections on the research process as a way of becoming aware of, and transcending, personal bias.

If you choose to use your professional diary as a source of evidence it is important that you find some method of distinguishing between the various classes of information it can contain. Virginia Winter (whose research was discussed above) describes her research diary as follows:

> My research diary contained substantive (factual) accounts of events in lessons, methodological accounts giving biographical details [of interviews and the children interviewed] and analytical (interpretive) accounts, in which ideas, hunches and questions were noted and anything else which might be of use in follow up interviews.
>
> (Winter, 1990, pp. 158–9)

Winter's diary contained a mixture of facts and interpretations of the facts. Unless fact and interpretation are kept distinct in your diary you run the risk of using your interpretations of events in place of the observable facts. Methods for keeping facts and interpretations distinct are discussed in sub-section 4.3.

Another practical step you can take is to pilot, or try out in advance, any instruments and procedures that you are developing. Piloting is an excellent way of revealing hidden sources of bias in your research instruments.

Another strategy is a procedure known as 'triangulation'. Triangulation simply means comparing two or more views of the same thing so that data from different sources can be used to corroborate, elaborate or illumine the research in question. If, for example, you were carrying out an observational study in order to understand some aspect of classroom interaction, then you might choose to:

(a) observe a particular lesson acting as a non-participant observer;

(b) interview the pupils so as to record their impressions of the lesson;

(c) discuss your observations with the teacher who took the lesson to see if his or her perceptions and interpretation matched your own.

You can also compare documentary evidence (for example, formal records of meetings or statements of policy) with different individuals' oral interpretations and/or practice. If you are assessing pupils' learning, then you might want to employ both formal and informal assessment techniques. Whatever you choose to do, projects designed to use multiple cases and informants and more than one data-gathering technique are more likely to be accurate than those which do not, and will provide more support for the arguments and recommendations you may want to put forward.

RELIABILITY

In a broad sense, when we refer to an inquiry as 'reliable', it means that you can be confident that nearly identical conclusions would be reached if it were to be repeated at another time, either by yourself or someone else. Your findings, or those of someone else, should be similar if you choose to repeat your observations on the same people on a different occasion, or you were to carry out the inquiry again with a different sample of people drawn from the same population. In a narrower sense, reliability is particularly important when it comes to designing questionnaires and interview and observation schedules. For example, in order for a questionnaire to qualify as reliable, a person's answers to the questions should be the same if he or she is asked to complete it a second time. If their answers are not the same, it may mean that the questions are ambiguous and do not provide reliable information. Piloting is very necessary when designing things like questionnaires and structured interview schedules.

Observation schedules and the way you record observations also need to be reliable, that is they need to mean the same to others as they do to you. This is particularly important if you are going to ask someone to help you with your observations. You need to make sure that you negotiate with each other to arrive at mutually agreed definitions of the behaviours and situations you want to concentrate on. As Coolican points out:

> ... We know that each person's view of a situation is unique and that our perceptions can be biased by innumerable factors. An untrained observer might readily *evaluate* behaviour which the researcher wants reported as objectively as possible. Where the trained observer reports a hard blow, the novice might describe this as 'vicious'.
>
> (Coolican, 1990, p. 63)

Once again you can see how important it is to pilot instruments and methods.

VALIDITY

Although you may have taken great care to ensure that your methods are reliable, it is not always the case that they will give you true, or 'valid', information concerning the phenomenon you are interested in. For example, a questionnaire designed to obtain general information from staff about their views of the role of governors in the local management of schools might instead tap individual opinions about particular governors' ability to administer school resources. In this case you would not have a valid measure of the topic you are interested in. In an interview, the interviewee might try to please the interviewer by giving acceptable rather than honest answers. Again, the information you are obtaining does not provide a valid reflection of people's opinions on the topic you are interested in. Finally, observations are more likely to be valid reflections of people's behaviour when they are made in everyday contexts. For example, observing instances of children's aggression in the playground is more likely to give a valid measure of naturally occurring aggressive behaviour than observing an arranged boxing match where the aggression might be ritualistic rather than spontaneous.

You will find out more about bias, reliability and validity in the sections which follow this one. Also, the two books listed at the end of this section discuss these topics in greater detail.

1.7 RESEARCH PURPOSES

We are now going to look briefly at three different types of inquiry: exploratory, explanatory, and predictive. The difference between them lies in their purpose and in the way the initial research questions are formulated rather than in their inquiry methods. The main data-collection methods we describe in Sections 2–4 can be used for all three types of inquiry.

EXPLORATORY STUDIES

The purpose of exploratory studies is, as the name suggests, to explore or investigate little understood phenomena or behaviours and discover the important underlying patterns, themes, and factors which affect them. The information and insights resulting from exploratory studies often lead to the formulation of a more precise set of research questions and hypotheses.

An example is a study by John Cowgill, who was interested in equal opportunities. He observed that boys tend to dominate the girls in CDT, and also that girls underachieve in this area. He decided to focus on the different types of interactions that might be taking place between teachers and pupils in CDT and to compare these with interactions in home economics (HE) lessons. He wanted to *explore* the effects of gender on the interactions. His research questions were:

With special reference to gender in all observations and interactions: teacher–pupil, pupil–teacher, pupil–pupil:

(a) What type of interactions are taking place?

(b) How are these interactions dealt with in the different areas?

(c) Are there any similarities between the two areas?

John's research strategy was to carry out a planned series of observations of the way pupils and teachers interacted in CDT and HE lessons. He acted as a non-participant observer, after discussing with his colleagues which lessons and pupil groups it would be appropriate to observe.

EXPLANATORY STUDIES

In an explanatory study, the researcher is interested in explaining the forces causing a particular phenomenon, and in identifying important events, beliefs, attitudes, and/or policies which might be shaping the phenomenon.

For instance, Christina Wojtak wanted to *explain* the relationship between the quality of children's writing, the criteria the children used to select books for reading, and the criteria they used to judge their own written work. She also wanted to assess changes in the quality of writing and in children's attitudes to their own writing, resulting from discussions about different ways of constructing stories. Christina's project involved analysis of children's writing, interviews with individual children, tape recordings of discussions, and observations of children writing.

In practice it can be difficult to distinguish between exploratory and explanatory studies. Much practitioner research involves an element of both.

PREDICTIVE STUDIES

Finally, we come to predictive studies which, as the name suggests, involves the planned investigation of the outcome of a particular prediction or set of predictions. For example, Margaret Khomo and Keith Farley had the idea that an active learning approach might be more effective than a didactic one in teaching a migration module to pupils in a comprehensive school. They *predicted* that pupils' appreciation and understanding of the relationship between patterns of migration and British culture would be enhanced by teaching methods which drew on pupils' personal experience and family histories of migration.

In order to see if there was any support for their prediction, Margaret and Keith decided to compare two classes' understanding of the concept of migration using questionnaires, both before and after they had worked through the module. Margaret taught one class using active learning methods; she taught the other class, the control class, using a more didactic approach. Margaret carried out observations in both classes during the lessons where they were working on the module. Keith also interviewed individual pupils.

Margaret and Keith's study has the feel of an experimental design, although the data they collected were mainly qualitative. They made a firm prediction that could be stated in the form of an hypothesis: 'encouraging children's active learning will be a more effective way of teaching the concept of migration than more traditional methods'. Their techniques were to compare an experimental or 'research' class with a control class, and to use questionnaires to compare changes in children's understanding and learning. Their study was also partly exploratory: Keith and Margaret wanted to understand why active learning might be a better approach to teaching the module. Classroom observation and interviews with pupils were the research strategies they used to help them with this aspect.

These examples highlight a point that we made right at the beginning of this introduction: practitioner research can be carried out for a number of different purposes using a number of techniques. Very often several purposes and techniques are combined into a single study.

FURTHER READING

BELL, J. (1999) *Doing your Research Project,* Buckingham, Open University Press.

This has become something of a 'bible' for first-time researchers in social science. It assists students in carrying out their first research projects successfully, without wasting lots of time in trial and error. It helps students to develop sound techniques and good practice which will serve them well in future research projects and assumes no prior knowledge of research methodology or experience of carrying out research.

PRACTITIONER AND ACTION RESEARCH

FREEMAN, D. (1998) *Doing Teacher-Research: from inquiry to understanding* (Teacher source), Boston (Mass.), Heinle and Heinle.

This book examines the issue of teacher research from three perspectives: teachers' voices – authentic accounts of teachers' experiences; frameworks – comprehensive discussions of theoretical issues; and investigations – enquiry-based activities.

ROBSON, C. (1999) *Real World Research: a resource guide for social scientists and practitioner researchers,* Oxford, Blackwell.

Practitioners and professionals working with people (e.g. in education, health and the social services) are increasingly required to be involved in studies where they are called upon to carry out some form of enquiry outside the laboratory. This text gives advice and support in carrying out such real world research. It is an invaluable guide to all aspects of practitioner research in education, psychology and the social sciences.

GENERAL EDUCATIONAL RESEARCH

COHEN, L., MANION, L., and MORRISON, K. (2000) *Research Methods in Education,* London, Routledge.

This is the classic textbook on educational research methods. It has been updated to include current developments in research practice, action research, developments in ICT, questionnaire design, ethnographic research, conducting needs analysis, constructing and using tests, observational methods, reliability and validity, ethical issues and curriculum research.

2 GETTING INFORMATION FROM DOCUMENTS AND SCHOOL RESOURCES

2.1 INTRODUCTION

This section provides guidance on using written documents as evidence. 'Written documents' here means anything that is written down – however formal or informal.

This section covers the following topics:

- sub-section 2.2 deals with deciding what sort of documents to draw on and with problems of access;
- sub-section 2.3 looks at written documents other than classroom resources used with children (this may be anything related to your research interest, from government reports to a handwritten letter);
- sub-section 2.4 considers how you may draw on published facts and figures (national and local statistical information);
- sub-section 2.5 examines classroom resources used with children (books, posters, worksheets, etc.);
- sub-section 2.6 reviews the methods discussed in the section, considering their strengths and weaknesses.

The reason for separating classroom resources from 'non-classroom' documents is that, in practice, it is likely you will wish to ask different questions about them. Children's own written work, which is also a kind of document, is considered separately in Section 4, 'Seeing what people do'. This is because children's work is the outcome of activities they engage in – it seems sensible to consider the two things together.

Evidence from documents may complement that obtained from other sources. For instance, if you are interested in what happens in a meeting, you may be able to observe the meeting and/or interview one or two participants. But it may also be worth checking the minutes to see which items are officially recorded. If you are focusing on classroom practice, it may be useful to examine a written policy, or syllabus, or some of the resources used, as well as making observations of lessons.

The guidance provided here should help you choose an appropriate method, or methods, to collect evidence from documents.

2.2 DECIDING WHAT INFORMATION YOU NEED, AND WHAT SOURCES TO TURN TO

There is a variety of information you can glean from documents, but you will need to be selective, both in the range of documents you use and in the aspects of the documents you draw on for your research. Your selection of documents will depend, most obviously, on your research question(s), but other, more mundane, factors will have a bearing on what you are able to do. For instance, some documents may be less accessible than others, while some may be confidential or be restricted in their use.

I shall deal below with three factors that will affect your use of documents as evidence for your project. What information do you need? What types of question do you wish to ask of the documents? And what form of access will you be allowed?

WHAT INFORMATION DO YOU NEED?

There will be several possible documents you could draw on to provide evidence for your research. So the first point to consider is the type of document(s) you should select. If you are reviewing practice, or developing some aspect of policy in a department, do you want to look at existing policy documents, or classroom resources, or schemes of work, or all of these? Which will provide the most appropriate information for your research question(s)?

If you are faced with a large number of documents, you may need to construct an appropriate sample of these. For instance, if your interest is in classroom resources – say the selection of reading books available to children in a class – you probably will not wish to look at all of them. You could select a large sample of books and look at certain (limited) aspects of these. You could examine a small number of books in greater detail or even look at a single book (or worksheet, etc.) that was the focus of some work you were interested in. You will also need to decide how to construct your sample. Will you make a random sample of books, by, for instance, selecting every fifth book from the bookshelves? Or will you focus on books that are of interest for a particular reason, such as books that children select most frequently? Similar questions about sampling apply to documents other than classroom resources (see also sub-section 1.6).

Having selected your document(s), a further decision is which aspects of these to focus on. Are you interested in the content of documents (what is said and what isn't said), or in how information is conveyed, or in the format/presentation of the document (e.g. the layout of a worksheet), or in all of these? Will you focus on the text, or visual images, or both?

WHAT TYPES OF QUESTION WILL YOU ASK?

Having decided (more or less) what you're going to focus on, you need to decide what questions you're going to ask of the document(s). Do you have in mind very specific questions, or more open-ended questions? Example 2.1 shows what questions might be asked by a teacher with an interest in bilingual books. The example is based on a project carried out by a teacher working on an Open University INSET course.

Example 2.1 Questions about bilingual books

Carola Zeegen was a support teacher working with bilingual pupils in Harrow. She wanted to find out more about the bilingual books available in a local middle-school library. She wanted to know what children and parents thought about the books, and also how they used the books. She wanted to know what value teachers thought the books had, and how, if at all, they used them. And she wanted to look at the books themselves – what kinds of books were they? She aimed to make recommendations to the school about the purchase and use of such books.

Carola selected ten books, at random, from those available on the library shelves. She decided to look through the whole book in each case – text and illustrations. Given her interests, she could ask open-ended questions, such as what types of books were available in bilingual form, and in what respects, if any, they were distinctive (different from the range of English books).

As it happened, Carola had rather more specific questions in mind. She had taken these from published checklists designed to evaluate classroom resources. They included such questions as whether the book was fact or fiction, which age range it was appropriate for and whether it presented stereotyped images of ethnic minority groups.

The first, open-ended questions, suggest that the teacher should seek to gain a general impression of the books, and then begin to identify features that were of interest, given her overall aims. She would make notes on the books, and use these as the basis of a qualitative account, perhaps identifying what seemed to be key characteristics of the books.

The second, more specific, questions suggest that the teacher has already decided what features to look for. She can say whether a book possesses a certain characteristic or not. She can allocate books to different categories on the basis of each question. In some cases, allocating a book to one of a series of categories will be relatively unproblematical (e.g., saying whether the main character in a story is Asian, black or white). In other cases, such allocations are a matter of judgement, and others may disagree with your judgement (e.g., that an image is 'stereotyped'). This issue will be discussed below (see sub-section 2.5). Allocating books to categories provides quantitative information, that is, information that can be counted. In this case Carola Zeegen was able to say that the books were mainly fiction; that most were aimed at young children (below the age of 11 years); that most did not present stereotyped images of ethnic minority groups (though some showed gender stereotyping).

Throughout this section I shall make a similar distinction between open-ended notes on documents, which produce qualitative information for your report; and assigning documents, or aspects of documents, to certain categories, which may produce quantitative information. This does not mean, however, that the two methods are mutually exclusive. You may decide to make open-ended notes on documents as a way of identifying categories of information to look for. Or you may wish to supplement quantitative information about a set of documents with a qualitative account that provides a fuller description.

The distinction between qualitative and quantitative methods was discussed in Section 1, and will recur in other sections of this Handbook.

WHAT FORMS OF ACCESS WILL YOU BE ALLOWED?

You may wish to look at published documents. As long as these are available locally, there is no problem of access – the documents are in the public domain. Other documents may be more personal, or confidential. Use of such documents (perhaps notes from a meeting, lesson plans produced by another teacher, or a whole host of other documents) involves certain ethical considerations. You will need to negotiate access to such documents.

It is important to carry out such negotiations before beginning your research, otherwise your plans may be upset by someone unexpectedly refusing you permission to use something important to your work. You will need to identify whom to ask for permission (if this is not obvious). It is best to tell the person about your interests and then ascertain what form of access you can have to the relevant document(s) and what restrictions, if any, will be imposed on your use of them. The specific questions you need to ask will vary depending on the kind of documents in which you're interested – but they might include the following:

- Assuming you can have access, what use are you allowed to make of the information? For instance, will you be allowed to quote from documents?
- What degree of confidentiality, if any, is required? For example, do you need to use pseudonyms for any people or institutions mentioned?
- Who will be allowed to see your report? Can anyone see it, or are certain restrictions imposed?
- Does the person supplying the document wish to see your report before you allow others to see it?

Checking your account with someone else (perhaps the writer of a locally produced document) also allows you to check your analysis and may change the way you interpret the document (see also sub-section 1.4 on ethics).

While published documents don't present problems of access, you *may* need to think about copyright. Copyright is *not* an issue for work submitted for assessment. It *only* becomes an issue if:

- you wish to publish your report, or to make *multiple copies* (for distribution to colleagues),
- you *also* wish to quote *whole* documents (e.g. a poem) or *large parts* of documents. 'Large parts' of documents means:
  - a quotation of 400 words or more, or a quotation that constitutes more than 20 per cent of the whole document;
  - several quotations that together total 800 words or more, or that constitute more than 40 per cent of the whole document.

While it is highly unlikely you will wish to include lengthy quotations in the body of your report, copyright applies also to extracts in appendices if these are duplicated along with your report.

The selection of appropriate documents, deciding what questions to ask of documents, and problems of access need to be considered at an early stage in your work as they will affect the kind of information you collect and how you are able to use this.

2.3 USING DOCUMENTS OTHER THAN CLASSROOM RESOURCES

I mentioned above that a document, in the sense I'm using in this section, means virtually anything written down: local or national policy statements, government or LEA reports, examination board reports, newspaper articles, school brochures, schemes of work, minutes of meetings, letters, etc. Documents are a useful source of information about something you are not able to observe for yourself – perhaps events that occurred outside your own school, or before you began work on this project. In this case, they may provide a social or historical context for the work you wish to carry out. Documents may present a particular viewpoint – perhaps the 'official' view of a committee, or parents' views – that you wish to compare with information from another source. Documents may also be plans, or statements of intent (a lesson plan or a policy statement) that you can draw on alongside observations of practice.

Whatever kinds of documents you are interested in, it is important to bear in mind that they are not complete and impartial accounts of events. They may be deliberately designed to argue a certain case. Even when they seek to present a factual account they must necessarily be selective. You may be interested as much in what is not said as in what is included in the document.

MAKING NOTES ON DOCUMENTS

The most common way to use documents is simply to read them, noting down points of interest. Such notes will be relatively open-ended: your scrutiny of the documents will be guided by your research questions, but you won't have a pre-specified set of points to look out for. This sort of open-ended examination will provide qualitative information.

When making notes on documents it is important to distinguish between your notes on the *content* of documents, and any *comments* or *interpretations* that occur to you. A colleague said that she saw the value in this when watching someone else take notes at a seminar: he made two columns for his notes – a left-hand column for what the speaker said and a right-hand column for his own response:

> I now do this when making notes on documents, using two colours – one for noting the content and the other for my responses and interpretations. It's like having a dialogue with the document. It's

helped me become more critical in my reading and it also helps me relate what I'm reading to my research interests.

It's possible to draw on qualitative information in a variety of ways in your final report: you may wish to provide an account of relevant parts of the document in your own words, or to quote selected extracts, or to quote longer extracts, or the whole document if it is short (e.g., a letter) – perhaps subjecting this to a detailed commentary.

Example 2.2 comes from a published account of a study of English teaching. The researchers were interested in what constitutes the English curriculum in secondary schools, and how this varies between different schools. As well as carrying out classroom observation and interviewing pupils and teachers, the researchers examined the English syllabuses in use in several schools. In this extract, one of the researchers, Stephen Clarke, begins to characterize the different syllabuses.

Example 2.2 Using documents: the Downtown School syllabus

'Downtown School syllabus espouses a 'growth' model of language and learning and is concerned to show how different kinds of lessons in reading, writing and speaking can work together, each having a beneficial effect upon the others and leading to a broad improvement in language competence by pupils:

The development of language will arise out of exploration in reading, writing and speaking.

The actual content items to be learnt comprise a traditional list of writing skills such as spelling, paragraphing and punctuation, as well as speech skills, but these are not to be imposed on pupils in a way that would make them seem an alien or culturally strange set of requirements:

The aim should not be to alienate the child from the language he [*sic*] has grown up with, but to enlarge his repertoire so that he can meet new demands and situations and use standard forms when they are needed, a process which cannot be achieved overnight.'

(Clarke, 1984, pp. 154–5)

ASSIGNING INFORMATION FROM DOCUMENTS TO CATEGORIES

It is possible to examine the content of documents in a more structured way, looking out for certain categories of information. This method of examining documents is sometimes known as 'content analysis'. It provides quantitative information. Many studies of the media have involved content analysis. Researchers may, for instance, scan newspapers to see how often women and men are mentioned, and in what contexts. They may categorize the different contexts – reports of crime; sport; politics, etc. It is then possible to count the number of times women, and men, are represented in different contexts.

It is unlikely you will wish to subject educational documents to a quantitative analysis, but this method is mentioned here for the sake of completeness. Quantitative analyses have frequently been applied to classroom resources (see below).

2.4 DEALING WITH PUBLISHED FACTS AND FIGURES

You may be interested in statistical information collected either nationally or locally. Some researchers have used published statistics as their only or their main source of evidence. For example, it is possible to compare aspects of educational provision in different LEAs in England and Wales by drawing on statistics published by the authorities or by the DES. (Section 6 of this Handbook lists several sources of national statistics.)

INTERPRETING STATISTICAL INFORMATION

Published statistics are often presented in the form of tables. These are not always easy to use. They may not contain quite the information you want, or they may contain too much information for your purposes. Examples 2.3 and 2.4 below show two tables that provide information on the number of pupils that stay on at school after the age of 16, but they provide slightly different information and they present the information in different ways. Both examples give separate figures for pupils of different ages (16-, 17- and 18-year-olds or 16-, 17-, 18- and 19-year-olds). Both allow comparisons to be made between girls and boys, and between staying-on rates in different years (but not the same set of years).

Example 2.3 covers the whole of Great Britain (England, Scotland and Wales but not Northern Ireland). The table presents staying-on rates in the context of 16- to 18-year-olds' 'educational and economic activities'. It allows comparisons to be made between the percentage of young people who stay on at school and the percentages who are engaged in other activities. But different types of school are grouped together. (It is not clear whether the table includes special schools.)

Example 2.4 covers England and Wales. It gives figures for 16-, 17-, 18- and 19-year-olds as a percentage of the relevant cohort of 15-year-olds one, two, three or four years earlier. It does not give any information about what young people who aren't at school are doing. But it does distinguish between maintained and non-maintained schools. It also explicitly excludes information from special schools.

If you wanted to know, say, the percentage of 16-year-olds who stay on at school nationally, the tables give similar figures: 31 per cent in 1988 in Example 2.3 and 30.1 per cent in 1988 in Example 2.4. (The slight discrepancy may be because of differences in the samples drawn on in each table.) But Example 2.3 masks large overall differences between maintained and non-maintained schools, and a small gender difference in maintained schools that is reversed in non-maintained schools. Both tables mask regional variation in staying-on rates (another DES table gives this information) and variation between pupils from different social groups – except in so far as maintained and non-maintained schools are an indicator of this.

When drawing on published statistics, therefore, you need to check carefully what information is given. Does this have any limitations in relation to your own research questions? Is there another table that presents more appropriate information (e.g., information from a more appropriate sample of people or institutions)? It is important to look at any commentary offered by those who have compiled the statistics. This will enable you to see the basis on which information has been collected – what has been included and what has not. If you are using local (e.g. school or local authority) statistics it may be possible to obtain further information on these from the relevant school/local authority department.

DRAWING ON PUBLISHED STATISTICS IN YOUR REPORT

You may wish to reproduce published statistics in your report, but if these are complex tables it is probably better to simplify them in some way, to highlight the information that is relevant to your own research. Alternatively, you may wish to quote just one or two relevant figures.

Example 2.5 shows how the table in Example 2.3 has been adapted and simplified by June Statham and Donald Mackinnon (1991), authors of a book on educational facts and figures designed for Open University students. Statham and Mackinnon present information from the original table as a histogram. They give combined figures for girls and boys to show overall staying-on rates. But they import information from another table to enable them to make a comparison between 1988 and 1980. They comment: 'During the 1980s, there has been a

Example 2.3 How many pupils stay on at school after the age of 16?

Table showing 'educational and economic activities of 16- to 18-year-olds'

POST-COMPULSORY PARTICIPATION RATES

Educational and economic activities of 16-18 year olds(1)

TABLE 21

Great Britain

	16			17			18			16-18 age range		
	Boys	Girls	Total	Boys	Girls	Total	Boys	Girls	Total	Boys	Girls	Total
	January 1988			January 1988			January 1988			January 1988		
Population (thousands)(2)	435	412	847	429	408	837	441	422	863	1305	1242	2547
Percentage of the age group												
In Full-time education												
School	30	32	31	19	19	19	3	2	2	17	18	17
Further education(3)	13	19	16	10	16	13	6	7	6	10	14	12
Higher education(3)	-	-	-	1	1	1	10	9	10	4	4	4
In Employment (outside YTS)(4)	20	20	20	34	39	36	66	71	68	40	44	42
On YTS(5)	29	21	25	25	17	21	1	1	1	18	13	16
Unemployed(6)	9	7	8	11	9	10	14	11	13	12	9	10
Of which in part-time day education (included in employed/unemployed)(7)	7	3	5	10	4	7	13	5	9	10	4	7

	16-18 age range											
	Boys	Girls	Total	Boys	Girls	Total	Boys	Girls	Total	Boys	Girls	Total
	January 1976			January 1981			January 1986			January 1987		
Population (thousands)(2)	1231	1178	2409	1405	1343	2748	1349	1284	2633	1319	1257	2577
Percentage of the age group												
In Full-time education												
School	16	16	16	16	17	16	17	17	17	17	17	17
Further education(3)	7	9	8	7	11	9	8	13	11	8	13	11
Higher education(3)	3	3	3	3	3	3	4	3	3	4	3	4
In Employment (outside YTS)(4)	65	66	65	54	52	53	42	44	43	42	44	43
On YTS(5)	-	-	-	5	5	5	12	9	10	14	11	12
Unemployed(6)	9	7	8	14	12	13	17	13	15	15	12	14
Of which in part-time day education (included in employed/unemployed)(7)	22	5	14	19	5	13	12	5	8	11	4	8

(1) Age as at 31 August of the preceding year.
(2) Some 10 per cent of the age group attend evening only courses. These cannot be classified by education/employment status and are not shown separately in this table. See Table 22.
(3) Full-time and sandwich excluding private education outside school. Excludes those on YTS within colleges.
(4) Including in 1976 and 1981 the unregistered unemployed and those who were neither employed nor seeking work (eg because of domestic responsibilities) and for 1986-88 those who were seeking work but not claiming benefit and those who are neither employed nor seeking work.
(5) Including those on YOP in 1976 and 1981 and those in further education establishments attending YTS/YOP courses.
(6) Registered unemployed in 1976 and 1981 and claimant unemployed in 1986-88 (DES estimates).
(7) Public sector part-time day study only, excluding those attending YTS courses. In addition, DES estimate of employer provision outside Local Education Authority colleges or YTS is 4% of 16 year olds and 6% of 16-18 year olds in 1983-84 (source: Department of Employment: New Entrant Survey). The majority of part-time day students are in employment but some are receiving unemployment benefit under the "21 hour rule".

(Source: Government Statistical Service, 1990, Table 21)

Example 2.4 How many pupils stay on at school after the age of 16?

Table showing 'percentage of pupils remaining at school beyond the statutory leaving age by type of school'

TABLE A14/89

PERCENTAGE OF PUPILS REMAINING AT SCHOOL BEYOND THE STATUTORY LEAVING AGE(1)

(A) BY TYPE OF SCHOOL: TIME SERIES 1985 TO 1989(2)

	Maintained schools			Non-maintained schools			All schools		
	Boys	Girls	Total	Boys	Girls	Total	Boys	Girls	Total
Age at 31 August of preceding year									
Aged 16									
1985	25.2	28.3	26.7	75.0	66.6	71.2	28.8	30.7	29.7
1986	25.5	28.3	26.9	76.1	68.1	72.5	29.1	30.8	29.9
1987	25.0	27.5	26.3	75.6	69.8	72.9	28.8	30.3	29.5
1988	25.4	27.9	26.6	75.6	71.7	73.8	29.3	30.9	30.1
1989	27.8	31.2	29.5	78.6	73.6	76.3	31.9	34.2	33.0
Aged 17									
1985	16.0	17.2	16.6	59.8	50.6	55.6	19.1	19.3	19.2
1986	15.9	16.7	16.3	59.7	52.4	56.4	19.0	18.9	18.9
1987	15.9	16.7	16.3	60.7	54.9	58.1	19.1	19.1	19.1
1988	15.7	16.4	16.0	63.2	57.6	60.7	19.2	19.1	19.1
1989	16.7	17.9	17.3	64.7	59.6	62.3	20.4	20.7	20.6
Aged 18									
1985	2.3	1.9	2.1	7.4	5.7	6.7	2.6	2.1	2.4
1986	2.3	1.9	2.1	7.9	6.5	7.3	2.7	2.1	2.4
1987	2.2	1.7	1.9	7.9	6.9	7.4	2.6	2.1	2.3
1988	2.0	1.7	1.8	8.0	7.0	7.6	2.4	2.0	2.2
1989	2.0	1.9	2.0	8.5	7.7	8.1	2.5	2.2	2.4
Aged 19 and over									
1985	0.2	0.1	0.2	2.0	1.6	1.8	0.3	0.2	0.3
1986	0.2	0.1	0.2	1.8	1.6	1.7	0.3	0.2	0.3
1987	0.2	0.2	0.2	2.6	2.1	2.4	0.4	0.3	0.3
1988	0.2	0.2	0.2	2.5	2.3	2.4	0.3	0.3	0.3
1989	0.2	0.2	0.2	2.8	2.3	2.6	0.4	0.3	0.4

(1) Pupils aged 16,17,18,and 19 remaining at school in January of each year expressed as a percentage of the relevent cohort aged 15 one,two,three and four years earlier respectively - see paragraphs 19-21 of the explanatory notes.
(2) Excluding special schools.

(Source: DES, 1990, Table A14/89)

slight increase in the percentages of young people over 16 staying on at school.' The comparison is clear and easy to understand when information is presented in this form. Although Statham and Mackinnon have chosen to compare different years, other comparisons might be made if suitable information is available – one might compare the national picture with a particular region, for instance.

Statistical information may be presented in several other ways. Ways of presenting numerical information you have collected yourself are discussed in Section 5 of this Part. These could equally well be used for adapting information from published sources.

Any table, or set of figures, is bound to be partial. You increase this partiality when you further select and simplify published statistics for inclusion in a report. June Statham and Donald Mackinnon issue some cautions on interpreting the educational statistics they have compiled from several sources:

> First, and most obviously, [our] book is bound to contain errors. Some of these may come from our sources; others, alas, will be all our own work. We hope that these are few and trivial, but we are resigned to accepting that a book of this character will have some.
>
> Secondly, we have inevitably made choices about which facts to include, and which to leave out. Some of these have been slightly forced choices, because of gaps and limitations in the available data.

But much more often, we have had to decide what we considered most significant and telling from an embarrassment of information. This is where interpretation is unavoidable, and prejudice a very real danger. We cannot, of course, claim to be unprejudiced; people are not normally aware of their own prejudices. What we can and do say is that we have never knowingly excluded or modified any information in order to favour our own beliefs, values or political preferences.

Thirdly, even the categories in which data are presented depend on controversial judgements, and are open to unintended distortion. There are different ways of defining social class, for example, or of identifying ethnic groups, and these can lead to very different pictures of the class structure or ethnic composition of the country, and of the relationship between class or ethnicity and, say, educational attainment ... Choosing categories for presenting the facts is fraught with uncertainty and controversy.

Finally, we would like to warn against leaping too quickly to what may seem obvious interpretations of facts and their relationships, such as conclusions about cause and effect. Above all, we should be cautious about accepting plausible interpretations of one fact or set of facts in isolation, without at least checking that our interpretation fits in with other relevant information.

(Statham and Mackinnon, 1991, p. 2)

Not all those who use and compile statistics are so cautious or so candid about the limitations of facts and figures.

Example 2.5 How many pupils stay on at school after the age of 16?

Histogram showing 'percentage of population staying on at school after 16, 1980 and 1988'

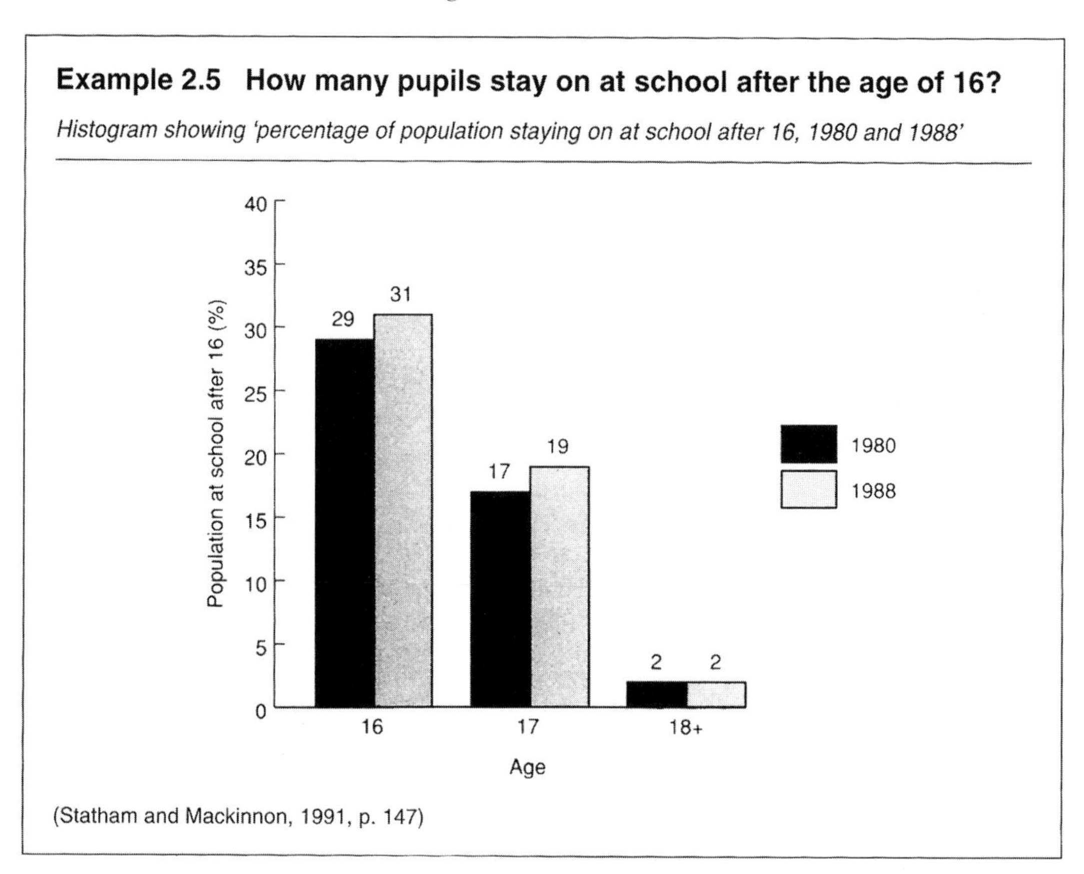

(Statham and Mackinnon, 1991, p. 147)

2.5 USING CLASSROOM RESOURCES

If your interest is in the curriculum, or in how children learn, you may wish to include an examination of the range of resources available in the classroom. The methods mentioned here have most frequently been applied to children's books in the classroom, but similar methods may be applied to other classroom resources (particularly print resources such as worksheets, posters, etc.) or resources in other areas (e.g., the school hall or library).

I mentioned at the beginning of this section that an examination of existing resources may be particularly relevant if you are interested in developing some aspect of the curriculum or school policy. Information about classroom resources may supplement information derived from other sources, such as observations of how children use the resources, or interviews to find out what children think of them. Children may themselves be involved in monitoring resources.

MAKING NOTES ON CLASSROOM RESOURCES

As with other documents, you may wish to scan classroom resources noting points of interest. This will be particularly appropriate if you wish to look at the teaching approach adopted, or at how certain issues are treated, without a specific set of categories to look for. You may have questions such as: How are people represented? How do textbooks deal with certain issues, such as environmental issues? What approach do they take to teaching a particular subject? How open-ended are tasks on worksheets? Do they give pupils scope to use their own initiative? These sorts of questions are probably best dealt with, at least initially, by open-ended scrutiny of the resources. This will provide qualitative information for your project.

You may wish to carry out a detailed analysis of a single book or resource item. Ciaran Tyndall was using the book *Comfort Herself* (Kaye, 1985) as a reader with a group of young secondary-school children. The book is about an 11-year-old girl with a white mother and a black Ghanaian father. Ciaran Tyndall became concerned about the imagery in the book, which she felt perpetuated cultural stereotypes. She made a careful examination of the text, as a prelude to preparing materials for her pupils to analyse it.

Among other things, Ciaran Tyndall's scrutiny revealed disparities between what she terms 'black imagery' and 'white imagery'. Example 2.6 shows how she documented this by selecting examples of images.

Example 2.6 Identifying 'black' and 'white' imagery in a children's story

Black imagery	*White imagery*
There were no streetlights and night was like a black blanket laid against the cottage windows.	Granny's hair was all fluffy and white round her head like a dandelion clock
Darkness creeping over the marsh like black water ... the window was a black square now.	Round white clouds like cherubs.
Palm tree tops which looked like great black spiders.	The cabin was bright white like vanilla ice-cream.
The black backdrop of an African night.	Achimota school – white buildings with graceful rounded doorways.
The citrus trees floated like black wreckage on a white sea.	As Comfort cleaned the cooking place, daubing white clay along it.
There was drumming now, a soft throbbing that was part of the Wanwangeri darkness.	The garri was made and stored away in a sack like white sand.

Comfort wrote in her diary pressing hard and dark.	Abla's smile flashed white.
The struts which supported it were riddled with black termite holes. burnt black shell	White clay was smeared round a deep cut on his leg ... his leg has been covered with a white bandage and he has been given pills white and gritty.
The anger in her grandmother's eyes, shining black like stones. Spare parts are Kalabule, black market.	Dry Leaf Fall' shone white on the bonnet of the lorry.

(Tyndall, 1988, p. 16)

As with other documents, notes on classroom resources should distinguish between what the resource says, or depicts, and how you interpret this. You will be able to draw on both sets of notes in your report. Ciaran Tyndall includes her tabulation of black and white imagery in an account of her study, alongside her interpretations of these images:

> The 'black' imagery is completely negative, used to convey feelings of fear or loneliness, ignorance or decay, whereas the 'white' imagery is always positive, carrying the sense of warmth, security, cleansing or healing.
>
> (Tyndall, 1988, p. 16)

ASSIGNING INFORMATION FROM CLASSROOM RESOURCES TO CATEGORIES

Classroom resources, or aspects of classroom resources, may, like other published documents, be allocated to a set of (pre-specified) categories. This provides quantitative information – you can count the number of books, or whatever, that fall into each category. Such an analysis may complement information you derive from a more open-ended examination.

As with other documents, it is possible to focus on any aspects of books or resources. Researchers may look at the printed text, or visual images, or both. They may be interested in the content of resources, in how information is presented, or in what tasks are required of readers. For instance, if you have examined worksheets in your class to see how far they encourage pupils to use their own initiative, you may decide that it is possible to allocate resources to one of three categories: 'contains only open-ended tasks'; 'contains a mixture of tightly-specified and open-ended tasks'; 'contains only tightly-specified tasks'. You may be able to combine the quantitative information you obtain from such an analysis with a qualitative account of the approach taken by some of the worksheets.

Books are often categorized using a more detailed checklist. Many published checklists have been produced to detect some form of imbalance in texts, such as gender, ethnic group or class imbalances. Example 2.7 shows a checklist devised by a group of teachers concerned about gender imbalances in modern languages textbooks.

Example 2.7 allows various numerical comparisons to be made between female and male characters. For instance, of 136 characters/examples in a textbook, 71 (52 per cent) may be male; 54 (40 per cent) female; and 11 (8 per cent) indeterminate. Giving results as percentages allows comparisons to be made between different books.

Many checklists rely on you making a judgement of some kind as was mentioned briefly above. This can be a problem as it may not be apparent why you are making a certain judgement, and someone else completing the same checklist may come to a different judgement. The checklist in Example 2.7 tries to solve this problem in two ways. First, it breaks down major categories into sub-categories that are more specific and more readily identifiable: 'subordination' is thus broken down into eight sub-categories. Secondly, it gives examples of those sub-categories thought to require further clarification: 'dependence' on another character is exemplified as 'Peter's secretary', 'John and his girlfriend', 'so and so's wife'. This makes it easier to check on the validity of the categories. Anyone else using the checklist, or a reader of a study based on this checklist, can see whether they think 'John and his girlfriend' actually is an example of women's dependence on men. It is also likely that these specific categories make the checklist relatively reliable so that two people using the checklist with the same book will reach a higher level of agreement on their results. You will still need to check on this, however, by piloting your checklist. (See also sub-section 1.6 on reliability and validity.)

It is best to pilot your checklist with a few books that represent the range you are interested in. Trying out your checklist in this way may reveal ambiguities in your categories or you may find the categories do not fit your data (so that you end up with a large set of items you cannot categorize, or that go into 'other'). You can check the reliability of categories by asking a colleague to help test your checklist, or by trying it out on the same book on two separate occasions. Finally, piloting will enable you to see if you are generating too much information. (This is a danger with the checklist in Example 2.7.) If you collect too much information it may be time-consuming to analyse.

2.6 REVIEWING METHODS

In this section I have discussed several ways in which you may draw on documents to provide evidence for your project. No documents provide perfect sources of evidence, and nor is any method of collecting evidence perfect. I shall summarize here the strengths and limitations of the methods I have referred to.

Example 2.7
Checklist to detect gender imbalances in modern languages textbooks

CHECKLIST 3

AN EXAMPLE OF SUBJECT-SPECIFIC CHECKLIST

MODERN LANGUAGES TEXT BOOKS
(Devised by a group working at the Modern Languages Teachers' Centre)

Name of school ....

Filled in by .... Date completed ....

Title of book/course ....
Chapter/unit/page reference ....
Publisher ....
Publication date ....
Name of reviewer ....

I SEXISM BY EXCLUSION OR OMISSION	F	M
(Are women or girls absent from texts or less represented than men or boys?)		
• Number of female characters or females mentioned in the texts		
• Number of male characters or males mentioned in the text		
ANONYMITY		
• Number of nameless females		
• Number of nameless males		
II SEXISM BY SUBORDINATION (Who has the more dominant role?)		
• Number of females initiating a conversation		
• Number of males initiating a conversation		
Taking 'Turn' in dialogues		
• Number of contributions made by females		
• Number of contributions made by males		
• Number of women dependent on men, e.g. Peter's secretary, John and his girlfriend, so and so's wife etc		
• Number of men dependent on women		
• Number of women mentioned in their own right, e.g. not as so and so's wife		
• Number of men mentioned in their own right		
Jobs and occupations		
• Number of women doing a paid job		
• Number of men doing a paid job		
• Number of women involved in housework or looking after children		
• Number of men doing housework or looking after the children		
• Number of women involved in intellectual activities		
• Number of men involved in intellectual activities		
• Number of women with a high status job or occupation		
• Number of men with a high status job or occupation		
III SEXISM BY DISTORTION		
• Number of females presented as being emotional, weepy, irrational, irresponsible, etc.		
• Number of males presented as being emotional, weepy, etc.		
• Number of females who have a passive or negative role, e.g. doing as they are told, appearing helpless, being mentioned for their looks rather than for their actions		
• Number of men who have a passive role		
• Number of females involved in physical activities: leisure and work, e.g. doing sports, driving cars, decorating the house, etc.		
Number of males involved in physical activities		
IV SEXISM BY DEGRADATION		
• Number of women presented as sex objects		
• Number of men presented as sex objects		
• Number of females shown as talking too much, chatting and wasting time		
• Number of males shown as talking too much, chatting and wasting time		
• Number of females presented as stupid, mindless, spending money carelessly etc		
• Number of males presented as stupid, mindless, spending money carelessly etc		
ANY EXAMPLES where women are shown as inferior to men, patronised by, e.g. 'Not bad for a girl', or 'sponging' off men		

(Myers, 1987, pp. 113–4)

DOCUMENTS AS A SOURCE OF EVIDENCE

Documents other than classroom resources

Evidence the document can provide	*Limitations*
Gives access to information you can't find more directly (e.g. by observation).	Will inevitably provide a partial account.
May provide a particular (authoritative?) viewpoint (e.g. an official statement).	May be biased.

Published facts and figures

Evidence the document can provide	*Limitations*
Provides numerical information – may provide a context for your own work.	Published tables are not always easy to use. They probably contain too much information that you need to select from and may not contain exactly the information you want.
Allows you to make comparisons between different contexts or different groups of people.	Information may be misleading. Need to check the basis of the statistics (how information was collected; from what sources; what is included and what is not) to ensure any comparison is valid.

Classroom resources

Evidence the document can provide	*Limitations*
Provides information on what is available for children to use – characteristics of resources.	Cannot tell you how resources are used, or how responded to by pupils – needs to be supplemented by other sources of evidence if this is of interest.

OPEN-ENDED SCRUTINY VERSUS CATEGORIZATION

In sub-sections 2.3 and 2.5, I distinguished between making open-ended notes on documents, which provides qualitative information; and categorizing documents, or aspects of documents, in some way, which normally provides quantitative information. Both types of method have advantages and limitations. I shall give their main features below.

Making open-ended notes

- Provides a general impression of the content, style, approach, etc. of the document.
- Allows you to take account of anything of interest that you spot.
- Particularly useful if you do not know what specific features to look out for, or do not want to be restricted to specific categories of information.
- You may draw on your notes to provide a summary of relevant parts of the document, or quote directly from the document to support points you wish to make.
- This sort of note-taking is selective, and two researchers with the same research questions may (legitimately) note down different things about a document.

- You need to check that you don't bias your account by, for instance, quoting something 'out of context' or omitting counter-evidence.

Assigning documents to categories

- Allows you to look out for certain specific features of the document that are relevant to your research question(s).
- Provides numerical information about a document (e.g. in a set of worksheets a certain proportion of tasks are 'open-ended' and a certain proportion 'tightly specified').
- Allows numerical comparison between different documents (e.g. one set of worksheets has a higher proportion of 'open-ended' tasks than another).
- You will miss anything of interest that doesn't form part of your category system.
- Some category systems can be applied reliably so that two researchers will produce a similar analysis of the same document; where personal judgement is involved, this tends to lessen the reliability of the category system.
- Assigning information to categories abstracts the information from its context. You need to take account of this in interpreting your results (e.g. you may detect a numerical imbalance between female and male characters, but interpreting this depends upon contextual factors).

Although I have contrasted these two ways of collecting information, I stressed earlier that the two methods may be used together to provide complementary information about a document.

FURTHER READING

ALTHEIDE, D.L (1996) *Qualitative Media Analysis (Qualitative Research Methods Paper) Volume 38*, Thousand Oaks (Calif.), Sage.

> This book is a short guide to media studies and includes advice on content and document analysis of newspapers, magazines, television programmes and other forms of media.

DENSCOMBE, M. (1998) *The Good Research Guide*, Buckingham, Open University Press.

> This book is written for undergraduate, postgraduate and professional students in education who need to undertake reearch projects. It offers a pragmatic approach particularly suitable for those interested in how to use research methods for a specific piece of small-scale research and for whom time is extremely limited. It has a chapter on documentary analysis and useful checklists.

DENZIN, N.K. and LINCOLN, Y.S. (eds.) (1998) *Strategies of Qualitative Inquiry*, Thousand Oaks (Calif.), Sage.

> This book covers case study, ethnography, grounded theory, participative inquiry and much more. Chapter 9 on 'Historical social science' offers an interesting account of using historical documentation in research.

HITCHCOCK, G. and HUGHES, D. (1989) *Research and the Teacher: a qualitative introduction to school-based research*, London, Routledge.

> This book provides useful guidance on various aspects of practitioner research. It includes a discussion of 'life history' and historical approaches to documentary sources.

ILEA (1985) *Everyone Counts: looking for bias and insensitivity in primary mathematics materials*, London, ILEA Learning Resources Branch.

As the title suggests, this book provides guidance on analysing mathematics texts, focusing on various forms of 'bias'. Many published checklists for analysing published material focus on bias of one form or another (gender, 'race' or class).

It is worth enquiring locally (contacting, perhaps, local authority equal opportunities advisers or subject advisers) for guidance that relates to your own concerns.

LEE, R. M. (2000) *unobtrusive Methods in Social Research,* Buckingham, Open University Press.

This book describes all kinds of unobtrusive ways of collecting data such as obtaining archival material and other forms of documentary evidence.

MYERS, K. (1992) *Genderwatch! Self-assessment schedules for use in schools,* London, SCDC Publications. Available from Genderwatch Publications, PO Box 423, Amersham, Bucks, HP8 4UJ.

Contains checklists and schedules for looking at all aspects of school and classroom life.

3 GETTING INFORMATION FROM PEOPLE

3.1 INTRODUCTION

This section examines how you can collect evidence for your project by obtaining information from people and recording it in some way. It is possible to obtain information from people in a number of ways. Sometimes it can be collected directly, as is the case with individual and group interviews; sometimes it can be collected indirectly by asking people to keep diaries or to complete questionnaires.

As you saw in Section 1, in order to provide evidence for your project, information needs to be collected and recorded systematically. Some of the methods suggested here may require little more than formalizing something which is already part of your teaching role or administrative routine. Others require more time – perhaps time to liaise with colleagues. You may also require additional resources, such as a tape recorder or a computer. The method(s) you select will depend on the nature of your research and what is practicable in your circumstances.

3.2 DECIDING WHAT INFORMATION YOU NEED AND HOW BEST TO OBTAIN IT

You may already have some of the information you require, derived from informal discussions with your colleagues and/or from documentary sources. In deciding what new information you require, there are four points to consider: *what type* of information is required; *whom* you will approach to obtain this information; *what to tell* your informants about your study; and *how* you are going to get the information.

This sub-section considers the first three points, later sub-sections discuss how to set about obtaining information from adults and children.

WHAT TYPE OF INFORMATION IS REQUIRED?

Section 1 identified three different types of inquiry: exploratory, explanatory, and predictive. In this section I shall show how specific research questions relate to the purpose of your study and the type of information you need to collect. Thinking about the relationship between the purpose of your study, the information you need to collect and your research questions will help with the design of your research activities. As was pointed out in Section 1, inquiries may have more than one purpose, and the distinction between exploratory, explanatory and predictive inquiries is not always clear cut. In the examples which follow, I shall pretend, for the sake of clarity, that it is clear cut.

Example 3.1 Staff and school development

The head of an inner-city primary school wanted to initiate discussions about formulating a school development plan (SDP). She thought that this was an important step because SDPs are a recognized means of managing change in schools faced with innovations in curriculum and assessment and with the introduction of local financial management of schools (LMS). The head began with a brainstorm by the staff. This raised staff development as a major concern. As a result of this consultation the head decided to draw up a self-completion questionnaire that was given to each member of the staff and which sought information about each individual's needs for professional development.

You can see from this example that the purpose of the head's inquiry is to produce a school development plan. When staff raised their professional development as a concern, the head came up with a specific question: 'What are our priorities for staff development in relation to the SDP?' In order to answer this question she needs to find some way of surveying the attitudes and opinions of all her staff. Individual interviews would be very time-consuming and would require a great deal of timetabling and organization. Her solution is to design a questionnaire which staff can complete in their own time. Questionnaires are discussed in sub-section 3.5.

Now let's look at an example of a predictive study. You will remember from Section 1 that predictive studies allow one to test hypotheses about causal relationships. Example 3.2 describes a predictive study carried out by a group of advisory teachers responsible for co-ordinating induction programmes for probationary teachers. They were recruited by their LEA to investigate why some school-based induction programmes were more successful than others.

Example 3.2 What makes school-based induction effective?

An induction scheme had been in operation within the local authority for five years. An earlier authority-wide survey of probationers had indicated that probationary teachers expressed a high measure of satisfaction with the provision made for them by teachers' centres but that the provision within schools was much less satisfactory and experience was much more variable. It was apparent that probationers judged some aspects of school-based induction as being more important than others. One important factor was whether or not the probationer obtained a regular release from teaching and another one was thought to be connected with the role of the 'teacher-tutor' responsible for facilitating induction within the school. Other factors were also identified, such as whether the probationers were on temporary or permanent contracts. The induction co-ordinators needed to find out more about the relative importance of these different factors. They decided to conduct in-depth interviews with a new sample of probationers from schools in their authority. They also decided to supplement the information they gained from these interviews with their own observations in these probationers' schools.

This example shows how information resulting from an initial exploratory study (the authority-wide survey), can lead to a more focused predictive inquiry. The induction co-ordinators were able to formulate a specific hypothesis: 'Successful school-based induction programmes depend first on probationary teachers being allowed a significant amount of release time, and secondly on them establishing a good relationship with their teacher tutor'. If this hypothesis held good for a new sample of probationers, then the induction co-ordinators would be able to make some specific recommendations to their LEA.

In order to test this hypothesis they needed to establish whether the majority of their new sample of probationers identified the same factors as the probationers taking part in the original survey. As a further test the co-ordinators decided to check the information they obtained from the interviews with information from their own observations. Unlike Example 3.1, where it was not feasible for one head to interview all staff, in this example time-consuming, in-depth interviews were appropriate, as there was a team of people to do them. Sub-section 3.4 gives advice on conducting interviews and designing interview schedules. You can find out more about observation in Section 4.

Finally, let's take a look at an example of an explanatory study (this example comes from an ILEA report, *Developing Evaluation in the LEA*).

Example 3.3 Why are pupils dissatisfied and disaffected?

'[Miss Ray, the teacher with responsibility for BTEC courses at Kenley Manor, was extremely concerned about the fourth-year pupils.] Throughout the year on the BTEC course, [these pupils] were dissatisfied and disaffected. At the suggestion of the evaluation consultant, the deputy head agreed to relieve Miss Ray for four afternoon sessions to investigate the causes of pupils' dissatisfaction and to suggest changes. Miss Ray was to visit a nearby school to look into their BTEC course where it was supposedly very popular. Miss Ray, who had often complained about 'directed time' and lack of management interest in the BTEC course, got so involved in the project that she gave a lot of her own time (about 45 minutes interviewing each pupil after school in addition to group discussions and meetings with staff) and produced a report with some recommendations to the senior management. The main grievance of the BTEC pupils was the low status of the course as perceived by other 4th years. The room allocated to BTEC was previously used by the special needs department and two of their teachers were probationers and according to one pupil had 'no control' over them.'

(ILEA Research and Statistics Branch, 1990, pp. 10–11)

Miss Ray's study sought an explanation of why the BTEC course was not popular so that she could make appropriate recommendations for change to the senior management team in her school. Miss Ray obviously needed to sample pupils' opinions on the course. Individual interviews with pupils in her own school provided her with this information. To gain a broader picture, however, she was advised to compare her school's course with a similar, but more successful, course at another school. She needed to find out how the other school's BTEC course was taught and group discussions with staff provided this information. Sub-section 3.4 gives advice on interviewing children and discusses how to manage and record group interviews.

When you have decided what sort of information to collect, you will need to think about the types of questions to ask your informants. In this section, I shall make a distinction between *open-ended questions,* which allow your informants to give you information that they feel is relevant, and *closed questions,* which impose a limitation on the responses your informants can make. This is a useful distinction, though it isn't always clear cut (people don't always respond as you intend them to). Open-ended questions will provide you with *qualitative* information. Closed questions may provide information that you can *quantify* in some way (you can say how many people favour a certain option, or you can make a numerical comparison between different groups of informants).

Information that you collect in the form of diaries or logs kept by others, and much of the information from face-to-face interviews, is likely to be qualitative. It is possible to design questionnaires so that you quantify the information they provide if you wish. (See also 'The qualitative/quantitative distinction' in sub-section 1.5.)

WHO WILL PROVIDE THE INFORMATION?

As you can see from the three examples discussed above, deciding who can provide you with information is as important as deciding what information you need. You would have to make similar decisions in all three cases about who to approach, how many people to approach, when to approach them and so on.

You first need to identify who has the information that you require, then to obtain access. Setting up interviews, arranging group meetings, and getting permission to interview pupils or staff in another school can eat into valuable research time before you have even collected any information. You will need to consider this alongside the time which you have available for data collection (carrying out interviews, chasing up questionnaires and so on), which is also time-consuming. You may need to limit your study and not collect all the information that you would ideally like.

Consider carefully whether the compromises you consider will undermine either the validity or reliability of your research. In connection with the former you have to be assured that the information you obtain does address the questions you pose. How can you be sure of this? You will need to weigh up various approaches at this stage. One approach may be more time-consuming than another, but the information may be more valid. Do not compromise where the validity of your study is at risk.

As far as the reliability of the information is concerned, you need to be sure that your informants are representative of the population you are investigating. If you feel you might be compromising the reliability of the data by covering too wide a population, limit your research by focusing on one particular group. It is important that you have a sufficient number in your sample if you wish to make general claims that apply to a larger population. Make a note of any limitations in the size and nature of your sample at the stage of data collection and be sure to take these into account when you come to the analysis and writing your report. If, for example, you can only approach a limited number of people for information you will have to be very tentative about your findings.

When deciding whom to approach, refer back to your research question(s). In Example 3.1 above, you can see how important it would be to have the initial reactions of *all* members of the staff to the formation of a school development plan, and I discussed why questionnaires were a more appropriate means of data collection in this case.

In Example 3.2, there would need to be a sufficiently large number of probationers in the study to be able to make generalizations about the probationers' experience of induction with any degree of confidence. It would also be important for those selected to be representative of the total population of probationers. If the intention was to compare the experience of different groups of probationers, for example probationers in primary and secondary schools, it would be necessary to select a sample representative of both these sectors.

In Examples 3.1 and 3.2, identifying who to ask for information was straightforward. In Example 3.3, however, it was important for the teacher concerned to identify key informants both inside and outside her school. She was aided by her local evaluation consultant who was able to tell her about a nearby school where the BTEC course was popular with pupils. Sometimes it is relatively easy to find out who is likely to be of help to you just by asking around. If you draw a blank with informal contacts, however, you may find that key people can be identified by looking through policy documents, records, and lists of the names of members of various committees. Section 6 gives advice on how to get access to documentary information, and also gives the names and addresses of a number of national educational organizations.

WHAT TO TELL PEOPLE

Collecting information from people raises ethical issues which need to be considered from the outset. Whether you can offer a guarantee of confidentiality about the information you are requesting will influence the presentation of your findings. Some points to consider are:

- *Should you tell people what your research is really about?* Bound up with this question is your desire to be honest about your research interest. At the same time, however, you do not want to influence or bias the information which people give you. Sometimes informants, particularly pupils in school, think there are 'right' answers to interview questions. One way of getting over this is to make a very general statement about the focus of your research before the interview and then to share your findings with your informants at a later stage.
- *Should you identify the sources of your information when you write up your research?* In Example 3.2, the study of probationary teachers, it was fairly straightforward to offer a guarantee of confidentiality to those who participated: large numbers of probationers were involved and anonymity could be ensured. Where practitioners are doing research within their own institution, as in Example 3.3, guaranteeing anonymity and confidentiality can be more of a problem. In this example, the names of the teacher and school have been changed, but you can imagine that in a local context it would be fairly easy to identify people and institutions. One way of dealing with this problem is to show your informants your record of what they have said, tell them the context in which you want to use it and seek their consent to that use. In discussing your interpretation of the data with them you will be able to check your understanding of the situation with theirs. Any comments that they make may also furnish you with additional information.

Deciding what information you need, who to ask and what degree of confidentiality you can offer informants will affect how you plan your research. Try to make some *preliminary* decisions on these points before reading the sub-sections that follow.

3.3 KEEPING DIARIES

Section 1 discussed how practitioner-researchers can use research diaries to record their own observations and reflections. It is also possible to get other people to keep diaries or logs over a set period of time and to use these written accounts as a source of data. This method relies very heavily on the co-operation of the informants. Its attraction as a method of data collection is that it can provide quite detailed information about situations which you may not have easy access to, such as someone else's classroom. Burgess gives some useful guidance as to how diaries in particular might be used as research instruments:

> ... Researchers might ... ask informants to keep diaries about what they do on particular days and in particular lessons. Teachers and pupils could be asked to record the activities in which they engage and the people with whom they interact. In short, what they do (and do not do) in particular social situations. In these circumstances, subjects of the research become more than observers and informants: they are co-researchers as they keep chronological records of their activities.

> The diarists (whether they are teachers or pupils) will need to be given a series of instructions to write a diary. These might take the form of notes and suggestions for keeping a continuous record that answers the questions: When? Where? What? Who? Such questions help to focus down the observations that can be recorded. Meanwhile, a diary may be sub-divided into chronological periods within the day so that records may be kept for the morning, the afternoon and the evening. Further sub-divisions can be made in respect of diaries directed towards activities that occur within the school and classroom. Here, the day may be sub-divided into the divisions of the formal timetable with morning, afternoon and lunch breaks. Indeed within traditional thirty-five or forty-minute lessons further sub-divisions can be made in respect of the activities that occur within particular time zones.
>
> (Burgess, 1984, pp. 202–203)

The form the diary takes (whether it is highly structured, partially structured, or totally unstructured) and what other instructions are given to the informant depends on what is appropriate in relation to your research question(s).

Often, asking people to keep a log or record of their activities can be just as useful to you, and not as time-consuming for them, as asking for a diary. Logs can provide substantial amounts of information. They tend to be organized chronologically, and can detail the course and number of events over brief periods of time (a day or a week), or they can provide less detailed records over longer time intervals (a term or even a whole year). Examples 3.4 and 3.5 illustrate some possible uses for diaries and logs.

Example 3.5 (drawn from Enright, 1981, pp. 37–51) shows how a diary can be used to explore certain phenomena in detail. It was not desirable in this instance to be prescriptive about what should be recorded or to impose any structure on the diary. This diary was kept by an individual teacher for his own use but the observations were shared with another teacher who also taught the class.

Example 3.4 Using a staff log to support a home–school liaison project

A junior school (with 130 children in six classes) had obtained an INSET grant of £1,000 for a one-year project entitled 'home–school liaison' within the school development plan. There was a history of lack of liaison with parents and the teaching staff were aware that this needed to be rectified. The head hoped that the liaison proposed would bring about changes in other areas of the school. The school had a stable teaching staff but there had been many changes at management level. There was some discontent, discouragement and disunity among the teaching staff.

Staff kept a log for one year in which they recorded initiatives designed to involve parents in school life (shown in Figure 2). Positive and negative reactions were also recorded and discussed. The log provided the staff with a cumulative record which helped the reviewing, planning and formative evaluation of the project.

Example 3.5 Keeping a diary to share with a colleague

The teacher kept a diary, written up in considerable detail every evening, over a seven-week period at the beginning of the summer term. He repeated the exercise the following year, for the same period with the same class. He shared the information with another teacher who taught the same class and who added her own comments.

The detailed information recorded in the diaries enabled the teachers to explore questions and illuminated key issues which enabled some conclusions to be reached. For example, some insight was gained as to how good discussion among children can be effected.

2 May	appointment of teacher with special responsibilities (incentive A) for SDP. She will undertake 3 hours home visiting weekly and co-ordinate all the work.
4 May	social evening: parents, teacher, governors and friends. Discussion (informal): development planned. shared reading. friends association (including community).
June - July	6 Wednesday afternoons. Topic: Olympic games. children split across ages into 8 groups with a teacher. parents invited to join us each week.
Activities offered:	fresco production, computer skills, flags and design, sports and athletics, gymnastic dance, science themes and construction skills. history of Olympic games and sportswear design. sports equipment and rules (practical and art).
19 July	Consultant Evaluator met full staff for initial review of progress with SDP. SDP as part of full school learning. priority to set up a new room for parents. positive spin-off of shared open afternoons. Children had enjoyed these. Discussion about the importance of strategies to bring parents into school - to develop a coherent and common approach to the children's learning.
October - November	6 open afternoons with cross-school groupings and parents invited. Skills: wood work. computer skills. puppet making. patch-work. cookery. art. model construction.

Autumn term: Development of shared-reading scheme. Work on class reading corners. Meetings with parents. Home visiting continued throughout the term.

13 October:	Consultant Evaluator met head teacher and deputy head. Objective discussion on events so far. Problem - of involving parents. slow pace of change. facilitating staff reflections.
26 January	Consultant Evaluator met head teacher and deputy head. Thoughts about National Curriculum and overall long term planning across curriculum areas. what has been achieved/learned? where do we focus next? has the quality of education been improved for the children? has the SDP contributed to needs of staff/school/wider community.

Figure 2 Part of the school's log.

In both of these examples the log and diary were kept over a considerable period of time, and yielded a lot of valuable information. Diaries and logs do not have to be kept for long periods in order to be useful, however. Asking people to keep a record over a few days or a couple of weeks can be just as revealing. Also, it may already be the practice in your school for teachers to keep *informal* day-to-day records of children's progress or what happens in their classroom. Gaining access to these accounts and just looking at a limited sample over a week or so can provide you with a great deal of information. *Formal* written records, such as developmental guides or observations made of children's behaviour, are highly confidential, and you will probably need to seek formal permission in order to use them as a source of evidence.

Older children may also be asked to keep diaries. In Example 3.3, Miss Ray could have asked a selected number of her BTEC pupils to keep diaries of what happened during their lesson times as an alternative to interviewing them. As with all practitioner research, it is important to respect people's rights to anonymity and confidentiality when asking them to share their diaries and logs with you. This is just as important a principle when dealing with children as when dealing with adults.

3.4 FACE-TO-FACE INTERVIEWING

Interviewing is one of the most popular methods of obtaining information from people, and researchers frequently have to weigh up the advantages and disadvantages of using interviews as opposed to questionnaires. In general, the attraction of the interview is that it is a two-way process which allows you to interact with the informant(s), thus facilitating a more probing investigation than could be undertaken with a questionnaire. The use of individual interviews, however, is very time-consuming.

I set out below some general advice on the use of interviews, whether individual or group. The approach you adopt will depend on the nature of your research questions and the time and facilities that you have available.

INDIVIDUAL INTERVIEWS

When you interview someone you are establishing a relationship with them, however briefly. Interviews are not simply a means of extracting 'pure' information from someone, or eliciting their 'real' beliefs and attitudes. What your informant tells you will depend upon their perceptions of you and of your inquiry, upon how they interpret your questions, and upon how they wish to present themselves. This is not to suggest that your informant is deceitful, but that they will provide you with the version of the information that they think is appropriate.

With this qualification, it is possible to provide some practical guidance on planning and conducting interviews.

Designing the interview schedule

1 First, set out the information you require. Depending on your research question, this may be a very detailed list or it may simply be some broad areas which you expect to cover in the interview (an *aide-mémoire*).

2 Place the information or areas in some logical sequence. Begin with a non-threatening question which will help to put the interviewee at ease. Leave the more sensitive questions to the end.

3 Decide on a preamble which will tell your informant what the research is about, and say how you anticipate using the information. If you are able to do so, give a guarantee about confidentiality. Whether you can do this or not you should in any case offer the interviewee the opportunity to see either your transcript (if you are using a tape recorder) or that part of your report which uses the information they have provided. At the end of the interview ask the interviewee whether there is anything they would

like to add to what they have said. Also, ask whether there is anything further that they would like to ask you about the study, thank them for their co-operation, and tell them when you will be in touch again to let them know the outcome.

4 Consider the phrasing of the questions. Do not use 'leading' questions. Use language which is easily understood by the informant(s). Do not use multiple questions. Only address one question at a time.

For example, a leading question might be: 'How often do you punish your pupils for late attendance?' A more appropriate non-leading version of this question would be, 'How do you deal with problems of late attendance in your classroom?' An example of a multiple question would be, 'Does your child do any writing at home, and if so what do you do when she or he asks you how to spell a word?' This question would be much better dealt with in two parts, 'Does your child do any writing at home?' and 'What do you do when your child asks you how to spell a word?'

5 Decide whether to use open-ended or closed questions or a combination of the two. Closed questions limit the range and type of answer that people can give. Often people are asked to choose one of a set of pre-determined options as an answer to the question. For example, a survey of how English primary school teachers plan their work might include the following question:

'When planning your work for the term do you:

(a) first choose which national curriculum statements of attainment you wish to cover and then plan your work round them?

(b) plan your work first and then fit the statements of attainment to your chosen activities or topic?

Neither of these?'

Because closed questions limit the range of possible answers, analysing the information you collect is much easier than when people have given you a wide variety of answers to each question. This can be important if you have to interview a large number of people. The other side of the coin is, of course, that the alternatives you provide may not contain answers which reflect your interviewee's attitudes, opinions and practice. Your interviewee may choose the option which most nearly matches their viewpoint, or they may choose an option like (c) above. In either case, the validity of your interview data is at risk, because you are failing to get some information people would provide if they had the opportunity.

An open-ended version of the question above might be phrased:

> 'When planning your work for each term, how do you make provision for covering the appropriate national curriculum statements of attainment?'

Open-ended questions have several advantages. People are free to respond as they wish, and to give as much detail as they feel is appropriate. Where their answers are not clear the interviewer can ask for clarification; and more detailed and accurate answers should build up a more insightful and valid picture of the topic. Open-ended interviews are, however, likely to take longer than those based on a series of closed questions. You will need to tape-record the interview (if possible) or take detailed rough notes, and transcribe the tapes or write up your notes afterwards. You will obtain large amounts of data which you may later find difficult to categorize and analyse.

You may wish to use open-ended questions, followed by a series of prompts if necessary, as well as some more closed questions.

6 Once you have decided on your questions you will find it helpful if you can consult other people about the wording of the questions. Their

comments might point out ambiguities and difficulties with phrasing which you have not spotted yourself. It is always wise to conduct a pilot and revise the schedule before you start interviewing for real.

7 If you are working collaboratively, each interviewer needs to conduct a pilot run. You will need to compare notes to see that you both interpret the questions in the same way.

8 Finally, you must consider how you will process and analyse the data.

Setting up the interview

1 First, you must obtain permission to interview pupils, staff, or other personnel.

2 Next you need to think how to approach the people concerned to arrange the interviews. Will you use a letter, the phone or approach them in person?

3 Where will the interview take place? How long will it take? You need to negotiate these arrangements with those concerned.

4 Will you use a tape recorder? If so, you should seek the permission of the interviewee to use it. Will you need an electric socket or rely on batteries? Is the recording likely to be affected by extraneous noise? All these things need to be planned in advance.

Conducting the interview

1 Before you actually carry out an interview check whether the time you have arranged is still convenient. If it is not, and this can frequently be the case, you will have to adjust your schedule.

2 As an interviewer, you need to be able to manage the interaction and also to respond to the interests of the interviewee. It can be useful to indicate to the interviewee at the start of the interview the broad areas that you wish to cover and, if the need arises, glance down to indicate that you want to move on to another area. Also, allow for silences – don't rush the interview. It is important to establish a good relationship with the person you are interviewing.

3 If you are using a tape recorder, check from time to time that it is recording.

After the interview

1 Reflect on how the interview went. Did you establish good rapport with the interviewee? Did you feel that the information you obtained was affected by your relationship with the interviewee? In what way? (Consider, for example, your sex, age, status and ethnicity in relation to those of the interviewee.)

2 Make a note of any problems experienced, such as frequent interruptions.

3 Record any observations which you felt were significant in relation to the general ambience of the interview.

4 Make a note of any information which was imparted after the interview was formally completed. Decide how you will treat this information.

5 Write to thank the interviewees for their help with your study and promise feedback as appropriate.

INTERVIEWING CHILDREN

Interviewing children may be a problem if you are also their teacher. Children will be affected by the way they normally relate to you. It can be difficult for them (and you) to step back from this and adopt a different role. If children regard you as an authority figure, it will be hard to adopt a more egalitarian relationship in an interview. They may also be unwilling to talk about certain subjects. It is particularly important to try out interviews with children, maybe comparing different contexts, or individual and group interviews to see which works best.

Below I have set out a few points of guidance on interviewing children.

1. Open-ended questions often work best. Decide what questions you would like to ask in advance, but don't stick too rigidly to them once the child really gets going. Making the child feel that you are listening and responding to his or her answers is more important than sticking rigidly to your schedule.
2. Children are very observant and very honest. It is important that they feel at ease, so that they can talk freely. Deciding where to conduct the interview, therefore, is very important. Very young children may find it easier to talk to you in the classroom where you can relate the discussion to concrete objects, work on the wall, etc. Older children may be easier to interview on their own away from the gaze of their peers.
3. Decide whether to interview the child alone or in a pair. Children are sometimes franker alone, but may feel more relaxed with a friend.
4. You may need to ask someone to interview the child on your behalf (or arrange for someone to look after the class while you do the interviewing).
5. Start off by telling the child why you want to interview her or him. Here it is very important that you explain:
   (a) that the interview is not a hidden test of some kind;
   (b) that you are genuinely interested in what he or she has to say and want to learn from it (so often in the classroom teachers ask questions which are not for this purpose – children don't expect it);
   (c) that what he or she says will be treated in confidence and not discussed with anyone else without permission.
6. During the interview either make notes or tape record (if the child is in agreement).
7. If you make notes, the best technique is to scribble as much as possible verbatim, using private shorthand, continuing to be a good listener meanwhile (difficult but not impossible). Then within 24 hours read through your notes and fill them out. Remember, if you are not a good listener the child will stop talking!
8. After the interview, show the child your notes and ask if it will be all right for you to discuss what has been said with other people. Be ready to accept the answer 'no' to part of the discussion (though this is rare in practice).

GROUP INTERVIEWS

The guidance given above on individual interviews and interviewing children is also relevant to group interviews. A group interview may be used in preference to individual interviews in some situations. Children may prefer to be interviewed in groups. Or there may be a naturally occurring group (e.g., members of a working group) that you wish to interview together. Group interviews may be useful at the beginning of your research, enabling you to test some ideas or gauge reactions to new developments or proposals. Initial group interviews of this nature can give you broad coverage and generate a lot of information and, perhaps, new ideas. Often in this situation the answers from one participant trigger off responses from another, giving you a range of ideas and suggestions. This can be more productive than interviewing individuals before you have sufficient knowledge of the area of investigation. Much depends on the time you have available for your research. Using a group whose knowledge or expertise you can tap can be a fruitful and time-saving means of obtaining information. There are, however, some points to bear in mind when running group interviews.

The group dynamic

A group is different from the sum of its parts. The composition of the group is important. Do people know one another? Will some people be in awe of others' opinions? May some fear a hidden agenda?

Groups, it is said, typically 'form, storm, norm, perform and mourn' (Mulford *et al.*, 1980). You need to take this into account for group interviews to be successful. For the group to 'form' there needs to be some way of including everyone, making them feel that they are members of the group. Each person needs to say something within the first five minutes, if only to introduce themselves. Typically there follows a period of 'storming', when the group is working out the issues of power and control and when personalities emerge. A 'brainstorm' of issues could be quite fruitful at this stage. 'Norming' happens as people settle down and recognize that it is permissible to hold different opinions. The group is then ready to 'perform' and the questions on your schedule can be addressed. There should be a feeling of constructive activity. As the interview nears its end, the stage of 'mourning' is reached. This is a vital point. It is a process that has to be managed by the person convening the interview to indicate to the group that it is almost complete. At this point you could ask whether there is anything else that anyone wants to say, or whether there is anything else that they want to ask about your study or the interview itself.

A good group is one that reaches the 'performing' stage. The most basic ingredient for this to happen is for there to be an atmosphere of trust within the group. Recognizing the natural stages in the formation of a group, however, will help you facilitate the formation of a good group. It will also help you to sort out the information obtained at different stages of the interview. Not all information will be useful to you. The comments and responses people make during the 'storming' and 'performing' stages are likely to be more valuable than those occurring during the 'forming' or 'mourning' stages.

The composition of the group

A group should number no more than eight people. You need to consider whom you invite to participate. You may wish to ask people who are likely to have different points of view, as such interviews are useful for exploring issues.

Organizational factors

The group interview needs to be arranged so that it will not be disturbed. Contextual factors, such as where you hold the interview and the seating arrangements are also very important. You need to consider whether you want to create an informal friendly atmosphere, or a more formal, 'round-table', 'business-like' atmosphere. Who should sit next to each other? Where are you going to sit? And so on.

Recording information

Consider how you will record the discussion. It is much harder to transcribe a tape of a group interview than of an individual interview, but, if the group agrees, it is still worth the effort to record it. If you can arrange it, you might consider asking another person to take notes and look after the tape recorder for you, leaving you free to concentrate on establishing a rapport with the group.

It is worth practising recording and transcribing before recording your actual interview. You may find it hard to tell what is happening, or who is speaking, especially if more than one person speaks at a time. Asking people to identifythemselves before they speak can make transcribing easier. (See also sub-section 4.7 on transcribing from audio- and video-recordings.)

Managing the discussion

In a group interview, it can be difficult to ensure that you cover what you had planned and still allow for some flexibility. You will need good memory and concentration so that you can remember what has been covered and link in new topics and issues. Try also to involve all members of the group. If you feel that the discussion is moving too far away from your brief, use a deferring statement – say you have a number of questions on this subject that you will come to later, but that you would like to explore A and B now. Avoid getting locked into a discussion with one person as this isolates the others. You have to balance breadth with depth. Watch for non-verbal cues from members of the group who are showing signs of frustration or boredom.

Many of the observations discussed above draw on the experience and expertise developed by Social and Community Planning Research (see Robson, 1986).

Now let's take a look at some practical examples of the use of interviews. In Example 3.6, from Kingsmead Primary School in London, parents, teachers and children were interviewed individually following a series of conferences which had been set up in the school. The ILEA Primary Language Record handbook (ILEA/CLPE, 1988) recommends holding language and literacy conferences to give children the chance to talk to their teachers about their experiences, achievements, likes and dislikes as language users. The conferences help teachers make formative assessments of children's progress, find out about their concerns, suggest new learning strategies, and so on. At Kingsmead it had been decided to try including children's parents in these conferences. Here members of staff wanted to evaluate how useful the conferences had been to all concerned.

As you can see, Example 3.6 (overleaf) uses fairly informal open-ended interview techniques, but the interview schedules were given a standard format because it was important that each child, parent and teacher was asked the same set of questions. As you can imagine, this example involved considerable numbers of people and took quite some time to carry out. An alternative to interviewing the parents and staff might have been to give them written questionnaires, and it is to these that we turn next.

3.5 USING QUESTIONNAIRES

Employing written questionnaires which people can take away and fill out is generally seen as fairly economical with time. However, this method does assume, first, that the respondents understand the questions in the terms intended and that they understand what information is required; and, secondly, that they have this information and are willing to divulge it. If the first condition is not met then the data will not be valid and worth processing. If the second condition is not met, and your questionnaire has a low response, the information you obtain may come from an unrepresentative sample of the population you want to survey, and will be unreliable. In either case, the value of any findings is undermined. It is a fairly skilled task to design a questionnaire relevant to your research question(s), and yet appropriate for the people to whom it will be administered.

Quite often you will need to weigh up the relative advantages and disadvantages of using questionnaires as opposed to interviews. The use of a questionnaire administered by the researcher '*in situ*' discussed below has some of the features of an interview. This method allows you to interact with the respondents and explain what is expected of them and, if necessary, clarify the questions. The response rate for *in situ* questionnaires is much higher than for postal questionnaires.

Example 3.6
Using interviews to evaluate language and literacy conferences

Questions asked of parents

1. What did you think of the Conference?
2. Successful because_______
   Unsuccessful because_____
3. Did you have any fears about it?
4. Did it change your understanding of what happens in school?
5. After seeing the teacher, has your child been affected in any way?
6. Would you repeat this exercise or change it?

Questions asked of children

1. What happened when your mum/dad got home after the Conference?
2. Will this meeting between your parent and your teacher help you in school?
3. After the meeting, did it change you in how you should behave in school?
4. Do you think it's a good idea to have meetings with your parents and teachers about you?
5. Do you want another one?

Questions asked of teachers

1. Was the P.T.C. Conference useful?
2. Would you like to repeat the exercise again?
3. Would you change the format?
4. Has it taught you anything about the parents?
5. Has it taught you anything about the children?
6. Will the information affect and influence your teaching?

Below I shall consider some general points about the use of questionnaires, whether administered individually or *in situ* with a group. What form your questionnaire takes and how you administer it will depend upon your research question(s) and the people you want information from. I shall give some examples of different types of questionnaire towards the end of this sub-section.

QUESTIONNAIRES ADMINISTERED INDIVIDUALLY

Some preliminary points to consider

The following considerations will influence what you ask and the way you ask it.

- How will you administer the questionnaire? Is it to be posted, or, perhaps, handed to colleagues? If it is for people you know this will affect the style of the questionnaire and the approach you adopt.
- How do you persuade people to respond? Who will own the information – you, your department, your school? How will it be used? Of what value could it be to the respondents? Don't ask for more information than you need, and don't expect too much of the respondents or you may not gain their co-operation.
- Will the questionnaire be anonymous? Is this likely to affect the way in which people respond? How will responses from staff be affected if they know that the head of department, head or principal might see these? Even where questionnaires are anonymous, it may still be possible to identify individuals by their answers which may indicate their role within the institution or local authority. In this case, how will you treat this data? As always you need to be scrupulous about preserving people's anonymity and/or confidences.
- When is the questionnaire to be administered? For example, suppose you want to evaluate an in-service course, at what point do you use a questionnaire? Before the course, during the course, or on completion? How will you deal with those people who drop out? You could consider using a telephone follow-up with a small sample of those who do not complete the course to find out why.
- How are you going to process the information and analyse it? Consider the facilities, the time and skills available. If you are going to collect quantitative data you may need to use some sort of statistical analysis. If this is the case it may be necessary to get advice before you collect the data. If you are going to collect qualitative information, how will you process it? Section 5 of this Handbook gives advice on these issues.
- It is useful to find out whether any studies have been undertaken previously in your area of interest. What did they find? Could you use or adapt any questionnaires employed before? It is most unlikely that you will be able to use exactly the same questionnaire, but it is common practice to use other researchers' questions where these are relevant to your study as this allows you to compare your findings with those of other people.
- Have you made arrangements to pilot your questionnaire? This will help you spot any likely problems in administering the questionnaire, and any difficulties or ambiguities in question wording.

Devising questions

- As a first step you should list the information you require: sort this under broad headings, then identify specific items.
- When you start formulating questions you must take care over choice of language: don't make this too complex, or too simple for your respondents. You should avoid obscure terminology, acronyms and abbreviations. Don't use vague or over-general terms that are likely to be interpreted differently by different people, e.g. 'democracy', an 'effective' course. Sometimes it is useful to break down the idea you are trying to get at into items that typify what you mean. For example, if you were interested in how democratic decision-making processes were in a school, you might identify several specific questions that you felt would provide evidence of this, such as:

(a) Are parents involved in any of the school's key decision-making processes?
(If 'yes', which one(s)?)

(b) Are children involved in any of the school's key decision-making processes?
(If 'yes', which one(s)?)

(c) How are your governors elected?

(d) At meetings does everyone have a chance to have their say?

- Remember that it is worth trying out individual questions on other people to get the wording right, as well as trying out the whole questionnaire.
- Are there equal opportunities implications to consider? Are there, for example, standard ways in your local authority of asking people for information about ethnicity and gender?
- Will the replies tell you what you want to know? How do you know? If they do not, then this will affect the validity of your data and undermine the whole research exercise. Check for bias and leading questions.
- As with interviews, your questions should be clear, concise and unambiguous. You should try not to use multiple questions, and should avoid double negatives.
- You should consider grouping questions about similar issues together.
- Sometimes you may want to use a four or five-point scale as a way of getting answers to your questions. For example, you can ask your respondents whether a particular event happens '*never, occasionally, frequently, always* (please ring the term that most nearly applies)'. Example 3.9 provides an illustration of scales used in a questionnaire designed for young children.
- Are you using 'closed' or 'open-ended' questions? When it comes to written questionnaires issued to a large number of respondents use the latter sparingly – they take a lot of time to process.

The design of the questionnaire

- Use only one side of the paper.
- Give the questionnaire a heading showing what it is about.
- If the questionnaire is not to be administered personally, you should provide a covering letter or a paragraph of introduction at the beginning.
- Keep the questionnaire as short as possible. Space out the items. (Dense print is off-putting and will affect the response rate.)
- Do you need to insert a column on the right-hand side to help you process and analyse the information?
- Give clear instructions in capital letters, e.g. 'TICK' and 'WRITE IN'.
- Where the information you are requesting is of a sensitive nature you should give people the choice to opt out. For example, if asking for the ethnic background of the respondent you could have a category 'I prefer not to answer this question'.
- Order the questions so that the straightforward non-controversial questions come first and the more sensitive ones last.
- Try to order the questions so that they come in a logical sequence.
- You may need a 'Don't know' or 'Not applicable' category.
- It may be useful to have an 'Other' category with a 'PLEASE SPECIFY'.
- It is a nice gesture to finish the questionnaire with 'THANK YOU FOR YOUR HELP WITH OUR STUDY'.
- Always review your questionnaire periodically in the light of the information gathered and any feedback respondents provide about difficulties in completing it.

Questionnaires are never perfect. Ideally they should be custom-built for a specific purpose. Beware of 'off-the-shelf' versions – as pointed out above, these will require adaptation, a pilot and (usually) revision.

QUESTIONNAIRES IN SITU WITH A GROUP

The guidance above on questionnaires administered individually also applies to questionnaires given to a group or class *in situ*. Here I shall consider one or two points that are specific to questionnaires so administered.

There are many advantages to the practitioner-researcher in administering questionnaires to a class or a group. In the first place, there is an enormous saving in time and possibly also in cost. Secondly, the response rate is almost certainly going to be much higher and the information obtained will be much more representative of the population and is, therefore, likely to be more reliable. Thirdly, if you administer questionnaires yourself, you will be alerted to any difficulties people experience with the wording or format. You will be able to explain to the respondents what is required. If the exercise is not taken seriously you will know that the data you have collected should be discarded as they are unreliable. This could happen if a class was disruptive, or if another member of staff acted to influence pupils' attitudes towards the study, as in Example 3.7 (overleaf).

There are some particular points you need to consider when using questionnaires *in situ*.

- *Organizational factors*: There needs to be a suitable place and adequate time to complete the questionnaire.
- *The person(s) administering the questionnaire*: It will be clear from Example 3.7 that, ideally, you should administer the questionnaire yourself. Where this is not possible, you need to brief an alternative (suitable) person.
- *Absentees*: While the response rate is likely to be very high for questionnaires administered in this way, you still need to take account of people who are absent on the day the questionnaire is given. This absence could bias the information you obtain. For example, if a study of absenteeism in the fifth year were undertaken in which pupils were asked about their attitudes to the curriculum, the staff and other pupils, it is likely that the pupils present in class would be unrepresentative of the fifth-year group as a whole. You would need to follow up pupils who were absent on the day of the survey to obtain their views.

Let us examine some examples of the use of questionnaires by teacher-researchers in the field.

Example 3.9 (p. 182) is part of a questionnaire which was given *in situ* to eight-year-olds. Here the researcher was interested in whether the adoption of a developmental approach to teaching literacy would have an impact on children's enjoyment of reading and writing. The questionnaire was administered jointly by the children's class teacher and the researcher. As you can see, it did not necessitate any writing by the children. Children were asked a question for each numbered row (e.g., 'How much do you like writing a story?) and they had to tick the face indicating their response.

Example 3.10 (p. 183) is taken from a postal questionnaire sent to a sample of probationary teachers. This postal questionnaire was later followed up by in-depth interviews with a new sample of probationary teachers, as mentioned in Example 3.2.

Example 3.7 Problems in administering a questionnaire

A researcher wanted to discover whether a course on job opportunities would influence secondary school pupils' attitudes towards different types of work. In particular, she was interested in whether pupils' attitudes towards women's and men's domestic and work roles would change if they were taught subjects and acquired skills in 'non-traditional' fields (for instance, girls in CDT and boys in 'homecraft'). She devised the questionnaire shown in Figure 3, which was given *in situ* to classes of secondary pupils before they started their course on job opportunities. Another, identical, questionnaire was given on completion of the course. The skills pupils were learning about in the course related to the list of jobs given in the questionnaire.

SECTION II

The following questions are about jobs which people do outside of the home. Again for each job we would like you to say whether YOU THINK it is

very much a MAN'S job
more of a MAN's job
either a MAN or a WOMAN's job
more of a WOMAN's job
very much a WOMAN's job

There are no right or wrong answers. It is not a test, it is what YOU THINK which is important. For each job tick the box which most nearly matches YOUR VIEW.

	very much a man's job	more of a man's job	either a man or a woman's job	more of a woman's job	very much a woman's job
garage mechanic (repairing cars)	❑	❑	❑	❑	❑
electrician (wiring a house)	❑	❑	❑	❑	❑
painter and decorator	❑	❑	❑	❑	❑
printer (printing books)	❑	❑	❑	❑	❑

Figure 3
Questionnaire on gender attitudes (from ILEA Research and Statistics Branch, 1985a).

When piloting the course in a secondary school the researcher was present when a male class teacher who had been asked to administer the pilot questionnaires gave them out and instructed the class to 'fill in this rubbish and get on with some work'. The researcher realized that if the information in the main study was to be reliable then the administration of the questionnaires *in situ* had to be undertaken by the person responsible for the evaluation, *not* the class or subject teacher.

Example 3.8 Questionnaire to assess staff development needs

During the production of a school development plan, it became apparent that there was a need for information about the staff's perceptions of their needs for professional development.

The questionnaire in Figure 4 was designed by the staff development committee and the format agreed at a staff meeting. It was circulated to individual staff members through the internal mail.

Name:______________________ Role:____________________

Date:______________________

SECTION A

1. In the context of your present job description which aspects of your role give you most satisfaction and why? Please be as specific as you can

2. Which aspects of your job description do you find most irksome and why?

3. Are there parts of your present job description for which you would like more training? Please give details of why and how you feel those needs could be met.

Figure 4 A staff development questionnaire (from Hilary Street, London).

Example 3.9 Questionnaire administered to primary school pupils

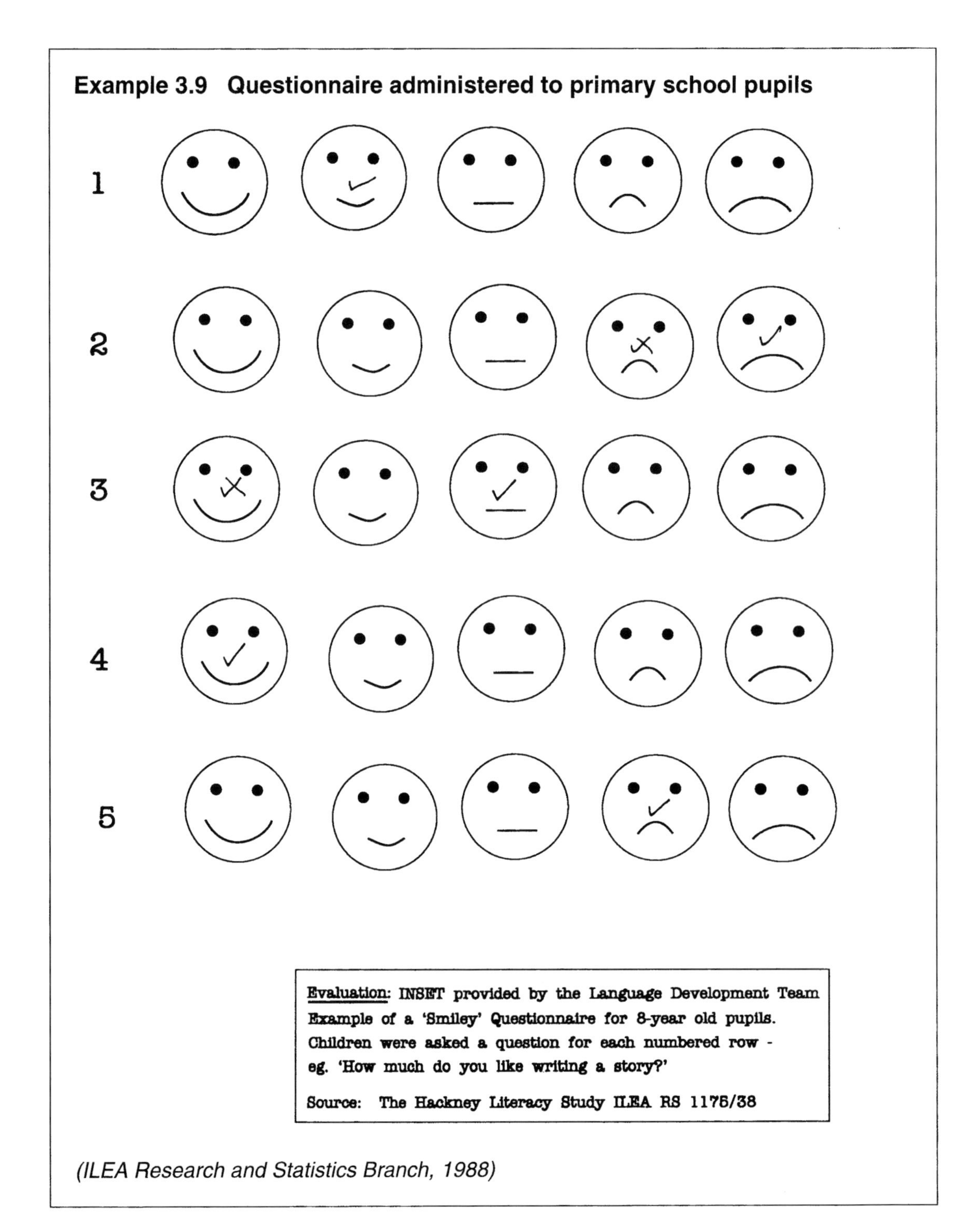

(ILEA Research and Statistics Branch, 1988)

These examples provide a range of questionnaire styles and techniques. Some, like the one in Example 3.8, are relatively open-ended and unstructured and will provide qualitative information. Others, such as the one in Example 3.10, are very highly structured and will give you quantitative information. The type of questionnaire you design will depend very much on who you want to get information from and what your research question is. Advice on analysing both quantitative and qualitative information from questionnaires is given in Section 5.

Example 3.10
Questionnaire on an induction programme for probationary teachers

We would like to know whether any of the following aspects of living and teaching in London are causing you difficulty:

	Much difficulty	Some difficulty	Little difficulty	No difficulty at all	
Having suitable living accommodation	❐	❐	❐	❐	(56)
Having sufficient money	❐	❐	❐	❐	(57)
Transport difficulties	❐	❐	❐	❐	(58)
Tiredness, feeling fatigued	❐	❐	❐	❐	(59)
Lack of social life	❐	❐	❐	❐	(60)
Holding the children's interest	❐	❐	❐	❐	(61)
Discipline problems	❐	❐	❐	❐	(62)
Conflict with school staff	❐	❐	❐	❐	(63)
Getting professional advice	❐	❐	❐	❐	(64)
Obtaining suitable teaching materials	❐	❐	❐	❐	(65)
Devising a suitable classroom organisation	❐	❐	❐	❐	(66)
Other (specify)	❐	❐	❐	❐	(67)

THANK YOU FOR YOUR CO-OPERATION WITH OUR SURVEY OF EDUCATION EXPERIENCE

(ILEA Research and Statistics Branch, 1985b)

3.6 REVIEWING METHODS

It will be clear from the examples above that the various methods of obtaining information from people – diaries, interviews and questionnaires – can take very different forms. Each method can be structured, semi-structured, or completely unstructured.

Which method you decide to adopt, and what form it will take, will depend very much on your research question(s) and on whether your study is predictive, exploratory or explanatory. If your study is predictive or explanatory, then it is likely that the instruments you adopt will be more structured than if it is exploratory.

Remember that adopting more than one method is often advantageous. Your prime consideration is the most appropriate method given your circumstances and the resources available (your time and that of colleagues, the expertise required and, possibly, also finance and equipment). I set out below the main advantages of the approaches discussed in this section and also some of the pitfalls associated with them.

WAYS OF COLLECTING INFORMATION

Diaries and logs

What the method can do	*Limitations*
Enables you to gain information about events you cannot observe.	You may get different amounts and types of information from different respondents.
Can be used flexibly.	Probably time-consuming to analyse.

Individual interviews

What the method can do	*Limitations*
Does not run the risk (as with questionnaires) of low response rate.	Takes time to administer.
Allows you to probe particular issues in depth.	Respondents will be affected by their perceptions of you and your research, and what responses they feel are appropriate.
Likely to generate a lot of information.	Takes time to write up and analyse.

Group interviews

What the method can do	*Limitations*
More economical on time than several individual interviews.	It may be hard to manage a group discussion.
Some respondents (e.g. children) may prefer to be interviewed as a group.	Respondents will be affected by others present in the interview.
May allow you to 'brain-storm' and explore ideas.	Note-taking may not be easy. Writing up notes and analysis is relatively time-consuming.

Questionnaires (posted and handed out)

What the method can do	*Limitations*
Questionnaires do not take much time to administer, so useful for a large sample.	Response rate may be low and you could get a biased sample.
Everyone is asked the same questions.	Danger of differing interpretations of the same questions – respondents cannot ask for explanations.
Can be designed so that analysis is relatively simple.	People's preferred responses may not be allowed for in your questionnaire.

Questionnaires in situ

What the method can do	*Limitations*
Take less time to administer than individual interviews.	Less flexible than individual interviews.
Higher response rate than postal questionnaires. If need be, you can ask others to administer the questionnaire.	If you are not present while the questionnaire is administered, responses may be affected by something you aren't aware of.

OPEN-ENDED VERSUS CLOSED QUESTIONS

I made a distinction above between asking open-ended questions, which provides qualitative information, and asking closed questions, which may provide information you can quantify. The main features of each approach are set out below.

Open-ended questions

- Allow your informants some degree of flexibility in their responses – they can select what seems relevant.
- Particularly useful if you're not able, or don't wish to anticipate the range of possible responses from informants.
- You may discover something unexpected – providing greater insight into the subject of your investigation.
- In interviews, you can probe – ask informants for clarification or further information.
- Open-ended interviews probably take longer to administer; you will also need to write up a set of interview notes, which takes time.
- Analysing open-ended information from interviews or questionnaires is relatively time-consuming.

Closed questions

- Limit the response(s) your informant can give.
- The choice of responses you allow may not cover your informants' preferred response(s).
- Probably take less time to administer in interviews.
- Analysis takes relatively little time.

In this section I've also stressed that it may be beneficial to use a combination of open-ended and closed questions, depending upon your research interests.

FURTHER READING

BURGESS, R. (1984) 'Keeping a research diary' in BELL, J., BUSH, T., FOX, A., GOODEY, J., GOLDING, S. (eds) (1984) *Conducting Small-scale Investigations in Education Management,* London, Harper and Row/The Open University.

Robert Burgess discusses the use of different kinds of diaries in educational research, including diaries kept by researchers and by informants. He also considers how diaries may be used as the basis of interviews with informants.

KEATS, D. (2000) *Interviewing: a practical guide for students and professionals*, Buckingham, Open University Press.

This book is very accessible and is packed with practical advice on how to get the best out of an interview. It includes chapters on interviewing children and adolescents, people with disabilities and interviewing across cultures.

LEWIS, A. and LINDSAY, G. (1999) *Researching Children's Perspectives*, Buckingham, Open University Press.

This book addresses the issues and practicalities surrounding the obtaining of children's views, particularly in the research context.

MIDDLEWOOD, D., COLEMAN, M. and LUMBY, J. (1999) *Practitioner Research in Education: making a difference*, London, Paul Chapman.

This book explores the effects of teachers' and lecturers' research on organizational improvement. It includes material on how to conduct research in school and college settings when investigating topics such as the management of people, the management of the curriculum and researching the effects of organizational change.

PETERSON, R. A. (2000) *Constructing Effective Questionnaires*, Thousand Oaks, California, Sage.

This book provides practical advice to both new and experienced researchers on all aspects of questionnaire design.

SEIDMAN, I. (1998) *Interviewing as Qualitative Research: a guide for researchers in education and the social sciences*, New York, Teachers College Press.

This volume provides guidance for new and experienced interviewers to help them develop, shape and reflect on interviewing as a qualitative research process. It offers examples of interviewing techniques as well as a discussion of the complexities of interviewing and its connections with the broader issues of qualitative research.

WARREN, C. A. and HACKNEY, J. K. (2000) *Gender Issues in Ethnography*, Thousand Oaks, California, Sage.

This book summarizes the state of the art of gender issues in fieldwork. Warren and Hackney show how the researcher's gender affects fieldwork relationships and the production of ethnography.

4 SEEING WHAT PEOPLE DO

4.1 INTRODUCTION

This section examines how you can collect evidence by watching, and recording in some way, what people do: what activities they engage in; how they behave as they carry out certain activities; how they talk; what kinds of work they do. The section also looks at the outcome of children's work – using children's writing as a main example: what can you say about children's work, and how can this be used as a source of evidence for your project?

You are already, necessarily, observing as part of your teaching. Your observations are recorded formally when you assess children or comment on their work. In addition to such formal observations, it is likely that you continually notice how children are behaving, or reflect on how a lesson has gone. Such observations may not be formally recorded, but will probably inform future work, such as how to group children so that they collaborate better or how to follow up a particular piece of work.

In order to provide evidence, you need to observe systematically and to record this in some way. Some of the methods suggested in this section will formalize what you already do as a part of teaching. Others require more time, or access to additional resources – perhaps a cassette recorder, or a colleague you can work with. The method(s) you select must depend upon your own professional context (including other commitments and demands upon your time) and on the nature of your research.

4.2 DECIDING WHAT AND HOW TO OBSERVE

You may derive ideas for making observations from other published studies you've read, or from discussing your research with colleagues – but the most important factor to consider is how the observations can fit in with your own professional context, and inform your own research questions. Four points to consider are *what to observe*, *what types of observation* to carry out; to what extent you should *participate* in the event you're observing; and *what to tell* those you are observing about what you are doing.

WHAT TO OBSERVE

Since you cannot observe everything that is going on you will need to sample, that is, to select people, activities or events to look at.

People

If you're observing pupils, or pupils and a teacher in class, which pupils, or groups of pupils, do you want to focus on?

- Do you want to look at a whole class? If you teach several classes, which one(s) will you observe? Are you going to focus on the pupils, or the teacher, or both?
- Do you want to focus on a small group working together? Will this be a pre-existing group, or will you ask certain pupils to work together? Will you select children at random, or do you want to look at certain children, or types of children? (For instance, is it important that the group contains girls and boys? If you teach a mixed-age group, do you want to look at older and younger children working together?)

- Is your focus to be on one or more individual children? How will you select the child(ren)? Is there a child with particular needs that you'd like to observe more closely?

Similar decisions need to be made if your focus is on teachers (or other people) in a range of contexts. For instance:

- Do you want to observe the whole staff (e.g. in a staff meeting)?
- Do you want to 'trail' an individual colleague?

Activities and events

You will also have to make decisions about the contexts you wish to observe, when to make observations and what types of activity to focus on.

- If observing in class, which lessons, or parts of the day, will you look at?
- Will you focus on certain pre-selected activities or look at what happens in the normal course of events? In the latter case you will need to consider how far what you observe is typical of the normal course of events – what counts as a 'typical' afternoon, for instance?
- If you're looking at children's work, how will you select this?
- If you're looking at meetings, how will you decide which to observe?

In each case, it is important to consider why you should focus on any activity, or group of pupils, etc. How is this relevant to your research question(s) and professional context? (See also 'Sampling' in sub-section 1.6.)

WHAT TYPE OF OBSERVATION?

When you have decided what to observe, you need to consider what kind(s) of observation to carry out, for instance whether to use *qualitative* or *quantitative* methods. Examples 4.1 and 4.2 illustrate these. Both are examples of observations carried out by teachers.

Example 4.1 Observing children writing

Christina Wojtak, from Hertfordshire, was interested in how young (six-year-old) children judged their own and others' writing, and whether their judgements would change after certain types of teaching. She worked with the children to help them produce their own books, which would be displayed in the book corner. Christina observed the children to see how they responded to their writing tasks.

There are several questions one could ask about children's responses. Some may be open-ended, such as how the children behaved as they wrote. How (if at all) would their behaviour change over the few weeks of the project?

Other questions may be quite specific, such as how many pieces of writing different children produced. Over certain (specified) periods, how much time did each child spend (a) working alone; (b) discussing with other pupils?

Example 4.2 Monitoring classroom interaction

Staff in a CDT department wanted to encourage more girls to take up technology but were worried about the male image of the subject. They had also noticed that boys seemed to dominate interaction during lessons. John Cowgill, head of CDT, decided to monitor classroom interaction more closely – comparing Year 8 pupils' behaviour in CDT and home economics.

As with Example 4.1, questions about interaction may be open-ended, such as how girls and boys behaved in whole-class question-and-answer sessions. How were they grouped for practical work, and how did they behave as they carried out such work?

> Other questions may require more specific information, such as how often the teacher asked questions of boys as opposed to girls. How did different pupils get to speak during question-and-answer sessions: by raising their hands and being selected by the teacher, by 'chipping in' with a response, or by some other means?

In both examples the initial open-ended questions would lead the observer towards the use of qualitative methods, to noting down what was going on. The observer's detailed field-notes would form the basis of their account of the lessons.

The more specific questions would lead the observer towards the use of quantitative methods, to recording instances of certain specified behaviour. The information can be presented numerically: a certain number of pupils behaved in this way; 70 per cent of pupils used this equipment, 40 per cent used that equipment, etc.

In the event, Christina opted for open-ended notes and John opted to focus on particular types of behaviour.

The examples above are concerned with observations of activities and of classroom interaction, but the same principle applies to observations of pupils, or teachers or other adults, in other contexts, and to looking at children's work. Depending on your research questions, you may wish to use qualitative or quantitative observation methods, or a combination of both. Used in combination, quantitative and qualitative methods may complement one another, producing a more complete picture of an event. Open-ended observations may suggest particular categories of behaviour to look for in future observations. Or initial quantitative research may suggest something is going on that you wish to explore in more detail using qualitative methods. (See also the discussion of the qualitative/quantitative distinction in sub-section 1.5.)

I shall discuss below examples of observations using quantitative and qualitative methods. I shall make a broad distinction between field-notes and observation schedules. Field-notes allow you to collect qualitative information. Observation schedules are *normally* used to collect quantitative information, but some provide qualitative information. Section 4.9 reviews the methods I have discussed and considers what they can and what they cannot tell you.

TO PARTICIPATE OR NOT TO PARTICIPATE?

A distinction is commonly made in research between *participant* and *non-participant* observation. A 'participant observer' is someone who takes part in the event she or he is observing. A 'non-participant observer' does not take part. In practice, this distinction is not so straightforward. By virtue of being in a classroom (or meeting, etc.) and watching what is going on, you are, to some extent, a participant. When observing in your own institution, it is particularly hard to maintain the stance of a non-participant observer, to separate your role as observer from your usual role as teacher. John Cowgill commented that, although observing in other colleagues' lessons, he was interrupted by pupils and occasionally found himself intervening to help a pupil, or on safety grounds.

Michael Armstrong, whose study *Closely Observed Children* documents the intellectual growth and development of children in a primary school classroom, comments as follows:

> I was acutely conscious ... that teaching and observation are not easy to reconcile. On the one hand, the pressures of classroom life make it exceptionally difficult for an individual teacher to describe the intellectual experience of his pupils at length, in detail and with a sufficient detachment. Conversely ... to observe a class of children without teaching them is to deprive oneself of a prime source of

> knowledge: the knowledge that comes from asking questions, engaging in conversations, discussing, informing, criticising, correcting and being corrected, demonstrating, interpreting, helping, instructing or collaborating – in short, from teaching.
>
> (Armstrong, 1980, p.4)

Michael Armstrong's solution was to work alongside another teacher, to give himself more time for sustained observation, and to write up detailed notes of his observations, interpretations and speculations at the end of the school day.

As part of your planning, you need to decide whether to combine observation with your normal teaching or whether you wish (and are able) to make special arrangements that free you from other duties and give you more time to observe. This will affect what you observe and what methods of observation you choose.

WHAT TO TELL PEOPLE

Watching people, and writing down what they do, has certain ethical implications. If you are observing adults – say in a staff meeting – it may seem obvious that you need to get their permission first. But it is equally important to consider the ethical implications of observing young children in a classroom. Such issues need to be considered as part of planning an observation, because they will have an impact on what you observe, how you carry out the observation, and how you interpret the results of the observation. Some points to consider are:

- *Should you ask people's permission to observe them?* This must depend on the context and purpose of the observation. For instance, if the observation were being carried out entirely for the observer's benefit, it might seem necessary to ask permission (perhaps from parents in the case of very young children). At the other end of the spectrum, you probably feel it is a normal part of teaching to keep a note of how pupils are progressing, not something that would require special permission.
- *Should you tell people they are being observed?* Bound up with this question is the notion of the observer's paradox: the act of observing is inclined to change the behaviour of those being observed. It is likely that the more you tell people about your observation, the more their behaviour will be affected. Some researchers compromise: they tell people they are being observed, but are rather vague about the object of the observation. They may say more about this after the event. You may feel that you can afford to be more open; or that, as a colleague or teacher (rather than a researcher from outside), it is important to retain an atmosphere of trust between yourself and those you work with.
- *Should you discuss the results of your observation with those you have observed?* This is partly an ethical question of whether people have a right to know what you're saying about them. But discussing observations with others also lets you check your interpretations against theirs. It may give you a different understanding of something you have observed.
- *Should you identify those you have observed?* In writing reports, researchers often give pseudonyms to people they have observed or institutions in which they have carried out observations. As a teacher, you may find it more difficult to maintain confidentiality in this way – the identity of those you refer to may still be apparent to other colleagues, for instance. One solution may be to discuss with colleagues or pupils how much confidentiality they feel is necessary, and how this may be maintained.

(See also sub-section 1.4, 'Ethics and practitioner research'.)

Decisions about sampling, what types of observation to make, how far you will participate in the events you're observing, and what you will tell those you observe will affect the type of research you can carry out.

4.3 MONITORING CLASS OR GROUP ACTIVITIES

This sub-section discusses a variety of ways in which you can watch what people do or the activities they are involved in. Several examples come from classrooms. However, any method of observation will need to be tailored to your own context. Something that works in one classroom may not in another. Many of the ideas suggested here may also be used in other contexts, such as assemblies or meetings, corridors or playgrounds.

RECOLLECTIONS

If you are teaching a class, you will necessarily be observing what is going on. You can focus these observations on the research question(s) you are investigating. If you have sole responsibility for the class, however, you will probably find it difficult to take notes while actually teaching. How difficult this is depends on a variety of factors: the pupils themselves, the type of lesson you are interested in, how work is organized, and so on. If the class is working independently (for instance, in groups) you may be able to use this time to jot down observations about one particular group, or one or two pupils. If you are working with the whole class or a group, you will probably be thinking on your feet. In this case, it is unlikely that you will be able to take notes at the same time.

Observations made under such circumstances may still provide useful evidence. You will need to make a mental note of relevant events and write these up as field-notes as soon as possible afterwards. This was the method adopted by Michael Armstrong, whose work I mentioned above. To aid your recollections it helps to make very rough notes (enough to jog your memory) shortly after the lesson and write these up fully later in the day.

Example 4.3 (p. 193) shows extracts from field-notes based on recollections. Will Swann, who wrote these notes, wanted to document the introduction of group poetry writing to children in a school for pupils with physical disabilities and associated learning difficulties. The notes formed the basis of a case study written for The Open University course E242 *Learning for All.*

It helps to develop a consistent format for your notes. This is particularly important if they are to form a major source of evidence, as in Example 4.3. Here, the observer has dated the notes, and provided contextual information – about the nature of the lesson, children who were present, and so on (only extracts from this information are given in Example 4.3). The observer has decided to record observations as a series of 'episodes' – significant aspects of a lesson that might be followed up in some way (e.g., by discussions with colleagues or in planning the next lesson).

The notes in Example 4.3 provide an interpretive account of parts of a lesson. Such accounts are frequently used by teachers documenting work in which they are actively participating. In this case, the teacher's reflections and interpretations during the lesson are themselves part of the data. For instance, 'Episode 2' records an *observation*: children joined in reading the witches poem, with Lee especially vocal. This is followed by an *interpretation*: 'I don't think he saw his contributions as changes to what I had written, they were more of a sign of his active involvement in the poem.' This interpretation serves as an explanation for what happens next: 'I ... asked if they wanted me to change the poem ... They generated two alternative last lines, and finally settled on one.'

An alternative format for field-notes is to make a formal separation between observations (what happened) and a commentary containing reflections and interpretations. The field-notes in Example 4.4 (p. 194) attempt to do this.

Any recording system is partial in that you cannot and will not wish to record everything. An added drawback with field-notes based on recollections is that you are bound to collect less information than someone taking notes as they go along. There is also a danger of biasing your recording: observers may see what they want to see while observing and having to remember significant events may introduce further bias. For this reason it helps to check out your observations by collecting information from at least one other source, for example by asking pupils about a lesson or looking at children's work. (See also 'Bias' in sub-section 1.6.)

On the other hand, this sort of observation intrudes very little on your teaching, and you do not need access to any other resources. For this reason alone you should be able to observe a larger sample of lessons (or track something of interest over a longer sequence of lessons) than someone who needs to make special arrangements to observe and record.

USING FIELD-NOTES TO RECORD ACTIVITIES AS THEY HAPPEN

Field-notes can also be used to record events as they happen. I mentioned above the difficulty of making notes while teaching but said that this might be possible during certain types of lesson or certain portions of a lesson. Alternatively, you may be able to enlist the help of a colleague, or a pupil, to observe in your class. In certain cases, you may be observing in a colleague's class. Or you may wish to use field-notes to record information in other contexts, such as assemblies or the playground.

This sort of observation is normally open-ended, in that you can jot down points of interest as they arise. You would need to focus on your research question(s), and this would necessarily affect what counted as points of interest. Field-notes can be contrasted with observation schedules, which structure your observations and may require you to observe specified categories of behaviour (observation schedules are discussed below).

Example 4.4 shows extracts from field-notes made by an Open University researcher, Janet Maybin, while watching an assembly in a middle school. Janet Maybin's observations form part of a larger study of children's collaborative language practices in school. In this case, she was interested in identifying the values laid down in school assemblies. She wanted to see whether, and how, these might resurface later in children's talk in other contexts.

As Janet Maybin was not taking an active part in the assembly, she could jot down observations and brief comments at the time. She also tape-recorded the assembly for later analysis (she occasionally jots down counter numbers in her field-notes). After school, she wrote up her field-notes, separating observations (what actually happened) from a commentary (her questions, reflections, interpretations, ideas for things to follow up later). Compare this with the 'interpretive' format in Example 4.3.

Separating 'observation' from 'commentary' is a useful exercise: it encourages the observer to think carefully about what they have observed, and to try out different interpretations. Bear in mind, however, that no observation is entirely free from interpretation: what you focus on and how you describe events will depend on an implicit interpretive framework (an assumption about what is going on).

It may be easier to attempt a separation if you are observing as a non-participant, but in principle either of the formats adopted in Example 4.3 and Example 4.4 may be used by participant and non-participant observers, and by those basing their field-notes on recollections, or on notes made at the time.

When writing up research reports that include observations based on field-notes, researchers frequently quote selectively from their notes, as in Example 4.5 (p. 195). These observations were made by Sara Delamont in a girls' school in Scotland. The observations form part of a larger study of classroom interaction. In this example, Sara Delamont documents some of the strategies pupils use to find out about a geography test.

Example 4.3 Group poems in a special school

Friday 29.10.90

Context: A short session this week 9.00 - 10.30. One of a series of weekly sessions introducing the kids to poetry, using drama to build up their own ideas and language, which are then put into a poem written up by me

Only some of the group in - Holley, Alastair, Ajmol, Andrew, Claire, Lee

Episode 1: While gathering their ideas and words on the board after the improvisation, Andrew decided to take his socks and shoes off again. He passed them to me one at a time. Disconcerted to get socks tossed at me while trying to listen to the others, [illegible]

Episode 2: I wrote the poem, including as many of their ideas and language as possible over break. Read it to them when I came back. Last week when we did the first group poem about Giants, I had to rewrite it slightly because Alastair insisted that his Giant had been bigger than a block of flats, not the ceiling. I'd hoped to avoid anyone claiming ownership of individual verses, so had not considered the possibilities that his intervention created. This week, as soon as I began to read the Witches poem, they joined in, with Lee especially vocal. I don't think he saw his contributions as changes to what I had written, they were more a sign of his active involvement in the poem. I then asked if they wanted me to change the poem. All the changes to the end improved it. They generated two alternative last lines, and finally settled on one. In future I'll build this into the session and talk explicitly about redrafting

Example 4.4 Field-notes of an assembly

'Sharing assembly' 22/11/90

Tape Counter	Notes	Comments/questions
134	3 children take it in turn to read out poems about animals which they have written. Seated classes quiet and attentive.	I can't hear any of this – neither I suspect can most other children in the assembly. What is being communicated here?
	1 child asks teachers to come and sit on two rows of chairs placed diagonally at the front. Teachers go up to the chairs, acting as if reluctant (sounds of 'Oh no').	I immediately realise teachers are being asked to pretend to be pupils, and the child will be their teacher. Air of puzzled anticipation among seated children. Maybe they aren't familiar with this kind of 'role-reversal' sketch?
142	Teachers mess about, pretending to punch each other, pull hair, tip chairs etc. Child 'teacher' stands in front looking embarrassed. Seated children laugh and make occasional comments.	Seated children don't seem at ease with this situation and don't quite know how to react. Who exactly is in authority, now? Teachers' acting out of pupil unruliness is exaggerated – to make it unreal?
	The child at the front is pretending to try and restore order to his 'class'.	The child 'teacher' in acting out his role is managing to remain respectful to his teacher 'pupils', so he's really acting two roles simultaneously (pupil and teacher)?
	The seated children watching now start to freely imitate the antics of the teachers at the front, and several sniggers break out as the noise level rises.	It's difficult for the watching children to cope with these two conflicting systems – teachers = fonts of authority v. teachers = naughty pupils. They seem very confused.
	Mr. Brown quickly steps out of the role of naughty pupil, and gives the watching children a threatening look as he says 'sh'.	Watching children seem almost relieved that traditional power relations are restored. They settle down very quickly.
150	Some children echo this 'sh', and the hall quickly becomes quiet. The teachers at the front stop messing about, and their pupil 'teacher' reads them rewritten versions of Jack and the Beanstalk, Goldilocks, and The 3 Little Pigs. Some whispering among seated children during the story.	The stories read by the 'teacher' to his 'class' are suitable for a younger agegroup than any classes in this school. Another way of making the event as 'unreal'?

Example 4.5 Extract from an account of a geography lesson

'On the third Wednesday of my fieldwork I went to the top geography set. The lesson opened with Mrs Hill being buttonholed by Jill with an involved query about fish farming. Then Mrs Hill called the class to order and announced a test on 'all Scotland' for the following week, giving them the rest of that lesson to revise for it. My notes continue:

A chorus of groans, protests and objections breaks out – dies away – to be replaced by questions on the nature of the test.

JACKIE: What type of questions? Short answer or essay?

MRS HILL: Short answer mostly.

JILL: Why do we have to have tests all the time?

LORRAINE: Will we be asked to draw anything?

KAREN: Will it be on the board, or are you going to read them out?

MRS HILL: (Says she'll read them out, and tells them they may have to draw. Then tells them to quieten down or she'll go on to the next topic – Newcastle.)

The girls were silenced, and the rest of the period consisted of revision, with girls asking questions about geography as they found points they were not sure of.

The following week I watched the test, which consisted of short answer questions read aloud, such as 'Name two coal-fired power stations in Scotland'. Once it was over the girls swapped papers and marked their neighbour's script.'

(Delamont, 1983, pp. 105–106)

There are several other ways in which field-notes can be drawn on in research reports. Example 4.6 is an extract from a chart that resulted from observing a primary school class. It was designed to identify problems that would be posed for a deaf child who was shortly to join this class – so the observations have been supplemented by identified problems and solutions. In this extract, *Siân* refers to the class teacher; *Ben*, to the deaf child; *Judi*, to a member of the support staff; and *Lorraine*, to Lorraine Fletcher, Ben's mother, who made the observations.

Recording at the time allows you to make fuller notes than recollections. It shares with recollections the problem of selectivity, and scope for unintended bias. It also has the advantage that, because it is open-ended, it leaves you free to note down anything of interest – you may spot something entirely unexpected.

USING AN OBSERVATION SCHEDULE

Observation schedules allow you to look out for certain specified types of behaviour, or participation in specified activities. Several observation schedules have been designed to record younger children's participation in a range of activities. The schedule in Example 4.7 (p. 197) was devised by Glen McDougall for use in a nursery school.

The list in this schedule contains all the activities available to children in the school in which it was developed. It was intended to be completed by staff at 30 minute intervals, but it proved impossible to maintain this degree of regularity. Staff therefore ticked the list at random intervals. In Example 4.7 five separate observations have been made. Some children have fewer than five ticks because they were out of the room for part of the time.

Glen McDougall used her schedule to identify differences in activities selected by girls and boys. (She wrote an account of her work – see Thomas, 1986.) But the schedule could be used as a record of activities selected by individual children over a certain period. It could also be adapted for use in other areas of the

Example 4.6 Observation of classroom activities presented as a chart

Observation of classroom activities: Tuesday 18 June 1985

1. *Pre-9.10* Children arrive. Informal relaxed time, lots of social interaction between Siân and children and amongst the children. No problems.

2. *9.10* Assembly. Usual format.
Problem: suggest assembly is inappropriate for Ben; may be a good time for computer work with Judi.

3. *9.30* (a) Children return. Preparation for TV: *Let's Go Maths*. Children sit round TV, teacher-led discussion about light and heavy. Lots of ideas emerge; all participating.
Problem: Extremely difficult to include Ben and Judi here. Suggest good preparation essential. The teacher's booklet contains a brief summary of content of the programme plus very useful ideas for activities and further reading. Judi needs to be very familiar with the content of the programme and ideas behind it before the class watch it.
Solution: Judi sees resource material in advance and discusses it with Siân. Children watch the second transmission. Lorraine records the first, takes notes for Judi, and watches the programme with Ben at home before he sees it at school.
(b) Siân explains activities planned for after TV. A lot of instruction given orally.
Problem: Instructions are quite detailed and complex.
Solution: Judi has her own copy of the timetable and lesson plans, with explanation of the aims of the activity.

4. *9.44* TV. The programme contains songs, a story as well as mathematical experiments. No problem if adequately prepared as outlined above.

5. *9.58* Siân directs children to activities. Discussion between Siân and children to make sure all know what to do. No problem if Judi is familiar with activities.

6. *10.00* Activities carried out in groups:
   - pictures of light and heavy things
   - working with a balance, finding out what balances 100 g weight, estimating first, with pre-printed charts to fill in; children work in pairs or together
   - weighing everyone in the class and making up a bar chart of the results

   Children very busy and active. Lots of talk about what they are doing.
Problem: Only that Ben would miss out on the very productive chat between children.
Solution: Plenty of discussion with Judi about what he is doing and everyone else is doing and why.

7. *10.15* Siân walks around groups. She supervises and chats with children about their work. No problem: easy to check that Judi and Ben are OK.

8. *10.20* Milk. Two children serve milk while the others are still working. People are finishing, chatting, helping each other, talking about what they've done, going round to see what others are doing. Maybe this would be an opportunity, as children finish their work, for Ben and Judi to talk to them about it, to encourage communication between the children and Ben and to make sure that Ben understands as much as possible of what has been happening.

9. *10.40* Playtime.

10. *11.00* Same activities, different children: groups rotate. Siân hears reading.

11. *11.40* Five minute warning. Children advised to finish off work. No problem: this is easy for Siân to sign.

(Downs *et al.*, 1987, pp. 53–4)

Example 4.7 Observation schedule for nursery activities

Date 2/7/84 . . . . Indoor Activities

	Home Corner	Music Corner	Book Corner	Creative	Pliable	Drawing	Construct-ional	Manipul-ative	Imagin-ative	Maths	Games	Sand	Water	Puzzles
Marina														
Robyn						present		but	outdoors					
Tamara	••••		•											
Danielle	••		•											
Aleah	•													
Charlene	•													
Sasha	•		•											
Tahira	••••													
Julie	••••		•											
Zoe					•									
Nicola					absent									
Natasha	••													
Adaora	•				•									
Nikki														
Rosalind	•••													
Clare					present		but	outdoors						
Rommel							••		•					
Tay							••		•					
Faisal	•								•					
George	•											•		
Rupesh							•							
Adam	•						•							
Nathan					present		but	outdoors						
Shalohuddin	•			•					•			••		
Nou					absent									

school, such as the playground. Similar schedules may be used whether your focus is on activities or on pupils – schedules can identify how often, or by whom, particular pieces of equipment are used, as well as what particular children do during the day.

An alternative way of recording activities, particularly in the playground, or in open-plan areas, is mapping: drawing a plan of an area showing the location of different activities or pieces of equipment. Such a plan can be used as background information for observations since it shows where, for instance, different pieces of equipment are in relation to one another. The plan may also be used to record observations: an observer can mark on it which children are in particular locations, and what activities they are carrying out. In this case you are getting a snapshot of behaviour at any one time. You would need to decide when to carry out the observations and would have to use a new plan for each observation.

Observation schedules may also be used to monitor pupils' behaviour in a more open-ended way. The schedule in Example 4.8 provides a means of recording pupils' activities in small groups. Observers are advised to prepare several copies of the schedule to observe in a lesson, and to conduct observations as follows:

- When you start your observation, pick one group of pupils – the farthest away from you to your left. Note the time, what activities the female pupils are engaged in, and the names. Note anything about behaviour and record any teacher intervention. Then, using the same group, repeat the observations for the male pupils in the group.
- When you've written notes on your first group, move round the room repeating the observations for each group. Go round the groups as many times as you can during the lesson.

(Myers, 1987, p. 25)

Example 4.8, like Example 4.7, is meant to allow comparison between girls' and boys' behaviours (several published schedules have been devised with similar aims). But the schedule could be used to monitor the behaviour of individual pupils working in groups.

Both schedules involve time-sampling. An observer is meant to write down what a pupil, or pupils, are doing at one particular time. The schedule in Example 4.7 specified a regular sampling every 30 minutes (though this regularity wasn't maintained). Example 4.8 doesn't specify particular sampling intervals, but the assumption underlying such a schedule is that practised observers will develop a regular 'rhythm' as they pass from group to group. With such methods only a certain proportion of pupils' behaviour is being sampled. The more frequently an observer samples, the more complete a picture they obtain, but it is still 'snapshots' that are being collected. It is not possible to follow through connected sequences of behaviour. Also, time-sampling will highlight frequently occurring behaviour, but this is not necessarily what is most important in a lesson. Something highly significant may happen only once – when you are jotting down notes about another pupil.

Example 4.7 specifies particular categories to look out for – involvement in certain activities. The schedule provides quantitative information. Glen McDougall, in producing her report of observations carried out in different classes, is able to say that more boys than girls participated in certain activities and more girls than boys in others. Example 4.8 does not provide quantitative information, but on reading through the notes afterwards an observer may identify certain patterns in the way pupils behave that merit discussion in any written report.

Sometimes researchers try to code open-ended observations such as those that might come from using the schedule in Example 4.8. They allocate behaviour they have observed to specific categories, such as talking to another pupil; talking to the teacher; listening to another pupil or the teacher; handling equipment; other 'on task' behaviour; mucking about, etc. By coding observations you can transform qualitative information into quantitative information – you can say how many pupils behaved in a certain way, or you can compare how different pupils behave. It can be difficult to use pre-specified categories – it may be best if categories grow out of the observations themselves. It may also be difficult to code written observations after the event and there is no way of going back to check on pupils' behaviour. Coding is likely to be more reliable if you have access to a video-recording (see sub-section 4.6). In this case you could also ask a colleague to check your coding.

Example 4.8 Observation schedule to monitor groups

CLASSROOM INTERACTION/OBSERVATION

FORM A - SMALL-GROUP WORK

Name of school . . . . Filled in by . . . . Date completed . . . .

	FEMALE PUPILS					MALE PUPILS			
Time	Activities	Names	Comments	Teacher Intervention		Activities	Names	Comments	Teacher Intervention

(Browne and France, 1986)

I've given examples of two schedules, each one tailored to particular needs. It is unlikely you will be able to find an observation schedule you can use off the peg. You will need to: identify carefully what kinds of behaviour you wish to observe, and in which contexts (open-ended observation using field-notes may help in this); draft, or adapt, a schedule to suit your own interests; then pilot this to make sure it works before using it 'for real'.

4.4 MONITORING CLASS OR GROUP DISCUSSION

I have just discussed ways of monitoring children's behaviour in a whole class or as members of groups. But your focus may be less on *what* children, or adults, are doing and more on *how* they are interacting. Talk is quite pervasive, and a very good source of evidence for a variety of research questions. There are several ways in which you can find out about talk. This section focuses on observing interactions *between* people. Examples include talk between a teacher and pupils; small-group talk in the classroom; and talk between a group of people in other contexts, such as meetings. If your focus is on an *individual* speaker (for instance, looking at their talk in different contexts), see also sub-section 4.5, 'Monitoring an individual'. If you wish to ask people to provide information about their talk (for instance, asking pupils to keep 'talk diaries') see also Section 3, 'Getting information from people'. If you wish to analyse formal records of discussions (such as minutes of meetings), see Section 2, 'Getting information from documents and school resources'.

This sub-section discusses techniques of monitoring talk as it happens using methods similar to those used to monitor other activities or aspects of behaviour. Such methods provide an overview of talk, which may be what your project requires. If you wish to look in more detail at what is said, or at how people interact, you will need to use an audio- or video-recording (see Part 3, Section 2). You may also wish to transcribe extracts of talk for close analysis (in which case, see Part 3, Section 2).

As with observing activities in a classroom, it is very difficult to carry out observations of talk as it happens if you are also an active participant. If you are involved in classroom talk as a teacher, you may be able to make notes from recollections after the event, but these are likely to be of the most general kind, for instance: what was talked about; who seemed to have a lot to say; any particularly salient feature, such as a dispute that broke out. If you wish to look at talk in any more detail you will need to observe on the spot as a non-participant – to observe while someone else is teaching, or to observe a small group working independently.

If you are chairing a meeting you will be in a similar position to a teacher taking a leading role in class discussion. It will be difficult to take systematic notes, but you may be able to ask a colleague to help. If you are a participant in a meeting (but not the chair), you may be able to note down main points that are relevant to your research question(s). You will still find, however, that it is difficult to take an active part in discussion while taking notes – you may find you note down points made by everyone except yourself! You need, therefore, to balance the needs of your recording against your wish to have a say in what is discussed.

The examples of observation methods in this section are all designed for observers who are not (simultaneously) taking a leading part in discussion.

USING FIELD-NOTES TO RECORD TALK

An observer may use field-notes to jot down points of interest about any interaction. Such notes may be your main source of information, or they may supplement other forms of recording. If you are taking notes on the spot, you will find that the talk flows very rapidly. This is likely to be the case particularly in informal talk, such as talk between pupils in a group. More formal talk is often easier to observe on the spot. In whole-class discussion led by a teacher, or in formal meetings, usually only one person talks at a time, and participants may wait to talk until nominated by the teacher or chair. The teacher or chair may rephrase or summarize what other speakers have said. The slightly more ordered nature of such talk gives an observer more breathing space to take notes.

Example 4.9 provides an example of detailed field-notes made at a school governors' meeting. The notes were made by Rosemary Deem, from The Open University. Rosemary Deem was collecting evidence for a research project on school governing bodies, carried out with two other researchers, Sue Hemmings and Kevin Brehony. As well as observing governors' meetings, the researchers issued questionnaires to a sample of governors and interviewed some chairs of governing bodies and head teachers. Observations of meetings provided information on how governors coped with their responsibilities (how they dealt with issues that were referred to them; whether issues were resolved in meetings or referred to the head, or to a governors' sub-group, etc.); on power relations in meetings (e.g., who contributed and how often); and on the roles taken by lay people and professionals.

The notes in Example 4.9 begin with the head's suggestion that governors attach themselves to houses within school. This gives rise to concern about the level and nature of governors' involvement in school life.

In these notes, Rosemary Deem has tried to note down, as near verbatim as possible, the points people made. She also wrote up recollections after the meeting in a research diary. To help in her analysis she created an index of issues that were discussed, and that she could track through subsequent meetings. In this case, she would index changes in school structure (the introduction of a new house system) and governor involvement in school life.

USING AN OBSERVATION SCHEDULE TO RECORD TALK

You can use an observation schedule to help you structure your observations of talk. You may be interested in who talks, or how much people talk. In this case, you could simply list participants' names, and make a tick alongside each name whenever the person *begins* speaking.

Schedules that record the number of contributions someone makes to a discussion can help you to identify very general patterns in the distribution of talk between different participants. This has the limitation that the number of contributions is only one measure of the amount someone talks. Someone may make very few but long contributions or frequent one-word responses.

Some schedules permit the observation of different categories of talk. The distinctions you're able to make will depend upon the type of talk you're observing. In teacher–pupil question and answer sessions you may be able to distinguish between pupils' contributions that are responses to a teacher's question or spontaneous contributions. Other distinctions may be appropriate in practical sessions when the teacher is walking from group to group checking on progress or offering help.

The schedule in Example 4.10 was devised by Jim McGonigal while working with a class of 12-year-old pupils in a school in Glasgow. Jim McGonigal wanted to assess children's contributions to group discussion in English lessons. He devised a system of 'doodles' to distinguish different types of talk. He allocated each child a box, divided into four sections, one for each five-minute portion of the talk he observed. Example 4.10 shows the pattern of talk for the first ten minutes.

Example 4.9 Field-notes from a governors' meeting

Cotswold School 19/2/91 7.00 p.m. – 9.40 p.m. shortest ever (!)

Seating plan

Room hot; min attendance
Parent ♂ AB
Co-opted ♂ vice-chair DJ
LEA Officer in attendance LR
Headteacher ♂ DM
Chair (parent) ♂ PB
Clerk ♀ JS
Teacher governor ♀ ML
Co-opted ♂ EN
LEA ♀ SH new councillor/governor
Deputy head ♂ observer
Parent ♂ BM
Co-opted ♀ BB
researcher

Usual seats except new governor. Politicos missing

DM Report next meeting – house structure – Govs cd form view themselves by visit or attachment cd put you all down for a house

BM Many govs cd be involved further in sch life

ML More useful than curric visits – 2 yr gps each house so gives better understanding of curric & small no staff so govs get to know them. Hses provide microcosm of sch

BB I think it is good idea – hve we had paper on hse structure?

DM Cd give you one.

BB Don't want to make wk – is there anything already

DJ If govs do this, need strategy – not just go for chat – must know from staff what they hope for.

PB Shall we just put names against houses – 2 govs per hse

BM Need to be clear a/b purpose – no reltnshp to gov subgps or other staff gps – hses x cut this + for one small gp. How do we monitor this in gov body

PB I perceive concern – no govs involved or sp resps etc. – are we getting into schl in ways giving us reasonable picture life sch in student/teacher view – when visited clroom, first time seen sch at wk in that way – help govs be involved – + cd tailor to own needs

BB I know I don't come into sch at all & as governor I should

BM No enthusiasm – reached capacity govs to visit – if devise new scheme

BB There's more to being gov than meetings.

Example 4.10
Record of a group discussion, distinguishing different categories of talk

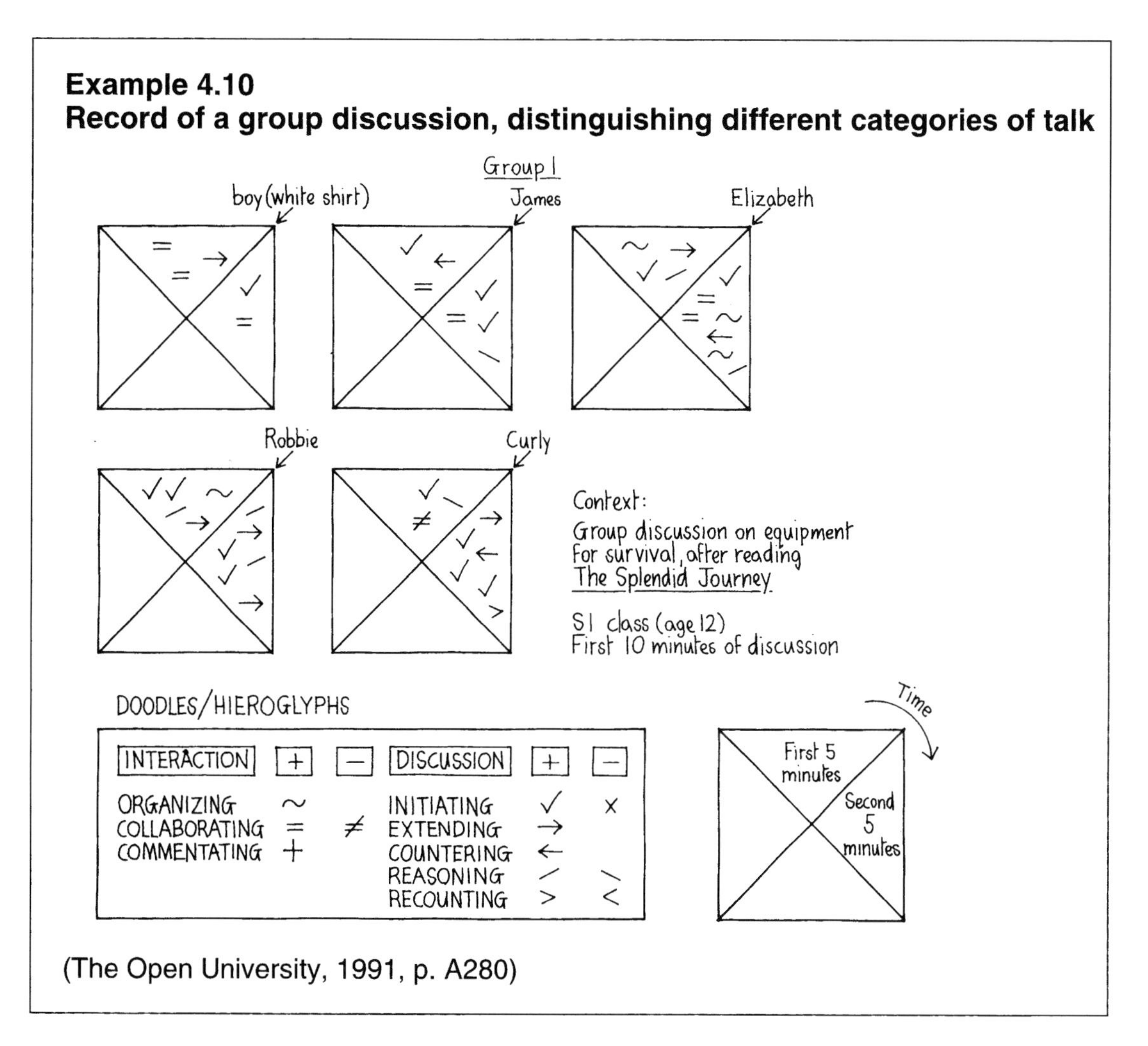

(The Open University, 1991, p. A280)

Jim McGonigal describes how he came by his doodles:

> The boxes I had drawn were too small to record all the functions in writing as they occurred, and I found myself using an imitative quasi-hieroglyphic doodle to note each occurrence. For *organizing* (identifying the task, directing, concluding) I used ~ which seemed a smoothing, facilitating form. *Collaborating* (agreeing, encouraging, yielding turns, moderating personal views in the light of other contributions) was drawn as an = sign. *Commentating* (a relatively rare and sophisticated skill, involving monitoring the speaker's own or others' contributions) seemed a +. *Initiating* (a good idea-producing move at the start of a stage of the discussion) was a ✓, and a ✗ would serve contrary-wise for negatively disruptive comments.
>
> We were well into discursive skills now (although interactive skills continued to play their vital role throughout) and the children were *extending* each other's ideas through rephrasing or additional detail (→), or *countering them* rationally (←) by raising objections or qualifying previous statements. As they were forced by the context to select from and choose between many items of potential usefulness for survival, *reasoning* skills (explaining, justifying, comparing, hypothesizing, generalizing) came into play and were recorded / (flawed reasoning or chop-logic got a \ ). *Recounting* (using relevant coherent anecdote or paraphrasing events in the text) was set down similarly as >), by raising objections or qualifying previous statements. As they were forced by the context to select from and choose between many items of potential usefulness for survival, *reasoning* skills (explaining, justifying, comparing, hypothesizing, generalizing) came into play and were recorded / (flawed reasoning or chop-logic got a \). *Recounting* (using relevant coherent anecdote or paraphrasing events in the

> text) was set down similarly as >, with < for fruitless anecdotal timewasting (though none of that occurred in the time I spent with the groups).
>
> (The Open University, 1991, p. A280)

If you wish to devise an observation schedule, it is useful to do some form of open-ended observation to identify appropriate categories of talk. You'll also find it is difficult to categorize talk in any very complex way when observing and recording on the spot. If you wish to look at different types of talk in detail, it is necessary to use an audio-or video-recording.

The further reading list at the end of this section gives references to published schedules. Most of these have been tried and tested, but you will probably still wish to adapt published schedules for your own purposes. Some published interaction schedules are difficult to use, and a schedule that works perfectly well in one context may not in another. If you do use a published observation schedule, it is important to practise first. If you devise your own schedule you should pilot this to check that it works and provides the sort of information you want.

4.5 MONITORING AN INDIVIDUAL

The different types of observation mentioned in sub-sections 4.3 and 4.4 could allow you to identify activities carried out by individuals: field-notes are likely to mention pupils by name, and some observation schedules allow pupils' names to be specified. But you may wish to focus more closely on the behaviour of one or more individual pupils – or teachers, or other adults.

You will probably already be carrying out observations of individual pupils as part of record-keeping and assessment, but whereas assessing pupils normally involves keeping track of their progress over a school year, or at least a term, in monitoring one or more individual pupils as part of your project you will be involved in a more short-term (but possibly more detailed) exercise. Nevertheless, similar principles apply, in that you will need to decide which activities to observe and when, and to devise an appropriate format for recording your observations.

USING FIELD-NOTES TO OBSERVE AN INDIVIDUAL

You could use field-notes to jot down observations about a particular child while he or she carries out an activity. The ILEA Primary Language Record suggests one format for recording a diary of observations of pupils' language use (with separate sections for speaking and listening, as opposed to reading and writing) to support the assessment of a pupil's language. Example 4.11 shows observations made about a pupil's writing.

A more recent book, *Patterns of Learning* (CLPE, 1990) suggests how the Primary Language Record may be adapted to cover other subject areas within the framework of the national curriculum.

If you want to use the Primary Language Record, it is important to refer to the *Handbook for Teachers*, which gives guidance on completing the record itself and the accompanying diary of observations. But it is likely that you will wish to select your own format in line with your research questions. You will also need to decide how often, during which activities, and for how long, you wish to observe the child you're focusing on.

Field-notes may also be used to record an adult's behaviour. Example 4.12 is a 'condensed account of two hours' in the life of a primary head teacher. The notes were made by Marie Stacey, then a project co-ordinator in the National Writing Project, who was work-shadowing the head.

Example 4.11 Record of a child's writing

2 **Reading and Writing**: diary of observations
(reading and writing in English and/or other community languages)

Dates	Reading
	Record actual examples of the child's reading (including wider experiences of story) across a range of contexts.
1st week of term.	K. shows little inclination to look at books when in the book corner. He enjoys conversation with other children at this time.
2.10.87.	M. (K's cousin) read 'The Cat Sat on the Mat' with him. K. became greatly excited, "Miss, can I read it to you?" He took the book home to read.
16.10.87.	K. returned to 'Cat on the Mat' after quite a long gap – asked me to listen to him reading it. Confidently recalled the story.
2.11.87.	K. read a small caption which accompanied a drawing of a sycamore 'wing' on the nature table.
13.11.87.	Browsing in the book corner he became excited by finding the smaller version of 'The Hungry Giant'. "It's the same as this book!" pointing to the 'big book'.
16.11.87.	K. brought in 3 pages from a Hindi date calendar for our 'Home Writing' Board'.

	Writing
	Record actual examples of the child's writing (including stories dictated by the child) across a range of contexts.
Sept.	K. tried to make his first book (other children were making some so he wanted to join in). Tried to write his name but became frustrated.
2.10.87	K. asked me to help him write his name. We talked about it and practised each letter. Finally managed a 'K'. He was delighted.
6.10.87.	Father sent in a Hindi/English alphabet & put it on the noticeboard.
9.10.87.	Big breakthrough – K. managed to copy his name today.
14.10.87.	K's first attempts at 'independent writing'. "I'm going to write a story." Echoes of 'The Hungry Giant' storychest story. Evidence of letters from his name in his writing.
15.10.87.	K. suggested a notice for our bottle collection & dictated it to me. Drew a bottle to illustrate the notice.
16.10.87.	Playing in the class shop 'Mr. Baker's Sandwich Bar' he took orders on the telephone & wrote on the jotter pad.

K *Reception — boy*
Languages: ***Hindi, English***

(ILEA/CLPE, 1988, p. 42)

Example 4.12 Record of two hours in the life of a primary head

'Opens post; signs cheques; organises his secretary's tasks; updates staff noticeboard; discusses dangerously cracked wall in playground with caretaker; discusses assembly with colleagues; examines leak on the electricity junction box; discusses problems over timing of parents' appointments; reads letters infants have written following visit to clinic; discusses discipline problems with temporary teacher; answers phone; amends addresses on child's record card; takes phone call from fellow head; sees teacher who wants time off; child reads to him; marks record and discusses reading; answers letters left over from yesterday; caretaker reports on wall – the Authority has promised to send someone; into Infants' assembly to warn them about danger from wall; sends note for Junior assembly about wall; secretary arrives, discusses her tasks; goes through his governors' report; goes through catalogue for staple guns; lists his own priorities for the day; tries to phone swimming instructor over a disciplinary problem (line engaged: this is his third attempt); phones pastoral adviser (line engaged); tries swimming instructor again (she's out); phones pastoral adviser re staffing; head refused telephone request for fundraising; wet playtime – he walks around, talks to children; inspects wall anxiously.'

(Stacey, 1989, p. 15)

As a result of the whole observation Marie Stacey is able to make comments about aspects of the head's professional life, such as the amount of routine administration he is obliged to do.

USING AN OBSERVATION SCHEDULE TO OBSERVE AN INDIVIDUAL

You may want to carry out more structured observations of specific activities or types of behaviour. Of the observation schedules mentioned above, Examples 4.7, 4.8 and 4.10 provide information about the behaviour of individuals. Alternatively, you could construct your own schedule focusing on the types of behaviour you are interested in.

Beate Schmidt-Rohlfing, a teacher from Leeds, trailed a seven-year-old girl, Asima, for a school day. The girl was deaf but, along with other deaf children, attended a mainstream school. Some lessons were spent in a special 'base' with other deaf pupils, others in a classroom with hearing pupils. The school had a bilingual policy – deaf pupils used British Sign Language as well as English. Beate Schmidt-Rohlfing wanted to see who this particular girl communicated with over a day. She noted down how often the girl initiated communication with others (members of the school staff and deaf and hearing peers) and how often others initiated communication with her. The information was written up as a case study for the Open University pack P535 *Talk and Learning 5–16*. The results of the observation were presented as a chart, reproduced as Example 4.13.

For a discussion of recording and transcribing talk, see Section 2 of Part 3 of this Handbook.

4.6 USING CHILDREN'S WORK

So far in this section I have discussed how you can observe children and adults, documenting their behaviour or the range of activities they engage in. But what if there is a tangible outcome to children's activities, a piece of work that you want to use as evidence in your project?

Pupils' work forms a useful source of evidence of their responses to a lesson, or of their knowledge, understanding or interests. It is something tangible that you can discuss with colleagues or pupils, so you can compare your interpretations with others'. You may find colleagues can supply you with examples of the same pupil's work from different contexts, though in this case you will lack contextual information on how the work was produced.

In considering ways of recording impressions of children's work, a similar distinction can be observed to that in previous sub-sections – between open-ended scrutiny of children's work (as with field-notes) and using a fixed set of categories to examine children's work (more akin to using an observation schedule). Children's written work is used as an example throughout this sub-section, but the general principles discussed will apply to other forms of work (drawings, models, etc.).

Example 4.13 Chart showing whom a child communicated with

	'A' to deaf peers	deaf peers to 'A'	'A' to hearing peers	hearing peers to 'A'	'A' to deaf Instructor	deaf Instructor to 'A'	'A' to support staff	Support staff to 'A'	'A' to class teacher	class teacher to 'A'
1. session base 9 – 9.40	26	24			17	12				
2. session classroom 9.40 – 10.30	14	15	3	6			18	21	0	1
playground	8	5	4	3						
3. session base 10.50 – 11.55	21	23					16	22		
lunch 12.00 – 12.20	12	12	4	6						
4. session classroom 1.05 – 2.25	25	26	4	7			23	15	2	2
playground	5	7	2	5						
5. session base 2.45 – 3.15	9	8			10	10				

(The Open University, 1991, p. A101)

Focusing on the tangible product of children's work necessarily provides a partial picture of what children can do. You may also wish to know how children carry out their work. In this case, you will need to look at one or more of sub-sections 4.3–4.5, depending on which aspects of behaviour interest you. You may wish to know what children think about their work, in which case, see Section 3, 'Getting information from people'. It is often useful to combine information from one or other of these sources with information derived from the product of children's work.

OPEN-ENDED SCRUTINY OF CHILDREN'S WORK

The Primary Language Record (PLR) illustrated in Example 4.11 provides one format for drawing on a combination of methods – it allows a teacher to record observations about the way a child writes as well as impressions about the written work itself. The PLR is not totally open-ended. It highlights certain aspects of writing to look for. In the same way, your own scrutiny of children's work will be guided by your research questions – it is unlikely to be completely open. You may intend to focus on formal conventions of writing (e.g. a child's developing use of punctuation), on content, or style, or on a combination of features.

When writing up an account of children's writing, teacher-researchers often include extracts from writing to support a point they wish to make, or they may include one or more whole pieces of writing with an attached commentary. Example 4.14 is part of a case study of the writing development of a four-year-old child, Christopher. It was written by Margaret J. Meek, a co-ordinator with the National Writing Project, who observed the context of Christopher's writing as well as looking at the finished product.

If you wish to refer to work other than a piece of writing (or drawing) in your report it may be difficult to include examples. You could include photographs, or you may need to resort to a description of the work.

Example 4.14 Using a child's writing as evidence

On another occasion, Christopher's teacher asked a group of children to illustrate their favourite nursery rhyme. She intended to accompany these by writing out the rhymes (alongside) herself, but Christopher wrote his own version of 'Humpty Dumpty' quite unaided. Later, he asked his teacher to write out the rhyme correctly — the first time he had acknowledged the difference between his writing and that of adults.

What does he know about writing?

- that rhymes are arranged in a particular way on the page
- that print usually starts at the top of the page and moves downwards
- how to write a large range of capital and lower case letters
- how to represent each sound in a word with a letter, although he occasionally uses one letter only to stand for a whole word, eg *K* for *'King's'* and *s* for *'sat'*.
- that words carry a consistent phonic pattern — *ol* is used to represent *'all'* in *'fall'* and *'all'*
- how to hold a long piece of text in his head as he writes

(Meek, 1989, pp. 77–8)

ASSIGNING CHILDREN'S WORK TO A SET OF CATEGORIES

You may wish to examine a single piece of work according to a set of categories, but it is more likely you will want to use this method to compare a range of work, perhaps the writing produced by a child in different contexts, or work from several pupils.

Some teachers involved in the Sheffield Writing Project wanted to find out about the range of writing produced by upper-primary and lower-secondary school pupils during a normal week of school. They collected all the writing produced by a sample of pupils (including rough notes and 'scribbles'). To compare the *amount* pupils wrote in different subjects, they simply counted the total number of words produced in English, history, and so on.

The teachers also wanted to record certain characteristics of children's writing: the extent to which pupils used their own words; how much control pupils had over what they wrote; how 'engaged' pupils seemed to be in their writing; whether the process or the product of writing was emphasized; and how teachers responded to pupils' writing. Example 4.15 shows a chart they devised to record the extent to which pupils used their own words.

Example 4.15 Record of a ten-year-old pupil's work for one week

Origin of words			
Derivative <..> Pupil's own			
Totally	*Mostly*	*Mostly*	*Totally*
Maths 1		Geography	History 1
Maths 2		French 2	History 2
French 1		Science 2	English
			Science 1

Note: 'French 1' = first piece of work completed in French.

In this case, the Sheffield teachers identified four categories of work: 'totally derivative', 'mostly derivative', 'mostly pupil's own', 'totally pupil's own'. The categories form a continuum. The teachers provided a description of each category:

> *Totally derivative* includes not only directly copied or dictated writing, but the writing in which a pupil may be required to fill in blanks with words from a given text as in a comprehension exercise.
>
> *Mostly derivative* indicates that there is limited scope for pupils to use some words of their own choice or, for example, to write up in discursive prose some information on which notes had previously been dictated. The most common example in the data was sentence length answers where pupils had to extract information from a text.
>
> *Mostly pupil's own* might include, as an example, a poem in which pupils had to include a given repeated line.
>
> *Totally pupil's own* indicates that the pupils were free to choose their own means of expression, although, for example, class discussion may have preceded the writing.
>
> (Harris *et al.*, 1986, p. 6)

Specifying the characteristics of each category in this way will probably make a coding system more reliable, but there is still scope for disagreement between coders. This is particularly likely between categories such as 'mostly derivative' and 'mostly pupils' own', where some personal judgement is called for.

When devising a category system it is important to try this out to see if it is appropriate for the children's work you want to examine. Trying it twice with the same pieces of work, or asking a colleague to use it, also acts as a test of your system's reliability.

Assigning pupils' work to a set of categories provides you with quantitative information: the Sheffield Writing Project teachers were able to specify, for each school subject, the number of pieces of pupils' written work that fell into each of their categories. They could then discuss, for instance, the extent to which pupils used their own words in different subjects.

When discussing quantitative information like this, it is possible to quote 'raw' figures – the tallies made of pupils' writing. But it is often better to give percentage figures when making comparisons between groups. Figures may also be presented as a table or histogram. Section 5 provides advice on presenting numerical information.

4.7 REVIEWING METHODS

This section discusses several ways of 'seeing what people do'. No method is perfect – each has strengths and weaknesses. What follows is a summary of what each method can do and what its limitations are.

WAYS OF COLLECTING EVIDENCE

Recollections

What the method can do	*Limitations*
Allows you to reflect after the event on part of the school day, or a meeting. You are likely to recall episodes that stand out.	There is a danger of unintended bias, exacerbated if you rely on recollections.
Does not require any special arrangements for the observation.	You cannot go back and check on any observations you are not sure of.
Interferes very little with normal teaching or participation in a meeting.	You will not be able to remember events in detail.
Because it can be fitted in with everyday work, you may be able to carry out more	On any occasion, you will collect less information than someone recording extensive observations at the time.

Observation at the time of activities, of talk, or of a particular individual

What the method can do	*Limitations*
Allows you to observe points of interest as they occur. You can observe across a whole lesson/meeting or at selected intervals.	You only have a short time to decide what to record.
Requires preparation – pen and paper, perhaps a schedule – but no special hardware.	You cannot go back and check your observations afterwards.
On any occasion, you will be able to make fuller observations than someone relying on recollections.	You cannot do as detailed an analysis as would be possible with an audio- or video-recording.

May be carried out in your lesson by a colleague or pupil.	Is difficult to carry out while teaching or taking an active part in a discussion or activity.
You can observe in a colleague's lesson.	You need a relationship based on trust – and you may still be intrusive. Pupils may interrupt to ask for help.

Children's work

What the method can do	Limitations
Can provide partial evidence of how your teaching has gone, or of pupils' knowledge and/or understanding.	Focuses on product of work – you may want additional evidence on process.
Data can be collected by someone else.	Work may be hard to interpret if you don't know the context in which it was produced.
You can return to, and reconsider, the evidence, and share interpretations with a colleague/pupils.	Extensive scrutiny of children's work is time-consuming.

FIELD-NOTES VERSUS OBSERVATION SCHEDULES

Throughout this section I have made a broad distinction between open-ended observation (using field-notes or open-ended scrutiny of children's work) to provide qualitative information; and more structured observation (using an observation schedule or assigning children's work to specific categories) which usually provides quantitative information. The main features of the two approaches include:

Field-notes (or open-ended scrutiny of children's work)

- Field-notes are open-ended. Observers note down points of interest. Anything can be noted down (though researchers will clearly be guided by their research questions).
- Sometimes observations may be unexpected, or things may be noted down that only begin to make sense later when mulled over and compared with other information. Such flexibility is useful, particularly when you feel it is too early to stipulate exactly what you want to look for.
- The information provided is qualitative. One of the commonest ways of using such information is to quote from field-notes (or transcripts, or examples of children's work) to support a point you want to make.
- Open-ended observation is selective – two different observers may (legitimately) notice different things about the same event/talk/piece of work, or make different interpretations of events.
- There is a danger of bias, in that observers may see what they want to see, or ignore counter-evidence.

Observation schedules (or assigning children's work to categories)

- Schedules focus on peoples' participation in specified activities, or on specific features of talk or pieces of work.
- They produce quantitative information that can be represented numerically (for instance, as a table or bar chart).
- They allow systematic comparisons to be made between people or between contexts.
- They may be constructed so as to be relatively reliable so that two different observers would get similar results from the same observations.

- When they involve making a personal judgement about something, they are likely to be less reliable.
- They necessarily restrict what an observer can observe – important information not included in the schedule may be missed.

When deciding how to carry out your research, it is often useful to draw on a combination of methods – these may complement one another and provide a more complete picture of an event.

This section should have given you some ideas for how to analyse the data you collect (how to make sense of it and how to sort it so that you can select information to use as evidence in your report). Section 5 provides further advice on analysing data and presenting your results to others.

FURTHER READING

ATKINSON, P. and HAMMERSLEY, M. (1998) 'Ethnography and participant observation' in N. K. DENZIN and Y. S. LINCOLN (eds.) *Strategies of Qualitative Inquiry*, Thousand Oaks, California, Sage.

BASSEY, M. (1999) *Case Study Research in Educational Settings*, Buckingham, Open University Press

This book takes the reader through the various stages in conducting case study research and includes a helpful account of data collection and data analysis methods.

CAVENDISH, S., GALTON, M., HARGREAVES, L. and HARLEN, W. (1990) *Observing Activities*, London, Paul Chapman.

A detailed account of observations carried out in primary schools in the Science Teacher Action Research (STAR) project. The book provides some general discussion of classroom observation and describes the Science Process Observation Categories (SPOC) system devised for STAR.

COOLICAN, H. (1990) *Research Methods and Statistics in Psychology*, London, Hodder and Stoughton.

This contains a very useful section on observation and coding. It is written for the novice researcher and is clear and easy to follow.

CORSARO, W. A. and MOLINARI, L. (2000) 'Entering and observing in children's worlds: a reflection on a longitudinal ethnography of early education in Italy' in P. CHRISTENSEN and A. JAMES (eds.) *Research with Children: perspectives and practices*, London, Falmer Press.

A resource book on the methodology of childhood research. The chapter by Corsaro and Molinari is written by two leading researchers in the field of child observation and ethnography.

MYERS, K. (1987) *Genderwatch! Self-assessment schedules for use in schools* (see full reference and description in the further reading list for Section 2).

The *Genderwatch!* schedules also cover classroom, school and playground observations.

ROBSON, C. (1999) *Real World Research: a resource guide for social scientists and practitioner researchers*, Oxford, Blackwell.

Chapter 8 covers all aspects of observational methods.

THE OPEN UNIVERSITY (1991) *PE 635 Working with Under Fives: an in-service training pack*, Milton Keynes, The Open University.

This pack provides detailed guidance on observing young children, and includes video activities.

WRAGG, E. C. (1999, 2nd edn) *An Introduction to Classroom Research*, London, Routledge.

A best-selling book written in clear and accessible language. It shows how various people study lessons for different purposes and in different contexts. It contains numerous examples of coding schemes as well as discussing how to develop them.

5 INFORMATION AND DATA: ANALYSIS AND PRESENTATION

5.1 INTRODUCTION

This section of the Handbook contains general advice on the analysis and presentation of data. You will probably have realised from reading the other sections that processes of analysis and interpretation begin to take place as soon as you make a start on collecting your data. During the initial phases of your project you will find yourself making decisions about what to observe and record, which questions to ask in interviews, which documents to select and so on. In a sense these decisions are a preliminary form of analysis as you are beginning to identify potentially important concepts and hypotheses which will aid later analysis and explanation.

During the course of carrying out a piece of research, something unexpected may occur which causes a change in direction and the formulation of new research questions or hypotheses. When this happens, researchers try to analyse why things departed from the expected. Was the original focus of the research inappropriate? What implications can be drawn from the new information? Should the research instruments (questionnaires, interview and observation schedules) be redesigned to take account of the unexpected? Usually this type of exploratory analysis happens during the pilot stage.

As soon as you begin to collect your data you can start to explore what it is telling you, although the picture will probably keep changing as you collect more information. During this phase researchers often begin to formulate preliminary hypotheses about what the data might mean.

The main business of analysis begins once all the information or data has been collected. This is the most exciting phase of the project. All the hard work of data collection has been completed. Now you can start to look for patterns, meaning and orderings across the complete data set which could form the basis of explanations, new hypotheses and even theories.

Analysing and interpreting data is a very personal thing. No one can tell you precisely how to set about it, although, as you have seen in previous sections, guidelines do exist. For quantitative data, things are a little easier as there are standard ways of analysing and presenting numerical information.

This section contains some very general guidelines and examples of the analysis of information. The section also includes advice about presenting data in your project report. First of all I shall discuss how to deal with 'unstructured' information from informal interviews, open-ended questionnaires, field-notes and the like. Then I shall take a look at how more structured information, such as that from interview and observation schedules, can be tackled. In the latter case it is usually possible to quantify the information and present it as tables and/or graphs. A set of further readings is given at the end of the section. These can give more detailed guidance on the topics covered here.

You should read this section while you are still designing your study and before you begin to collect any data. You will find it most useful to read through the whole section quickly, and then to go back to the sub-sections which you need to read in more detail when you are deciding which methods to use for your project. You will need to return to this section once you have collected your data. This time you will probably want to concentrate only on those sub-sections of direct relevance to your project.

5.2 DESCRIPTION, ANALYSIS, EXPLANATION AND RECOMMENDATION

Data can be used in two ways: *descriptively* or *analytically* (to support interpretations). In practitioner research the main purpose of analysis and interpretation, whether the data are qualitative or quantitative, is to move from *description* to *explanation* and/or *theory*, and then to *action* and/or *recommendation*. Let's look at some extracts from Margaret Khomo's project report in order to illustrate this.

Example 5.1 Moving from description to recommendation

In her report, Margaret gives the following account of pupils' reactions to recording their family histories on tape:

> The pupils were very enthusiastic when they had to record their findings about their family. Even sensitive information – for example revealing that a mother had been adopted – was included. Most of the pupils couldn't wait to hear the finished tape-recording, the only ones who did not were those pupils who did not like the sound of their voices on tape. Listening to the tape caused amusement.

This is a descriptive piece of writing drawn from Margaret's record of her classroom observations. She also, however, tried to analyse why it was that her 'active learning' approach generated so much interest and enthusiasm from pupils, particularly the 'less able' pupils:

> The active learning approaches used ... created a working situation in which the pupils were sharing their findings and working out their answer(s) together. This appeared to generate a sense of unity within the class whereas within the control group it was very much a case of each individual completing his or her work without a sense of class involvement ...
>
> The active learning approaches used provided more opportunities for the less able pupils ... to contribute positively to the work of the class.

Here Margaret has been able to propose an explanation as to why 'active learning' is an effective way of teaching about migration. It encourages a sense of unity among pupils by providing a co-operative learning environment where all pupils, including the less able, feel able to share their own personal knowledge and make positive and valued contributions.

Finally, as a result of her observations Margaret was able to make recommendations concerning the management of an active learning environment. Her main recommendation was that active learning was an extremely effective method of teaching history, and that it had particular benefits for less able pupils. When using active learning methods, however, teachers needed to be aware that lesson plans must be more tightly structured than when a more didactic approach is used. Also, time limits need to be set for each activity if pupils are to get through all the work.

I have been able to present neat and tidy excerpts from Margaret's final report. What I have not been able to show are the processes of sifting, sorting and organizing her data that she went through to arrive at these explanations and recommendations. So just what do you do when faced with analysing and interpreting pages of field-notes, notes on documents, diary excerpts, observations, records of interviews, transcripts and the like? The next sub-section gives some guidelines.

5.3 DEALING WITH QUALITATIVE DATA

When dealing with qualitative data you have to impose order on it and organize it so that meanings and categories begin to emerge. One of the most commonly used methods for doing this is known as the method of constant comparison. Hutchinson explains this method as follows:

> While coding and analysing the data, the researcher looks for patterns. He [*sic*] compares incident with incident, incident with category, and finally, category with category ... By this method the analyst distinguishes similarities and differences amongst incidents. By comparing similar incidents, the basic properties of a category ... are defined. Differences between instances establish coding boundaries, and relationships among categories are gradually clarified.
>
> (Hutchinson, 1988, p. 135)

The main aims of this method are to simplify your data by establishing categories, properties of categories, and relationships between categories which will help you explain behaviours, actions and events. This in turn may lead to new theoretical understanding. In qualitative data analysis, looking for and predicting relationships between categories is the first step towards forming new theories.

In Section 1 I mentioned the notion of 'grounded theory' (Glaser and Strauss, 1967) as this applied to qualitative research. What this means is that, in comparison to quantitative or predictive studies where the researcher starts off with an hypothesis based on an existing theory, in qualitative research it is possible to construct and test hypotheses and theories after the data collection has begun. These new theories are 'grounded' in, or arise from, the data.

IDENTIFYING INCIDENTS

In the quotation above, when Hutchinson talks about an 'incident' she is referring to observations or records of segments of activity, behaviour or talk. Identifying where one incident or segment leaves off and another begins is important when analysing qualitative data. The examples of different kinds of field-notes in sub-section 4.3 illustrate some of the many ways in which researchers identify incidents.

In Example 4.3, Will Swann uses 'event-sampling' to identify two episodes or incidents which took place during his lesson. One was an incident where a pupil took off his shoes and socks during an improvization session. The second described children's participation in reading the poem that came out of the improvization session.

In Example 4.4, Janet Maybin organized her field-notes into a series of incidents which took place during a school assembly. This is another example of 'event-sampling'. Note how Janet used the tape counter to help her find each incident.

In Example 4.6, Lorraine Fletcher used a 'time-sampling' strategy to record a series of classroom activities over specified time periods. In this case, however, each segment of time may contain a number of incidents which must be identified.

An incident is not an arbitrary slice or piece of activity, as is a ten-minute section of time. It is a constituent part of an identifiable whole where the whole could be a lesson, an interview, a classroom day, an assembly, a meeting, a consultation and so on. When identifying where one incident begins and another leaves off (or where one topic begins and ends, if you are dealing with talk), you will find that events within an incident are more related to one another than they are to events outside the incident.

IDENTIFYING CATEGORIES

Once you have identified the incidents then you can begin to sort and categorize them. The process of categorization can probably be explained most clearly by an example.

Example 5.2 Identifying categories

In her paper in *Practitioner Research in the Primary School* (Webb, 1990), Susan Wright describes how she carried out an investigation of language use in the teaching and learning of mathematics. She conducted a 'closely focused case study of six middle infant children', and collected her data during normal maths teaching sessions over six months. In particular she concentrated on the topics of time, length and weighing. Her data consisted of tape-recordings, an observation diary and children's worksheets and maths notebooks.

Even before Wright started to collect her data, however, she categorized her research questions into the following four groups:

Questioning

For example,

What kind of questions do I ask?
What kind of questions do the children ask?
What kind of response do the various questions elicit?

Word usage

For example

Which words do children actually use?
Are there any mathematical words which cause particular difficulty?

Shared meanings and misunderstandings

For example:

Is there any discernible pattern in the areas of misunderstanding?
Can I as a teacher learn anything from this?

Non-linguistic evidence of understanding

What factors other than language indicate comprehension?

(adapted from Wright, 1990, pp. 127–8)

Once she had collected the data and started to analyse her transcripts she discovered further categories. For example, when Wright looked at her questions to children (there were some 750 examples of these), they could be grouped as follows:

Factual knowledge questions
Personal questions
Prompting questions
Reasoning or hypothetical questions

(Wright, 1990, pp. 130–31)

Similarly, she found she could fit the questions the children asked into these categories:

Checking up questions
Tentative answers
Requests for information
Miscellaneous questions
[Pupils' open questions to each other.]

(Wright, 1990, p. 133)

Wright concluded that,

> There should be greater use of reasoning questions by the teacher and more opportunity for children to hypothesize about their work; children's active use of mathematical vocabulary should be encouraged together with an awareness of the need to extend the personal vocabularies of some children ...
>
> (Wright, 1990, p. 151)

In this example, the 'incidents' that Wright was particularly interested in were questions: the questions the children asked of each other and of their teacher, and the questions the teacher asked the children. When categorizing these questions Wright probably proceeded as follows:

1. Listened to tapes of the lessons, or read through transcripts and made a note of all examples of 'questions'.
2. Sorted these examples into three piles:
   (a) teacher's questions;
   (b) children's questions to teacher;
   (c) children's questions to each other.
3. Sifted through each pile in turn to see if categories of question could be identified.
4. Once categories were identified, sorted the questions into further piles under each category.
5. Saw whether any questions which were left over formed a further category, or whether the first set of categories needed to be modified to accommodate these.

Sub-sections 2.3, 2.5, 4.3, 4.4 and 4.6 give further examples of how to construct categories.

As I mentioned at the beginning of this session there are no hard-and-fast rules about analysing qualitative data. As a starting point most researchers recommend actual physical sorting of the data into basic categories. They do this by writing up each incident on a separate piece of paper or index card which can then be arranged and rearranged into various piles as categorization proceeds. Wolcott (1990) advises that one should 'begin sorting by finding a few categories sufficiently comprehensive to allow you to sort all your data' (p. 33). For example, you could sort all the data from interviews with men into one pile, and that from women into another. Or you could differentiate talk produced by adults from talk produced by children; information from government documents with information from local documents, data collected in one school or class from data collected in another and so on.

If your data include samples of talk, you may find there are examples of *indigenous categories* which reflect a classification system used by the people in the setting you are studying. For example, children might categorize themselves as either 'brainy types' or 'sporty types'. Where indigenous categories exist in the data, then analysis involves discovering the properties of these categories, and offering explanations for their derivation.

Wright's categories in Example 5.2 are examples of *researchers' categories*, that is, categories you create for yourself. As you construct more detailed sub-categories within your original all-embracing categories you will probably find some incidents and statements that fall into more than one category, and some that will not fit at all. Some categories may have to be redefined or even abandoned either if they contain too few entries, or if they are becoming too large. If you have used triangulation (see sub-section 1.6) you will have a means of checking the validity of your categories. If they are valid they should be able to cope with data from different sources.

Finally, you can use *pre-specified* categories which others have used and published before you. Section 4 contains examples of these, such as the nursery observation schedule by Glen McDougall (Example 4.7).

The books in the further reading list at the end of this section give more detailed advice and techniques on analysing qualitative data. You should not feel bound to use the methods set out in this Handbook if you come across something which is more appropriate.

5.4 PRESENTING QUALITATIVE DATA IN YOUR REPORT

The selection of material to include in your report is one of the main tasks facing you when writing about qualitative data. Coolican offers the following advice:

> A qualitative research report will contain raw data and summaries of it, analysis, inference and, in the case of participant observation, perhaps feelings and reactions of the observer at the time significant events occurred. These are all valid components for inclusion but it is important that analysis, inference and feeling are clearly separated and labelled as such.
>
> (Coolican, 1990, p. 236)

The main body of your report should contain summaries of your data rather than the actual data itself, unless you want to discuss a particular piece of data in depth (such as a section from a transcript or examples of children's work). For the most part, raw data such as field-notes, accounts of meetings and interviews, transcripts and the like should be included as appendices. Your report should include brief interpretive accounts of how you analysed and categorized your data, and definitions of your categories. Well-chosen illustrative examples will help readers understand your choice of categories.

When you come to select data to summarize for your report, it is worth while remembering that if you have collected a lot of information, then you will not be able to include summaries of all of it in your report. You should go back to your original research questions for guidance on what to select. Data which answers these questions should be included; data which is interesting in itself, but which does not answer or throw new light on the original questions should be discarded.

While most of what you will include in your report will be summaries of your data, this does not mean that we do not want you to put *any* raw data in the report. Qualitative reports are brought to life by quotations. Here is Coolican again:

> The final report of qualitative findings will usually include verbatim quotations from participants which will bring the reader into the reality of the situation studied ... The quotes themselves are selections from the raw data which 'tell it like it is'. Very often comments just stick with us to perfectly encapsulate people's position, on some issue or stance in life, which they appear to hold.
>
> (Coolican, 1990, pp. 235–6)

Carefully chosen quotations can play a very important part in reports based on qualitative data. If you want to include quotations in your report then you must make them work for you. Brief quotations which go straight to the heart of the matter have much more impact than longer, more rambling ones, even if the latter do make important points.

No one can really tell you what to select to put into your report. You should, however, try to observe Coolican's guidelines about making clear distinctions between summaries of data, analysis, and interpretation.

5.5 DEALING WITH QUANTITATIVE DATA

The two principal methods of obtaining quantitative data are measuring and counting.

In sub-section 1.5, we defined as quantitative data anything that could be 'quantified' on some numerical basis. As an example, we gave children's scores on a reading test. Here, it is reading performance that is being measured, and the measure is the numerical score obtained from the test. A second type of quantification we referred to was the assignment of children to groups or categories.

For example, on the basis of the individual reading performance of 28 children, you might want to assign 8 to the category of 'above average reading ability', 15 to the category 'average reading ability' and 5 to the 'below average reading ability' category. In this instance you are counting how many instances or cases fall into categories you have selected beforehand.

In this sub-section we shall be dealing mainly with structured data generated by questionnaires, interview schedules, observation schedules, checklists, test scores, marks of children's work, rating scales and the like. Test scores, marks and rating scales all yield numerical data and are therefore quantitative by definition. The kind of information you collect when you are using an observation schedule, checklist or questionnaire is more likely to be in the form of ticks and crosses, and this data has to be converted to numbers before you can start analysing it.

As I mentioned above, qualitative data can be quantified by assigning instances to categories, and then counting up the number of instances in each category. This is a particularly useful technique for dealing with structured data. There is no reason why categories generated from the analysis of the type of unstructured data discussed in sub-section 5.3 cannot be treated in the same way so as to allow numerical comparisons to be made. However, this approach to unstructured data is less common in practice than the qualitative methods discussed in sub-section 5.3.

Discovering categories and assigning incidents to categories simplifies qualitative data and can help you discover patterns and relationships which lead to new hypotheses and interpretations. The same can be said of quantitative data, except that here we have to introduce some new ideas about how to describe the data.

Categories and variables

When you are planning your investigation two things you need to decide at an early stage are:

> What you intend to measure or count;
>
> What units of measurements you should use.

Here it is conventional to distinguish categories from variables. Categories have already been discussed in sub-section 5.3. Here we shall concentrate mainly on variables. Alan Graham (1990) describes the differences between categories and variables as follows:

> Whereas categories are labelled with names, variables are measured with numbers. Variables are so called because they vary, i.e. they can take different values. For example, age and family size are variables

> because age varies from one person to another just as family size varies from one family to another.
>
> ... You may have noticed that it is impossible to measure someone's age with perfect accuracy – you might know it to the nearest minute perhaps, but what about the seconds, tenths of seconds, thousandths of a second ... ? With family size, on the other hand, perfect accuracy is possible, because there is a basic unit – people – and they tend to come in whole numbers!
>
> ... All variables like age, which can be subdivided into infinitely small units are often called continuous variables. The other type of variable, of which family size is an example, comes in discrete chunks, and is called a discrete variable.
>
> (Graham, 1990, pp. 17–18)

When you are designing your study it is very important to work out whether your methods of data collection are going to give you discrete or continuous data, as this will influence the kind of analysis you are able to do and how you present your data. Unlike variables, which can be either continuous or discrete, categories are always discrete. For example, in a questionnaire about people's political attitudes, 'vote labour', 'vote conservative', etc., are names for discrete qualitative categories. Counting up the number of instances, or the number of people responding positively to each category, quantifies the data.

Analysing category data

Let's look at an example of some category data to see how we can begin to analyse it. Example 5.3 shows one of the observation schedules used by a student for a project on gender and classroom interaction in CDT and home economics (HE) lessons.

The observation schedules contained three main categories – teacher addresses pupil (teacher–pupil); pupil addresses teacher (pupil–teacher); and pupils address each other (pupil–pupil). The schedule in Example 5.3 is a record of interactions in an HE lesson on textiles. This lesson centred round the three activities shown on the lefthand side of the schedule. For each activity, under the appropriate category heading, the observer noted the number of times interactions take place between ten boys, five girls and their teacher. Each interaction (represented by a tick or a cross) occurs as a *discrete* instance of the behaviour being recorded. Note how the observer also recorded his own impressions to help him interpret the data later.

Once you have quantified your data, as I have done in Table 1, then there are a number of things that you can do with them. Figure 5 and Table 1 contain raw data. Without further analysis, raw data alone cannot tell you very much. Let's see what the category data in Table 1 can tell us when we start to analyse them further.

When I looked at Table 1, I approached it in the following way. First I added up the total number of observations in the table. This came to 134. Next I added up the total number of observations for the girls (48), and for the boys (86) and worked out what these were as a *percentage* of the total number. For the boys this came to 64 per cent (86/134 × 100), and for the girls it came to 36 per cent (48/134 × 100).

This was an interesting finding. On the face of it, it looked as if, in this lesson, the boys dominated classroom interaction and spoke, or were spoken to, twice as often as the girls. Before jumping to conclusions, however, I took another look at the table and noticed that there were *twice as many boys (10) as there were girls (5)* in this class. It is not really surprising, therefore, that there were more interactions generated by boys.

To confirm this I worked out the average or mean number of interactions per pupil by dividing the total number of interactions (134) by the total number of pupils (15). This comes to a mean of 8.9 interactions per pupil. Next I worked out

Example 5.3 Coping with categories

OBSERVATION SHEET NO. 2 CLASSROOM INTERACTIONS

✓ = BOY X = GIRL	TEACHER/PUPIL	PUPIL/TEACHER	PUPIL/PUPIL
ACTIVITIES IRONING/PRESSING	✓✓✓✓✓✓xxxx ✓✓✓xx✓	✓✓✓x✓✓xx✓✓✓ xx✓	✓✓✓xx✓x✓✓✓✓x ✓✓xx
SETTING UP SEWING MACHINE	✓✓xx ✓✓✓xx✓x ✓x✓	✓✓✓✓ xx✓xxx ✓✓✓xx✓✓	✓✓✓✓xx✓✓✓✓x xx✓
CUTTING-OUT PATTERN	✓✓✓✓xx✓✓x ✓✓x✓✓✓✓	✓✓x ✓✓✓xx✓ ✓✓x	✓✓✓✓✓✓xxx ✓✓✓xx✓
GENERAL COMMENTS BOY ✓ GIRL X	TEACHER TRIES TO INTERACT WITH ALL PUPILS BOYS DEMANDING.	BOYS SEEK/ASK FOR/DEMAND HELP/ADVICE GIRLS GET ON WITH WORK NEED SPECIFIC HELP/ADVICE	A LOT OF INTERACTING NOT CONCERNED WITH WORK ESPECIALLY BOYS

CLASS 2R	LESSON HOME ECONOMICS TEXTILES	GROUP 4	NO. OF BOYS 10	NO. OF GIRLS 5	DATE 14.5.90

Figure 5 One of John Cowgill's observation schedules.

When you count up the number of ticks and crosses in each cell of Figure 5 you arrive at the figures in Table 1.

Table 1
The total number of interactions between pupils and teachers in an HE lesson.

	Type of interaction					
	Teacher–pupil		*Pupil–teacher*		*Pupil–pupil*	
Activities	*Boys*	*Girls*	*Boys*	*Girls*	*Boys*	*Girls*
Ironing/pressing	10	6	9	5	10	6
Setting up sewing machine	8	6	10	7	9	5
Cutting out pattern	12	4	8	4	10	5
Totals	30	16	27	16	29	16

Total no. of interactions = 134 (86 boys, 48 girls)

No. of girls = 5; no. of boys = 10

The number of interactions per category for boys and girls (bottom two rows of Table 1) can be converted into the percentages shown in Table 2.

Table 2 The percentage of interactions attributed to boys and girls according to type of interaction.

	Teacher–pupil	Pupil–teacher	Pupil–pupil
Boys	34.8	31.4	33.7
Girls	33.3	33.3	33.3

the mean number of interactions generated by boys, which came to 8.6 (86/10), and by girls, 9.6 (48/5).

While it is not strictly legitimate to calculate means when you have discrete data, as you cannot have 0.6 of an interaction, working out the means has told us something very useful. Boys and girls were equally likely to engage in some form of classroom interaction in this HE lesson. If anything, the girls engaged in more interactions on average (9.6) than the boys (8.6), and my first impression, that it was the boys who were doing all the talking, was wrong.

Of course, we cannot draw firm conclusions about patterns of classroom interactions on the basis of a single observation session of one lesson and one group of pupils. The student actually collected data from six lessons over a two-week period, which gave him a richer data base to work with. His analyses led him to the conclusion that, 'The opportunities for interactions within the lessons observed were equal for both boys and girls'.

Next I looked to see if the patterns of interaction were different depending on who was doing the talking. Did teachers address more remarks to boys or to girls? Did the girls talk among themselves more than the boys? Using the data at the bottom of Table 1, I worked out the percentages of interactions attributed to boys and girls in each category (see Table 2). Again, the pattern is quite clear. The 48 interactions attributed to the girls were equally divided between the three categories. The boys were addressed by their teacher slightly more frequently than the girls (34.8 per cent versus 33.3 per cent) and spoke to the teacher marginally less often than girls (31.4 per cent as opposed to 33.3 per cent). These differences between boys and girls are not sufficiently large to claim that there is a real difference between them.

You can see by this example that working out *percentages* and *means* are two very useful techniques for analysing category data, although as I explained above you must be careful when using means because of the discrete nature of the data. Means are more useful when it comes to dealing with data in the form of continuous variables. Converting things to percentages allows you to make direct comparisons of discrete data from unequally sized groups.

When you are dealing with this type of data the trick is to simplify it so that patterns begin to emerge. I did this for Example 5.3 by converting the data to percentages and means. Also, I looked at overall totals across Table 1 rather than the numbers in each individual cell. Looking at overall totals across categories is known as *collapsing the data*, and is a useful way of looking for patterns and relationships in quantitative data. Wolcott (1990) advises you to look for the broadest possible category divisions when you begin to analyse qualitative data (see sub-section 5.3). Similarly, collapsing categories is a good way to start looking at quantitative data.

Analysing variables

Example 5.4 gives a *summary table* of some data collected by Renfrow when she evaluated the effects of two different art training programmes for gifted children. Based on her own observations and observations in published literature, this study is an example of a predictive experimental study. Renfrow wanted to evaluate different methods of teaching art to gifted children, and to see how their drawing skills could be improved. Her own ideas about teaching art as well as those in published research reports led her to formulate the following hypothesis: '... Given nine weeks of systematic training in perception and copying, gifted ... students between the ages of eight and 11 would be able to draw the head of a human being more realistically than gifted students receiving traditional art instruction ... (Renfrow, 1983, p.28).

In this study the variables were (a) children's age; (b) two different types of art instruction and (c) two sets of scores on a drawing test. Variables (a) and (b) are known as independent variables. Independent variables are those which researchers are free to control or 'manipulate'. For example, Renfrow was free to choose the art instruction programmes and the ages of the children she wanted to test. Variable (c) is known as a dependent variable because the effects it measures are dependent on the researcher's manipulations of the independent variable (or variables). In Renfrow's experiment, how well children performed on the drawing test *depended* on their age and the type of instruction they were given. In experimental research the dependent variable is always the one that is being measured.

To test her hypothesis, Renfrow's experimental group were given 18 forty-minute art lessons over nine weeks and worked on tasks such as copying upside-down line drawings; recording perspective; expressing shape through shadow; and copying photographs and drawings. The control group also had 18 forty-minute traditional art lessons and used a variety of media to explore texture, line, colour and composition. Renfrow taught the experimental group, one of her colleagues taught the control group.

Example 5.4 Coping with variables

Table 3 gives the data from the 36 children taking part in Renfrow's experiment. There were nine children in each of the two age-groups and 18 children in each of an experimental and a control group. The pre- and post-test scores in the table are the marks out of 20 given to drawings the children produced at the beginning and end of the experiment.

Table 3 Total (T) and mean (M) pre- and post-test scores for older and younger children's drawings in the experimental and control groups (N=36, n=9; maximum scores=20).

		Experimental group			*Control group*		
Age (years)		*Pre-test scores*	*Post-test scores*	*Pre-test/ post-test gain*	*Pre-test scores*	*Post-test scores*	*Pre-test/ post-test gain*
8–9	*T*	55.5	126.5	71.0	51.5	60.0	8.5
	M	6.2	14.1	7.9	5.7	6.6	0.9
10–11	*T*	82.5	138.0	55.5	68.0	93.0	25.0
	M	9.2	15.3	6.1	7.6	10.3	2.7
Overall	*T*	138.0	264.5	126.5	119.5	153.0	33.5
Overall	*M*	7.7	14.7	7.0	6.6	8.5	1.9

N stands for total number of children; n stands for the number in each group.

(adapted from Renfrow, 1983, pp. 30–31)

At the beginning of the nine-week programme all the children made a drawing of a human head. This pre-test established how well they could draw before the programme started. At the end of the programme they produced another drawing of a human head. This was the post-test. Drawings from the pre- and post-test were then randomly ordered so that it was impossible to tell which test or group of children they had come from. The drawings were given marks out of 20 by two teachers not involved in the training programme. Here 'marks out of 20' is an example of a continuous variable.

Although Table 3 is not raw data (raw data here would be each child's marks out of 20 on the pre- and post-test), it still contains too much information for you to see any patterns between the variables. Let's use it to try to extract the information which will allow us to compare children's pre- and post-test gains in the two groups.

If you look at the bottom of columns 2 and 5 in Table 3, you can see that the overall mean post-test score for the experimental group was 14.7 as against 8.5

for the control group. This means that after nine weeks of experimental art training this group of children's drawings were given higher marks than those of children following the traditional programme.

Before you can make any claim that the experimental art programme is superior, however, you need to look at the pre-test/post-test gains for each group. You need to do this because it is just possible that the children allocated to the experimental group were better at drawing in the first place. Subtracting the pre-test scores from the post-test scores gives a measure of how much improvement there has been. Looking at the bottom of columns 3 and 6, you can see that, on average, children's scores in the experimental group have improved by 7 marks, while those in the control group have only improved by 1.9 marks.

Next we can look to see whether the experimental programme was as effective for the younger children as for the older children. I found it useful to draw up another table here, again using the information in columns 3 and 6 of Table 3.

Table 4 Mean pre-test and post-test gains for older and younger children in the experimental and control groups.

Age (years)	*Experimental group*	*Control group*
8–9	7.9	0.9
10–11	6.1	2.7

Table 4 immediately shows that improvements in drawing skills were much greater for younger and older children in the experimental group than for children in the control group, in spite of the fact that both groups had nine weeks of art lessons. It also shows that the experimental programme was relatively more beneficial for the eight- to nine-year-olds (mean gain = 7.9) than for the older children (mean gain = 6.1). By contrast, the traditional art programme hardly improved the younger children's scores at all (mean gain = 0.9), and only had a small effect on the older children (mean gain = 2.7).

As with the student's data in Example 5.3, when you analyse raw quantitative data, it is best to try and simplify them first by drawing up a summary table of totals and means. You can then extract information selectively to help answer your research questions and hypotheses. Data like Renfrow's are suitable for statistical analysis.

5.6 PRESENTING QUANTITATIVE DATA IN YOUR REPORT

You should not include raw data from questionnaires, observation schedules and the like in the main body of your report. For example, you would not put Figure 5 in your report. As with qualitative data, raw data belongs in the appendices. There are a number of standard techniques for presenting quantitative data in reports. These include tables, graphs, bar and pie charts and histograms.

WHEN TO USE TABLES

You can see from Examples 5.3 and 5.4 above that tables which summarize raw data can be useful aids to analysis and interpretation. They are also useful for presenting your findings in your project report. You can use tables to display both category and variable data. If you choose to display your data in the form of a table, however, you need to make sure that it is clearly labelled with all the information your readers will need in order to interpret it for themselves.

In Tables 1 and 3 note that both the rows and the columns are clearly labelled. Both tables give information about the number of children taking part in the study and what the numbers in the table represent. Some of this information is given in the caption for the table and some in the table itself. Writing an appropriate caption for a table is very important, as captions should contain information which helps the reader interpret the table.

The caption for Table 1 tells you that the figures in the table represent *the number of interactions* observed in the various categories. The caption for Table 2 tells you that the numbers in the cells are *percentages*. The caption for Table 3 tells you that the figures contained in the table are *total and mean scores* on a drawing test. Your readers need all of this information if they are to understand your arguments. If, for example, you do not know how old the children are, or what the maximum test score is in Table 3, then the information it contains is not very useful. Clearly labelled tables with well-written captions speak for themselves; they save you having to describe your data in words.

Another thing to remember when using a table is that it should not contain too much information. Drawing up tables like Tables 1 and 3 is a useful exercise for you, but does it help your reader? Less complex tables such as Tables 2 and 4 have much more impact, even though they contain information that can be extrapolated from their larger parent tables.

WHEN TO USE BAR CHARTS, PIE CHARTS AND HISTOGRAMS

Bar charts, pie charts and histograms are sometimes more effective ways of representing data than tables. Bar and pie charts should be used to represent discrete category data. Histograms are normally used for continuous data. Bar charts represent categories as columns and are commonly used to draw attention to differences between two or more categories.

Like bar charts, pie charts are useful for presenting discrete data. Each slice of the pie represents a particular category. The number of slices depends on the number of categories in the raw data (make sure you don't have too many or too few). The size of each slice is determined by measuring the angle it makes at the centre of the pie. If one category contains 10 per cent of the total number of cases, its angle will be one-tenth of 360 degrees, or 36 degrees. Pie charts are extremely useful for representing data expressed as percentages.

If you want to compare two pies, as in Figure 7 (p. 227), the size of each circle must be in proportion to the number of cases it contains. In Figure 7, for example, there are fewer females in part-time higher education than males. The circle representing information about female students, therefore is proportionally smaller than the one for males. As you can see from this example, pie charts can be useful for presenting statistical information from published sources.

The histogram in Example 5.7 (p. 228) shows that staff opinion in the 25–35 year age range is strongly polarized with almost equal percentages agreeing and disagreeing with the statement. A significant percentage of 36–45 year-olds also agree with the statement, but a higher percentage disagree, and in the two older age groups, the majority of staff members favour schools remaining in local authority control.

Histograms should be used whenever you have continuous data. The main difference between a histogram and a bar chart is that the columns of a histogram are allowed to touch, whereas the bars of a bar chart should not touch. This is because the scale on the horizontal axis of a histogram should always describe a continuous variable (such as 'age group' in Figure 8, p. 228), whereas on a bar chart, the horizontal axis should describe a discrete category. As with tables, the labelling of the axes of bar charts, pie charts and histograms needs to be accurate, and captions must be thought out carefully.

WHEN TO USE GRAPHS

As well as histograms, graphs can be used to plot continuous data. They should not be used for discrete data because it makes no sense to draw lines joining discrete data points. Graphs, however, are very useful for looking at relationships between continuous variables.

When the information from Table 4 is presented as a graph, the different effects the two art programmes had on younger and older children are immediately apparent. Note that both axes are clearly labelled. When you plan graphs, choosing the scales for the axes is all important. Large effects can be diminished by an inappropriate scale. Conversely, small effects can be exaggerated, as Example 5.9 (p. 229) shows.

Example 5.5 Using a bar chart to represent data

As part of a project designed to explore why some children found using the school computers easier than others, a primary school teacher collected information about how many children in each class had regular access to a computer at home. Of the 125 children in the school, 47 had access to computers (see Table 5)

Table 5 Number of children with access to home computers.

Reception	10	(no. in class = 18)
Class One	7	(no. in class = 24)
Class Two	3	(no. in class = 20)
Class Three	12	(no. in class = 23)
Class Four	9	(no. in class = 21)
Class Five	6	(no. in class = 19)

The information in Table 5 could be presented as the bar chart shown in Figure 6.

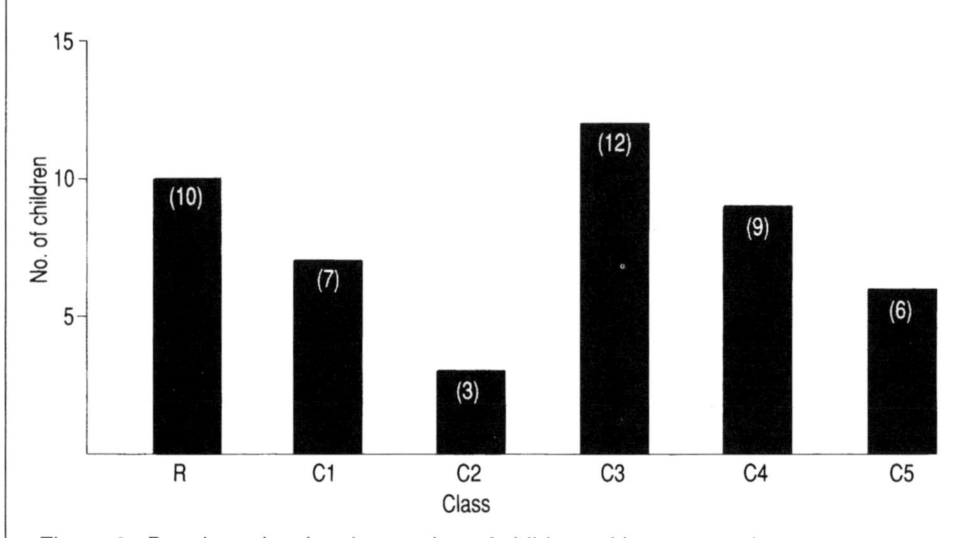

Figure 6 Bar chart showing the number of children with access to home computers.

If you compare the height of the bars in Figure 6, you can see that there is no obvious relationship between age and whether or not children have access to a computer. Reception class children's homes have the second highest number of computers, and the oldest children have the second lowest number of home computers. As there are approximately equal numbers of children in each class, computer ownership must be related to some factor other than children's age; parental income or occupation perhaps.

Figure 10a (p. 230), which has been plotted using reasonable scales on each axis, shows that there is quite a large difference between the two schools in terms of their examination scores. It also shows that while there is not much difference between the maths and English scores over three years for School A, School B's English results are better than their maths results. The maths results, however, appear to be improving.

If you were basing your interpretation on Figure 10b (p. 230), however, you might be tempted to think that School A's maths exam results show a pronounced decline over the years 1988–90, whereas those of School B show a marked improvement. This is because in Figure 10b the scale of the vertical and horizontal axes is not appropriate. Points on the vertical are too far apart and points on the horizontal axis are too close. In actual fact, School A's maths results decline from a mean of 69.6 in 1988 to a mean of 67.4 in 1990, a mean difference of 2.2 marks. For School B, however, there is a mean increase of 4.6 marks between 1988 and 1990. Without using some form of statistical analysis it is not possible to say whether these trends represent significant changes in maths performance or whether they are due to chance. The example does illustrate, however, how it is possible for graphs to give false impressions about data.

You can find out more about the construction of tables, bar and pie charts, histograms and graphs in Coolican (1990) and Graham (1990) (see the further reading list on p. 230).

Example 5.6 Using a pie chart to represent data

Figure 7 shows how government statistics about the number of part-time students in higher education in the years 1986/87 can be represented using a pie chart.

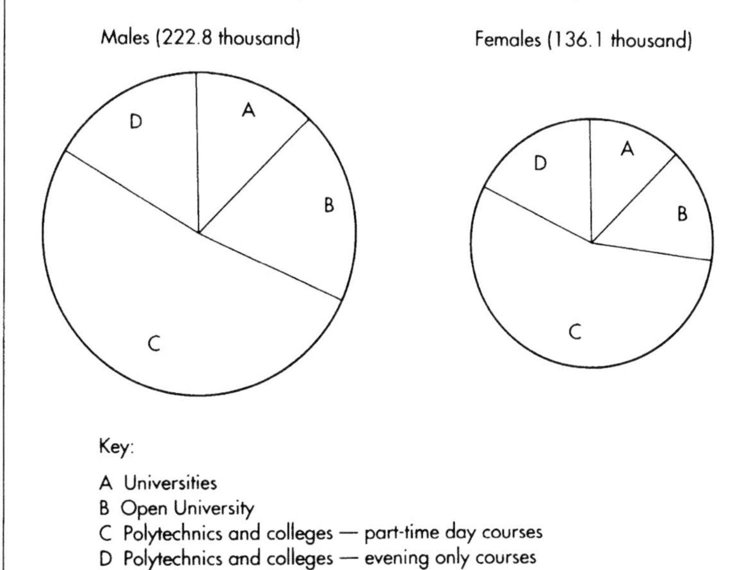

Source: Central Statistical Office, *Social Trends 19*, London, HMSO, 1989, p. 60

Figure 7 Part-time students in higher education 1986/7 (from Graham, 1990, p. 31).

Example 5.7 Using histograms

Supposing you had drawn up a structured questionnaire using a five-point rating scale to measure staff's attitudes to recent changes in the way schools are managed. The questionnaire is sent to 200 staff in local schools, and 186 people return it. One of the statements contained in this questionnaire is:

Statement 6: *Comprehensive schools should opt out of local authority control.*

Strongly agree
Agree
Neither agree or disagree
Disagree
Strongly disagree

Responses to this statement from staff in different age groups might be as shown in Table 6.

Table 6
Numbers of teachers responding to Statement 6 by level of agreement.

Age (years)	Agree/ strongly agree	Neither agree nor disagree	Disagree/ strongly disagree
25–35 (n = 41)	18	5	18
36–45 (n = 80)	32	2	46
46–55 (n = 46)	10	7	29
56–65 (n = 19)	5	3	11
Totals	65	17	104

In this table I have collapsed the categories 'agree'and 'strongly agree' into one as there were not enough numbers in each. I have also done this for the 'disagree' and 'strongly disagree' categories. Using the total number of responses in each age group, I can convert the information in the table to percentages and represent it in the four-part histogram shown in Figure 8.

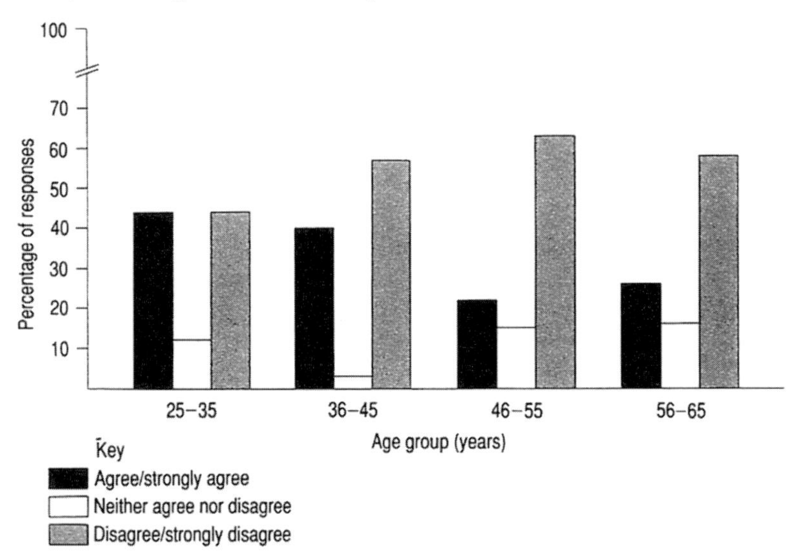

Figure 8 Percentages of staff responses to Statement 6 by age group.

Example 5.8 Using graphs

The data from Renfrow's experiment given in Table 4 could equally well be presented as the graph shown in Figure 9.

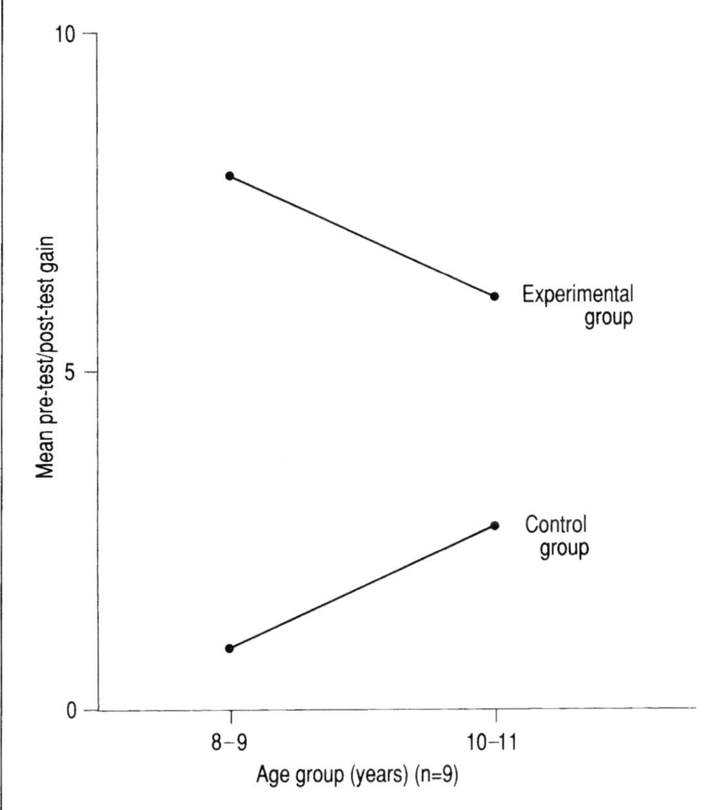

Figure 9 Mean pre- and post-test gains in drawing scores as a function of age and experimental condition.

Example 5.9 Plotting graphs

Table 7 Mean end-of-year examination marks (out of 100) in maths and English for two hypothetical schools over a three-year period.

	1988	*1989*	*1990*
School A			
Maths	69.6	68.5	67.4
English	68.0	69.5	69.8
School B			
Maths	53.4	56.7	58.9
English	61.7	63.2	62.8

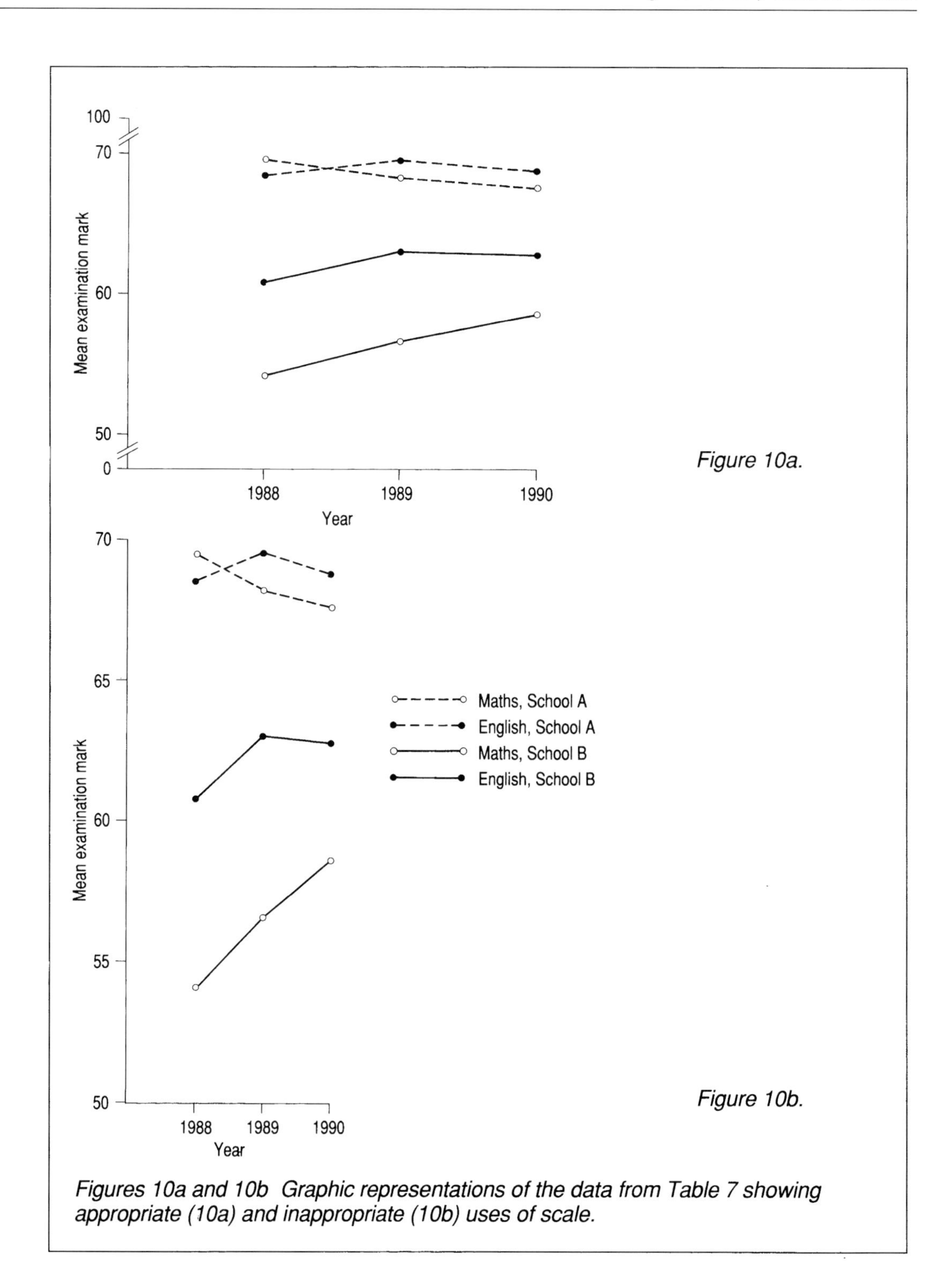

Figures 10a and 10b Graphic representations of the data from Table 7 showing appropriate (10a) and inappropriate (10b) uses of scale.

5.7 CONCLUSION

This section has described how to analyse and interpret qualitative and quantitative data. Throughout I have tried to illustrate the kind of reasoning processes you must engage in when you begin to analyse your data. As I mentioned at the outset, analysing and writing about qualitative data is very much a question of personal style, and you will have to develop methods and techniques you feel comfortable with. When it comes to analysing quantitative data, there is less scope for individuality. Certain conventions have to be observed. Discrete category data must be treated in a different way from data obtained from the measurement of continuous variables. Nevertheless, even here people develop different styles of presenting their data. I personally find it easier to interpret data when I can draw a picture of them, and I therefore prefer graphs to tables. I hope this section will encourage you to develop your own style of analysis and presentation.

FURTHER READING

BRYMAN, A. and BURGESS, R. G. (eds) *Analysing Qualitative Data*, London, Routledge.

This is a comprehensive, state-of-the-art reader for students.

COOLICAN, H. (1990) *Research Methods and Statistics in Psychology*, London, Hodder and Stoughton.

This book gives good advice on analysing both qualitative and quantitative data. It is easy to read and contains exercises which can be worked through. It is written for the novice researcher.

NORTHEDGE, A. (1990) *The Good Study Guide*, Milton Keynes, The Open University.

This book gives advice on study skills in general, and includes a useful chapter on how to handle numbers and interpret statistical data. It also contains two chapters on writing techniques. It has been specifically written for adults studying part-time and for people returning to study after a long break.

ROBSON, C. (1996) *Real World Research: a resource for social scientists and practitioner researchers*, Oxford, Blackwell.

Part V of this highly accessible text discusses how to report research enquiries and presents several different report writing formats for research reports.

ROWNTREE, D. (1981) *Statistics Without Tears: a primer for non-mathematicians*, New York, Charles Scribner and Sons.

This is another user-friendly text about how to use statistics. It introduces the main concepts and terminology of statistics but without allowing the reader to get bogged down in formulae and calculations.

WOLCOTT, H.F. (1990) *Writing up Qualitative Research*, Qualitative Research Methods Vol. 20, Thousand Oaks, California, Sage.

This book is a very readable introduction to analysing and writing up qualitative data. It gives good advice on how to approach report writing, and recognizes that, for the beginner, this is not an easy task.

WOODS, P. (1999) *Successful Writing for Qualitative Researchers*, London, Routledge.

This book discusses all aspects of the writing process and like Wolcott helps with the difficult bits. It is an excellent, accessible source.

REFERENCES

ARMSTRONG, M. (1980) *Closely Observed Children: the diary of a primary classroom*, London, Writers and Readers in association with Chameleon.

BASSEY, M. (1990) 'On the nature of research in education (part 1)', *Research Intelligence*, BERA Newsletter no. 36, Summer, pp. 35–8.

BROWNE, N. and FRANCE, P. (1986) *Untying the Apron Strings: anti-sexist provision for the under-fives*, Buckingham, Open University Press.

BURGESS, R. (1984) 'Keeping a research diary' in BELL, J., BUSH, T., FOX, A., GOODEY, J. and GOULDING, S. (eds) *Conducting Small-scale Investigations in Education Management*, London, Harper and Row/The Open University.

CENTRAL ADVISORY COUNCIL FOR EDUCATION (ENGLAND) (1967) *Children and their Primary Schools*, London, HMSO (the Plowden Report).

CENTRE FOR LANGUAGE IN PRIMARY EDUCATION (CLPE) (1990) *Patterns of Learning*, London, CLPE.

CINAMON, D. (1986) 'Reading in context', *Issues in Race and Education*, no. 47, Spring, pp. 5–7.

CLARKE, S. (1984) 'Language and comprehension in the fifth year' in BARNES, D.L. and BARNES, D.R. with CLARKE, S., *Versions of English*, London, Heinemann Educational Books.

COOLICAN, H. (1990) *Research Methods and Statistics in Psychology*, London, Hodder and Stoughton.

DELAMONT, S. (1983) *Interaction in the Classroom*, London, Methuen.

DEPARTMENT OF EDUCATION AND SCIENCE (DES) (1982) *Mathematics Counts*, London, HMSO (the Cockroft Report).

DEPARTMENT OF EDUCATION AND SCIENCE (DES) (1989) *Science in the National Curriculum*, London, HMSO.

DEPARTMENT OF EDUCATION AND SCIENCE (DES) (1990) *Statistics of Education: Schools, January 1989*, London, HMSO.

DOWNS, S., FLETCHER, A. and FLETCHER, L. (1987) 'Ben' in BOOTH, T. and SWANN, W. (eds) *Including Pupils with Disabilities*, Milton Keynes, Open University Press/The Open University.

ELLIOT, J. (1981) *Action research: framework for self evaluation in schools. TIQL working paper no. 1*, Cambridge, University of Cambridge Institute of Education, mimeo.

ENRIGHT, L. (1981) 'The diary of a classroom' in NIXON, J. (ed.) *A Teacher's Guide to Action Research*, London, Grant Macintyre.

GATES, P. (1989) ' Developing consciousness and pedagogical knowledge through mutual observation' in WOODS, P. (ed.) *Working for Teacher Development*, Dereham (Norfolk), Peter Francis Publishers.

GLASER, B. and STRAUSS, A. (1967) *The Discovery of Grounded Theory*, Chicago, Aldine.

GOVERNMENT STATISTICAL SERVICE (1990) *Educational Statistics for the United Kingdom 1989*, London, HMSO.

GRAHAM, A. (1990) *Investigating Statistics: a beginner's guide*, London, Hodder and Stoughton.

HARRIS, J., HORNER, S. and TUNNARD, L. (1986) *All in a Week's Work: a report on the first stage of the Sheffield Writing in Transition Project*, London, SCDC Publications.

HOPKINS, D. (1985) *A Teacher's Guide to Classroom Research,* Milton Keynes, Open University Press.

HUTCHINSON, S. (1988) 'Education and grounded theory' in SHERMAN, R.R. and WEBB, R.B. (eds) (1988) *Qualitative Research in Education: focus and methods,* Lewes, Falmer Press.

INNER LONDON EDUCATION AUTHORITY AND CENTRE FOR LANGUAGE IN PRIMARY EDUCATION (ILEA/CLPE) (1988) *The Primary Language Record: a handbook for teachers*, London, ILEA/CLPE.

INNER LONDON EDUCATION AUTHORITY RESEARCH AND STATISTICS BRANCH (1985a) *Equal Opportunities in the Curriculum in Single-sex Schools*, RS 973/85, London, ILEA.

INNER LONDON EDUCATION AUTHORITY RESEARCH AND STATISTICS BRANCH (1985b) *ILEA Induction Scheme: five years on*, RS 10051/85, London, ILEA.

INNER LONDON EDUCATION AUTHORITY RESEARCH AND STATISTICS BRANCH (1988) *The Hackney Literacy Study*, RS 1175/88, London, ILEA.

INNER LONDON EDUCATION AUTHORITY RESEARCH AND STATISTICS BRANCH (1990) *Developing Evaluation in the LEA*, RS 1284/90, London, ILEA.

KAYE, G. (1985) *Comfort Herself*, London, Deutsch.

KEMMIS, S. and MCTAGGART, R. (1981) *The Action Research Planner*, Victoria (Australia), Deakin University Press.

MEEK, M. J. (1989) 'One child's development' in NATIONAL WRITING PROJECT (1989) *Becoming a Writer*, Walton-on-Thames, Nelson.

MINNS, H. (1990) *Read It to Me Now! Learning at home and at school,* London, Virago Press.

MORRIS, C. (1991) 'Opening doors: learning history through talk' in BOOTH, T., SWANN, W., MASTERTON, M. and POTTS, P. (eds) *Curricula for Diversity in Education*, London, Routledge/The Open University.

MULFORD, W., WATSON, H. J. and VALLEE, J. (1980) *Structured Experiences and Group Development,* Canberra, Canberra Curriculum Development Centre.

MYERS, K. (1987) *Genderwatch! Self-assessment schedules for use in schools*, London, SCDC Publications.

NIAS, J. (1988) 'Introduction' in NIAS, J. and GROUNDWATER-SMITH, S. (eds) *The Enquiring Teacher: supporting and sustaining teacher research,* Lewes, Falmer Press.

NIXON, J. (ed) (1981) *A Teacher's Guide to Action Research,* London, Grant McIntyre.

OLIVER, E. and SCOTT, K. (1989) 'Developing arguments: yes, but how?', *Talk*, no. 2, Autumn, pp. 6–8.

THE OPEN UNIVERSITY (1976) E203 *Curriculum Design and Development,* Unit 28 *Innovation at the Classroom Level: a case study of the Ford Teaching Project,* Milton Keynes, Open University Press.

THE OPEN UNIVERSITY (1991) P535 *Talk and Learning 5–16*, Milton Keynes, The Open University.

PHILLIPS, T. (1988) 'On a related matter: why "successful" small-group talk depends on not keeping to the point' in MACLURE, M., PHILLIPS, T. and WILKINSON, A. (eds) *Oracy Matters*, Milton Keynes, Open University Press.

RENFROW, M. (1983) 'Accurate drawing as a function of training of gifted children in copying and perception', *Education Research Quarterly,* vol. 8, no. 31, pp. 27–32.

ROBSON, S. (1986) 'Group discussions' in RITCHIE, J. and SYKES, W. (eds) *Advanced Workshop in Applied Qualitative Research*, LONDON, SOCIAL AND COMMUNITY PLANNING RESEARCH.

SHERMAN, R.R. and WEBB, R.B. (eds) (1988) *Qualitative Research in Education: Focus and Methods,* Lewes, The Falmer Press.

STACEY, M. (1989) 'Looking forward', *About Writing,* vol. 11, Autumn 1989.

STATHAM, J. and MACKINNON, D. with CATHCART, H. and HALES, M. (1991) (second edition), *The Education Fact File*, London, Hodder and Stoughton/The Open University.

STENHOUSE, L. (1975) *An Introduction to Curriculum Research and Development,* London, Heinemann.

STENHOUSE, L. (1978) *Curriculum Research and Development in Action,* London, Heinemann.

THOMAS, G. (1986) ' "Hallo, Miss Scatterbrain. Hallo, Mr Strong" ': assessing nursery attitudes and behaviour' in BROWNE, N. and FRANCE, P. (eds) *Untying the Apron Strings: anti-sexist provision for the under-fives,* Milton Keynes, Open University Press.

TYNDALL, C. (1988) 'No comfort here', *Issues in Race and Education*, no. 55, Autumn, pp. 14–16.

WALKER, R. (1989) *Doing Research: a handbook for teachers,* London, Routledge.

WEBB, R. (ed.) (1990) *Practitioner Research in the Primary School,* Basingstoke, Falmer Press.

WINTER, V. (1990) 'A process approach to science' in R. WEBB (ed.), *Practitioner Research in the Primary School,* Basingstoke, Falmer Press.

WOLCOTT, H.F. (1990) *Writing up Qualitative Research,* Qualitative Research Methods Series 20, Newbury Park, California, Sage Publications.

WOODS, P. (1988) 'Educational ethnography in Britain' in SHERMAN, R.R. and WEBB, R.B. (eds) (1988) *Qualitative Research in Education: focus and methods,* Lewes, The Falmer Press.

WRIGHT, S.(1990) 'Language counts in the teaching of mathematics' in WEBB, R. (ed.) *Practioner Research in the Primary School,* Basingstoke, Falmer Press.

YARD, L. (1991) 'Why talk in art' in THE OPEN UNIVERSITY, P535 *Talk and Learning 5–16*, Milton Keynes, The Open University.

PART 3 RESOURCES FOR THE ANALYSIS OF TALK AS DATA

CONTENTS

INTRODUCTION

In this third and final part of the Handbook, we provide an introduction to issues concerned with analysing talk. In Section 1, Neil Mercer looks at the different approaches found in educational research, and compares their advantages and disadvantages. In Section 2, Joan Swann looks at the practicalities of recording and transcribing talk for the purposes of analysis. Here she extends and develops the discussion of these issues in Part 2.

1 THE ANALYSIS OF TALK AS DATA IN EDUCATIONAL SETTINGS

1.1 INTRODUCTION

My main aim in this section is to provide a basic guide to ways of analysing talk which can be used in educational research. I begin with a review of approaches and methods, and then discuss some of the key issues involved in making methodological choices. Given limited space, I have not attempted to go into detail about any of the methods involved. The section should be read in conjunction with Section 2, 'Recording and transcribing talk in educational settings', where you will find examples from several of the approaches I describe here. For a thorough and comparative discussion of methods, I recommend Edwards and Westgate's (1994) book *Investigating Classroom Talk*.

1.2 APPROACHES AND METHODS

Researchers from a range of disciplinary backgrounds – including psychologists, sociologists, anthropologists, linguists – have studied talk in educational settings, and they have used a variety of methods to do so. The methods they have used reflect their research interests and orientations to research. That is, particular methods are associated with particular research perspectives or approaches; and each approach always, even if only implicitly, embodies some assumptions about the nature of spoken language and how it can be analysed. I will describe eight approaches which have provided analytic methods used in educational research:

1 systematic observation
2 ethnography
3 sociolinguistic analysis
4 'linguistic' discourse analysis
5 socio-cultural discourse analysis
6 conversation analysis
7 discursive psychology
8 computer-based text analysis.

Before doing so, I should make it very clear that – for the sake of offering a clear introductory view – my categorization is fairly crude. In practice, approaches overlap, and researchers often (and increasingly often) use more than one method.

1 *SYSTEMATIC OBSERVATION*

A well-established type of research on classroom interaction is known as 'systematic observation'. It essentially involves allocating observed talk (and sometimes non-verbal activity such as gesture) to a set of previously specified categories. The aim is usually to provide quantitative results. For example, the observer may record the relative number of 'talk turns' taken by teachers and pupils in lessons, or measure the extent to which teachers use different types of question as defined by the researcher's categories. Early research of this kind was responsible for the famous 'two thirds rule': that two thirds of the time in a classroom lesson someone is usually talking, and that two thirds of the talk in a classroom is normally contributed by the teacher (see for example Flanders, 1970). The basic procedure for setting up systematic observation is that researchers use their research interests and initial observations of classroom life to construct a set of categories into which all relevant talk (and any other communicative activity) can be classified. Observers are then trained to identify talk corresponding to each category, so that they can sit in classrooms and assign what they see and hear to the categories. Today, researchers may develop their own categorizing system, or they may take one 'off the shelf' (see, for example, Underwood and Underwood, 1999).

A positive feature of this method is that a lot of data can be processed fairly quickly. It allows researchers to survey life in a large sample of classrooms without transcribing it, to move fairly quickly and easily from observations to numerical data (the talk may not even be tape-recorded) and then to combine data from many classrooms into quantitative data which can be analysed statistically. Systematic observation has continued to provide interesting and useful findings about norms of teaching style and organization within and across cultures (see for example Galton *et al.*, 1980; Rutter *et al.*, 1979; Galton *et al.*, 1999). It has also been used to study interactions amongst children working in pairs or groups (e.g. Bennett and Cass, 1989; Underwood and Underwood, 1999). In Britain, its findings about teacher-talk have had a significant influence on educational policy-making and the training of teachers (for example, in constructing guides for good practice, see Wragg and Brown, 1993).

2 *ETHNOGRAPHY*

The ethnographic approach to analysing educational interaction emerged in the late 1960s and early 1970s. It was an adaptation of methods already used by social anthropologists and some sociologists in non-educational fields (see Hammersley, 1982, for accounts of this). Ethnographic analysis aims for a rich, detailed description of observed events, which can be used to explain the social processes which are involved. In early studies, ethnographers often only took field-notes of what was said and done, but fairly soon it became common practice for them to tape-record talk, to transcribe those recordings, and to report their analysis by including short extracts from their transcriptions. Ethnographers are normally concerned with understanding social life as a whole, and while they will record what is said in observed events, language use may not be their main concern. Their methods do not therefore usually attend to talk in the same detail as do, say, those of discourse analysts or conversation analysts (as discussed below).

Early ethnographic research helped to undermine two long-standing assumptions about communication in the classroom: first, that full, meaningful participation in classroom discourse is equally accessible to all children, so long as they are of normal intelligence and are native speakers of the language used in school (Philips, 1972); and second, that teachers ask questions simply to find out what children know (Hammersley, 1974). It has also revealed how cultural factors affected the nature and quality of talk and interaction between teachers and children, and how ways of communicating may vary significantly between home communities and schools (as in the classic research by Heath, 1982). Ethnographic studies have been important too for showing how teachers use talk to control classes, how classroom talk constrains pupils' participation (Mehan, 1979; Canagarajah, 2001; Chick, 2001) and how children express a range of social identities through talk in the classroom and playground (Maybin, 1994).

3 SOCIOLINGUISTIC ANALYSIS

Some research on talk in educational contexts has its roots in sociolinguistics. Sociolinguistics is concerned, broadly, with the relationship between language and society. (See Swann *et al.*, 2000, for a general introduction to this field). Sociolinguists are interested in the status and meaning of different language varieties (e.g. accents and dialects, different languages in bilingual communities) and in how these are used, and to what effect, by speakers (or members of different social/cultural groups). Sociolinguists have carried out empirical research in school or classroom settings; but sociolinguistic research carried out in other settings has also implications for educational policy and practice (for example, research on the language of children's home lives). In classroom research, sociolinguists have investigated such topics as language use in bilingual classrooms (Martyn-Jones, 1995; Jayalakshmi, 1996), language use and gender relations (Swann and Graddol, 1994) and language and ethnicity (Edwards and Sienkewicz, 1990). Both qualitative or quantitative methods may be used. For example, researchers have compared the extent to which girls and boys dominate interactions (French and French, 1988; Swann, 1993), and recorded the incidence of switches from one language to another in the course of a lesson (Edwards and Sienkewicz, 1990). Qualitative sociolinguistics sometimes resembles ethnographic research, but can also incorporate the methods of descriptive linguistics – such as the identification of distinctive sound patterns (phonology), grammatical constructions or vocabulary items.

4 LINGUISTIC DISCOURSE ANALYSIS

The term 'discourse analysis' has no precise meaning; it is used to refer to several different approaches to analysing language (both spoken and written) and hence to some quite different methods. Within linguistics, it usually indicates an interest in the way language is organized in units longer than sentences. Educational research following this approach has focused on the structural organization of classroom talk. The classic investigation of Sinclair and Coulthard (1975) showed that in teacher-led lessons the language has characteristics which mark it out as a distinct, situated language variety, and one which assigns particular roles to speakers (see also Stubbs, 1983; Willes, 1983). They devised a method for categorising all talk in a lesson into a hierarchical system of 'acts', 'moves' and 'exchanges' and 'transactions'. The basic unit of teacher–pupil communication in this system is the 'IRF exchange', in which a teacher *initiates* an interaction (typically by asking a question), the student *responds* (usually by providing an answer) and the teacher then provides some *follow-up* or *feedback* (for example, by confirming that the answer was correct). The IRF concept has since been used by many classroom researchers, although few employ the whole of Sinclair and Coulthard's rather complex hierarchical system. For recent evaluations of the educational significance of the IRF exchange, see for example Mercer (1995, chapter 3) and Wells (2000, chapter 5).

A rather different linguistics-based approach to analysing talk is based on *systemic functional grammar* (SFG), the creation of the linguist Michael Halliday (Halliday, 1976 and 1978). As the name implies, an SFG-based approach to analysing spoken language allows a researcher to consider how the special educational functions of classroom language relate to its grammatical structure and its textual organization (Iedema, 1996; Gibbons, 2000).

5 'SOCIO-CULTURAL' DISCOURSE ANALYSIS

The term 'socio-cultural' has become associated with research which draws explicitly on the developmental psychology of Lev Vygotsky (1978; see also Wertsch, 1985). It represents an approach in which language is considered a 'cultural tool' for learning, and which each parental generation of a society uses to guide the cognitive and social development of its children. 'Socio-cultural' discourse analysis differs from 'linguistic' discourse analysis in being less concerned with the organizational structure of spoken language, and more with its content, function and the ways shared understanding is developed, in social context, over time.

Although he would not then have called himself a 'socio-cultural' researcher, back in the 1970s Douglas Barnes (1976) was one of the first to use this kind of method for studying teaching and learning. Since then, socio-cultural analyses of talk have been used to study teacher–student interactions (Edwards and Mercer, 1987; Erickson, 1996; Hughes and Westgate, 1998; Rojas-Drummond, 2000) and the development of students' understanding in science, maths and other subjects (Driver, 1983; Lemke, 1990; Brown and Renshaw, 2000). As with ethnography and conversation analysis, reports of such research are usually illustrated by selected extracts of transcribed talk, to which the analyst provides a commentary.

Also building on Barnes's work (Barnes and Todd, 1977, 1995), a socio-cultural approach has been used to analyse and evaluate the talk of children working together in pairs or groups (Lyle, 1993, 1996; Hicks, 1996), sometimes on computer-based activities (Wegerif and Scrimshaw, 1997). Mercer *et al.*, (1999) used this approach, along with other methods, in an action research project aimed at improving the quality of primary children's use of language as a tool for reasoning.

6 CONVERSATION ANALYSIS

Conversation analysis (CA) grew out of a radical sociology called ethnomethodology, which was founded on a dissatisfaction with the focus of conventional sociology on studying the structural organization of society on a grand scale. Ethnomethodologists aimed instead to explain how the social world operates by focusing on the micro-level of social interaction. The more specific goal conversation analysts pursue is understanding how social interaction is achieved, minute by minute, through everyday talk and non-verbal communication.

CA is a demanding methodology, because it uses a very detailed and laborious style of transcription (for an example, see Section 2); and sets very strict criteria for the kinds of interpretations which an analyst can make from the data of recorded talk. Widely used in the analysis of talk in work-related settings (see, for example, Drew and Heritage, 1992), it has still to be applied to any great extent in classroom research (but see Baker, 1997; Stokoe, 2000).

7 DISCURSIVE PSYCHOLOGY

Discursive psychology is a particular approach within social psychology concerned with how people use language to account for their actions, pursue their interests and get things done. It involves the study of rhetoric, or language as a persuasive medium. Not used to any great extent as an approach to studying classroom interaction, its most obvious relevance to educational research is for the analysis of the talk of interviews (see Potter and Wetherell, 1994; Edwards and Potter, 1992).

8 COMPUTER-BASED TEXT ANALYSIS

Research in linguistics has recently been revolutionized by the development of computer facilities for analysing large databases of written or spoken (transcribed) language. Software packages known as 'concordancers' enable any text file to be scanned easily for all instances of particular target words. Not only can their frequency of occurrence be measured, but the analysis can also indicate which words tend to occur together, and so help reveal the way words gather meanings by 'the company that they keep'. The results of such searches can be presented as tabular *concordances*. One practical application of this method (outside educational research) has been in compiling dictionaries. Lexicographers can now base their definitions on an analysis of how words are actually used in a large databank (or 'corpus') of naturally occurring written and/or spoken language. Concordances can reveal some of the more subtle meanings that words have gathered in use, meanings which are not captured by literal definitions.

Once recorded talk has been transcribed into a word file, a concordancer allows a researcher to move almost instantly between occurrences of particular words and the whole transcription. This enables particular words of special interest to be 'hunted' in the data, and their relative incidence and form of use in particular contexts to be compared. The basic data for this kind of analysis, throughout, remains the whole transcription. By integrating this method with other methods, the analysis can be both qualitative (analysing particular interactions, by, say, using discourse analysis) and quantitative (comparing the relative incidence of 'key words', or of types of interaction, as might a systematic observer). Initial exploratory work on particular short texts (or text extracts) can be used to generate hypotheses which can then be tested systematically on a large text or series of related texts. For example, a researcher may want to see if a technical term introduced by a teacher is taken up by students later in a lesson, or in their group-based activity. By locating all instances of the term in the transcription file, the ways it is used by teachers and students can then be considered (see, for example, Monaghan, 1999; Wegerif and Mercer, 1997; Mercer, 2000, chapter 3).

SOME COMPARATIVE COMMENTS ON THESE APPROACHES

Each of the approaches I have described has its own strengths and weaknesses – and of course its own advocates and critics. Systematic observation has obvious appeal for those who like 'data which can be presented in quantitative form and which can be summarized and related to other data using statistical techniques' (Croll, 1986, p. 5). If you wish to survey some specific features of interaction in a very large sample of classrooms, then this method is also an attractive option. The most common criticisms of systematic observation focus on the fact that speech data is usually reduced to categorical frequency counts at an early stage of analysis. Some critics question the validity of a method in which researchers are committed to recording only those events which have been specified in advance by their category scheme (Hamilton and Delamont, 1974). Others have argued that analyses based on discrete categories of types of interaction ignore the essential cumulative nature of classroom talk as a continuous, contextualized process (Edwards and Mercer, 1987). However, defenders of systematic observation respond that it should be judged for what it claims to do, in its own terms – and by the self-evident value of the findings it offers (McIntyre, 1980; Croll, 1986, chapter 7).

In contrast, qualitative approaches such as ethnography and socio-cultural discourse analysis can claim greater sensitivity to culture, context, and the ways talk enables educational activity to progress, minute by minute. In their comprehensive review of methods for researching talk in classrooms, Edwards and Westgate (1994) suggest that one of the strengths of these methods is that they enable a researcher to see beneath the surface of classroom interaction, and so heighten critical awareness of what is taking place; and that the value of this can be seen in the fact that teachers seem to readily appreciate the insights gained from ethnographic and socio-cultural research (Edwards and Westgate, 1994, p. 58). If you are interested in the content and structure of classroom talk as it is pursued minute by minute as a finely co-ordinated process of interaction, then your choice of method is likely to include some variant of ethnography, discourse analysis or conversation analysis.

Of course, qualitative approaches have their own weaknesses and limitations, which are admitted by experienced practitioners (see Hammersley, 1992, Wegerif and Mercer, 1997). One obvious problem is the seemingly intuitive nature of the analytic procedures involved. The process of doing ethnography, for example, of moving from observations to descriptions to interpretations, is hard to make explicit. It is impossible to show that all possible reasonable interpretations of the original data were considered. And because it is normal for ethnographers, discourse analysts and conversation analysts to base their research reports only on short, selected extracts of transcript evidence, readers have to trust that these are indeed as representative as claimed. Stubbs (1994) argues that while research reports based on the presentation of selected extracts of recorded talk can be insightful and plausible, they are unconvincing as the basis for drawing generalized conclusions. He uses this position to argue for the use of 'linguistic' discourse analysis and computer-based text analysis.

Conversation analysts claim, with some justification, that one strength of their method compared with others is that it ensures the most direct and detailed attention to the actual language spoken, including intonations and pauses, and so enables the researcher to see how social interaction is actually achieved. They also claim that their concern with revealing 'participants' categories' (that is, the ways participants themselves make sense of social life) rather than imposing 'analysts' categories' (that is, the theoretical concepts that most researchers use to explain what they observe) is the mark of a superior empirical approach (Schegloff, 1997). CA practitioners place a high value on evidence for analytic claims being visible in the talk, and take issue with sociolinguistic and socio-cultural analyses which invoke cultural factors, background knowledge, aims or attitudes of speakers. For instance, factors such as 'gender' and 'race' would only be considered relevant themes by conversation analysts if it could be shown that speakers attended to these factors *as topics* in their conversation. However, researchers who favour other approaches question this tenet of CA methodology, as it denies the possibility that social and cultural variables can be implicit in, or contextual to, the talk. Moreover, it can be argued (Wetherell, 1998) that whether or not a factor is 'visible' as a topic in talk may depend on an analyst's arbitrary decision about where the talk sample begins and ends. For example, patterns of interaction between male and female students recorded while working in a group may reflect the history of their past conversations, unrecorded by the analyst, in which issues of gender dominance were explicitly raised.

QUANTITATIVE AND QUALITATIVE METHODS

The most common contrast made between methods for analysing talk is whether they provide quantitative or qualitative results. The relative strengths and weaknesses of the various quantitative and qualitative methods for analysing talk can be summarised as follows:

Quantitative analysis

Most obviously includes systematic observation, but also sociolinguistic methods, systemic analysis and computer-based text analysis if used to measure relative frequencies of occurrence of particular words or patterns of language use.

Strengths:

- an efficient way of handling a lot of data; for example a researcher can 'survey' a lot of classroom language relatively quickly;

- enables numerical comparisons to be made, which can perhaps then be subjected to a statistical analysis.

Weaknesses:

- actual talk, as data, may be lost early in the analysis: all you work with are your categories;
- pre-determined categories or other target items will limit analysts' sensitivity to what actually happens;
- the analysis cannot handle the ways that meaning is constructed amongst speakers, over time, through interaction.

Qualitative analysis

Includes ethnography, socio-cultural discourse analysis, conversation analysis.

Strengths:

- the talk remains throughout the analysis;
- any categories emerging are generated by the research (i.e. are outcomes), not prior assumptions;
- the examples of talk you can provide to any reader of your research are real: you do not ask them to take on trust the validity of your abstracted categorization;
- the development of joint understanding, or the persistence of apparent misunderstandings or different points of view, can be pursued through the continuous data of recorded/transcribed talk;
- the analysis can be expanded to include consideration of non-verbal aspects of communication recorded on video or audiotape.

Weaknesses:

- it is difficult to use these methods to handle large sets of data, because they are so time-consuming: it is commonly estimated that transcribing and analysing one hour of talk using such methods will take between five and fifteen hours of research time;
- it is difficult to use such analyses to make convincing generalizations. Researchers are open to charges of selecting particular examples to make a case.

COMBINING METHODS

With their various strengths and weaknesses, it may seem logical to use two or more methods of analysing talk in a complementary way. In doing so, however, it is important to recall a point I made earlier in this chapter – that different methods may embody different conceptions of the nature of talk and what counts as a valid analysis. Nevertheless, there are ways of combining at least some methods which will satisfy most reasonable concerns about validity and methodological consistency. Thus Gibbons (2001) combined a socio–cultural approach with one based on systemic functional grammar in research on teaching English as a second language. Wegerif and Mercer (1997) combined socio-cultural analysis with computer-based text analysis in their research on the talk of primary school children working together at the computer. They suggest that this allows a fine-grained qualitative analysis of talk to be related to a statistical analysis of quantitative results, with the different analytic methods informing each other and so providing findings which are both context-sensitive and generalizable. One other striking example is O'Connor and Michaels' (1996) study of children's group-based activity, in which they combined elements of ethnography, conversation analysis and both 'linguistic' and 'socio–cultural' approaches to discourse analysis. The crucial methodological issue is that judgements about the appropriateness of any methods take account of the nature of language itself and its functions in educational settings; and it is to that topic that I turn now.

1.3 THE FUNCTIONS OF SPOKEN LANGUAGE IN EDUCATIONAL SETTINGS

Whatever our motive for observing and recording talk, we must use methods for its analysis which do justice to its nature as a medium of communication, and to its special uses in educational settings. At a conceptual level, we can distinguish between language as the medium of education, and language as the subject of education. Research may be concerned with either, or both, of these functions. Language is at the heart of education, because it is the principal means of communication between teachers and learners. As a physical, observable representation of the process of teaching and learning, talk is an attractive source of data. But as analysts of classroom talk, we should beware of treating it naively, as simply a medium for transmitting information. While language does of course enable teachers and students to exchange information, the process is rarely one of 'transmission'. Any teacher knows that they can instruct a class in how to carry out a task and find that their instructions have been interpreted in several different ways. Language also has more subtle functions than the mere exchange of information. Teachers and learners use language not only to share experience and information, but also to jointly make sense of it; it is a tool for collective thinking, and any new understanding that emerges from a classroom interaction is a joint achievement by its participants. Moreover, teachers use talk to guide, enthuse, control, confuse and embarrass students.

In the most immediate sense, 'becoming educated' means becoming able to make sense of and participate in the language practices of school. In a wider sense, it means becoming able to use language as a specialized tool for the pursuit of literature, science, and other kinds of intellectual endeavour. Language is a part of the curriculum in every subject; from art to engineering, one has to learn a specialized way of using language. This may provide reasons for analysing talk – not only when students are learning a second or other language, but also when they are learning new ways of using their native tongue. And of course education is also often intended to help students use language more effectively in their everyday lives in wider society.

We also need to take account of the temporal, cumulative nature of making meaning through talk. The process of teaching and learning is often a long-term enterprise. Education can be considered as one 'long conversation' between teachers and learners that continues through hours, days, months, even years (Maybin, 1994). As researchers, limited to sampling relatively short stretches of classroom life, we can neither cope completely with this temporal quality of educational talk nor afford to ignore it.

1.4 ANALYSING THE TALK OF INTERVIEWS

Researchers differ in their reasons for analysing talk as data, and some functions and features of language may seem more or less significant to the questions which motivate the research. But we must try to ensure that the methods we use for observing and analysing the process of communication are sensitive to the way that the meaning is shaped by particular social contexts. Such considerations do not only apply if the data is of classroom interaction. A researcher may be interested in teachers' or learners' accounts of their educational experience, or their explanations of their behaviour – in which case the data may be the talk in interviews. In such investigations, a vital concern should again be to recognize that interviews never simply involve the transmission of ideas from one person to another. It is fairly obvious that the questions an interviewer asks will shape interviewees' responses. But taking account of this will involve more than trying to avoid putting words into respondents' mouths. Interviews are best thought of as dialogues in which both participants contribute to the responses which are recorded (Kvale, 1996). Respondents never simply 'speak their minds' to an interviewer, they engage in a conversation with another person who they will perceive as playing some role, of more or less importance, in their lives. As in any conversation, one function of talk will be for participants to account for themselves to a listener, and the kinds of accounts that are provided will inevitably be influenced by the speaker's conception of their audience. It is on this basis that some researchers argue that both interviewees' and interviewers' talk should be included in any analysis (Potter and Wetherell, 1994).

1.5 CONCLUSION

The methodological problems of dealing with the rich and messy data of educational talk are unavoidable, but that does not mean that they are insoluble. A range of approaches now exist, as I have described, each offering practical methods that have already yielded interesting and valuable findings. Anyone who is planning to use talk as data needs to consider whether the methods of observation and analysis they propose to use are sufficiently sensitive to the nature of spoken language and how it is used in their research settings. There are of course no easy answers to this question, and, as I have explained, researchers disagree about whether or not particular methods are satisfactory. But educational researchers have no excuse for treating talk data naively. Some consideration of the issues I have discussed, especially at the planning stage, may help avoid that happening.

Perhaps what is most required is a willingness to consider a range of methodological options for addressing any research questions, to make explicit one's reasons for selecting or combining methods, and most of all to avoid reducing methodological problems to simplistic choices, such as that between 'quantitative' and 'qualitative' methods. As Hammersley says:

> the same dilemmas – between adopting sensitising and definitive concepts, between focusing on the typical or the atypical, between studying a small sample in depth and or a large sample more superficially, etc. – face all researchers, whatever tradition they identify with. We will stand much more chance of finding effective solutions to the problems of classroom research if we recognize this and are prepared to learn from one another than if we simply bolster confidence in our own preferred strategies by castigating those who have made different choices.
>
> (Hammersley, 1986, p. 47)

REFERENCES

BAKER, C. (1997) 'Ethnomethodological studies of talk in educational settings' in Davies, B. and Corson, D. (eds) *Encyclopedia of Language and Education, Vol. 3: oral discourse and education,* The Hague, Netherlands, Kluwer.

BARNES, D. (1976) *From Communication to Curriculum,* Harmondsworth, Penguin.

BARNES, D. and TODD, F. (1977) *Communication and Learning in Small Groups,* London, Routledge and Kegan Paul.

BARNES, D. and TODD, F. (1995) *Communication and Learning Revisited,* Portsmouth, N.H., Heinemann.

BENNETT, N. and CASS, A. (1989) 'The effects of group composition on group interactive processes and pupil understanding', *British Educational Research Journal,* vol. 15, no. 1, pp. 19–32.

BROWN, R. and RENSHAW, P. (2000) 'Collective argumentation: a sociocultural approach to reframing classroom teaching and learning' in H. Cowie and D. van der Aalsvoort (eds) *Social Interaction in Learning and Instruction: the meaning of discourse for the construction of knowledge,* Amsterdam, Pergamon.

CANAGARAJAH, A.S. (2001) 'Critical ethnography of a Sri Lankan classroom; ambiguities in student opposition to reproduction through ESOL' in Candlin, C. N. and Mercer, N.M., *English Language Teaching in its Social Context,* London, Routledge/The Open University.

CHICK, J.K. (2001) 'Safe-talk: collusion in apartheid education' in Candlin, C. N. and Mercer, N.M., *English Language Teaching in its Social Context,* London, Routledge/The Open University.

CROLL, P. (1986) *Systematic Classroom Observation,* Lewes, Sussex, Falmer Press.

DELAMONT, S. and HAMILTON, D. (1984) 'Revisiting classroom research: a continuing cautionary tale' in Delamont, S. (ed.) *Readings on Interaction in the Classroom,* London, Methuen.

DREW, P. and HERITAGE, J. (eds) (1992) *Talk at Work,* Cambridge, Cambridge University Press.

DRIVER, R. (1983) *The Pupil as Scientist?,* Milton Keynes, Open University Press.

EDWARDS, A.D. and WESTGATE, D.P.G. (1994, 2nd edn) *Investigating Classroom Talk,* London, Falmer Press.

EDWARDS, D. and MERCER, N.M. (1987) *Common Knowledge: the development of understanding in the classroom,* London, Methuen/Routledge.

Edwards, D. and POTTER, J. (1992) *Discursive Psychology,* London, Sage.

EDWARDS, V. and SIENKEWICZ, T. (1990) *Oral Cultures Past and Present: rappin' and Homer,* Oxford, Basil Blackwell.

ERICKSON, F. (1996) 'Going for the zone: the social and cognitive ecology of teacher–student interaction in classroom conversations' in Hicks, D. (ed.) *Discourse, Learning and Schooling,* Cambridge, Cambridge University Press.

FLANDERS, N.A. (1970) *Analysing Teacher Behavior,* Reading (Mass.), Addison-Wesley.

FRENCH, J. and FRENCH, P. (1988) 'Sociolinguistics and gender divisions' in Mercer, N.M. (ed.) *Language and Literacy from an Educational Perspective, vol. 1: Language Studies,* Milton Keynes, Open University Press.

GALTON, M., SIMON, B. and CROLL, P. (1980) *Inside the Primary Classroom,* London, Routledge and Kegan Paul.

GALTON, M. (1987) 'Grouping and group work' in C. Rogers and P. Kutnick (eds) *The Social Psychology of the Primary School,* London: Routledge.

GALTON, M., HARGREAVES, L., COMBER, C. WALL, D. and PELL, T. (1999) 'Changes in patterns of teacher interaction in primary classrooms: 1976–96', *British Educational Research Journal,* vol. 25, no. 1, pp. 23–38.

GIBBONS, P. (2001) 'Learning a new register in a second language' in Candlin, C.N. and Mercer, N.M., *English Language Teaching in its Social Context,* London, Routledge with the Open University.

HALLIDAY, M. (1976) *System and Function in Language,* London, Oxford University Press.

HALLIDAY, M. (1978) *Language as a Social Semiotic,* London, Edward Arnold.

HALLIDAY, M.A.K. (1994, 2nd edn) *An Introduction to Functional Grammar* London, Arnold.

HAMILTON, D. and DELAMONT, S. (1974) 'Classroom research; a cautionary tale, Research in Education, vol. 11, pp. 1–16.

HAMMERSLEY, M. (1974) 'The organisation of pupil participation', *Sociological Review*, vol. 22, no. 3, pp. 355–68. (Reprinted in Hargreaves, A. and Woods, P. (eds) (1984) *Classrooms and Staffrooms,* Milton Keynes, Open University Press.)

HAMMERSLEY, M. (1982) 'The sociology of the classroom' in Hartnett, A. (ed.) *The Social Sciences in Educational Studies,* London, Heinemann.

HAMMERSLEY, M. (1986) 'Revisiting Hamilton and Delamont: a cautionary note on the relationship between "systematic observation" and ethnography' in Hammersley, M. (ed.) *Controversies in Classroom Research,* Milton Keynes, Open University Press.

HAMMERSLEY, M. (1992) *What's Wrong with Ethnography?,* London, Routledge.

HEATH, S.B. (1983) *Ways with Words: language, life and work in communities and classrooms,* Cambridge, Cambridge University Press.

HICKS, D. (1996) 'Contextual enquiries: a discourse-oriented study of classroom learning' in Hicks, D. (ed.) *Discourse, Learning and Schooling,* Cambridge, Cambridge University Press.

HUGHES, M. and WESTGATE, D. (1998) 'Possible enabling strategies in teacher-led talk with young pupils', *Language and Education*, vol. 12, no. 3, pp. 174–91.

IEDEMA, R. (1996) 'Save the talk for after the listening: the realisation of regulative discourse in teacher talk', *Language and Education,* vol. 10, no. 1, pp. 83.

JAYALAKSHMI, G.D. (1996) 'One cup of newspaper and one cup of tea' in Mercer, N.M. and Swann, J. (eds) *Learning English: development and diversity,* London, Routledge with the Open University.

KVALE, S. (1996) *Interviews: an introduction to qualitative research interviewing,* London, Sage.

LEMKE, J. (1990) *Talking Science: language, learning and values,* Norwood, New Jersey, Ablex.

LYLE, S. (1993) 'An investigation into ways in which children "talk themselves into meaning" ', *Language and Education,* vol. 7, no. 3, pp.181–97.

LYLE, S. (1996) 'An analysis of collaborative group work in the primary school and the factors relevant to its success', *Language and Education,* vol. 10, no. 1, pp. 13–32.

MARTYN-JONES, M. (1995) 'Code-switching in the classroom' in Milroy, L. and Muysken, P. (eds) *One Speaker, Two Languages: cross-disciplinary perspectives on code-switching,* Cambridge, Cambridge University Press.

MAYBIN, J. (1994) 'Children's voices: talk, knowledge and identity' in Graddol, D., Maybin, J. and Stierer, B. (eds) *Researching Language and Literacy in Social Context,* Clevedon, Multilingual Matters/The Open University.

MEHAN, H. (1979) *Learning Lessons: social organization in the classroom,* Cambridge (Mass.), Harvard University Press.

MERCER, N.M. (1995) *The Guided Construction of Knowledge: talk amongst teachers and learners,* Clevedon, Multilingual Matters.

MERCER, N.M. (2000) *Words and Minds: how we use language to think together*, London, Routledge.

MERCER, N.M., WEGERIF, R. and DAWES, L. (1999) 'Children's talk and the development of reasoning in the classroom', *British Educational Research Journal*, vol. 25, no. 1, pp. 95–111.

MONAGHAN, F. (1999) 'Judging a word by the company its keeps: the use of concordancing software to explore aspects of the mathematics register', *Language and Education*, vol. 13, no.1, pp. 59–70.

O'CONNOR, C. and MICHAELS, S. (1996) 'Shifting participant frameworks: orchestrating thinking practices in group discussion' in Hicks, D. (ed.) *Discourse, Learning and Schooling*, pp. 63–103, Cambridge, Cambridge University Press.

PHILIPS, S. (1972) 'Particant structures and communicative competence' in Cazden, C. (ed.) *The Functions of Language in the Classroom,* New York, Teachers' College Press, Columbia University.

POTTER, J. and WETHERELL, M. (1994) *Discourse and Social Psychology,* London: Sage.

ROJAS-DRUMMOND, S. (2000) 'Guided participation, discourse and the construction of knowledge in Mexican classrooms' in Cowie, H. and Aalsvoort, D. van der (eds) *Social Interaction in Learning and Instruction: the meaning of discourse for the construction of knowledge,* Amsterdam, Pergamon.

Rutter, M., Maugham, B., Mortimore, P. and OUSTON, J. (1979) *Fifteen Thousand Hours,* London, Open Books.

SCHEGLOFF, E. (1997) 'Whose text? Whose context?', *Discourse and Society,* vol. 8, no. 2. pp. 165–87.

SINCLAIR, J. and COULTHARD, M. (1975) *Towards an Analysis of Discourse: the English used by teachers and pupils,* London, Oxford University Press.

STOKOE, E. (2000) 'Constructing topicality in university students' small-group discussion; a conversation analytic approach', *Language and Education,* vol. 14, no. 3, pp. 184–203.

STUBBS, M (1986) *Educational Linguistics,* Oxford, Basil Blackwell.

STUBBS, M. (1983) *Discourse Analysis: the sociolinguistic analysis of natural language,* Oxford, Basil Blackwell.

STUBBS, M. (1994) 'Grammar, text and ideology: computer-assisted methods in the linguistics of representation', *Applied Linguistics,* vol. 15, no. 2, pp. 202–23.

SWANN, J., MESTHRIE, R., DEUMERT, A. and LEAP, W. (2000) *Introducing Sociolinguistics,* Edinburgh, Edinburgh University Press.

SWANN, J. (1992) *Girls, Boys and Language,* Oxford, Blackwell.

SWANN, J. and GRADDOL. D. (1994) 'Gender inequalities in classroom talk' in Graddol, D., Maybin, J. and Stierer, B. (eds) *Researching Language and Literacy in Social Context,* Clevedon, Multilingual Matters/The Open University.

UNDERWOOD, J. and UNDERWOOD, G. (1999) 'Task effects in co-operative and collaborative learning with computers' in Littleton, K. and Light, P., *Learning with Computers: analysing productive interaction,* London, Routledge.

VYGOTSKY, L.S. (1978) *Mind in Society,* London, Harvard University Press.

WEGERIF, R. and SCRIMSHAW, P. (1997) (eds) *Computers and Talk in the Primary Classroom,* Clevedon, Multilingual Matters.

WEGERIF, R., and MERCER. N.M. (1997) 'Using computer-based text analysis to integrate quantitative and qualitative methods in the investigation of collaborative learning', *Language and Education,* vol. 11, no. 4, pp. 271–86.

WELLS, G. (1999) *Dialogic Enquiry: towards a sociocultural practice and theory of education,* Cambridge, Cambridge University Press.

WERTSCH, J.V. (1985) (ed.) *Culture, Communication and Cognition: Vygotskian perspectives,* Cambridge, Cambridge University Press.

WETHERELL, M. (1998) 'Positioning and interpretative repertoires: conversation analysis and post-structuralism in dialogue', *Discourse and Society,* vol. 9, no. 3, pp. 387–412.

WILLES, M. (1983) *Children into Pupils: a study of language in early schooling,* London, Routledge and Kegan Paul.

WOODS, P.(1983) *The Sociology of the School,* London, Routledge and Kegan Paul.

WRAGG, T. and BROWN, G. (1993) *Explaining,* London, Routledge.

2 RECORDING AND TRANSCRIBING TALK IN EDUCATIONAL SETTINGS

2.1 INTRODUCTION

This section provides guidance for those who wish to carry out an investigation into aspects of spoken language. It is designed mainly for use in educational settings, and will probably be particularly appropriate for teachers and other educationists engaged on small-scale research projects. Many of the techniques and principles it discusses, however, apply equally well to investigations of spoken language in non-educational contexts.

I shall discuss factors to take into account when making audio and video-recordings of spoken language, then look at different ways of making a written transcript from these recordings. The section does not provide detailed guidance on analysis but suggests points to take into account when you are considering how to analyse your data.

2.2 PRELIMINARIES: DECIDING WHAT INFORMATION YOU NEED AND HOW TO COLLECT THIS

I am assuming that, as a reader of this section, you will already have in mind a clear purpose for recording and analysing spoken language – that you will have identified certain issues to focus on, perhaps specified, in a formal project, as a set of research questions. These questions will affect the setting in which you carry out your research, the people and events you decide to observe and record, the stance you adopt towards others involved in your research, the particular types of recording you make and how you transcribe and analyse these.

SELECTING A SAMPLE OF PEOPLE AND EVENTS

Since you cannot, and will not wish to record everything that is going on you will need to select people and events to focus on. If your interest is in aspects of classroom talk, you may wish to focus on talk between the teacher (yourself or a colleague) and pupils, or between different pupils, or both. You may be interested in whole-class discussion or small-group talk. You may wish to compare contributions from a small number of pupils in different contexts, or to monitor one child closely in a range of activities.

You will also need to think about the representativeness of the types of talk you wish to examine. For instance, how are you selecting the types of activity that you wish to record and analyse? Do these cover the full range of activities normally encountered? Or are you contrasting contexts you think are distinctive in some way?

If you are carrying out a small-scale investigation focusing on talk in one or two contexts, there are two important points to bear in mind about the samples of talk you eventually come up with:

- Your observations may provide great insights into people's conversational strategies, the way they manage certain activities or their understanding of certain concepts – but you cannot make broad generalizations on the basis of a small number of observations. For instance, observations of people's behaviour in one set of contexts do not provide evidence of how they 'generally' behave.
- A related point is that there are problems in making inferences about people's abilities or understanding on the basis of what they happen to do when you are recording them. For instance, just because students do not produce certain types of talk does not mean they cannot. On the other hand, students may develop coping strategies that make it appear they understand more than they do.

ADOPTING A RESEARCHER STANCE

A distinction is commonly made in research between *participant* and *non-participant* observation. A participant observer is someone who takes part in the event she or he is observing; a non-participant observer does not take part. There are practical difficulties with this distinction: for instance, by virtue of being in a classroom (or meeting, etc.), or by setting up recording equipment, you are to some extent a participant – and you are likely to have an effect on people's language behaviour. The linguist Labov identified what he termed 'the observer's paradox' (Labov, 1970) – that the mere act of observing people's language behaviour (or, for that matter, other aspects of their behaviour) is inclined to change that behaviour. Different effects are likely to be produced by different observers (it may matter whether an observer is female or male, or perceived as relatively senior or junior). Many linguistic researchers (such as Labov himself) have attempted, in various ways, to minimize the intrusion of their observations in order to obtain more 'authentic' data. Others have argued that such detachment is not a reasonable research goal:

> We inevitably bring our biographies and our subjectivities to every stage of the research process, and this influences the questions we ask and the ways in which we try to find answers. Our view is that the subjectivity of the observer should not be seen as a regrettable disturbance but as one element in the human interactions that comprise our object of study. Similarly, research subjects themselves are active and reflexive beings who have insights into their situations and experiences. They cannot be observed as if they were asteroids, inanimate lumps of matter: they have to be interacted with.
>
> (Cameron *et al.*, 1992, p. 5)

For educationists researching in their own institutions, or institutions with which they have a close association, it will probably be impossible to act as a completely detached observer. It will be impossible, for instance, to maintain a strict separation between your role as an observer and your usual role as a teacher or a colleague. When interpreting the talk you collect you will need to take account of the effect your own presence, and the way you carried out the observations, may have had on your data.

It is also important to consider, more generally, the relationship you have, or that you enter into, with those who participate in your research and allow you to observe their language behaviour. I have used the term *researcher stance* to refer to this more general relationship – the way a researcher behaves towards the people and events she or he is observing. Cameron *et al.* (1992) distinguish between three kinds of relationship, or researcher stance:

- 'ethical research', in which a researcher bears in mind the interests of research participants – e.g. minimizing any inconvenience caused, protecting privacy – but still carries out research on participants: in this case, it is the researcher who sets the agenda, not other research participants;
- 'advocacy', in which researchers carry out research on and for participants – e.g. regarding themselves as accountable to participants and being willing to use their expert knowledge on participants' behalf (when required by participants to do so);
- 'empowering research', in which researchers carry out research on, for and with other participants – e.g. being completely open about the aims and methods of the research, recognizing the importance of participants' own agendas, empowering participants by giving them direct access to expert knowledge.

The kind of researcher stance you feel able to adopt will affect the overall conduct of your research – what you research, the specific methods you adopt, how you interpret your results, the forms in which you disseminate research findings. Points to consider include:

- *What kind of talk is it reasonable to record?* Only 'public' talk or also casual, or 'private' conversation?
- *Do you always need permission to record talk?* Researchers would usually gain permission to make recordings (perhaps from parents in the case of young children), whereas talk may be recorded by teachers as a part of 'normal' teaching activity that does not require permission. But what if the teacher is also a researcher, or if s/he wishes to make use of 'routine' recordings for research purposes?
- *How open should you be about the purposes of your recordings?* Bound up with this question is the notion of the observer's paradox: it is likely that the more you tell people about your research the more their behaviour will be affected. Some researchers compromise: they are rather vague about the precise purposes of their research, though they may say more after completing their recording. 'Empowering' research would require greater openness and consultation. You may also feel that, if you are observing as a colleague or a teacher, it is important to retain an atmosphere of trust between yourself and those you work with.
- *To what extent should you discuss your recordings with research participants?* This has to do partly with the researcher stance you adopt. Discussing recordings with others also lets you check your interpretations against theirs, and may give you a different understanding of your data.
- *How should you identify those you have recorded?* In writing reports, researchers often give pseudonyms to institutions in which they have carried out research, or people whose words they quote. If you have worked more collaboratively with participants, however, they may wish to be identified by name. If you do wish to maintain confidentiality it may be hard to do this where you are observing in your own institution – the identity of those you refer to may be apparent to other colleagues. One solution is to discuss with colleagues or students how much confidentiality they feel is necessary and how this may be maintained.

- *In what ways should you consult those you have recorded about the dissemination and further use of your work?* People may give permission to be recorded for a certain purpose, but what if your purposes change? E.g. you may wish to disseminate your work to a wider audience, or to use a video obtained for your research in a professional development session with local teachers.

For those interested in the relationships between researchers and 'the researched', Cameron *et al.* (1992) is a useful source. Professional organizations also provide research guidelines – see for instance the British Association for Applied Linguistics (1994) *Recommendations on Good Practice in Applied Linguistics.*

The rest of this section provides practical guidance on making audio and video-recordings, making field-notes to supplement these recordings, and transcribing talk for detailed analysis.

2.3 MAKING AUDIO AND VIDEO-RECORDINGS

Plan to allow enough time to record talk in classrooms or other educational settings. You may need to allow time to collect, set up and check equipment. You will also need to pilot your data collection methods to ensure that it is possible to record clearly the kinds of data you are interested in. When you have made your recordings you will need time to play and replay these to become familiar with your data and to make transcriptions.

An initial decision concerns whether to make *audio* or *video*-recordings. Videos are particularly useful for those with an interest in non-verbal behaviour; they are also useful for showing how certain activities are carried out, or certain equipment used. On the other hand, video cameras are likely to be more intrusive then audio recorders, and you may also find it harder to obtain a clear recording of speech.

I have set out below some practical points to bear in mind when making a choice between audio and video-recordings.

Audio or video-recordings?

Audio-recordings

- An audio-cassette recorder can be intrusive – though this is less likely to be the case in classrooms where pupils are used to being recorded, or recording themselves. Intrusiveness is more of a problem if cassette recorders are used in contexts where talk is not normally recorded, and where there is not the opportunity for recording to become routine (e.g. staff or other meetings).
- Intrusiveness can be lessened by keeping the technology simple and unobtrusive, for example by using a small, battery-operated cassette recorder with a built-in microphone. This also avoids the danger of trailing wires, and the problem of finding appropriate sockets.
- It is also better to use a fairly simple cassette recorder if pupils are recording themselves. In this case, go for a machine with a small number of controls, and check that young pupils can operate the buttons easily.
- There is a trade-off between lack of intrusiveness/ease of use and quality of recording: more sophisticated machines, used with separate microphones, will produce a better quality recording. This is a consideration if you intend to use the recordings with others, for example in a professional development session.
- A single cassette recorder is not suitable for recording whole-class discussion, unless you focus on the teacher's talk. The recorder will pick up loud voices, or voices that are near to it, and probably lose the rest behind background noise (scraping chairs and so on). Even when recording a small group, background noise is a problem. It is worth checking this by piloting your recording arrangements: speakers may need to be located in a quieter area outside the classroom.

- With audio-recordings you lose important non-verbal and contextual information. Unless you are familiar with the speakers you may also find it difficult to distinguish between different voices. Wherever possible, supplement audio-recordings with field-notes or a diary providing contextual information.

Video-recordings

- Video cameras are more intrusive than audio-cassette recorders. In contexts such as classrooms, intrusiveness can be lessened by leaving the recorder around for a while (switched off).
- A video camera is highly selective – it cannot pick up everything that is going on in a large room such as a classroom. If you move it around the classroom you will get an impression of what is going on, but will not pick up much data you can actually use for analysis. A video camera may be used to focus on the teacher's behaviour. When used to record pupils, it is best to select a small group, carrying out an activity in which they don't need to move around too much.
- As with audio-recordings, it is best to have the group in a quiet area where their work will not be disrupted by onlookers.
- The recording will be more usable if you check that the camera has all that you want in view and then leave it running. If you move the camera around you may lose important information, and you may introduce bias (by focusing selectively on certain pupils or actions).
- Video cameras with built-in microphones don't always produce good sound recordings. You will need to check this. A common problem is that you may need to locate a camera a long way from the group you are observing both to obtain a suitable angle of view, and to keep the apparatus unobtrusive. If it is important that you hear precisely what each person says, you may need to make a separate audio-recording or use an external microphone plugged into the video camera.

After you have made recordings, it is useful to make a separate note of the date, time and context of each sequence, and then summarize the content (use the cassette player counter to make an index of your tape and help you locate extracts again).

2.4 MAKING FIELD-NOTES

Field-notes allow you to jot down, in a systematic way, your observations on activities and events. They provide useful contextual support for audio and video-recordings, and may also be an important source of information in their own right. For instance, if your focus is on students in a particular lesson, you may wish to make notes on a (related) discussion between teachers; on other lessons you are unable to record; or on the lesson you are focusing on, to supplement your recordings. You may also wish to make notes on the recordings themselves, as a prelude to (and a context for) transcription.

If you are taking notes of a discussion or lesson on the spot, you will find that the talk flows very rapidly. This is likely to be the case particularly in informal talk, such as talk between students in a group. More formal talk is often easier to observe on the spot. In whole-class discussion led by a teacher, or in formal meetings, usually only one person talks at a time, and participants may wait to talk until nominated by the teacher or chair. The teacher or chair may rephrase or summarize what others speakers have said. The slightly more ordered nature of such talk gives an observer more breathing space to take notes.

It is usual to date notes and to provide brief contextual information. The format adopted is highly variable – depending on particular research interests and personal preferences. Example 4.4 in Part 1, sub-section 4.3, shows extracts from field-notes made while a researcher was observing a school assembly.

2.5 MAKING A TRANSCRIPT

In order to analyse spoken language at any level of detail, you will need to make a written transcript. Transcription is, however, very time-consuming. Edwards and Westgate (1994) suggest that every hour's recording may require fifteen hours for transcription. I find that I can make a rough transcript more quickly than this, but a detailed transcript may take far longer, particularly if a lot of non-verbal or contextual information is included.

In small-scale research, transcripts may be used selectively. For instance, you could transcribe (timed) extracts – say ten minutes from a longer interaction. You could use field-notes to identify certain extracts for transcription; or you could make a rough transcript of an interaction to identify general points of interest, then more detailed transcripts of relevant extracts.

While transcripts allow a relatively detailed examination of spoken language, they only provide a partial record: they cannot faithfully reproduce every aspect of talk. Transcribers will tend to pay attention to different aspects depending upon their interests, which means that a transcript is already an interpretation of the event it seeks to record. Elinor Ochs, in a now classic account of 'Transcription as theory', suggests that 'transcription is a selective process reflecting theoretical goals and definitions' (1979, p. 44). This point is illustrated by the sample layouts and transcription conventions discussed below.

TRANSCRIPTION CONVENTIONS

Many published transcripts use conventions of written language such as punctuation in representing speech. But because written down speech is not the same as writing it can be quite hard to punctuate.

If you do wish to punctuate a transcript bear in mind that in so doing you are giving the speech a particular interpretation. Compare the following two methods of punctuating a teacher's question(s):

> Now, think very carefully. What would happen if we cut one of those hollow balls in half? What would we find inside?
>
> Now, think very carefully what would happen if we cut one of those hollow balls in half. What would we find inside?

Use of punctuation represents a trade off between legibility and accessibility of the transcript and what might be a premature and impressionistic analysis of the data. It is probably best at least initially to use as little conventional punctuation as possible. Several sets of transcription conventions are available to indicate features of spoken language. Some of these are high detailed, allowing transcribers to record intakes of breath, increased volume, stress, syllable lengthening, etc. (see, for instance, Sacks *et al.*, 1974; Ochs, 1979). Such conventions are designed to produce accurate transcriptions, but there is a danger that they will lend a misleading sense of scientific objectivity to the exercise. Rather than being 'objectively identified' such features of speech are likely to correspond to the transcriber's initial interpretations of their data.

Bearing in mind this caveat, Figure 1 illustrates a simple set of conventions for transcribing spoken language.

Further transcription conventions may be added if need be. Alternatively, as in Figure 1, you can leave a wide margin to comment on features such as loudness, whispering, or other noises that add to the meaning of the talk (as with other aspects of transcription these will necessarily be selective).

Teacher begins by telling class the lesson is to be about toy animals. She arranges some stuffed toy animals on her desk, then asks the class 'Have you got any toy animals at home?' Students are selected individually to respond. Teacher first asks a girl, and makes her repeat carefully 'I have got many toy animals at home.' Then turns to a boy, S1.

		Transcription	Notes
1	T:	You [student's name] have you got	
2		many toy animals at home	
3	S1:	Yes I have { (.) I have a got	
4	T:	{ mmh	
5	S1:	many toy animals at home	
6	T:	That's good that's right what toy	
7		animals have you got at home (.)	
8		what name for animals (.)	
9		[student's name] what toy animals	low voice
10		have you got at home (.) I'm like a tiger	
11	Ss:	<laughter>	
12	T:	What yes	
13	S2:	I have { I have got { (.) I	T nods; lowers S2's
14	T:	{ mmh {mmh a (.)	hand and places on
15		or maybe two or { maybe three	desk
16	S2:	{ I have got a many	
17		toy animals	
18	T:	mmh I have got { many toy animals	
19	S2:	{ many toy animals	

Key

T	= Teacher
S	= Student (S1 = Student 1, etc)
student's name	underlining indicates any feature you wish to comment on
(.)	brief pause
(1sec)	timed pause
{maybe {I have got	brackets indicate the start of overlapping speech
<laughter>	transcription of a sound etc. that forms part of the utterance

Figure 1 Transcription of teacher–student talk.

In Figure 1 I have used an extract from field-notes to contextualize the transcript. In the transcript itself, I have followed the frequently used convention of referring to the speakers simply as teacher and students. An alternative is to give speakers pseudonyms (see the discussion of confidentiality under 'Adopting a researcher stance' above). The sequence in Figure 1 comes from an English lesson carried out with seven-year-old students in a school in Moscow, in Russia. The students are being encouraged to rehearse certain vocabulary and structures. The teacher addresses each student directly to ensure they contribute and uses features such as humour ('I'm like a tiger') to further encourage the students. In this extract Student 2 seems unsure of how to respond to the teacher's question (as indicated by his hesitation). In an attempt to help, the teacher offers him suggestions for the next word in his sentence (*a*, *two*, or *three* – presumably toy animals). This may be what leads to the student's error (*a many toy animals*) which is subsequently corrected by the teacher.

LAYING OUT A TRANSCRIPT

The most commonly used layout, which I shall call a 'standard' layout, is set out rather like a dialogue in a play, with speaking turns following one another in sequence. This is the layout adopted in Figure 1. One of the better known alternatives to this layout is a 'column' layout, in which each speaker is allocated a separate column for their speaking turns.

Figures 2 and 3 illustrate respectively 'standard' and 'column' layouts applied to the same brief extract of talk. This comes from one of a series of English lessons in a secondary school in Denmark, near Copenhagen (Dam and Lentz, 1998). The class of 15-year-old mixed-ability students were carrying out a project on 'England and the English'. The extract shows a group of students, two girls and two boys, beginning to plan what to do for their homework. The students are seated round a table, the girls opposite the boys.

Transcription			**Notes**
1	G1:	What are we going to do at home	addresses group
2		(.) any ideas	directly
3	B1:	Yes (.) I take this (.) I take	refers to book which
4		this <general laughter> yes yes	he holds up
5		I take it mmh and I see and I	
6		see if there's something I can	
7		use (.)	
8	G1?:	We can use	
9	B1:	We can use	
10	B2:	So what (would) we do ( )	question towards
11		read it at home (.) the	girls?
12		questionnaire	
13		{ (.) read it at home	
14	B1	{ ( )	
		[. . .]	
15	G2:	Maybe I can get some materials	
16		for this	
17	G1:	From (mother)	
18	G2:	Yes	
19	B1?:	from where	
20	G2	from my mother (.) from the	
21		travel agency	

Key

As in Figure 1 with, in addition:

G, B	= Girl, Boy
(would)	transcription uncertain: a guess
( )	unclear speech – impossible to transcribe
[...]	excision – some data excluded

Figure 2 Transcription of small group talk: standard layout.

In group talk it's often interesting to look at the role taken by different students. In this case, the group seemed to collaborate fairly well and to be generally supportive of one another. Girl 1 seemed to play an organizing or chairing role – e.g. by asking for ideas from the rest of the group; by 'correcting' Boy 1, reminding him that his work is for the group as a whole (line 8 of the standard layout); and by completing Girl 2's turn (line 17 of the standard layout). I would be interested in looking further at this group's work to see if Girl 1 maintained this role or if it was also taken on by other students.

The way transcription is laid out may highlight certain features of the talk, for instance:

- The standard layout suggests a connected sequence, in which one turn follows on from the preceding one. This does seem to happen in the extract transcribed in Figures 2 and 3 but it is not always the case. In young children's speech, for instance, speaking turns may not follow on directly from a preceding turn. I shall also give an example of more informal talk below in which it is harder to distinguish a series of sequential turns.

- Column transcripts allow you to track one speaker's contributions: you can look at the number and types of contribution made by a speaker (e.g. Girl 1's 'organizing' contributions), or track the topics they focus on – or whatever else is of interest.
- In a column transcript, it's important to bear in mind which column you allocate to each speaker. Because of factors such as the left–right orientation in European scripts, and associated conventions of page layout, we may give priority to information located on the left-hand side. Ochs (1979) points out that, in column transcripts of adult-child talk, the adult is nearly always allocated the left-hand column, suggesting they are the initiator of the conversation. In Figure 3 I began with Girl 1, probably because she spoke first, but I also grouped the girls and then the boys together. This may be useful if your interest is, say, in gender issues, but it's important to consider why you are adopting a particular order and not to regard this as, somehow, 'natural'.

	G1	G2	B1	B2	Notes
1	What are we going				addresses group
2	to do at home (.)				directly
3	any ideas				
4			Yes (.) I take		refers to book
5			<u>this</u> (.) I take		which he holds
6			this <general		up
7			laughter> yes yes		
8			I take it mmh and		
9			I see and I see		
10			if there's		
11			something I can		
12			use (.)		
13	We can use (?)				
14			We can use		
15				So what (would)	question
16				we do ( ) read	towards girls?
17				it at home (.)	
18				the questionnaire	
19			( )	(.) read it at	
20				home	
	[. . .]				
21		Maybe I can get			
22		some materials			
23		for this			
24	From (mother)				
25		Yes			
26				from where (?)	
27		from my mother			
28		(.) from the			
29		travel agency			

Key

As in Figure 2 with, in addition:

(?) Guess at speaker

Figure 3 Transcription of small group talk: column layout.

Accounts of conversational turn-taking have often assumed that one person talks at a time (e.g. Sacks *et al.*, 1974). As I suggested above, however, this is not always the case, particularly in young children's talk, or in more informal discussion where there is lots of overlapping talk and where speakers frequently complete one another's turns. In her analysis of informal talk amongst women friends, Jennifer Coates developed a method of transcription in which she used a 'stave' layout (by analogy with musical staves) to represent the joint construction of speaking turns (see, for instance, Coates, 1996). Stave transcription has not been used frequently in educational contexts but may be adopted to illustrate highly collaborative talk in small groups. Figure 4 below comes from a study made by Julia Davies (2000) of English lessons in three secondary schools in Sheffield, in the north of England. Davies was particularly interested in gender issues – in how girls and boys worked together in single-sex and mixed-sex groups. Figure 4 shows a group of four teenage girls reflecting on their earlier experiences of school. Davies found (like Coates) that the girls' talk was particularly collaborative (e.g. it contained overlapping speech, joint construction of turns and several indicators of conversational support).

1	Bel	Right/anything else? / everyone {have a think/right/
	Jan	{everyone have a think
	Lou	
	Rosa	
2	Bel	
	Jan	about their important memories /
	Lou	
	Rosa	
3	Bel	I've got one (.) /right I remember (.)
	Jan	
	Lou	
	Rosa	
4	Bel	{<laughs> Jan AGAIN/
	Jan	I've got this important {memory of school was-/I got
	Lou	
	Rosa	
5	Bel	
	Jan	{this effort trophy at middle school (.) /
	Lou	{Jan again/ yeah?/
	Rosa	
6	Bel	
	Jan	and I-/oh and I were-/and I was dead chuffed/I thought it were great/
	Lou	
	Rosa	
7	Bel	
	Jan	an effort trophy?/ it were great weren't it?/
	Lou	I got one of them/ yeah/
	Rosa	
8	Bel	
	Jan	{it were great/
	Lou	{at the fourth year of juniors/
	Rosa	

Key

As Figure 3 with, in addition:

Yeah/	A slash represents the end of a tone group, or chunk of talk
Yeah?/	A question mark indicates the end of a chunk analysed as a question
AGAIN	Capital letters indicate a word uttered with emphasis

Staves are numbered and separated by horizontal lines; all the talk within a stave is to be read together, sequentially from left to right.

Figure 4 Transcription of group talk: stave layout (adapted from Davies, 2000, p. 290).

Note

This figure is adapted from Davies's original. Davies follows Coates in representing, within a stave, only those students who are speaking. Here I have included all students throughout the transcription – which illustrates, for instance, that one student, Rosa, does not speak at all in this sequence. Rosa may have been contributing in other ways, e.g. non-verbally, and she does speak later in the discussion.

The layout you choose for a transcript will depend on what you are transcribing and why. Here I have tried to show how different layouts highlight certain aspects of talk and play down others. You will need to try out, and probably adapt, layouts till you find one that suits your purposes – bearing in mind, as ever, that such decisions are already leading you towards a particular interpretation of your data.

INCLUDING NON-VERBAL AND CONTEXTUAL INFORMATION

Transcriptions tend to highlight verbal information, though I have indicated above how non-verbal information can be shown in a 'notes' column, or by typographical conventions such as capital letters for emphasis or loudness. If you are particularly interested in non-verbal information you may wish to adopt transcription conventions that highlight this in some way. As examples, Figure 5 below shows how a storyteller uses a number of non-verbal features in her performance of a Nigerian story ('A man amongst men'); and Figure 6 shows how a teacher uses gaze to nominate female or male students to respond to her questions.

	Transcript	**Notes**
1	[Once upon a time] a | long | long | long | long | long time ago there was a | hunter a [very well-known and respected hunter]	spreading gesture to start story; downward gestures used for rhythm;
	*every day he would go | out into the | bush he would catch whatever meat he needed for the village, he would carry it on his back he would bring it into the village he would throw it down on the floor the people	*facing A, or orienting towards A even when embodying actions
	they would see him *they would start clapping their hands <claps, A. claps>	*hands out to A; A also invited by direct gaze, head movement, general body orientation.

Key

[Once upon a time]	Square brackets indicate beginning and end of large spreading gesture
| long	Vertical slash indicates downward gesture accompanying a word
*every day	Asterisk indicates something that is commented on in the 'Notes' column
catch whatever meat	Underlined speech indicates that the storyteller also mimes the actions she describes
<claps>	As in transcripts above, indicates sound/action that forms part of the utterance
A	Audience

Figure 5 Representation of non-verbal features in an oral narrative.

Teacher: If you have a pendulum (.) which we established last week was a weight a mass (.) suspended from a string or whatever
(.) and watch I'm holding it with my hand so it's at rest at the moment (.) what is it that makes the pendulum swing in a downward direction for instance till it gets to there? [1]?
{ (.) just watch it
Mathew: gravity }
Teacher: What is it Mathew? [2]
Mathew: Gravity
Teacher: { Yes (.) } now we mentioned gravity when we were
Boy: { ( ) }
Teacher: actually doing the experiments but we didn't discuss it too much (.) OK so it's gravity then that pulls it down (.) what causes it to go up again at the other side? [3]
Boy: { Force the force
Boy: The string Miss }

Key

~~~~~ means gaze to boys
——— means gaze to girls
{ } overlap
(.) pause
( ) unclear

Figure 6 Representation of teacher's gaze towards female and male students (Swann and Graddol, 1989/1994, pp. 157–9).

Note

The full transcript from which Figure 6 is extracted shows that the teacher's gaze is more frequently directed towards the boys at critical points in the interaction, such as when a question is to be answered.

REPRESENTING DIFFERENT LANGUAGE VARIETIES

The transcripts of classroom talk I have illustrated so far come from contexts in which English is being used as a medium of instruction. In many contexts, however, even where English is used as a classroom language, teachers and students may also use another language, such as the students' first or main language, for certain purposes. In this case, it may be interesting to see when a teacher or student uses each language.

There are many different ways of representing the alternation between different language varieties. Figures 7 and 8 below show how researchers have represented languages in their original form whilst also offering an English translation. Figure 7, from research carried out by Antoinette Camilleri in bilingual classrooms in Malta, shows a teacher alternating between English and Maltese, where Maltese is used to amplify or explain (rather than simply translate) an English sentence read from a textbook. In this case, an English translation of the Maltese utterances is given in a separate column. Figure 8, from research carried out by G. D. Jayalakshmi in Bihar, in northern India, shows how a teacher uses Sanskrit partly to demonstrate his knowledge and also 'because he believes that his function is to instruct students not only in language but also, more generally, in life' (Jayalakshmi, 1996, p. 145). In this case, an English translation is given in brackets beneath the Sanskrit.
~~~~~

England Australia New Zealand and Argentina are the best producers of wool *dawk l-aktar li għandhom* farms *li jrabbu n-nagħag għas-suf* *O.K.* England *tgħiduli minn licma post* England *għandhom* Scotland *magħrufin* *tant għall*-wool *u ġersijiet* *tagħhom O.K.*	they have the largest number of farms and the largest number of sheep for wool O.K. England where in England we really mean Scotland they are very well-known for their woollen products

Figure 7 Transcript illustrating alternation between English and Maltese (Camilleri, 1994; cited in Mercer, 1996, p. 134).

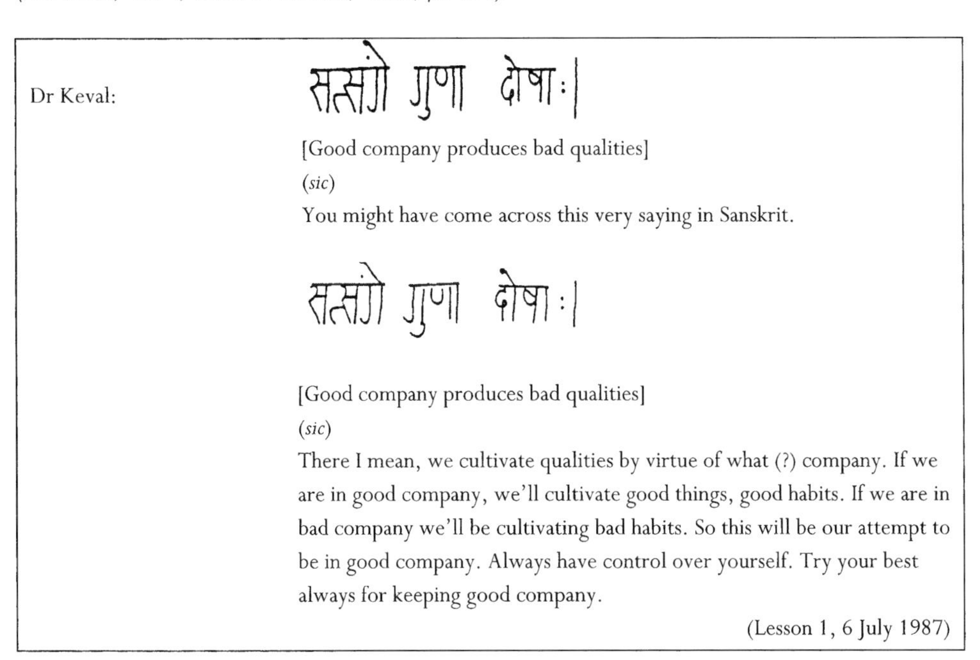
Dr Keval: सत्संगो गुणा दोषा:।

[Good company produces bad qualities]

(*sic*)

You might have come across this very saying in Sanskrit.

सत्संगो गुणा दोषा:।

[Good company produces bad qualities]

(*sic*)

There I mean, we cultivate qualities by virtue of what (?) company. If we are in good company, we'll cultivate good things, good habits. If we are in bad company we'll be cultivating bad habits. So this will be our attempt to be in good company. Always have control over yourself. Try your best always for keeping good company.

(Lesson 1, 6 July 1987)

Figure 8 Transcript illustrating alternation between Sanskrit and English (Jayalakshmi, 1996, p. 145).

Note

In this case there is an error in Dr Keval's Sanskrit. Jayalakshmi comments that he may have learnt quotations such as this by rote.

In Figure 8, Jayalakshmi represents Sanskrit in Devanagari script. It would also have been possible to represent it in transliteration, in Roman script. It is, however, more difficult to decide how to represent language varieties closely related to English, or different varieties of English, that do not have a conventional orthography. Figure 4 above represented non-standard grammar ('it were great') but did not attempt to represent the girls' accent. Some transcribers resort to 'eye dialect' (as in *we wuz jus' goin' 'ome*) to give an indication of pronunciation, but there is a danger here of representing certain speakers (working-class speakers, children, non-native speakers) as somehow deviant or incompetent.

Mark Sebba used a mixed system in his transcription of the speech of young Black speakers in London, who alternate between Creole (derived from Jamaican Creole) and London English. Creole utterances were underlined, London English utterances were not. Underlined utterances were, then, to be 'pronounced as if Creole' (1993, p. 163). Sebba also used some 'eye dialect' features to indicate the pronunciation of specific words or sounds; and certain 'one-off' conventions, such as the use of '%' to represent a glottal stop (the sound used as a variant of /t/ in certain linguistic contexts, and in certain varieties of English – sometimes represented as an apostrophe as in *bu'er* for *butter*). Figure 9 illustrates this. One point of interest is that the glottal stop, a feature of London English but not (usually) of Jamaican Creole, is here used within a Creole utterance (*invi%e*, line 4).

1	J:	did you go to Jackie's par%y?
	(1.0)	
	C:	who Jackie Lomax
	J:	yeah
	C:	no one never invi%e me
5	J:	I heard that she had a really nice par%y an' Cheryl said there was a lo% of boys there (0.6) you know and they (were) playin' pass the parcel an' that
	C:	is it?
	J:	yeah
10	C:	she invite you?
	J:	no
	C:	she never invite me neither an Leonie 'ave one as well never invite never tell me not'in' (0.4) me no business too!

Figure 9 Transcription of a conversation using Creole and London English (Sebba, 1993, pp. 19–20).

Sets of symbols such as the International Phonetic Alphabet (IPA) are used by phoneticians to give a systematic representation of the sounds of English and other languages. Such alphabets are hard for the non-expert to read and are not usually suitable for transcribing long conversational sequences. However if you are interested in learners' pronunciations of English, and you are familiar with the IPA or a similar alphabet, you could use phonetic symbols selectively for certain words, or to represent certain sounds.

Figure 10 illustrates the use of phonetic symbols to represent a young Russian student's pronunciation of the word *bushy* (this is taken from the same lesson as that transcribed in Figure 1).

Transcription	**Notes**
1 S: Its tail is short and [bɪʃi]	pronounced to rhyme with *fishy*
2 T: Bushy ([bʊʃi])	more conventional pronunciation
3 S: Bushy ([bʊʃi])	more conventional pronunciation

Figure 10 Representation of pronunciation using phonetic symbols.

2.6 TOWARDS AN ANALYSIS: QUANTITATIVE AND QUALITATIVE APPROACHES

Discussions of research methodology often make a distinction between quantitative and qualitative approaches to research. Broadly, quantitative approaches allow you to identify and count the distribution of certain linguistic features, or certain types of utterance. You can then draw a numerical comparison between, for instance, the types of talk produced in different contexts or by different students, or groups of students. Some forms of quantification can be carried out 'on the spot'. For instance, while observing a lesson you could count the number of times each student responded to a teacher's question. More complex patterns can be identified from scrutiny of audio or video recordings, or from a transcript. G. D. Jayalakshmi, for instance, whose research in Indian classrooms I referred to above, noticed that students participated less in 'traditional' teacher-directed lessons (drawing on textbooks) than in lessons based on videos which she had introduced. To check her impressions, she analysed recordings of a random sample of lessons, counting up the number of times a student initiated talk; and what types of talk this involved (whether the student was seeking clarification, asking about the meaning of a word, making a single word contribution, or making a longer contribution to discussion). She displayed her results in a table (cited as Table 1 below). Table 1 shows that, in the contexts analysed, students initiated more talk in video than traditional lessons, and they also made a large number of longer contributions.

Table 1 Number and type of student-initiated moves in two types of lesson.

Type of class	Number of student-initiated moves	Clarification seeking	Meaning of words	Single word contributions	Longer contributions
Traditional	11	3	2	5	0
Video Led	38	2	3	0	33

(Source: Jayalakshmi, 1993, p. 287)

By contrast, a qualitative approach tends to be used if the questions that are asked of a piece of data are more open-ended: if you wanted to know, for instance, what happened during a meeting; how students worked together in certain learning situations; how relationships were established and maintained; or how students achieved an understanding of certain concepts.

Within educational research there have been several debates about the relative merits of quantitative and qualitative approaches. The box below summarizes features of each as applied to the analysis of spoken language and some advantages and disadvantages that have traditionally been associated with them.

Quantitative and qualitative approaches to the analysis of spoken language

A quantitative approach allows you to represent your data in terms of numbers. You can make a numerical comparison between talk produced by different people or during different events.

When representing data that has been analysed using quantitative methods it is usual to display this in a table. Alternative forms of representation such as histograms or bar charts may be used to point up comparisons between people or events.

Data may be analysed using prespecified categories of talk. Alternatively, as in Jayalakshmi's research, categories may emerge from close scrutiny of data: e.g. from playing and replaying an audio or video-recording, or working slowly through a transcript. Such categories are not 'naturally' present in the data, but will depend upon your own research interests.

Representing talk in terms of numbers has the disadvantage that it is necessarily a reductive exercise: talk is reduced to a set of categories: it is abstracted from its original context; it is unambiguously pigeon-holed, masking the rather fluid, uncertain and negotiated meanings that are evident when talk is examined in context.

Talk may be recorded and analysed in a more open-ended way. Researchers adopting a qualitative approach to recording can note down and explore any interesting aspects of their data. What count as interesting aspects will depend upon the questions the researcher is concerned to investigate, but sometimes points emerge that are quite unexpected.

Aspects of the data may only begin to make sense when mulled over and compared with other information, or perhaps discussed with speakers. Sometimes interpretations may change, or you may want to allow for a number of different interpretations.

When presenting and discussing data that has been recorded and analysed using a qualitative approach, researchers frequently quote selectively from field-notes or transcripts to support points they wish to make. Transcripts may be supported by a detailed commentary.

Such ways of analysing and presenting data allow the researcher to preserve important contextual information that affects the meanings of utterances, and also to preserve the ambiguity and fluidity of these meanings. The approach is selective in that two researchers may (legitimately) notice different things about a stretch of talk or provide different interpretations of utterances. There is also a danger of unintended bias, in that researchers may notice features of talk that support a point they wish to make and ignore counter-evidence.

While some researchers argue for an integration of quantitative and qualitative approaches, it has also been suggested that they embody fundamentally different views of the meaning of spoken language (coding language into discrete categories, for instance, suggests that meanings are relatively fixed and unambiguous, whereas qualitative approaches often emphasize ambiguity in language and argue that utterances need to be interpreted in context). For an overview of this debate see, for instance, Edwards and Westgate (1994).

Wegerif and Mercer (1997) suggest that it is possible to progress beyond this apparent divide by drawing on corpus, or computer-based forms of analysis. Corpus-based analyses allow researchers to process huge amounts of spoken or written language and establish quantitative patterns of language use. They have frequently been used to identify meanings of words and phrases and to aid the compilation of dictionary entries. They may also be used to identify stylistic differences between different (literary) authors or different types of text. Wegerif and Mercer illustrate how corpus-based methods may be used with smaller amounts of data, and in combination with a qualitative exploration of language.

Wegerif and Mercer drew on this combination of methods as part of an ongoing study of exploratory talk in the classroom. They found that primary school children performed better on a standardized test of reasoning after they had been 'coached' in the use of exploratory talk. They also looked at transcript evidence of the quality of children's talk during problem solving activities carried out before and after the coaching intervention. Extracts from transcripts are used to show that, after the intervention, children spent more time discussing problems, considered alternative solutions, and eventually reached agreement on the correct answer. Wegerif and Mercer point out, however, that such evidence may not be seen as convincing because it consists only of one or two brief extracts from transcripts.

As a way of complementing their initial qualitative approach, Wegerif and Mercer used a computerized concordancing program. This identifies all instances of a word or expression used in a particular set of data, and displays these in their immediate linguistic context. In Figure 11 below, for instance, the words *'cos* and *because* are displayed in each speaking turn in which they occurred in one group's interaction before and after the intervention. Wegerif and Mercer suggest that *'cos* and *because* are used differently in the pre- and post-intervention interaction: in the post-intervention interactions they are more frequently used to link reasons to claims. They carried out similar analyses of other terms that might be seen as indicative of reasoning (e.g. *if* and *so* used to link a reason to an assertion).

Focal Group 1 pre-intervention task use of ''cos' or 'because'

Elaine: It isn't *'cos* look that's a square
Graham: No *'cos* look watch there all down there and they are all at the side and they are all up there
Elaine: Wait wait wait its that one *'cos* look it's them two and them two ( ) and them two
John: *'Cos* look that goes out like that –
Elaine: *'Cos* look that goes in
John: *'Cos* look that goes too far out
Graham: Look *'cos* that's got 4
Elaine: No . . . not that one not that one *because* it's got a little bit like that it's that one look – it goes in and then it goes out
John: No it's isn't *because* it's there
Elaine: No *because* it will come along like that
Elaine: Could be that one *because* look stops at the bottom and look
Elaine: It isn't it isn't *because* look
(12)

Focal Group 1 post-intervention task use of ''cos' or 'because'

Graham: Number 6 *'cos* 6 stops in there *'cos* look if you
Elaine: It can't be there *'cos* look if you done that
Elaine: It is look if that goes like that and then it has another one *'cos* those two make
Elaine: He doesn't say what they are *'cos* he might be wrong
Graham: Yeh *'cos* look
Elaine: *'Cos* it would go round
John: It is *'cos* it goes away *'cos* look that one goes like that
Elaine: No it can't be *'cos* look . . . with the square with the triangle you take away the triangle so you're left with the square so if you do just this and then again take that away it's going to end up, like that isn't it?
Graham: Actually *'cos* that's got a square and a circle round it
John: Yeh *'cos* it goes like that and then it takes that one away and does that
Elaine: No *'cos* look
Elaine: Probably one in the circle *'cos* there are only two circles
Graham: *'Cos* if they are lines and then they are going like that it is because they are wonky isn't it
Graham: No actually it ain't *'cos* then
Elaine: Yeh it's number 8 *because* those ones – those two came that those two make that
John: No *because* 1, 2, 3 1, 2, 3
John: No *because* that goes that way and that goes that way
Graham: No *because* it's that one
(21)

Figure 11 Incidence of 'cos *and* because *in primary school children's talk.*

This form of analysis provides quantifiable data (i.e. it is possible to calculate the frequency with which *'cos* and *because* are used in different contexts). It is also possible to see each instance of *'cos* and *because* in a limited linguistic context, which provides further information about their use in each case (as in Figure 11 above). And it is possible, for any one instance, to display further linguistic context (any number of preceding and following speaking turns) to allow a qualitative exploration of the data.

If this form of analysis interests you, it is possible to purchase concordancing software (or, in some cases, to download software from the internet). You will need, however, to be prepared to spend time exploring the software to see how it can be made to work most effectively for your own purposes. For further discussion and examples of corpus-based analysis see, for instance, Stubbs (1996).

2.7 CONCLUSION

In this section I have discussed various techniques you can use to record and transcribe spoken language. There is no 'ideal' way to do this, and I have tried to indicate the strengths and weaknesses of different approaches so that you can select the most appropriate method, or combination of methods, for your own purposes. It is beyond the scope of this section to consider, at any level of detail, ways of analysing spoken language, though I have suggested some initial considerations to bear in mind.

REFERENCES

BRITISH ASSOCIATION FOR APPLIED LINGUISTICS (BAAL) (1994) *Recommendations on Good Practice in Applied Linguistics*, BAAL.

CAMERON, D., FRASER, E., HARVEY, P., RAMPTON, M.B.H. and Richardson, K. (1992) Researching Language: Issues of Power and Method, London, Routledge.

CAMILLERI, A. (1994) 'Talking bilingually, writing monolingually', paper presented at the Socioloinguistcs Symposium, University of Lancaster, March.

COATES, J. (1996) *Women Talk*, Oxford, Blackwell Publishers.

DAM, L. and LENTZ, J. (1998) *It's up to Yourself if You Want to Learn: autonomous language learning at intermediate level*, Copenhagen, DLH (video and print).

DAVIES, J.A. (2000) *Expressions of Gender: an enquiry into the way gender impacts on the discourse styles of pupils involved in small group talk during GCSE English lesson, with particular reference to the under-achievement of boys,* Sheffield, University of Sheffield, unpublished PhD Thesis.

EDWARDS, A.D. and WESTGATE, D.P.G. (1994) *Investigating Classroom Talk*, London, Falmer Press (second edition).

JAYALAKSHMI, G.D. (1993) 'Video in the English curriculum of an Indian secondary school', Milton Keynes, The Open University, unpublished PhD thesis.

JAYALAKSHMI, G.D. (1996) 'One cup of newspaper and one cup of tea' in Mercer, N.M. and Swann, J. (eds) *Learning English: development and diversity*, London, Routledge/The Open University.

LABOV, W. (1970) 'The study of language in its social context' in W. Labov (1972) *Sociolinguistic Patterns*, Oxford, Basil Blackwell.

MERCER, N.M. (with contributions from Douglas Barnes) (1996) 'English as a classroom language' in Mercer, N.M. and Swann, J. (eds) *Learning English: development and diversity*, London, Routledge/The Open University.

OCHS, E. (1979) 'Transcription as theory' in Ochs, E. and Schieffelin, B.B. (eds) *Developmental Pragmatics*, London, Academic Press.

SACKS, H., SCHEGLOFF, E. and JEFFERSON, G. (1974) 'A simplest systematics for the organization of turn-taking for conversation, *Language*, vol. 50, no. 4, pp. 696–735.

SEBBA, M. (1993) *London Jamaican: language systems in interaction*, London, Longman.

STUBBS, M. (1996) *Text and Corpus Analysis: computer-assisted studies of language and culture*, Oxford, Blackwell.

SWANN, J. and GRADDOL, D. (1994) 'Gender inequalities in classroom talk' in Graddol D., Maybin, J. and Stierer, B. (eds) *Researching Language and Literacy in Social Context*, Clevedon, Multilingual Matters/The Open University.

WEGERIF, R. AND MERCER, N.M. (1997) 'Using computer-based text analysis to integrate qualitative and quantitative methods in research on collaborative learning', *Language and Education*, vol. 11, no. 4, pp. 271–86.

ACKNOWLEDGEMENTS

AUTHORS' ACKNOWLEDGEMENTS

PART 2

We are grateful to:

Hilary Claire, from The Open University, for her help in identifying checklists for resources.

Carola Zeegen, for allowing us to draw on her work on bilingual books.

Donald Mackinnon, from The Open University, for much helpful discussion about the examples drawn on in the book.

Will Swann, from The Open University, for allowing us to quote extracts from his field-notes.

Janet Maybin, from The Open University, for allowing us to quote extracts from her field-notes.

Glen McDougall, head teacher of Edward Wilson Primary School, City of Westminster, for allowing us to reprint her observation schedule.

Rosemary Deem, Sue Hemmings and Kevin Brehony for allowing us to quote from field-notes from their ESRC-funded project, 'Reform of school governing bodies: a sociological investigation'.

The E242 *Learning for All* course team for allowing us access to material collected for an audio-cassette.

Andrew Faulkner, from University College, London, for his help and advice on drafts of Sections 1 and 5.

Martyn Hammersley, from The Open University, for much helpful discussion about the content of Section 5.

Barbara Kinsella, from The Open University, for her help with the electronic production of this text and some of the illustrations.

PART 3

I am grateful to Rupert Wegerif for suggestions on computer-based methods of analysing spoken language discussed in Section 2.

REPRODUCTION OF OTHERS' MATERIAL

Grateful acknowledgement is made to the following for permission to reproduce material in this Handbook.

PART 1

Ball, S. J. (1981) *Beachside Comprehensive: a case study of secondary schooling*, Cambridge, Cambridge University Press, pp. xv and 29–34 and Tables 3, 4, 5 and 7; French, J. and French, P. (1984) 'Gender imbalances in the primary classroom: an interactional account', *Educational Research*, **26**(2), pp. 127–36, © National Foundation for Educational Research in England and Wales 1984; *Figure 3*: Gannaway, H. (1976) 'Making sense out of school' in Stubbs, M. and Delamont, S. (eds) *Explorations in Classroom Observation*, Chichester, John Wiley.

PART 2

Kemmis, S. and McTaggart, A. (1981) *The Action Research Planner*, Deakin University Press; *Figure 1:* Hopkins, D. (1985) *A Teacher's Guide to Classroom Research*, Open University Press; *Examples 2.3, 2.4 and 5.6:* Crown copyright material is reproduced under Class Licence Number C01W0000065 with the permission of the Controller of HMSO and the Queen's Printer for Scotland; *Example 2.6:* Tyndall, C. (1988) 'No comfort here', *Issues in Race and Education*, no. 55; *Example 2.7:* Myers, K. (1987) *Genderwatch!*, ©1987 by Kate Myers; *Example 3.6:* Questionnaire from *The Parent–Teacher–Child Conference*, reproduced by permission from Kingsmead Primary School, London; *Example 3.7:* Bird, M. and Varlaam, A. (1985) *Equal Opportunities in the Curriculum in Single Sex Schools*, London Metropolitan Archives; *Example 3.8:* Hilary Street, London Borough of Wandsworth; *Example 3.9:* Bird, M. and Norton, N. (1988) *The Hackney Literacy Study*, London Metropolitan Archives; *Example 3.10:* Bird, M. and Varlaam, A. (1985) *Induction Scheme: five years on*, London Metropolitan Archives; *Example 4.8:* Browne, N. and France, P. (1986) *Untying the Apron Strings: anti-sexist provision for the under-fives*, Open University Press; *Example 4.11: The Primary Language Record: a handbook for teachers* (1988), London Metropolitan Archives. *Example 4.11:* reproduced by permission of the Bay Area Writing Project, School of Education, University of California.

PART 3

Grateful acknowledgement is made to the following sources for permission to reproduce material in this book:

Table1: Swann, J. (2001) 'Recording and transcribing talk in educational settings' in *English Language Teaching in its Social Context: a Reader*, Candlin, C .N. and Mercer, N. (eds), Routledge in association with Macquarie University and the Open University; *Figures 1, 2, 3, 4, 5, 6, 7, 8, 9, 10 and 11:* Swann, J. (2001) 'Recording and transcribing talk in educational settings' in *English language Teaching in its Social Context: a Reader*, Candlin, C. N. and Mercer, N. (eds), Routledge in association with Macquarie University and the Open University.